ASP.NET

DEVELOPER'S COOKBOOK

Steven Smith
Rob Howard
The ASP Alliance

**DEVELOPER'S
LIBRARY**

Sams Publishing, 800 E. 96th Street, Indianapolis, Indiana 46240

ASP.NET Developer's Cookbook

International Standard Book Number: 0-672-32524-1

Library of Congress Catalog Card Number: 2003092438

Printed in the United States of America

First Printing: *June 2003*

Second Printing with corrections: *January 2004*

06 05 04   4 3 2

Sams Publishing offers excellent discounts on this book when ordered in quantity for bulk purchases or special sales. For more information, please contact

U.S. Corporate and Government Sales
1-800-382-3419
corpsales@pearsontechgroup.com

For sales outside of the U.S., please contact

International Sales
1-317-581-3793
international@pearsontechgroup.com

Trademarks

All terms mentioned in this book that are known to be trademarks or service marks have been appropriately capitalized. Sams Publishing cannot attest to the accuracy of this information. Use of a term in this book should not be regarded as affecting the validity of any trademark or service mark.

Warning and Disclaimer

Every effort has been made to make this book as complete and as accurate as possible, but no warranty or fitness is implied. The information provided is on an "as is" basis. The authors and the publisher shall have neither liability nor responsibility to any person or entity with respect to any loss or damages arising from the information contained in this book or from programs accompanying it.

Associate Publisher
Michael Stephens

Acquisitions Editor
Neil Rowe

Development Editor
Mark Renfrow

Managing Editor
Charlotte Clapp

Project Editor
Matthew Purcell

Copy Editor
Kezia Endsley

Indexer
John Sleeva

Proofreader
Tracy Donhardt

Technical Editor
Doug Holland

Team Coordinator
Cindy Teeters

Cover Designer
Alan Clements

Page Layout
Julie Parks

Graphics
Tammy Graham

❖

To my wife Michelle and daughter Ilyana,
for all the time they let me spend on writing books
and playing with cool technology.

− Steve

❖

Contents at a Glance

Table of Contents

**13 Rendering Data with ASP.NET Web
Controls   169**

About the Authors

Steven A. Smith, Microsoft ASP.NET MVP, is president and owner of ASPAlliance.com, LLC, the #1 ASP.NET developer community, which provides articles, forums, listservs, and sample code for ASP and ASP.NET developers. He is also the owner and head instructor for ASPSmith Ltd, a .NET-focused training company. Steve speaks at several conferences each year and has written articles for MSDN and AspNetPRO magazines in addition to his first book, ASP.NET By Example. Steve has a Master's degree in Business Administration and a Bachelor of Science degree in Computer Science Engineering. When he isn't working, Steve enjoys swimming, biking, and computer games. Steve lives in Ohio with his wife Michelle and daughter Ilyana. Steve can be reached at ssmith@aspalliance.com.

Rob Howard is a Program Manager on the Microsoft ASP.NET Team and is responsible for features such as Caching, Session State, Error Handling, and the Http Runtime. He additionally runs and maintains the www.asp.net web site and is the lead developer on the ASP.NET Forums source project. Rob has written or contributed to several books on ASP.NET, and is also a frequent presenter at conferences and user groups. He can be reached at rhoward@microsoft.com.

ASPAlliance.com Contributors

Brett Burridge is a Microsoft Certified Professional based in the United Kingdom. Since 1997, he has created websites and software applications for a range of public sector organizations, start up ventures and multinational companies. Brett has also written technical articles for ASPToday, ariadne.ac.uk and ASPAlliance.com. Brett's ASPAlliance column is at http://aspalliance.com/brettb/.

Robert Chartier has developed IT solutions for more than nine years with a diverse background in both software and hardware development. He is internationally recognized as an innovative thinker and leading IT architect with frequent speaking engagements showcasing his expertise. He's been an integral part of many open forums on cutting-edge technology, including the .NET Framework and Web Services. His current position as vice president of technology for Santra Technology (http://www.santra.com) has allowed him to focus on innovation within the Web Services market space.

He uses expertise with many Microsoft technologies, including .NET, and a strong background in Oracle, BEA Systems, Inc.'s BEA WebLogic, IBM, Java 2 Platform Enterprise Edition (J2EE), and similar technologies to support his award-winning writing. He frequently publishes to many of the leading developer and industry support Web sites and publications. He has a bachelor's degree in Computer Information Systems. Robert Chartier can be reached at rob@santra.com.

Jesudas Chinnathampi also known as Das, has been working with Active Server Pages since 1998. Currently he is working with Silicomm Corporation, http://silicomm.com. Das is also a member of the ASPElite, http://ASPElite.com, a select group of developers who help to manage the discussions at ASPFriends.com. Das started working with ASP.NET when its first beta was released.

Recently Das wrote chapters for two WROX books discussing working with ASP.NET and databases. You can view the details of his books at the following links:

co-author—Beginning ASP.NET Databases using VB.NET
http://www.amazon.com/exec/obidos/ASIN/1861006195

co-author—Beginning ASP.NET Databases using C#
http://www.amazon.com/exec/obidos/ASIN/1861007418

Also, Das has his own column at http://aspalliance.com/das/. Das has a Masters Degree in Computer Application. During leisures, he enjoys driving, playing chess and watching games (Cricket, Basketball, Shuttle Badminton).

Jose Fuentes likes to be thought of as a "do it guy"[md]when others say it can't be done, he finds a way. This is a guy that goes to bed and wakes up in the middle of the night with answers to his problems. Jose lives in Tallahassee, FL with his wife and young boy. He specializes in Windows application development using VB .NET, though he also handles all the ASP.NET that's thrown at him. He has worked in the development field as a professional for six years, but has been a hobby developer since he was 12 when he started using GWBasic. When he's not spending endless amounts of time developing, you can find Jose playing with his family. His other activities include computer art. His favorite motto is "if it can't be done, you haven't tried hard enough". He can be reached at dark7622@yahoo.com.

Chris Garrett is the Head of Technology for one of the larger european new media agencies, working with some of the worlds best known brands helping them develop web and interactive TV strategies. Chris started his obsession with programming when at around the age of ten he started learning BASIC on his Commodore VIC-20. The addiction has never been kicked and since 1994 has concentrated on the Internet, most recently using ASP.NET. When Chris isn't hunched over a computer screen or talking someones ear off about some new technology, he tries very hard to have a real life with his wife Clare, his daughter Amy and two overweight cats.

David Gottlieb is a web developer for EBSCO Subsidiary Web Services, a subsidiary of EBSCO Industries, Inc. in Birmingham, Alabama. His primary skills are ASP.NET with C#, Microsoft Commerce Server 2002, Microsoft Content Management Server 2002, Classic ASP and a little VB. He is an ASP Alliance columnist, a member of the AspElite at http://www.aspelite.com, and is a moderator of the ASP.NET Forums at www.asp.net.

Other books by David Gottlieb: Co-Author: ASP.NET Components Toolkit - Wrox Press - http://www.amazon.com/exec/obidos/ASIN/1861008023

Thomas Johansen is a young and promising developer from Norway. He has been programming since the age of 12 when he made simple programs in Basic. For the past 2 years Thomas has been developing windows and web application using the .NET framework. He is skilled in ASP, VBScript, JScript, C, C++, Java, C#, ASP.NET, GDI+ and Web Services. Developing custom controls for use in ASP.NET applications is one of things he enjoys the most. Thomas is frequently answering developers at the official ASP.NET forums, and he has a column at ASP Alliance (http://aspalliance.com/aylar/) where he posts his articles. Thomas can be reached at aylar@aspalliance.com.

Sreedhar Koganti is a Microsoft Certified Professional from Falls Church, VA. He has several years of experience in developing and implementing applications for Microsoft platforms as a consultant. As an author whenever he is free, he writes articles to various magazines and sites like MSDNAA and HardcoreWebservices magazine, and so on. He also got an opportunity to teach Microsoft related technologies at George Washington University, USDA, and so on, as a part time faculty. He has a free educational site (www.w3coder.com) that contains .NET-related content. He can be contacted at SreedharK@W3Coder.com.

Colt Kwong is a Microsoft MVP in ASP.NET and addict in anything about *.NET*. He's one of the Top 25 posters at the Microsoft Official ASP.NET Forums. He is also a moderator on the Microsoft's ASP.NET Forums and ASPAdvice List Server, ASPElite member, Microsoft Mobile Solutions Partner, guest speaker in Microsoft Hong Kong TechEd 2002, freelancer for Microsoft HK and the President of the Hong Kong .NET User Group. He's in the Winner's Circle for Microsoft's Asia Student.NET Online Challenge, earning perfect scores in Visual Studio .NET Advanced, Visual Studio.NET Intermediate, and Visual Studio .NET Basics. He has a Bachelor of Science Degree in Computer Science.

He co-authored a book for Wrox in Jan 2003: Beginning Dynamic Web Sites with Web Matrix (ISBN: 1861007922) and he can be reached at Colt@mvps.org.

Bjørn Lyngwa is a young developer hailing from Norway. He is self-taught, but hopes for admittance to Queensland University of Technology where he wishes to achieve the Bachelor of IT degree. In the here-and-now he is sporadically writing articles for his column at the ASPAlliance.

Haroon R. Malik is from Lahore, Pakistan. He has been working with ASP.NET since its Beta 2 version. He has a Master's degree in Computer Sciences with specialization in E-Commerce. He is also an MCP. He is a member columnist of the ASP Alliance team and regularly writes technical articles related to ASP.NET/SQL Server 2000.

Haroon has been teaching computer courses for the last 2 years and is now acting as a course instructor for the certification course of Microsoft Certified Application Developer (MCAD), at Infologix Institute of Technology, Lahore. Previously he has worked as a Web Administrator, Database Operator and Assistant Network Administrator.

Haroon enjoys his free time reviewing books, testing new technologies or surfing the Internet for R&D.

Andrew Mooney is a software developer from Illinois. He specializes in web development using Microsoft database technologies, especially SQL Server 2000 and Access 2000. He holds all of the Brainbench BCIP certifications, including Web Developer Database, Web Developer Client-Side, and Web Developer Server-Side.

Tim Musschoot is a Jr. Software Engineer from Roeselare, Belgium. During his studies at the University of Ghent, he got interested in software engineering. He started working as a freelancer in 1998. At first, he was a Visual C++ developer, but the interest in ASP came very soon after that. Especially the possibility of extending application usability by adding a webbased interface increased this interest even further. After being a beta tester for Lernout & Hauspie (L&H), he signed up for the Visual Studio .NET betatesting program in 2000, and came in touch with .NET. About 18 months ago Tim joined the AspFriends lists and a couple of months later he started writing articles related to web development (aspnl.com, aspalliance.com). Since 2002, he's also an active participant of the AspFriends community and a member of the AspElite team.

Daniel Olson is the principal software designer for trading operations at an investment company in Fort Worth, TX where he lives with his wife and four children. He has been developing applications in .Net since the beta version. Before that he developed applications in Java.

Philip Quinn is from Christchurch, New Zealand and has been deeply immersed in the world of programming for a number of years. Starting from BASIC and working his way up through VB, VBScript and now VB.NET and C++. He specializes in ASP and ASP.NET development (with VBScript and VB.NET).

Aside from programming he also spends too much time playing various games and exploring graphic design.

Chris Rickard is an independent software engineer living and working as a full time employee in Annapolis, Maryland. Chris has more than 16 years of development experience building web, n-tier, mobile and client server database applications. When he is not glued to the computer, you'll find him hanging out with his wife and two kids, playing fantasy football and hockey or pretending to be a real hockey player on some of Central Maryland's ice rinks.

Steve Sharrock is president of Stephen Sharrock Consulting, Inc. (http://www.sharkcode.com). Steve is a veteran software developer with over twenty years of experience and has been writing Web applications and Web Services using the .NET platform since the early beta days in 2000. Steve is a member of several developer community organizations including AspAlliance, AspElite, SDForum and his local CUG user groups. Steve lives in the San Francisco Bay Area. When he is not involved with his consulting business or speaking at a local user group, Steve is an avid inline skater and can usually be found on the skating trails around his community.

Jeff Widmer is lead developer for the Xbox.com Web site (http://www.xbox.com), where he works with Microsoft Content Management Server 2002, Microsoft Commerce Server 2002, and the .NET Framework to produce an international Web site that receives more than four million page views per month. Jeff has been working with VB .NET, C#, and ASP.NET since the first beta was released in 2000. He is a Microsoft Certified Application Developer for .NET and a Microsoft Certified Solution Developer. Jeff currently lives in Kirkland, WA with his beautiful wife Jill. He can be reached at jwidmer@aspalliance.com or at his Web site at http://www.jeffreywidmer.com.

Paul Wilson is a software architect in Atlanta, currently with a medical device company. He specializes in Microsoft technologies, including .NET, C#, ASP, SQL, COM+, and VB. His WilsonWebForm Control allows Multiple Forms and Non-PostBack Forms in ASP.NET. He is a Microsoft MVP in ASP.NET and is also recognized as an ASPFriend's ASPAce/ASPElite. He is a moderator on Microsoft's ASP.NET Forums, as well as one of the top posters. He is certified in .NET (MCAD), as well as also holding the MCSD, MCDBA, and MCSE. Please visit his website, www.WilsonDotNet.com, or email him at Paul@WilsonDotNet.com.

Remas Wojciechowski had his first computing experience with a ZX Spectrum when he typed "10 LET A = 3". Although he has a degree in business administration, he now devotes a large part of his professional life to (ASP).NET development. Currently he works for Bayer AG in Leverkusen, Germany, and is responsible for new technologies in the group's corporate finance. In his spare time (less and less) he writes articles (way too few) for his aspalliance.com column. Remas is a Polish national but he has lived in Germany since 1994.

Jeremy Zongker is a Microsoft Certified Solution Developer for Microsoft .NET (MCSD.NET) and a Microsoft Certified Systems Engineer (MCSE). He is the founder and president of Trilitech, LLC (www.trilitech.com), a web design, development and hosting company. He also runs www.DevelopIn.net, a site that provides resources for developers wanting to learn more about programming using the .Net framework. In addition Jeremy has written articles for ASP Alliance (www.aspalliance.com/jzongker) and CSharp Today (www.csharptoday.com). He has been programming on his own for over ten years and professionally for the last three. He has been working almost exclusively with Asp.Net since July of 2001. Jeremy is currently working as a Software Developer III at one of Oklahoma's largest banks. He lives in Broken Arrow, OK with his lovely wife Jeanette and beautiful daughter Katrina.

Acknowledgments

Like most books, this one is the result of a huge collaboration by many different people. More than most books, even, this one is the result of the efforts of many, since it involved the collaborative efforts of over two dozen individual contributors from Microsoft and ASPAlliance.com.

First of all, my acquisitions editor, Neil Rowe at Sams Publishing, was great to work with and really made the whole book-writing affair much easier than it might have been. He was especially patient with me throughout the whole process. In addition to Neil, Matt Purcell helped the book get through author review, and was also great to work with. Once the book was totally submitted to Sams, he helped ensure corrections and updates from Sams editors and technical reviewers were brought to the authors' attention and corrected in a timely fashion. Mark Renfrow, Development Editor, also helped ensure the book was done in a timely fashion and of the highest quality. Kezia, our copy editor, had the thankless task of taking the hodgepodge of strangely formatted recipes that I sent to her and making sure they were all formatted consistently. A big thank you goes to her.

Doug Holland tech reviewed the contents of the recipes, making sure they compiled and ran (and used the right programming language, in many cases). He caught a lot of errors in the text, ensuring that you the reader will have a much more pleasant experience when you put these recipes to use.

There were other members of the team at Sams whom I never directly interacted with, but without whom I'm sure this book could not have been produced. I'd like to thank them here as well.

I would like to thank Sterling Hughes and Andrei Zmievski, authors of the *PHP Developer's Cookbook*. Their book provided an excellent example for me to follow as I wrote the *ASP.NET Developer's Cookbook*, and although I haven't written a single line of PHP code, I found their book to be well-organized and full of examples for techniques and organizational ideas for this book.

I would like to extend a special thank-you to Scott Guthrie and the rest of the ASP.NET team, including Rob Howard, for their open-ness and support over the last several years. They have consistently bent over backwards to help community members and authors learn about their product and improve it with feedback and feature ideas. They regularly invite members of the community to Redmond where they spend huge amounts of their valuable time sharing their knowledge and listening to our ideas, and for that I am extremely grateful.

Thanks also to Rob Howard individually, for his work on this book. He is one of the busiest members of the ASP.NET team, regularly juggling core development on the product with side projects like the ASP.NET Forums, this book, community events and speaking engagements, and other community efforts. Somehow he manages to keep everything going, and I've really enjoyed working with him. I wasn't too keen to write another book so soon after completing my first book (*ASP.NET By Example*); it was the chance to work with Rob that made me agree to go forward with this project.

Many members of the ASP Alliance community contributed to this book and are listed as authors. In particular, I'd like to extend my thanks to Thomas Johansen, who built the recipe-management code that I used to coordinate the dozens of columnists who contributed recipes. I would also like to thank Jeremy Zongker, who really went above and beyond as the book was approaching its final completion date and submitted dozens of recipes in a very short timespan. Haroon Malik also contributed quite a few recipes, as well as feedback on the book's organization that helped make the final result better.

Thanks go my family, who has supported me while I've worked on this book. My daughter Ilyana just recently turned one, and thankfully she had begun sleeping through the night by the time I began serious work on the book. That allowed me to spend many all-nighters completing the book while she and my wife Michelle slept. Thanks also to my brother Chris, who was always available to help me procrastinate work on the book by playing games. To my parents, thanks for all of your love and support, and for helping to make me the person I am today. Last, but certainly not least, I'd like to thank my wife Michelle for putting up with me and loving me even when I'm taking a lot more than I'm giving. I love you.

—Steve Smith

We Want to Hear from You!

As the reader of this book, *you* are our most important critic and commentator. We value your opinion and want to know what we're doing right, what we could do better, what areas you'd like to see us publish in, and any other words of wisdom you're willing to pass our way.

As an associate publisher for Sams, I welcome your comments. You can email or write me directly to let me know what you did or didn't like about this book—as well as what we can do to make our books better.

Please note that I cannot help you with technical problems related to the *topic* of this book. We do have a User Services group, however, where I will forward specific technical questions related to the book.

When you write, please be sure to include this book's title and author as well as your name, email address, and phone number. I will carefully review your comments and share them with the author and editors who worked on the book.

Email: feedback@samspublishing.com
Mail: Michael Stephens
          Sams Publishing
          800 E. 96th Street
          Indianapolis, IN 46240 USA

For more information about this book or another Sams title, visit our Web site at www.samspublishing.com. Type the ISBN (excluding hyphens) or the title of a book in the Search field to find the page you're looking for.

Foreword

It is hard to believe that the first release of ASP.NET Version 1.0 is only a year old. In that relatively short amount of time, it has taken the Web-development world by storm. It now powers some of the largest sites on the Internet—some of the highlights include the MSN Portal, Dell.com, and the Home Shopping Network. More than one million Web developers now use ASP.NET daily for new projects.

One of the most attractive elements of ASP.NET is its incredibly rich feature set, and the broad depth of the .NET Framework class library that accompanies it. Traditional ASP offered developers 5 core objects to program against (Request, Response, Server, Application, Session). ASP.NET and the .NET Framework offer an additional 3,000 classes and utility libraries for developers to optionally take advantage of within their Web solutions. A short list of these code utilities included classes that send email, validate form input values, update performance counters, write event log messages, manipulate XML, output cache content, perform complex regular expressions, manipulate files, and much, much more.

These rich features and code libraries can save developers hundreds of hours when building Web sites and applications. Mastering them enables developers to dramatically increase their productivity, and deliver faster and more robust solutions.

This book provides an excellent guide through these code libraries of ASP.NET. It contains dozens of well-organized, task-oriented "code recipes" that enable developers to find specific code samples that demonstrate how to quickly get things done. It also provides a great roadmap for developers looking to explore the breadth of great features that ASP.NET has to offer.

The authors of this book have carefully assembled this list of code recipes from the thousands of hours they have spent participating in the online ASP.NET community. The great authors and columnists of ASP Alliance (www.aspalliance.com) are among the most dedicated users of ASP.NET, and have used and supported it from its very beginning. It would be hard to find a more qualified group of developers to learn ASP.NET from.

Scott Guthrie
Product Unit Manager
ASP.NET Development Team
Redmond, Washington

Introduction

THE FIRST THING I WOULD LIKE TO SAY about this book is that it is not a new idea, but an extension of an idea that has been tried and tested. A great deal of this book's format and structure has been adapted from previous cookbooks published by Sams. In particular, the *PHP Developer's Cookbook* served as a template as I wrote this book, and in fact influenced me to go ahead with this project when I was still uncertain about doing so. In it, the author states the purpose of that cookbook so well, that rather than attempt to reword it, I will quote it here for you:

> "I have an extensive library of books on the practice of programming—tomes of information in pristine condition sitting on my bookshelf. These books have influenced the way I program and the style of my programming. They are bibles; books around which programmers shape their whole philosophies.
>
> However, I also have another set of books. These books sit on my desk, my bed, and my living room couch. They are tattered, bent out of shape, and thoroughly coffee-stained. And that is the greatest honor that I can bestow upon them because they are meant for practical use; they are references for problems that I encounter every single day.
>
> This book is meant as such a text."
>
> —Sterling Hughes, *PHP Developer's Cookbook*

Although I'm sure Sterling and I would disagree about what the best technology is for developing dynamic Web sites, we do agree that some books provide the theory that is necessary to program well, whereas others provide the specific techniques required to accomplish specific tasks. This book is designed around the latter purpose, and it is my hope that this book will find its place on your desk, filled with sticky notes and bookmarks and highlights, and perhaps a few coffee stains. As you develop applications with ASP.NET, I hope that this book's table of contents will be one of the first places you turn (maybe even before Google) when you find that you have a specific task that you need to accomplish.

How to Use This Book

This book is designed to be a reference. It contains about 250 task-oriented *"recipes"* related to common ASP.NET programming tasks. This book features many tasks that are covered in the documentation, as well as many that are not found anywhere else. In every case, we have attempted to show the "best-practice" method of performing the task at hand, so that you as the reader can be confident that using examples from this text will result in correct code, not code that works fine in a quick demo but falls apart in a real application.

This book is not designed to be read from cover to cover. It should be used just like a real cookbook. That is, if you have some chicken that you want to make for dinner, you flip to the chicken section and scan through the recipes to find one that fits your tastes and needs. Similarly, if you have a DataGrid that you're trying to enhance to add sorting and updates, you should flip to the "Rendering Data with Web Controls" section (of the book, the index, or the table of contents) and scan the available recipes to find the one that meets your needs. Then it is a simple matter to adapt the recipe to your needs.

Most recipes also include references to find more information, either within this book or elsewhere. In addition to these references, the book's Web site will be updated with the latest corrected sample files and errata. The book's Web site is located at http://aspalliance.com/cookbook/.

Chapter Summaries

The book's chapters are organized according to the general task at hand. Because ASP.NET developers often need to use parts of the .NET Framework that are not themselves part of ASP.NET, the latter chapters of the book cover features of .NET whose usage is not limited to ASP.NET applications.

Chapter 1, "Web Form Basics," is about creating Web Forms using ASP.NET. The basic syntax and options are covered.

Chapter 2, "User Controls," describes how to create User Controls in ASP.NET. User Controls are very similar to Web Forms, and this chapter logically follows and builds on the Web Forms chapter.

Chapter 3, "Custom Controls," describes how to create your own custom controls for use in ASP.NET pages. Several common features of custom controls are described at a high level with code examples. However, this subject is large enough for its own book, so don't expect a lot of explanation to accompany these samples.

Chapter 4, "Caching," describes the many ways you can implement caching in ASP.NET. One of the most exciting features of ASP.NET, caching can radically improve the performance of almost any data-driven Web application. This chapter is full of examples that show how to take advantage of this feature.

Chapter 5, "Mobile Controls," is about the built-in mobile controls that ship with ASP.NET (or are available as a separate download in version 1.0).

Chapter 6, "ASP.NET Application Configuration," covers the many configuration options that are available for ASP.NET applications, focusing mainly on sections of the web.config file.

Chapter 7, "State Management," is all about storing and retrieving information about a user's interaction with the site using a variety of techniques. ASP.NET offers many options here, so it's easy to get confused about which ones to use and when. This chapter should help.

Chapter 8, "Security," is about setting up security options using the built-in security features of ASP.NET. It's primarily concerned with the common tasks associated with Web application security, and so does not delve into the more advanced code-level security and CLR security features available in the .NET Framework.

Chapter 9, "Error Handling and Debugging," describes how to set up debugging, logging, tracing, and friendly error handling in your ASP.NET applications.

Chapter 10, "Basic Data Operations with ADO.NET," is about the most common ADO.NET tasks that Web applications require.

Chapter 11, "Working with DataReaders and DataSets," builds on the previous chapter and demonstrates tasks specific to these two ADO.NET objects, which provide the backbone of most data access in .NET.

Chapter 12, "XML," is of course about XML and covers related protocols for working with XML data in ASP.NET.

Chapter 13, "Rendering Data with ASP.NET Web Controls," is all about displaying data on Web Forms using Web controls that ship with ASP.NET. This is probably one of the most useful chapters of the book for experienced ASP.NET developers. It also represents the last chapter in the book that is related specifically to ASP.NET; the rest of the chapters cover tasks and technology that is applicable to almost any .NET application, whether Web-based or not.

Chapter 14, "Working with Classes," is about classes and object-oriented development techniques, from a syntax and how-to perspective. This is not the place to learn proper object-oriented development techniques, but it does show how to apply them in .NET.

Chapter 15, "Manipulating Strings," describes the most common string and text-related tasks, and the easiest ways to accomplish them using the .NET Framework.

Chapter 16, "Working with Numbers, Dates, and Times," describes the most common tasks related to numbers, dates, and times, and how to accomplish them using the .NET Framework.

Chapter 17, "Working with Files and Folders," describes file system access using the .NET Framework.

Chapter 18, "Working with Collections," is about the many built-in collections that come with the .NET Framework and how to use them, as well as how to create your own custom collection objects.

Chapter 19, "Web Services," is about writing and consuming Web services using the .NET Framework.

Chapter 20, "LDAP/ADSI Directory Services," is about using and accessing directory stores like Active Directory and reading and writing information to and from them.

Chapter 21, "Internet Tasks and Techniques," is about common Internet-related tasks that ASP.NET developers face, such as "scraping" content from another Web site, sending email, or performing other network tasks.

Chapter 22, "Generating and Manipulating Images," is about the extensive support for image manipulation that is provided by the .NET Framework and available to ASP.NET developers.

Chapter 23, "Threading, Remoting, Reflection, and CodeDOM," provides a few examples of these advanced .NET Framework features that are required for some ASP.NET applications.

A Brief History of ASP.NET

ASP.NET's development began around the time Active Server Pages was first being released. At that time, Mark Anders and Scott Guthrie already believed that ASP had a number of inherent limitations that they wanted to address. Several years later, with the addition of the Common Language Runtime and the whole .NET Framework to build upon, their ideas for a better Web application development platform came to fruition with ASP.NET 1.0, which was released in early 2002.

For a 1.0 product, ASP.NET is truly awesome. The developer tools provided by Visual Studio .NET dwarf anything available for ASP 3.0 or Visual Basic 6, and free tools like the ASP.NET Web Matrix, which came out just after the official release of ASP.NET, have been incredibly popular with the developer community. Unlike ASP, which offered about half a dozen intrinsic objects, ASP.NET ships with *thousands* of objects available for developers to use on any Web page.

ASP.NET code is compiled, not interpreted. It's object-oriented, not script-based. It supports many languages and a common language framework, rather than just a few scripting languages. It eliminates COM dependencies and associated "DLL Hell," and makes it possible to deploy Web applications simply by copying them from one machine to another with minimal, if any, configuration required. In short, it is a vast improvement over its predecessor, with unheard of stability and security for a 1.0 product. With ASP.NET 1.1, many small bugs have been fixed and a few separate code libraries have been integrated into the product.

ASP.NET 2.0 is coming. Expect to see it add—in fact, almost double—the functionality of ASP.NET 1.x, with more Web controls and infrastructure to help you solve common problems and repetitive tasks. Expect to write less code to do the same things you do now in ASP.NET 1.x. It will not be nearly as drastic a change as ASP.NET 1.0 was compared to ASP 3.0, and it will support side-by-side installation, which will make upgrading a relatively simple process.

Finding Help

You'll find this book's samples, in both VB and C#, at the book's Web site (`http://aspalliance.com/cookbook/`). There you will also find any errata or bug fixes and contact information for the authors. Most of the examples in this book (except those that pose a security risk) are live and available for you to test on the book's Web site as well.

If you find anything wrong with this book, please let me know so that I can share it with others. If you would like to be notified about updates to the Web site (such as errors and bug fixes) or future editions of this book (such as for ASP.NET 2.0), you can sign up to receive this information on the Web site as well.

—Steven A. Smith

I

ASP.NET Pages

1

Web Form Basics

1.0. Introduction

The most basic part of an ASP.NET application is the ASPX page, or Web Form. With ASP.NET, Microsoft enables you to use compiled, event-driven, object-oriented methods for building dynamic Web applications. The Web Form differs from the typical legacy ASP script page in its design and function. Rather than executing top-down as an interpreted script, the Web Form is similar to a VB Form-based application. Each control raises events that are then wired to particular activities. In this chapter, you learn how to create a Web Form, and how to perform some fairly simple but commonly needed tasks. You learn more complicated recipes for enhancing your ASP.NET applications and Web Forms in later chapters.

1.1. Declaring an ASP.NET Page

You want to create an ASPX page (a Web Form).

Technique

To declare an ASP.NET page (a Web Form), you simply create a file with an .ASPX extension and place it in a Web folder. The ASPX page is as follows:

```
<%@ Page Language="VB" Explicit="true" Strict="true" %>
<html>
<body>
A simple ASP.NET Page.  All @Page attributes are optional.
</body>
</html>
```

Comments

The ASP.NET engine will process any ASPX page, even if it doesn't contain any code, just as is done in ASP. There are about 20 optional parameters you can set in the `Page` directive. The three listed in this example (`Language`, `Explicit`, and `Strict`) are optional, but are strongly recommended. If `Language` is omitted, the default language specified in the web.config file is used. Two additional items that are worth mentioning are the `Src` and `Codebehind` attributes. `Src` is used to specify a file to use for the codebehind class when the page is first requested. The class found at this location is compiled the first time the page is requested. The `Codebehind` attribute is similar—it is used at compile time by Visual Studio .NET to maintain a link between ASPX pages and their codebehind classes. Do not use both the `Src` and `Codebehind` attributes in a Visual Studio .NET project or you will get a duplicate class error; the same class is compiled and referenced twice. In addition to `Src` or `Codebehind`, you must also specify the `Inherits` attribute in order to use a codebehind class.

See Also

@Page—http://msdn.microsoft.com/library/en-us/cpgenref/html/
cpconpage.asp

1.2. Using a Codebehind File with an ASP.NET Page

You want to reference a codebehind file's class from your ASP.NET page (your .ASPX file).

Technique

Use the `Page` directive to specify the codebehind file. If you use the `Src` attribute, ASP.NET will compile the contents of the specified file when a user first requests this page. The ASPX page is as follows:

```
<%@ Page Language="vb" inherits="AspNetCookbook.myCodeBehind"
src="recipe0102vb.aspx.vb" %>
<html>
   <head>
      <title>Using CodeBehind</title>
   </head>
   <body>
      <form id="Form1" method="post" runat="server">
      </form>
   </body>
</html>
```

In codebehind:

```
Imports System

NameSpace AspNetCookbook
    Public Class myCodeBehind
        Inherits System.Web.UI.Page
        Sub Page_Load(byval sender As System.Object, e As System.EventArgs)
            Response.Write("This is my Codebehind page!")
        End Sub
    End Class
End NameSpace
```

Comments

ASP.NET allows you to separate your code and user interface (UI) into assemblies (.DLL files) and .ASPX pages, respectively. This way the programmers and the designers can work separately without interfering with each other's work on the same page. Because the code is separate from the main file it is called a *codebehind*. In the previous example, in the Page directive, Src specifies the codebehind file. The example assigns the value recipe0102vb.aspx.vb to the attribute Src. So, all the processing statements will reside inside the codebehind file, recipe0102vb.aspx.vb.

Note that you can have any name for the codebehind file. If you are using C#, your codebehind filename should end with .CS. Note that, if you use Visual Studio .NET, VS.NET will automatically use an attribute called Codebehind. This attribute will contain the codebehind filename. You should not combine the Codebehind attribute with the Src attribute in a single Web Form. You must ensure also that the class specified in the page's Inherits attribute is a descendent of the System.Web.UI.Page class.

See Also

Understanding codebehind—http://aspalliance.com/stevesmith/articles/ViewArticle.aspx?id=42

1.3. Dynamically Adding Literal Text or HTML to a Web Form

You want to dynamically add some text or HTML to your ASP.NET Web Form in a particular location.

Technique

Use the System.Web.UI.WebControls.Literal control to place literal text anywhere on a Web Form. The ASPX page is as follows:

```
<html>
  <head>
    <title><asp:Literal id="litTitle" runat="server" /></title>
  </head>
  <body></body>
</html>
```

In `<script runat="server" />` block or codebehind:

```
Sub Page_Load(sender As Object, e As EventArgs)
  litTitle.Text = "This is my page title."
End Sub
```

Comments

The easiest way to place some content on a Web page when you want to have absolute control over the formatting (for example, you don't want your text wrapped in a `<div>` tag or in other HTML tags) is to use the `Literal` control in the `System.Web.UI.WebControls` namespace. Another option that you can use is data-binding, which you use by adding `<%# VariableName %>` to the page and ensuring that `Me.DataBind()` is called somewhere in the page's execution (typically during `Page_Load`). Usually the `Literal` is a better solution, however, because data-binding the page will force all the controls on the page to data-bind as well, and this can cause unexpected results or inefficient use of your controls. You can also use the `Label` Web Server Control to display dynamic text.

See Also
Section 2.1, "Declaring a User Control"

1.4. Submitting Data to Another Page Using ASP.NET

You want to submit data to another Web page. The target Web page is not restricted to any particular type.

Technique

Submit the data directly from the client using a `form` `post` with the `action` attribute specifying the target Web page.

The ASPX page is as follows:

```
<form method="post" action="Recipe0104asp.asp">
  Price: <Input type="text" name="Price" value="22.50" /><br>
  Quantity: <Input type="text" name="Quantity" value="4" /><br>
```

```
      <Input type="submit" value="Submit Entire Form" />
   </form>
```

Submit the data through the query string using a redirect on the server. You do this after the client has posted back to the server with the data to be appended to the query string.

The ASPX page is as follows:

```
<form runat="server">
   Price: <asp:TextBox Runat="server" ID="Price" Text="22.50" /><br>
   Quantity: <asp:TextBox Runat="server" ID="Quantity" Text="4" /><br>
   <asp:Button Runat="server" ID="SubmitButton"
   Text="Postback and Redirect" OnClick="SubmitButton_Click"/><br>

   <asp:Button Runat="server" ID="WebRequestButton"
   Text="Submit by Web Request" OnClick="WebRequestButton_Click"/>
   <asp:Label Runat="server" ID="WebResponseLabel"/>
</form>
```

In `<script runat="server" />` block or codebehind:

```
Private Sub SubmitButton_Click(ByVal sender As System.Object, _
   ByVal e As System.EventArgs)
   Response.Redirect("Recipe0104asp.asp?Price=" & Price.Text & _
   "&Quantity=" & Quantity.Text)
End Sub
```

You create a Web request to post to the target Web page from within the postback and then display this information to the client, all within the same client-server round trip. In `<script runat="server" />` block or codebehind:

```
Private Sub WebRequestButton_Click(ByVal sender As System.Object, _
   ByVal e As System.EventArgs)
   Dim RequestUrl As String =
      Request.Url.GetLeftPart(System.UriPartial.Authority) & _
      Request.ApplicationPath & "/Recipe0104asp.asp"
   Dim Post As String = "Price=" & Price.Text & _
      "&Quantity=" & Quantity.Text
   Dim Writer As StreamWriter = Nothing

   Dim WebRequestObject As HttpWebRequest
   Dim sr As StreamReader
   Dim WebResponseObject As HttpWebResponse

   Try
      WebRequestObject = CType(WebRequest.Create(RequestUrl), HttpWebRequest)
      WebRequestObject.Method = "POST"
      WebRequestObject.ContentType = "application/x-www-form-urlencoded"
```

```
        WebRequestObject.ContentLength = Post.Length
        Writer = New StreamWriter(WebRequestObject.GetRequestStream())
        Writer.Write(Post)
        Writer.Close()

        WebResponseObject = CType(WebRequestObject.GetResponse(),
            HttpWebResponse)
        sr = New StreamReader(WebResponseObject.GetResponseStream)

        WebResponseLabel.Text = sr.ReadToEnd
    Finally
        Try
            sr.Close()
        Catch
        End Try

        Try
            WebResponseObject.Close()
            WebRequestObject.Abort()
        Catch
        End Try
    End Try
End Sub
```

Comments

There are three ways to submit data to another Web page:

- `Form post` from the client
- Postback to the server followed by redirect
- Postback to the server and create an `HttpWebRequest`

The first method involves a `form post` from the client. The `form` has the `action` attribute set to the target Web page. When the client clicks the Submit button, the entire form is posted to the target Web page directly from the client. The disadvantage to this method is that the data cannot be manipulated on the server before being posted to the target page.

The second method involves posting back to the server. During the postback event, the selected data is validated and then attached to the query string of the target Web page. The target Web page then extracts the data from the query string. The disadvantage of this method is that the data is visible in the query string and has size restrictions.

The third method involves creating an `HttpWebRequest` to submit the data to the target Web page and then receive the response immediately. This all occurs within the single postback, thus eliminating the redirect (which actually requires a round-trip to the client). The response from the target Web page can then be parsed and displayed to the client. This technique is described in Chapter 21, "Internet Tasks and Techniques."

See Also

Chapter 21, "Internet Tasks and Techniques"

1.5. Creating a Scrolling Table within a Web Form

You want to create a scrolling region inside your Web Form.

Technique

Using Cascading Style Sheets, it is simple to create a scrolling region inside a Web Form. In the ASPX page:

```
<table border="1" bgcolor="#EEEEEE">
<tr>
<td>Query Results:</td>
<td><div style="overflow-y:scroll; height=40;">
<table bgcolor="#FFFFFF">
<tr bgcolor="#CCCCCC">
<td>First Name</td><td>Last Name</td>
</tr>
<tr>
<td>Steve</td><td>Smith</td>
</tr>
<tr>
<td>Rob</td><td>Howard</td>
</tr>
<tr>
<td>ASPAlliance</td><td>Team</td>
</tr>
</table>
</div>
</td>
</tr>
</table>
```

Comments

This technique is not supported by all browsers, but will work with Internet Explorer 4.0 and later and should work with Netscape 6.0 and later. The `overflow` property has a number of options that you can set that many ASP.NET developers are unaware of. These options can provide very powerful benefits for your Web Form presentation.

See Also

Overflow CSS Property–http://htmlcompendium.org/properties-list/Coverflo.htm

1.6. Selectively Hiding or Revealing Portions of a Web Form Programmatically

You want to show or hide controls or parts of your Web Form programmatically.

Technique

Toggle the `Visible` property of controls that inherit from `System.Web.UI.Control`. The ASPX page:

```
<html>
<body>
<form runat="server">
<asp:panel id="pnlSample" runat="server">
<asp:Label id="lblSample" runat="server" Text="Sample Text" />
</asp:panel>
<asp:button runat="server" id="btnToggle" Text="Toggle Panel Visibility"
   OnClick="btnToggle_Click" />
</form>
</body>
</html>
```

In `<script runat="server" />` block or codebehind:

```
Sub btnToggle_Click(sender as object, e as EventArgs)
   pnlSample.Visible = Not pnlSample.Visible
End Sub
```

Comments

The Panel control used here can contain other controls. When setting the `Visible` property of the Panel, the change is reflected through the controls within the panel as well. Because all the Web Server Controls inherit from `System.Web.UI.Control`, you can utilize the `Visible` property of each of them. This property can be set to `True` or `False`.

1.7. Displaying a Calendar in a Web Form

> You want to display a calendar in your Web Form, perhaps to allow users to select a date.

Technique

You can use the `Calendar` Web Control to display a calendar on a page or as a selection tool on a form. Its sub-elements appearance can all be set using its properties. To display a calendar with notes on some days:

```
<script runat="server">
Sub PrettyCalendar_OnDayRender (Sender As Object, _
    e As System.Web.UI.WebControls.DayRenderEventArgs)
    If e.Day.Date = Today Then
        'Add a carriage return
        e.Cell.Controls.Add(new LiteralControl("<br />"))
        'Add a message of the day
        e.Cell.Controls.Add(new LiteralControl("Today!"))
    End If
End Sub
</script>
<form runat="server">
    <asp:Calendar ID="PrettyCalendar" Runat="server"
        OnDayRender="PrettyCalendar_OnDayRender">
        <TodayDayStyle ForeColor="Red" BackColor="Aqua"></TodayDayStyle>
        <DayStyle Font-Bold="True" HorizontalAlign="Left" Height="90px"
        BorderWidth="1px" BorderStyle="Solid" BorderColor="Blue" Width="100px"
        VerticalAlign="Top" BackColor="#80FFFF"></DayStyle>
        <NextPrevStyle ForeColor="Blue"></NextPrevStyle>
        <DayHeaderStyle Font-Size="Large" Font-Bold="True" BorderWidth="1px"
        ForeColor="Brown" BorderStyle="Solid" BorderColor="Black" Width="100px"
        BackColor="#00C0C0"></DayHeaderStyle>
        <TitleStyle Font-Size="Large" Font-Bold="True" BorderWidth="1px"
        BorderStyle="Solid" BorderColor="Black" BackColor="#80FFFF"></TitleStyle>
        <WeekendDayStyle BackColor="#C0C0FF"></WeekendDayStyle>
    </asp:Calendar>
</form>
```

To use a calendar for user input on a Web Form:

```
<%@ Page Language="VB" Explicit="true" Strict="true" %>
<HTML>
    <body>
        <script runat="server">
        Sub Page_Load(Sender As object, e As EventArgs)
```

```
        If Not IsPostBack Then
            DepartureDate.SelectedDate = System.DateTime.Today
        End If
    End Sub

    Sub SearchButton_Click(Sender As object, e As EventArgs)
        If DepartureDate.SelectedDate <= System.DateTime.Today Then
            ResultLabel.Text = _
                "You must selected a Departure Date in the future."
        ElseIf(ReturnDate.SelectedDate < DepartureDate.SelectedDate)
            ResultLabel.Text = "Return Date must follow the Departure Date."
        Else
            ResultLabel.Text = "Departing on " & _
                DepartureDate.SelectedDate.ToShortDateString() & _
                " and returning on " & _
                ReturnDate.SelectedDate.ToShortDateString()
        End If
    End Sub
    </script>
    <form runat="server" ID="Form1">
        <h1>Find a Flight</h1>
        <table>
            <tr>
                <td>Departure Date</td>
                <td><asp:Calendar ID="DepartureDate" Runat="server">
                    <DayStyle Font-Size="X-Small"></DayStyle>
                    <TitleStyle Font-Bold="True"></TitleStyle>
                  </asp:Calendar></td>
            </tr>
            <tr>
                <td>Return Date</td>
                <td><asp:Calendar ID="ReturnDate" Runat="server">
                    <DayStyle Font-Size="X-Small"></DayStyle>
                    <TitleStyle Font-Bold="True"></TitleStyle>
                  </asp:Calendar></td>
            </tr>
        </table>
        <asp:Button ID="SearchButton" Runat="server"
            Text="Search" OnClick="SearchButton_Click" />
        <br>
        <asp:Label ID="ResultLabel" Runat="server" />
    </form>
  </body>
</HTML>
```

Comments

You can extend the `Calendar` control a number of ways, such as allowing users to select certain weeks or months or ranges of dates. It can be used to display events on certain dates, and its appearance can be controlled by its properties or through the use of Cascading Style Sheets. It does not support the use of the standard validation controls, but a CustomValidator can be used to validate a calendar, if necessary.

See Also

ASP.NET Events Calendar—`http://ASPAlliance.com/events/`

1.8. Validating User Form Input

You want to validate your users' entries on a Web Form.

Technique

ASP.NET ships with a suite of validation controls that make form validation a relatively simple process for most rules. These include the following controls:

- `RequiredFieldValidator`
- `RangeValidator`
- `CompareValidatior`
- `RegularExpressionValidator`
- `CustomValidator`

In addition, display of error messages is eased by the use of the `ValidationSummary` control. The following code sample demonstrates each of these validators and includes comments describing their various properties where it may not be immediately obvious.

```
<%@ Page language="vb" %>
<%@ Import namespace="System.Web.UI.WebControls" %>
<script runat="server">
Public Sub button1_Click(sender As Object, e As System.EventArgs)
    Label1.Text = "Hello, the time is now " & DateTime.Now.ToLongTimeString() & _
        "<br>Page.IsValid = " & Page.IsValid
End Sub


Public Sub ServerValidate(sender As Object, args As ServerValidateEventArgs)
    Dim num As Integer = Int32.Parse(args.Value)
    If num Mod 2 = 0 Then
        args.IsValid = True
```

```
        Else
            args.IsValid = False
        End If
    End Sub
</script>
<script type="text/javascript">
function isEven(oSrc, args){
    //var _sqrt = Math.round(Math.sqrt(args.Value));
    args.IsValid = (args.Value % 2 == 0);
}
</script>
<html>
    <body>
        <form method="post" runat="server">
            <table>
                <tr>
                    <td>
                        RequiredFieldValidator
                    </td>
                    <td>
                        <asp:textbox id="TextBox1" runat="server" />
                    </td>
                    <td width="400">
                        <!--
These RequiredFieldValidator properties are common to all validators.
ControlToValidate links the validator to another Web control and is
required for all validators.
Text is displayed where the validator is located when there is a
ValidationSummary.
ErrorMessage is displayed in the ValidationSummary.
Display can be Static or Dynamic.
When it is static, the browser will hold
space for the validator's output.
When it's Dynamic, the browser will resize as
needed when the validator is triggered.

In addition, you can specify a value for InitialValue, which is useful
if you have a form element with some default text in it, such as
"Enter a value". Note that if a non-blank value is specified for
InitialValue,
a blank value will then be considered valid.
                        -->
                        <asp:RequiredFieldValidator id="TextBox1Required"
                        runat="server" ControlToValidate="TextBox1"
                        Text="*" Display="Static"
                        ErrorMessage="RequiredFieldValidator field is required." />
                    </td>
```

```
        </tr>
        <tr>
          <td>
             RangeValidator
          </td>
          <td>
             <asp:textbox id="TextBox2" runat="server" />
             <br>
          </td>
          <td>
             <!—
  The RangeValidator supports properties
  MinimumValue and MaximumValue, which are self-explanatory, and
  Type, which must be one of Currency, Date, Double, Integer, or String.
  —>
             <asp:RangeValidator id="TextBox2Range"
             ControlToValidate="TextBox2" MinimumValue="2"
             MaximumValue="5" Type="Integer" Text="Invalid!"
            runat="server" Display="Dynamic"
  ErrorMessage="RangeValidator value must be between 2 and 5 inclusive." />
          </td>
        </tr>
        <tr>
          <td>
             CompareValidator: Integer Field
          </td>
          <td>
             <asp:textbox id="TextBox3" runat="server" />
          </td>
          <td>
             <!—
  The CompareValidator adds the following properties:
  Operator - can be a comparison operator, such as Equal, GreaterThan,
  GreaterThanEqual, LessThan, LessThanEqual, NotEqual
  or can be DataTypeCheck as it is here.
  DataTypeCheck will simply validate that the value of the
  ControlToValidate is of the specified type.

  Not shown is the ValueToCompare, which can be used to specify
  a particular value to which the ControlToValidate should be compared.
  Not used for DataTypeCheck.
  —>
             <asp:CompareValidator id="TextBox3CompareInteger"
             ControlToValidate="TextBox3" Operator="DataTypeCheck"
             Type="Integer" Text="!" Display="Dynamic"
             ErrorMessage="CompareValidator - Value must be an integer."
             runat="server" />
```

```
        </td>
      </tr>
      <tr>
        <td>
          CompareValidator: One Integer field less than other
        </td>
        <td>
          <asp:textbox id="TextBox4" runat="server" />
          <br>
          <asp:textbox id="TextBox5" runat="server" />
        </td>
        <td>
          <!-
The CompareValidator can be used to compare the values of two controls by
specifying a control in the ControlToCompare property.  Note that
ControlToCompare
and ValueToCompare cannot both be set for a particular control.
          ->
          <asp:CompareValidator id="TextBox45Compare"
          ControlToValidate="TextBox4" ControlToCompare="TextBox5"
          Operator="LessThan" Type="Integer" Text="A must be < B"
          runat="server" Display="Dynamic"
ErrorMessage="CompareValidator: First field must be less than second field." />
        </td>
      </tr>
      <tr>
        <td>
          RegularExpressionValidator
        </td>
        <td>
          <asp:textbox id="TextBox6" runat="server" />
          <br>
        </td>
        <td>
          <!-
ValidationExpression refers to a valid regular expression.
The beginning of string (^)
and end of string characters ($) are optional for these expressions
and are always assumed by
the control. You'll find many sample regular expressions at
http://regexlib.com/.

Note that the Text property can also be set by placing a value between
the opening and closing
tags of a validator, as shown below.
          ->
```

```
              <asp:RegularExpressionValidator id="TextBox6Regex"
              runat="server" ControlToValidate="TextBox6"
              ValidationExpression="^\d{5}$" Display="Dynamic"
   ErrorMessage="RegularExpression:Zip code must be 5 numeric digits">
      *</asp:RegularExpressionValidator>
          </td>
        </tr>
        <tr>
          <td>
            CustomValidator: Even Number
          </td>
          <td>
              <asp:textbox id="TextBox7" text="3" runat="server" />
              <br>
          </td>
          <td>
            <!-
```

The CustomValidator supports one property and one event. The property
is   ClientValidationFunction and the event is ServerValidate. You
can specify a client-side function with the former property which will
be used for client-side validation, and you can handle the
ServerValidate event for server-side validation. The client and server
functions must follow the design shown in the <script> blocks at
the top of this listing.
            ->

```
              <asp:CustomValidator id="TextBox7Custom" runat="server"
              ControlToValidate="TextBox7"
              OnServerValidate="ServerValidate" Display="Dynamic"
              ErrorMessage="Must be an even number!"
              ClientValidationFunction="isEven">
      *</asp:CustomValidator>
          </td>
        </tr>
      </table>
      <p>
         <asp:Button id="Button1" onClick="Button1_Click"
         text="Save" runat="server" />
      <p>
         <asp:Label id="Label1" runat="server" />
      <p>
         <!-
```

The ValidationSummary control supports properties that control how it is
displayed, such as HeaderText, which controls the header.
DisplayMode must be one of BulletList, List, or SingleParagraph.

ShowMessageBox, when true, will display a JavaScript Alert with the
contents of the validation summary.

```
    ShowSummary, when false, will hide the summary on the page.
    This can be useful if no
    errors are to be output to the browser but the summary is to be logged,
    for instance.

    —>
            <asp:ValidationSummary ID="ValidationSummary1" runat="server"
            HeaderText="Error in the following field(s):"
            DisplayMode="BulletList" />
        </form>
    </body>
</html>
```

Comments

Remember that all validators run both client-side and server-side, and that you should always check `Page.IsValid` to ensure that its value is `True` before you perform any operations on the data that was submitted.

See Also

Regular Expressions—http://regexlib.com

Validation Control Samples—http://aspauthors.com/aspnetpro/validation/

1.9. Working With DropDownLists

You want to programmatically create a DropDownList, insert a blank row, and set the selected value.

Technique

The ASP.NET Web controls provide a rich object-oriented API to allow you to easily manipulate them. The following code instantiates a DropDownList and populates it with four items using several techniques. It also demonstrates how to dynamically set the selected item.

```
Private Sub Page_Load(ByVal sender As System.Object, _
    ByVal e As System.EventArgs)
    ' Instantiate the control
    ColorDropDownList = New DropDownList()
    ' Add an item using a string
    ColorDropDownList.Items.Add("Blue")
    ' Add an instance of a ListItem constructed with a string
    ColorDropDownList.Items.Add(New ListItem("Green"))
```

```
' Add an instance of a ListItem constructed with a text and a value
ColorDropDownList.Items.Add(New ListItem("Red", "Red"))
' Add a blank item to the top of the list
ColorDropDownList.Items.Insert(0, New ListItem(""))
' Set the selected item
ColorDropDownList.Items(0).Selected = True
' Add the control to a PlaceHolder on the page
PlaceHolder1.Controls.Add(ColorDropDownList)
End Sub
```

Comments

There are several ways to set the selected item, just as there are several ways to add items. You can also set the control's `SelectedIndex` to an appropriate value, or find a particular Item in its `Items` collection by using the Items collection's `FindByText` or `FindByValue` methods. These methods return a particular item in the list (if one exists that matches the criteria specified). Also note that inserting a blank first item is a common technique performed with data-bound DropDownLists, and that this must be done *after* the list has called its `DataBind()` method.

See Also

Section 14.2, "Data-binding to a DropDownList"

1.10. Creating Dependent DropDownList Controls

You want to create several DropDownList controls that depend upon one another.

Technique

You can solve this issue by:

- Dynamically filling the DropDownList controls with data
- Catching the `SelectedIndexChanged` event from the control where the selection changes

When you want the contents of a DropDownList control (referred to as the *slave* control) to depend on the contents of another DropDownList control (referred to as the *master* control), you need to signal this slave control when the selected item in the master control changes. The result of this is a rewrite of the contents of the slave control.

The ASPX page is as follows:

```
<html>
<body>
    <form id="dependingdropdowns" method="post" runat="server">
    <asp:DropDownList id="countryList" runat="server"
    AutoPostBack="True"
    OnSelectedIndexChanged="SelectedIndexChangedEventHandler"/>
    <asp:DropDownList id="cityList" runat="server" />
</form>
</body>
</html>
```

The master control has the `AutoPostBack` property set to `True`. This allows an immediate postback of the form when the selection changes. Otherwise, it is impossible to rewrite the contents of the slave control. When the selection changes in the master control, the `SelectedIndexChanged` event will be raised and the `SelectedIndexChangedEventHandler` function will be executed.

In `<script runat="server" />` block or codebehind:

```
Private Sub Page_Load(ByVal sender As System.Object, _
    ByVal e As System.EventArgs) Handles MyBase.Load
    If Not IsPostBack Then
        countryList.Items.Add(New ListItem("- Make a selection -"))
        countryList.Items.Add(New ListItem("Belgium", "B"))
        countryList.Items.Add(New ListItem("France", "F"))
    End If
End Sub
```

The first time the page is shown, the contents of the master control will be set. The initial selection will be the `Make a selection` option. In the same block or codebehind, you also have:

```
Private Sub SelectedIndexChangedEventHandler( _
    ByVal sender As System.Object, _
    ByVal e As System.EventArgs) Handles countryList.SelectedIndexChanged
    cityList.Items.Clear()
    If countryList.SelectedItem.Value = "B" Then
        cityList.Items.Add(New ListItem("Brussels"))
        cityList.Items.Add(New ListItem("Antwerp"))
        cityList.Items.Add(New ListItem("Ghent"))
    ElseIf countryList.SelectedItem.Value = "F" Then
        cityList.Items.Add(New ListItem("Paris"))
        cityList.Items.Add(New ListItem("Lyon"))
        cityList.Items.Add(New ListItem("Bordeaux"))
    End If
End Sub
```

This is the core of the process. In this code block, the contents of the slave control are set, depending on the selection in the master control. This happens only if a valid selection for the master control is made (in this case, when a country is selected). This function is called any time the selection in the master control changes.

Comments

This example covers the situation in which one slave control depends on one master control. The technique can be extended. When several slaves depend on one master control, you have to set the contents of all slave controls in the `SelectedIndexChanged` event handler. When you want a third control to depend on the second one, you have to set the `AutoPostBack` property to `True` for the second DropDownList, and add an event handler to the `SelectedIndexChanged` event for this control. The technique to rewrite this third combo is similar to the earlier technique. You simply have to make sure that when the selection of the first combo changes, both selections for the second and third are set to a valid option.

See Also

http://www.aspalliance.com/timmusschoot/aspdotnet/dropdownrewrite.aspx

1.11. Working with ListBoxes

You want to display a ListBox and, after a postback, determine which value or values a user has selected.

Technique

Use the `System.Web.UI.WebControls.ListBox` control to place a ListBox control. To allow multiple values to be chosen from the ListBox, set the `SelectionMode` property to `Multiple`. The default is `Single`. The `SelectedIndex` property can use used to determine whether the user has selected any items from the ListBox. The ASPX page is as follows:

```
<html>
    <head>
        <title>recipe0111vb</title>
    </head>
    <body>
    <form id="Form1" method="post" runat="server">
        <asp:ListBox
            ID="CountryListBox"
            Runat="server"
```

```
        SelectionMode="Multiple">
        <asp:ListItem Value=1>United States</asp:ListItem>
        <asp:ListItem Value=2>United Kingdom</asp:ListItem>
        <asp:ListItem Value=3>China</asp:ListItem>
        <asp:ListItem Value=4>India</asp:ListItem>
    </asp:ListBox><br>

    <asp:Button
        ID="SubmitButton"
        Runat="server"
        Text="Submit"
        OnClick="Verify">
    </asp:Button>

    <asp:Label
        ID="OutputLabel"
        Runat="server">
    </asp:Label>

  </form>
  </body>
</html>
```

In `<script runat="server" />` block or codebehind:

```
Public Sub Verify(sender As System.Object, e As System.EventArgs)

Dim myListItem As ListItem
If CountryListBox.SelectedIndex <> -1 Then
    OutputLabel.Text = "You selected: "
        If CountryListBox.SelectionMode = ListSelectionMode.Single Then
            OutputLabel.Text += "<b>" & _
                CountryListBox.SelectedItem.Text & "</b>"
        Else
            For Each myListItem In CountryListBox.Items
                    If myListItem.Selected Then
                        OutputLabel.Text += "<b>" & myListItem.Text & _
                            "</b>, "
                    End If
            Next
        End If
Else
        OutputLabel.Text = "You didn't selected any country!"
End If

End Sub
```

Comments

This example demonstrates how to determine which values a user selected from a multiple-selection ListBox. First, you start with an `If` statement, which verifies whether the user has selected an item. Then you parse through all the items in the ListBox to find the number of items selected. You also use a `Label` Web Server Control to display the output to the user. If you want to retrieve the value of the selected item, you use the following statement:

```
CountryListBox.SelectedItem.Value
```

Note that for a multiple-selection ListBox, this will only return the first value.

See Also

`http://aspalliance.com/das/tutorial/listbox.aspx`

1.12. Persisting Data on a Web Form between Postbacks

> You want to have your form controls automatically retain their values between postbacks.

Technique

By default, all ASP.NET HTML Controls and Web Controls will automatically persist their values between postbacks.

The following page demonstrates a standard HTML input box, an HtmlInputText control, and a TextBox control, and how the latter two will retain their values after each postback without any extra code.

```
<form id="StateDemo" method="post" runat="server">
    <p>Enter values for each box and press the button.</p>
    Input Type=Text box: <input type="text"><br/>
    Input Type=Text box with runat=server: <input type="text" id="Input1"
    runat="server" /> <br/>
    ASP TextBox Web Control: <asp:TextBox id="TextBox1" runat="server" /><br/>
    <asp:Button ID="Button1" Runat="server" Text="Postback!" />
</form>
```

Comments

Although in classic ASP, it was necessary to use in-line script to set the values of the HTML form elements, ASP.NET takes care of this tedious chore for you. This is one of the coolest and simplest features of ASP.NET. Non-form controls, such as Labels, also persist their values automatically using `ViewState`, and you can control this behavior by using the `EnableViewState` property of these controls.

1.13. Adding Client-Side Script to a Web Form

You want to add client-side scripting to a Web Form programmatically from your ASP.NET code.

Technique

Use three methods to emit client-side script: the `System.Web.UI.Page`'s `RegisterStartupScript` and `RegisterClientScriptBlock` methods, and the `System.Web.UI.WebControls.WebControl` (Button) `Attributes.Add` method.

This simple login example asks the users to enter their names and passwords and then click the Submit button. You first want to emit client-side JavaScript that will set the initial browser focus to the username field. You also want to emit client-side script that will require a confirmation from the users if the password field is blank.

The ASPX page is as follows:

```
<asp:TextBox id="UserNameTextBox" runat="server"></asp:TextBox>
<br>
<asp:TextBox id="PasswordTextBox" runat="server"
  TextMode="Password"></asp:TextBox>
<br>
<asp:Button id="SubmitButton" runat="server" Text="Submit"></asp:Button>
```

In `<script runat="server" />` block or codebehind:

```
Public Sub Page_Load(sender As [Object], e As EventArgs)

  ' emit script to set initial focus
  RegisterStartupScript("focus", _
    "<SCRIPT language='javascript'>" + _
    "form1.UserNameTextBox.focus()" + _
    "</" + "SCRIPT>")

  ' emit script to check for blank password
  RegisterClientScriptBlock("myscripts", _
    "<SCRIPT language='javascript'>" + _
    "function checkPwd(){" + _
    " if ( form1.PasswordTextBox.value == '')" + _
    "  if ( confirm('Are you sure about a blank password?'))" +
    "   return true;" + _
    "  else {" + _
    "   form1.PasswordTextBox.focus();" + _
    "   return false;" + _
    "  } else return true;" + _
    " } </" + "SCRIPT>")
```

```
' add submit button onclick event to call checkPwd function
SubmitButton.Attributes.Add("onclick", "javascript:return checkPwd()")

End Sub 'Page_Load
```

Comments

The `RegisterStartupScript` method emits the client-side JavaScript that sets the initial focus into the Web Form just before the closing tag of the `Page` object's `<form runat=server>` element, thus ensuring that the script will run when the page is first loaded. The `RegisterClientScriptBlock` method emits the JavaScript containing the `checkPwd` function just after the opening tag of the `Page` object's `<form runat=server>` element. Finally, you use the `SubmitButton` object's `Attributes.Add` method to add the button's `onclick` event, which calls the JavaScript `checkPwd` function.

See Also

Page.RegisterStartupScript—`http://msdn.microsoft.com/library/en-us/cpref/html/ frlrfsystemwebuipageclassregisterstartupscripttopic.asp`

Page.RegisterClientScriptBlock—`http://msdn.microsoft.com/library/en-us/cpref/html /frlrfsystemwebuipageclassregisterclientscriptblocktopic.asp`

Tidbits and ASP.NET FAQs (Set Focus)—`http://aspalliance.com/shark/articles/ NewbieFAQs/FAQDoc.aspx`

2

User Controls

2.0. Introduction

A great way to encapsulate functionality so that it can be used on multiple Web Forms in an application is with User Controls. User Controls offer a programming model that closely models that of Web Forms, making them very easy for ASP.NET developers to pick up once they are familiar with building Web Forms. The most frequent use for User Controls is to create navigation and other layout elements for an application that can be reused across many Web Forms. They have full support for properties and events, they can be built and deployed using just a text editor, and they can be built with separate HTML and code sections, unlike other custom controls.

One key limitation of User Controls, however, is that they cannot be referenced outside of their application domain for security reasons. If you need to span multiple applications, you will probably want to use a custom control instead.

In this chapter, you learn the most common tasks that are encountered when working with User Controls. You'll start with the basics, and work up to some advanced techniques that can be used to build dynamic Web sites such as Microsoft's IBuySpy portal.

2.1. Declaring a User Control

You want to create a User Control for use by your Web Forms.

Technique

Simply place the appropriate code inside of an .ASCX file. The ASCX page:

```
<%@ Control Language="VB" %>
<asp:label runat="server" id="lblSample" />
```

In `<script runat="server" />` block or codebehind:

```
Sub Page_Load(sender as object, e as EventArgs)
lblSample.Text = "Sample Control Text"
End Sub
```

Comments

User Controls are declared almost the same as normal Web Forms, except that they have the .ASCX extension and use @ Control directives instead of @ Page directives. Like the @ Page directive, the @ Control directive supports several parameters, all of which are optional. It is generally best not to include a server-side `form` tag in a User Control (for example, `<form runat="server">`), because there can be only one of these per Web Form. Also, User Controls that include form controls must be placed within a server-side form for these controls to work correctly. Also, codebehind classes for User Controls need to inherit from `System.Web.UI.UserControl`.

2.2. Adding a User Control to a Web Form

You want to add a User Control to a Web Form.

Technique

You must first register the User Control on the page before you can insert it like a regular control. At the top of the ASPX page, add the following:

```
<%@ Register TagPrefix="AspNetCookbook" TagName="SampleControl"
    Src="SampleControl.ascx" %>
```

In the ASPX page where you want to insert the control:

```
<AspNetCookbook:SampleControl runat="server" />
```

Comments

The @ Register directive allows you to specify the prefix of the tag (`TagPrefix`), the name of the tag (`TagName`), and the relative location of the User Control (`Src`) to associate with the specified tag prefix and tag name. The User Control is then inserted; for example, `<TagPrefix:TagName runat="server" />`.

Users of Visual Studio .NET will note that there is very limited designer support for user controls, and that in HTML view there is no code completion for prefixes specified in `<%@ Register %>` blocks on a page.

2.3. Getting and Setting User Control Properties

You want to read or write properties of a User Control from your Web Form.

Technique

User Control public properties can be set declaratively or programmatically from the page that contains them. Their values can also be read and used by the containing page. Full-property declaration should be used as a best practice, but for quick-and-dirty work, you might use public variables instead.

The User Control (recipe0203vb.ascx) is as follows:

```
<%@ Control Language="vb" %>
<script runat="server">
Private _title As String
Private _author As String
Private _renderDate As DateTime = System.DateTime.Now

Public Property Title() As String
   Get
      Return _title
   End Get
   Set
      _title = value
   End Set
End Property


Public Property Author() As String
   Get
      Return _author
   End Get
   Set
      _author = value
   End Set
End Property


Public ReadOnly Property RenderDate() As DateTime
   Get
      Return _renderDate
   End Get
End Property


Private Sub Page_Load(sender As Object, e As EventArgs)
   TitleLabel.Text = Title
   AuthorLabel.Text = Author
End Sub
```

```
</script>
<h1><asp:Label id="TitleLabel" runat="server" /></h1>
<h3><asp:Label id="AuthorLabel" runat="server" />
</h1>
```

This User Control is for a header of a story. It includes input parameters for the title and author of the story. It also exposes a `readonly` property for `RenderDate` that the calling page can use if it chooses to do so. The following page uses this control. It demonstrates how to set its `Title` property declaratively (in the HTML tag for the control) and how to set its `Author` property programmatically. It also reads the `RenderDate` and displays it in a Label. The ASPX page (`recipe0203vb.aspx`) is as follows:

```
<%@ Page Language="VB" %>
<%@ Register TagPrefix="ucl" TagName="header" Src="recipe0203vb.ascx" %>
<!DOCTYPE HTML PUBLIC "-//W3C//DTD HTML 4.0 Transitional//EN" >
<HTML>
  <HEAD>
    <title>User Controls</title>
    <Script Runat="Server">
    Private Sub Page_Load(sender As Object, e As System.EventArgs)
    header1.Author = "Snoopy"
    FooterLabel.Text = "Rendered " + header1.RenderDate
    End Sub 'Page_Load
    </Script>
  </HEAD>
  <body>
    <form id="dependingdropdowns" method="post" runat="server">
      <ucl:header id="header1" runat="server"
      Title="A Tale of Mystery"></ucl:header>
      <p>It was a dark and stormy night.</p>
      <hr />
      <asp:Label ID="FooterLabel" Runat="server" />
    </form>
  </body>
</HTML>
```

Comments

Note that these examples do not use codebehind files, so all class members are available locally. It is sometimes necessary to use reflection to access properties of User Controls that do not use codebehind from pages that do use codebehind. This is covered in section 2.8, "Programmatically Accessing Properties of a Late-Bound User Control."

See Also

Section 2.8, "Programmatically Accessing Properties of a Late-Bound User Control"

2.4. Partial Page Output Caching

You want to cache the output of a User Control.

Technique

```
<%@ OutputCache Duration="60" VaryByParam="none" %>
<script runat="server">
   Sub Page_Load(sender As Object, e As EventArgs)
      timestamp.Text = DateTime.Now.ToString()
   End Sub
</script>
<asp:Label id="timestamp" runat="server" />
```

Comments

Caching the entire contents of a page is not always desirable. Examples include:

- An application that executes per requested business logic
- An application that displays user-specific content (personalization)

Examples such as these are bad candidates for page output caching because the content can be reused only by the same user. Good candidates for partial page output caching include any dynamically generated content shared by all users, such as a menu or content served from a database.

See Section 4.2, "Partial Page Output Caching VaryByControl," for extensions to partial page caching.

2.5. Dynamically Adding User Controls to a Web Form

You want to programmatically insert a User Control into a Web Form.

Technique

You simply load the User Control into a `Control` object and add it to the page (or other control inherited from `System.Web.UI.Control`). In `<script runat="server">` or codebehind:

```
Sub Page_Load(sender as object, e as EventArgs)
Dim sampleControl as Control = LoadControl("recipe0201vb.ascx")
Controls.Add(sampleControl)
End Sub
```

You can also add an @ Reference directive at the top of the page to tell ASP.NET to dynamically compile and link the control at runtime. In the ASPX page:

```
<%@ Reference Control="recipe0201vb.ascx" %>
```

Comments

The `LoadControl` function takes the virtual path to the User Control (specified as the parameter) and returns a `Control` object. This object can then be loaded onto the page with `Controls.Add(control As System.Web.UI.Control)`. The `Controls.Add` function is also a member of any other control that inherits from `System.Web.UI.Control`.

This technique can allow you to dynamically create your entire Web site. The IBuySpy portal sample application makes extensive use of this technique.

> ### See Also
>
> Creating Instances of User Controls Programmatically—http://msdn.microsoft.com/library/
> en-us/cpguide/html/cpconinstantiatingusercontrolsprogrammatically.asp
>
> IBuySpy Portal—http://IBuySpyPortal.com

2.6. Raising Events from a User Control

You want to raise an event from a User Control and handle it in a Web Form.

Technique

User Controls support events using the same syntax as other classes in the .NET Framework. Simply declare the event using the following syntax.

In the User Control's `<script runat="server" />` block or codebehind:

```
Public Event MultipleReached(ByVal sender As Object, ByVal e As EventArgs)

Public Overridable Sub OnMultipleReached(ByVal e As EventArgs)
    RaiseEvent MultipleReached(Me, e)
End Sub
```

The page can wire up the event by specifying a function for the `OnMultipleReached` attribute of the User Control, as follows. The ASPX page:

```
<uc1:Recipe0206vb id="Recipe0206vb1" runat="server" Multiple="5"
    OnMultipleReached="MultipleReached"></ucl:Recipe0206vb>
```

The User Control needs to raise the event by calling `OnMultipleReached`, which in this case it does every *N*th time a counter is incremented.

In the User Control's `<script runat="server" />` block or codebehind:

```
' if number of hits is a multiple of Multiple, raise event
If Application("count") Mod Multiple = 0 Then
    OnMultipleReached(EventArgs.Empty)
End If
```

Finally, in the page, you can specify which action to take in response to the event that the event handler function specified.

In `<script runat="server" />` block or codebehind:

```
Sub MultipleReached(ByVal sender As Object, ByVal e As EventArgs)
   Message.Text="Congratulations!  You were the 5th visitor!"
End Sub
```

Comments

The syntax for raising and handling events is quite different for C# than for VB.NET. The C# version of this technique is available from this book's Web site.

See Also

Section 15.9, "Handling Events"

Developing Microsoft ASP.NET Server Controls and Components by Nikhil Kothari and Vandana Datye (Microsoft Press; ISBN 0735615829)

2.7. Sharing User Controls Across Application Domains

You want to share your User Controls across application domains.

Technique

By design, User Controls are inaccessible outside of the application domain in which they reside. This is for security reasons. However, this can be a limitation if you want to share User Controls across several applications on a server. A fairly straightforward workaround exists, which involves setting up a virtual directory within each application that needs to use the User Controls, and mapping that virtual directory to a single physical directory containing the User Controls. This solution is better than simply copying the User Controls from application to application, because that would quickly turn into a maintenance nightmare.

These steps were developed by readers of `AspAlliance.com`, and were first published in the article listed at the end of this section.

1. Create a Web application project to hold the User Controls, and place the shared User Controls in this project.

2. Create a virtual directory in each application that needs to use these shared User Controls. This is done in the IIS manager by right-clicking on the application and choosing New, Virtual Directory. Browse to the folder created for the Web application in Step 1, and name the directory the same as that folder.

3. Create a reference from each application that needs the shared controls to the shared controls. This is done in Visual Studio .NET from within the Solution Explorer by right-clicking and choosing Add Reference. Browse to the bin folder of the project created in Step 1 and select the DLL from that folder. (It should have the same name as the project by default.)

4. Drag-and-drop will not work for these shared User Controls in VS.NET. Instead, you must manually type the `<%@ Register %>` directive and specify the `Src` of the User Control, referring to the virtual directory you set up (see Section 2.2).

See Also

Reuse in ASP.NET Across Application Domains—`http://www.aspalliance.com/stevesmith/articles/netreuse1.asp`

Section 2.2, "Adding a User Control to a Web Form"

2.8. Programmatically Accessing Properties of a Late-Bound User Control

You want to programmatically access the properties and/or methods of a User Control that does not have a codebehind and is just-in-time(JIT) compiled on its first request.

Technique

In this example, you have a simple greeting User Control that exposes two properties and a method. You set one property using late binding and the other property using reflection. You then invoke the method using reflection. The User Control uses these properties to display a Label that holds a combination of these values. The code for the User Control is available from this book's support Web site. When you declare the User Control on the page, you also set its username property declaratively—this property will be overridden at runtime by the code in `Page_Load()`.

The ASPX page:

```
<form id="Test" method="post" runat="server">
  <ucl:Recipe0208vb id="Recipe0208vbl" runat="server"
  username="Steve"></ucl:Recipe0208vb>
</form>
```

In `<script runat="server" />` block or codebehind:

```
Protected Recipe0208vb1 As Object

Private Sub Page_Load(ByVal sender As System.Object, _
    ByVal e As System.EventArgs) Handles MyBase.Load
    'Late binding call will override declarative setting
    'Only works in VB, not C#
    Recipe0208vb1.UserName = "Rob"

    'Reflection
    Dim myControl As Control = Page.FindControl("Recipe0208vb1")
    Dim myControlType As Type = myControl.GetType()
    Dim GreetingProperty As PropertyInfo =
        myControlType.GetProperty("Greeting")
    GreetingProperty.SetValue(myControl, "Guten Tag, ", Nothing)

    Dim MessageMethod As MethodInfo = myControlType.GetMethod("AddMessage")
    Dim Params() As Object = New Object()
        {"This message was added using reflection!"}
    MessageMethod.Invoke(myControl, Params)
End Sub
```

Comments

There are two ways to do this. The first one only works in Visual Basic and uses *late binding*. It works only when `Option Strict` is turned off, and allows variables declared as `Object` to use methods and properties that are not known at compile time. In general, it is not a good idea to use late binding if you can avoid it. However, one of the advantages of VB over C# is that it supports late binding, which provides a much simpler mechanism than reflection for tasks like the one described in this section.

The second technique uses a process called *reflection*, which uses classes found in the `System.Reflection` namespace. The net effect is the same as with late binding, but the calls are much more explicit, and there is a lot more code. Because reflection is built into the .NET Framework, it will work with any .NET language.

See Also

Understanding User Controls, Part 2—

http://www.dotnetjunkies.com/tutorials.aspx?tutorialid=507

3

Custom Controls

3.0. Introduction

One of the most powerful features of ASP.NET is its support for custom server controls and components. ASP.NET ships with dozens of built-in controls, and developers can easily extend these controls or write their own controls from scratch. Server controls can be used to encapsulate complex user interface logic or business rules, and can benefit from design-time support like drag-and-drop and toolbox support and property builders. Custom controls pick up where User Controls leave off, providing greater flexibility, reusability, and a better design time experience, but with some added complexity. In this chapter you will find examples covering some of the most common server-control techniques.

Custom controls as a rule inherit directly or indirectly from the `System.Web.UI.Control` base class. Controls that are visible on a page should inherit directly or indirectly from `System.Web.UI.WebControls.WebControl`, which provides properties like `Style`, which you can use to determine the look of the control on the page. Custom controls can be built in a number of ways. Some simply override the `Render()` method, thus determining the HTML output in place of the control at run-time. Others, known as composite controls, act as containers for other controls. Others inherit from existing fully functional controls to create more specific versions of these controls or to enhance their functionality.

Controls in ASP.NET can support *data-binding* as well as *templates*. In fact, there is easily enough information about building controls to fill an entire book (and in fact such a book exists and is listed at the end of this section), so this chapter attempts to cover the most common techniques that you will use, leaving much of the theory to other books dedicated to control building.

See Also

Developing ASP.NET Server Controls and Components by Nikhil Kothari and Vandana Datye (Microsoft Press; ISBN 0735615829)

3.1. Declaring a Simple Custom Control

You want to create a simple custom control to output some text.

Technique

This example demonstrates how easy it is to create custom controls in ASP.NET, especially when compared to COM components. You simply create a class that inherits from `System.Web.UI.Control` or `System.Web.UI.WebControls.WebControl` and give it whatever properties and methods you need. In Visual Studio .NET, you would normally do this by creating a new Web Control Library project. You override its `Render()` method to control its output, and you have a very simple yet powerful tool for encapsulating and reusing user interface logic.

The `Recipe0301vb` class is as follows:

```
Imports System.ComponentModel
Imports System.Web.UI
Namespace AspNetCookbook

    <DefaultProperty("Text"), ToolboxData("<{0}:Recipe0301vb
        runat=server></{0}:Recipe0301vb>")> Public Class Recipe0301vb
        Inherits System.Web.UI.WebControls.WebControl

        Dim _text As String

        <Bindable(True), Category("Appearance"),
        DefaultValue("")> Property [Text]() As String
            Get
                Return _text
            End Get

            Set(ByVal Value As String)
                _text = Value
            End Set
        End Property

        Protected Overrides Sub Render(
            ByVal output As System.Web.UI.HtmlTextWriter)
            output.Write([Text])
        End Sub

    End Class
End Namespace
```

To reference a custom control on a Web Form, you need to add a `Register` directive to the page, and specify three parameters. The `TagPrefix` is used for all controls from this namespace and assembly when they are declared on the page, and can be anything but asp, which is reserved for the built-in Web Controls that ASP.NET provides. Next, the namespace in which the controls reside must be specified. Finally, the name of the assembly, without any path information or the .DLL extension, is specified for the Assembly parameter. An example of this follows:

```
<%@ Page language="VB" %>
<%@ Register TagPrefix="AspNetCookbook" Namespace="AspNetCookbook"
Assembly="RecipesVB" %>
...
<form id="Form1" method="post" runat="server">
  <AspNetCookbook:Recipe0301vb id="Recipe0301vb1" runat="server" />
</form>
```

Comments

Note that in Visual Studio .NET, a default namespace with the same name as the project is automatically prefixed to all Visual Basic class names. This is a frequent source of confusion and is inconsistent with how default namespaces are handled in C#, where they are inserted into each class file as a visible namespace. You can turn off this default behavior by setting the default namespace to an empty string in the Project Properties dialog box. You can determine the full namespace of a class by using the ILDASM.EXE command-line tool on the generated assembly, or by going into the class view utility in Visual Studio .NET.

3.2. Extending Existing Web Controls

You want to extend the functionality of an existing Web Control.

Technique

This example shows how to extend the functionality of an existing control—the Label control—and turn it into a RainbowLabel. This is accomplished through the use of *inheritance*—RainbowLabel is a *subclass* of the System.Web.UI.WebControls.Label class.

The RainbowLabel class is as follows:

```
Imports System
Imports System.Web.UI
Imports System.Web.UI.WebControls
Imports System.ComponentModel

Public Class RainbowLabel
  Inherits System.Web.UI.WebControls.Label
```

```
Public Property EnableRainbowMode() As Boolean
  Get
    If ViewState("EnableRainbowMode") Is Nothing Then
      Return True
    Else
      Return Boolean.Parse(CStr(ViewState("EnableRainbowMode")))
    End If
  End Get
  Set(ByVal Value As Boolean)
    ViewState("EnableRainbowMode") = Value
  End Set
End Property

Protected Overrides Sub Render(ByVal output As HtmlTextWriter)
  If EnableRainbowMode Then
    output.Write(ColorizeString([Text]))
  Else
    output.Write([Text])
  End If
End Sub  'Render

Private Function ColorizeString(ByVal input As String) As String
  Dim output As New System.Text.StringBuilder(input.Length)
  Dim rand As Random = New Random(DateTime.Now.Millisecond)

  Dim i As Integer
  For i = 0 To input.Length - 1
    Dim red As Integer = rand.Next(0, 255)
    Dim green As Integer = rand.Next(0, 255)
    Dim blue As Integer = rand.Next(0, 255)

    output.Append("<font color=""#")
    output.Append(Convert.ToString(red, 16))
    output.Append(Convert.ToString(green, 16))
    output.Append(Convert.ToString(blue, 16))
    output.Append(""">")
    output.Append(input.Substring(i, 1))
    output.Append("</font>")
  Next i

  Return output.ToString()
End Function
End Class
```

To use this control, you need to do the following:

```
<%@ Page language="VB" %>
<%@ Register TagPrefix="AspNetCookbook" Namespace="AspNetCookbook"
```

```
Assembly="AspNetCookbook" %>
<!DOCTYPE HTML PUBLIC "-//W3C//DTD HTML 4.0 Transitional//EN" >
<html>
<head>
<title>03 Custom Controls - 02 Extending Existing Web Controls</title>
</head>
<body>

<form id="Form1" method="post" runat="server">
  <AspNetCookbook:RainbowLabel text="This is a rainbow colored test string"
  runat="server"/><br />
  <AspNetCookbook:RainbowLabel EnableRainbowMode="false"
  text="This is a test string" runat="server"/>
</form>

</body>
</html>
```

Comments

This control creates a rainbow-ish pattern in the text it displays. This is accomplished by encapsulating each character in `<font>` tags. The color on each character is randomized. Although perhaps not the most useful control, it does demonstrate how easy it is to extend the functionality of existing Web Controls. It is worth noting that the Label control should not be overlooked as a powerful control on which to build—the validation controls all inherit from the simple Label control.

See Also

Section 3.1, "Declaring a Simple Custom Control"

Developing ASP.NET Server Controls and Components by Nikhil Kothari and Vandana Datye (Microsoft Press; ISBN 0735615829)

3.3. Creating ViewState-Enabled Control Properties

You want your control's properties to retain their state using `ViewState`.

Technique

This example shows you how to create properties for your controls that retain their state using `ViewState`.

The `ViewStateControl` class:

```
Imports System
Imports System.Web.UI
Imports System.Web.UI.WebControls
Imports System.ComponentModel

Public Class ViewStateControl
  Inherits System.Web.UI.WebControls.WebControl

  Public Property [Text]() As String
    Get
      Dim _text As String = CStr(ViewState("Text"))
      If _text Is Nothing Then
        Return String.Empty
      Else
        Return _text
      End If
    End Get
    Set(ByVal Value As String)
      ViewState("Text") = Value
    End Set
  End Property



  Protected Overrides Sub Render(ByVal writer As HtmlTextWriter)
    writer.Write([Text])
  End Sub
End Class
```

To use this control, you need to do the following:

```
<%@ Page language="VB" %>
<%@ Register TagPrefix="AspNetCookbook" Namespace="AspNetCookbook"
Assembly="AspNetCookbook" %>
<!DOCTYPE HTML PUBLIC "-//W3C//DTD HTML 4.0 Transitional//EN" >
<html>
<head>
<title>Recipe0303</title>
</head>
<body>

<script language="VB" runat="server">
Sub Page_Load(Sender As Object, E As EventArgs)
  If Not IsPostBack Then
    Dim RandomGenerator As Random
    RandomGenerator = New Random(DateTime.Now.Millisecond)

    ViewStateControl1.Text = RandomGenerator.Next(1,100)
  End If
```

```
End Sub
</script>

<form id="Form1" method="post" runat="server">
  <AspNetCookbook:ViewStateControl id="ViewStateControl1" runat="server"/>
  <asp:linkbutton text="PostBack test" runat="server"/>
</form>

</body>
</html>
```

Comments

This control property called Text will retain its state on postbacks—as you see, it is quite easy to get properties to retain their state by using the ViewState property, and this technique is recommended for most Web Control properties.

See Also

Section 3.1, "Declaring a Simple Custom Control"

3. 4. Creating a Composite Control

You want to combine two or more Web Controls into a single composite custom control.

Technique

This example shows you how to create a very simple yet useful composite control. The control is a composition of a TextBox and a validator, and the control can be used to validate email addresses. The EmailTextBox class is as follows:

```
Imports System
Imports System.Web.UI
Imports System.Web.UI.WebControls
Imports System.ComponentModel
Imports System.ComponentModel.Design

Namespace AspNetCookbook
  Public Class EmailTextBox
    Inherits System.Web.UI.WebControls.WebControl
    Implements INamingContainer

    Private textBox As textBox
    Private validator As RegularExpressionValidator
```

```
    Public Property Text() As String
      Get
        EnsureChildControls()
        Return textBox.Text
      End Get
      Set(ByVal Value As String)
        EnsureChildControls()
        textBox.Text = Value
      End Set
    End Property


    Public Property ErrorMessage() As String
      Get
        EnsureChildControls()
        Return validator.ErrorMessage
      End Get
      Set(ByVal Value As String)
        EnsureChildControls()
        validator.ErrorMessage = Value
      End Set
    End Property


    Public Overrides ReadOnly Property Controls() As ControlCollection
      Get
        EnsureChildControls()
        Return MyBase.Controls
      End Get
    End Property


    Protected Overrides Sub CreateChildControls()
      Controls.Clear()

      textBox = New TextBox
      validator = New RegularExpressionValidator

      Controls.Add(textBox)
      Controls.Add(validator)

      textBox.ID = "Email1"
      validator.ControlToValidate = textBox.ID
      'A typical email address regular expression
      validator.ValidationExpression = "^([a-zA-Z0-9_\-\.]+)@((\[[0-9]{1,3}
\.[0-9]{1,3}\.[0-9]{1,3}\.)|(([a-zA-Z0-9\-]+\.)+))
([a-zA-Z]{2,4}|[0-9]{1,3})(\]?)$"
```

```
      End Sub
   End Class
End Namespace
```

To use this control, you need to do the following:

```
<%@ Page language="VB" %>
<%@ Register TagPrefix="AspNetCookbook" Namespace="AspNetCookbook"
Assembly="AspNetCookbook" %>
<!DOCTYPE HTML PUBLIC "-//W3C//DTD HTML 4.0 Transitional//EN" >
<html>
<head>
<title>Recipe0304</title>
</head>
<body>

<form id="Form1" method="post" runat="server">
  <AspNetCookbook:EmailTextBox
    ID="EmailTextBox1"
    ErrorMessage="You must provide a valid email address!"
    runat="server"
  />
</form>

</body>
</html>
```

Comments

This control validates the input in the TextBox. If the input is not a valid email address an error message appears. Controls like this one are useful on pages that contain a lot of user input that needs to be validated. You can easily extend this control to use several validator types, allow the page developer to define his/her own validation expression, and so on.

See Also

Regular Expression Library—http://regexlib.com/

3.5. Creating a Data-bound Control

You want to create a custom control that supports data-binding.

Technique

This example shows you how to create a simple and original data-bound custom server control—a data-bound bulleted list. The CustomBulletedList class is as follows:

```
Imports System
Imports System.Web.UI
Imports System.Web.UI.WebControls
Imports System.ComponentModel
Imports System.Collections
Imports System.Text

Public Class CustomBulletedList
  Inherits System.Web.UI.WebControls.WebControl

  Private _html As New StringBuilder()
  Private _dataSource As IEnumerable

  Public Property DataSource() As IEnumerable
    Get
      Return _dataSource
    End Get
    Set(ByVal value As IEnumerable)
      _dataSource = value
    End Set
  End Property

  Private Sub CreateBulletedList()
    Dim dataSource As IEnumerable = Nothing

    Try
      dataSource = Me._dataSource
    Catch
    End Try

    If Not (dataSource Is Nothing) Then
      _html.Append("<ul>")
      Dim dataObject As Object
      For Each dataObject In dataSource
        _html.Append("<li>")
        _html.Append(dataObject)
        _html.Append("</li>")
      Next dataObject
      _html.Append("</ul>")
    End If
  End Sub
```

```vb
Public Overrides Sub DataBind()
  MyBase.OnDataBinding(EventArgs.Empty)

  CreateBulletedList()
End Sub


Protected Overrides Sub Render(ByVal output As HtmlTextWriter)
  output.Write(_html)
End Sub
End Class
```

To use this control, you need to do the following:

```vb
<%@ Page Language="VB" %>
<%@ Register TagPrefix="AspNetCookbook" Namespace="AspNetCookbook"
Assembly="AspNetCookbook" %>
<!DOCTYPE HTML PUBLIC "-//W3C//DTD HTML 4.0 Transitional//EN" >
<html>
<head>
<title>Data Bound Controls</title>
</head>
<body>
<script language="vb" runat="server">
Sub Page_Load(ByVal sender As System.Object, ByVal e As System.EventArgs)
  listControl.DataSource = New String() {"Test 1", "Test 2", "Test 3"}
  listControl.DataBind()
End Sub
</script>

<AspNetCookbook:CustomBulletedList id="listControl" runat="server"/>

</body>
</html>
```

Comments

This control allows you to data-bind any data source that is derived from IEnumerable to it—the content will be listed in bulleted format. Overriding the DataBind method is the critical point in this control. When this method is called, it is trying to bind to the data source and call the CreateBulletedList method.

CreateBulletedList loops through all of the data objects in the data source and saves them to be outputted as bulleted lines.

By overriding the Render method, you can control the rendering of the control, and render it exactly as you see fit. You should always opt for this approach when performance is an issue (and when isn't it?), because it is much faster than overriding the CreateChildControls method.

One last point you should take note of is that you should always use a StringBuilder instead of a regular string as the HTML output source. Using regular string objects will *seriously* degrade the performance of your custom control.

See Also

Section 3.6, "Creating a Templated Control"

3.6. Creating a Templated Control

You want to create a control that supports the use of templates.

Technique

This example creates a simple templated control. It displays the current time on the server on which it runs and allows you to add dynamic text and so on.

First, the main control class, `DateTimeControl`:

```
Imports System
Imports System.Web.UI
Imports System.Web.UI.WebControls
Imports System.ComponentModel

Namespace AspNetCookbook
  <ToolboxData("<{0}:DateTimeControl runat=server></{0}:DateTimeControl>"), _
  ParseChildren(True)> _
  Public Class DateTimeControl
    Inherits Control
    Implements INamingContainer
    Private _template As ITemplate
    Private _container As DateTimeContainer
    Private _text As String

    <TemplateContainer(GetType(DateTimeContainer))> _
    Public Overridable Property Template() As ITemplate
      Get
        Return _template
      End Get
      Set(ByVal Value As ITemplate)
        _template = Value
      End Set
    End Property

    Public Overridable ReadOnly Property Container() As DateTimeContainer
      Get
```

```
      Return _container
    End Get
  End Property


  Public Overridable Property Text() As String
    Get
      Return _text
    End Get
    Set(ByVal Value As String)
      _text = Value
    End Set
  End Property


  Public Overridable ReadOnly Property DateTime() As String
    Get
      Return System.DateTime.Now.ToShortTimeString()
    End Get
  End Property


  Protected Overrides Sub OnDataBinding(ByVal e As EventArgs)
    EnsureChildControls()
    MyBase.OnDataBinding(e)
  End Sub          'OnDataBinding


  Protected Overrides Sub CreateChildControls()
    If Not (Template Is Nothing) Then
      _container = New DateTimeContainer(Text, DateTime)
      Template.InstantiateIn(Container)
      Controls.Add(Container)
    Else
      Controls.Add(New LiteralControl("" + [Text] + " " + DateTime))
    End If
  End Sub
End Class
```

Now let's take a look at the container control `DateTimeContainer`. It enables you to use
`<%# Container.Text %>` and so forth.

```
  Public Class DateTimeContainer
    Inherits Control
    Implements INamingContainer
    Private _text As String
    Private _dateTime As String


    Public Sub New(ByVal text As String, ByVal dateTime As String)
```

```
      Me._text = text
      Me._dateTime = dateTime
    End Sub         'New


    Public ReadOnly Property Text() As String
      Get
        Return _text
      End Get
    End Property

    Public ReadOnly Property DateTime() As String
      Get
        Return _dateTime
      End Get
    End Property
  End Class
End Namespace
```

Comments

This control allows you to add a template and thus choose how you want the data to be presented. The control is built using two classes—DateTimeControl is the actual control you add to the page and DateTimeContainer is the container control that holds the actual template data. Use of a container class is, strictly speaking, not necessary if you don't want to use custom properties. If you just want to display static content, you can instantiate the control in a Panel control or a similar control.

See Also

Section 3.4, "Creating a Composite Control"

Section 3.5, "Creating a Data-bound Control"

3.7. Dynamically Adding Controls to a Web Form

You want to programmatically insert controls into a Web Form.

Technique

You can add controls to any class that exposes a Controls() collection property by using the Class.Controls.Add() method. In this example, the user chooses which control should be added to the page. The PlaceHolder control can be used to specify exactly where on a Web Form you want your new control to appear, but otherwise is not necessary for this technique to work.

The ASPX page is as follows:

```
<form id="Recipe0307" method="post" runat="server">
  <asp:DropDownList id="DropDownList1" runat="server">
    <asp:ListItem Value="Simple Text Control (Recipe0301)">
      Simple Text Control (Recipe0301)</asp:ListItem>
    <asp:ListItem Value="RainbowLabel (Recipe0302)">RainbowLabel
      (Recipe0302)</asp:ListItem>
  </asp:DropDownList>
  <asp:Button id="Button1" runat="server" Text="Select"
   onclick="Button1_Click"></asp:Button>
  <p>
    <asp:PlaceHolder id="PlaceHolder1" runat="server"></asp:PlaceHolder>
  </p>
</form>
```

In `<script runat="server" />` block or codebehind:

```
Sub Button1_Click(ByVal sender As Object, ByVal e As System.EventArgs)
' Initialize Placeholder
PlaceHolder1.Controls.Clear()

Select Case DropDownList1.SelectedIndex
  Case 0:
    Dim SimpleText As AspNetCookbook.Recipe0301vb = _
      New AspNetCookbook.Recipe0301vb()
    SimpleText.Text = "This is the simple text control from Recipe 3.01."
    PlaceHolder1.Controls.Add(SimpleText)
    Exit Select
  Case 1:
    Dim RainbowText As AspNetCookbook.RainbowLabel = _
      New AspNetCookbook.RainbowLabel()
    RainbowText.Text = "This is the RainbowText control from Recipe 3.02."
    PlaceHolder1.Controls.Add(RainbowText)
    Exit Select
End Select
End Sub
```

Comments

Dynamically creating and inserting controls onto a page is a very powerful technique that you can easily extend to create flexible page architectures.

3.8. Using the Treeview IE Web Control

You want to implement a tree view using the TreeView IE Web Control.

Technique

The first step is to install the IE Web Controls from Microsoft. The link to download and install these controls is as follows: `http://msdn.microsoft.com/downloads/samples/ internet/default.asp?url=/downloads/samples/internet/asp_dot_net_ servercontrols/webcontrols/default.asp`

The next step is to add a reference to the controls on your page:

```
<%@ Register TagPrefix="mytree" Namespace="Microsoft.Web.UI.WebControls"
Assembly="Microsoft.Web.UI.WebControls" %>
<%@ import namespace="Microsoft.Web.UI.WebControls" %>
```

Then you add the `TreeView` control to your page:

```
<mytree:treeview runat="server" id="myTree">
</mytree:treeview>
```

The last step is to add the node information to the TreeView. This is the list of items that will appear when you expand the tree:

```
<mytree:treeview runat="server" id="myTree">
  <mytree:treenode text="Cars">
    <mytree:treenode text="Ford" />
     <mytree:treenode text="Toyota" />
    <mytree:treenode text="Infiniti" />
      </mytree:treenode>
</mytree:treeview>
```

Here, we created one node called `Cars` and then added nodes within that node for different car manufacturers.

Comments

The TreeView IE Web Control is a very powerful and easy-to-use control. In this example, you saw how easy it was to create an explorer-like expandable tree. When adding nodes to the TreeView, you use a very XML-like approach whereby the nodes that are under a parent node are contained inside the parent node tag. If you encounter errors when trying to add a reference to your page, or you receive errors indicating that the Web Controls cannot be found, copy the Web Controls DLL to the `bin` directory of your application.

See Also

Basics of the TreeView Control—

`http://www.aspalliance.com/jamesavery/webcontrols/treeviewp1.aspx`

Section 3.11, "Data-binding a TreeView Control"

Overview of Treeview Control—

`http://msdn.microsoft.com/workshop/webcontrols/overview/treeview.asp`

3.9. Using the TabControl and PageView IE Web Controls

You want to implement a tabbed interface or a wizard-like form using the IE Web Controls TabControl and PageView.

Technique

The first step is to install the IE Web Controls from Microsoft. The link to download and install these controls is as follows: `http://msdn.microsoft.com/downloads/samples/internet/default.asp?url=/downloads/samples/internet/asp_dot_net_servercontrols/webcontrols/default.asp`

Next, you need to add a reference to the Web Controls on your page:

```
<%@ Register TagPrefix="ieControls"
Namespace="Microsoft.Web.UI.WebControls"
Assembly="Microsoft.Web.UI.WebControls" %>
<%@ import namespace="Microsoft.Web.UI.WebControls" %>
```

Then you add your tabstrip. This is the control that generates the tabs that users click to change pages:

```
<IECONTROLS:TABSTRIP id="myTabStrip" runat="server" TargetID="myMultiPage"
   Orientation="Vertical">
            <IECONTROLS:Tab Text="Tab 1"></IECONTROLS:Tab>
            <IECONTROLS:TabSeparator></IECONTROLS:TabSeparator>
            <IECONTROLS:Tab Text="Tab 2"></IECONTROLS:Tab>
            <IECONTROLS:TabSeparator DefaultStyle="height:100%;">
            </IECONTROLS:TabSeparator>
</IECONTROLS:TABSTRIP>
```

Lastly, you need to add your multipage control that contains the different pages that will be viewed when users select each tab:

```
<IECONTROLS:MULTIPAGE id="myMultiPage" runat="server">
  <IECONTROLS:PAGEVIEW>
            Page 1
```

```
   </IECONTROLS:PAGEVIEW>
   <IECONTROLS:PAGEVIEW>
                Page 2
   </IECONTROLS:PAGEVIEW>
</IECONTROLS:MULTIPAGE>
```

Comments

Notice that there is a property on the tabstrip control called `TargetID`. This must be set to the ID of the multipage control that will be working with the tabstrip. When the users click on the tab, the tabstrip will then tell the PageView to show the corresponding page. When working with the multipage control, you can add any type of ASP.NET or HTML between the opening and closing PageView tags. In this example, the tabstrip is running vertically, but you can also set this value to horizontal. To do so, you simply need to set the `Orientation` property to `horizontal`.

See Also

Overview of TabStrip Control—

http://msdn.microsoft.com/workshop/webcontrols/overview/tabstrip.asp

Overview of MultiPage Control—

http://msdn.microsoft.com/workshop/webcontrols/overview/multipage.asp

3.10. Using the ToolBar IE Web Control

You want to implement a toolbar using the ToolBar IE Web Control.

Technique

The first step is to install the IE Web Controls from Microsoft. The link to download and install these controls is as follows: http://msdn.microsoft.com/downloads/samples/internet/default.asp?url=/downloads/samples/internet/asp_dot_net_servercontrols/webcontrols/default.asp

   Next, you need to add a reference to the Web Controls on your page:

```
<%@ Register TagPrefix="ieControls"
Namespace="Microsoft.Web.UI.WebControls"
Assembly="Microsoft.Web.UI.WebControls" %>
<%@ import namespace="Microsoft.Web.UI.WebControls" %>
```

Then, you add the toolbar to your page:

```
<iecontrols:Toolbar id="myToolbar" runat="server">
</ie:Toolbar>
```

Lastly, you add the buttons that you want to appear on your toolbar:

```
<iecontrols:Toolbar id="myToolbar" runat="server">
   <iecontrols:ToolbarButton Text="First Button" />
   <iecontrols:ToolbarSeparator />
   <iecontrols:ToolbarButton Text="<b>Second Button</b>" />
</iecontrols:Toolbar>
```

Comments

The toolbar control is a quick way to get a nice-looking toolbar working on your site. Notice in this example that you can even add rich content to the button text. This enables you to use HTML on your buttons. You can also set the `ImageUrl` property of the button tag to use an image as your button.

See Also

Overview of ToolBar Control—
http://msdn.microsoft.com/workshop/webcontrols/overview/toolbar.asp

3.11. Data-binding a TreeView Control

You want to populate a treeview with data by using XML and the TreeView IE Web Control.

Technique

If you have not worked with the TreeView control before, refer to section 3.8 for basic TreeView information. First, you need to add the TreeView to your page and set the `treenodesrc` property to the XML file that you'll be creating.

```
<mytree:treeview runat="server" id="myTree" treenodesrc="cars.XML">
</mytree:treeview>
```

The next thing you need to do is create your XML file that you will use to bind the TreeView to:

```
<?xml version="1.0" encoding="utf-8" ?>
<TREENODES>
  <treenode text="Cars">
    <treenode text="Ford" />
    <treenode text="Toyota" />
    <treenode text="Infiniti" />
  </treenode>
</TREENODES>
```

When the page loads, the TreeView will generate its nodes from the XML file.

Comments

It is not possible to directly data-bind a dataset to the TreeView Web Control. The data must first be translated to XML. You can use `response.write`, which writes the XML, or use XSLT to transform the dataset into the correct XML. When using XSLT, you can specify the XSLT file using the `TreeNodeXsltSrc` property of the TreeView. In addition to using XML to define the actual nodes of the TreeView, you can also use XML to define the style types by using the `TreeNodeTypeSrc` property of the TreeView control.

See Also

Overview of Treeview Control—

`http://msdn.microsoft.com/workshop/webcontrols/overview/treeview.asp`

Creating Dynamic TreeViews—

`http://www.aspalliance.com/jamesavery/webcontrols/treeviewp2.aspx`

3.12. Installing a Component in the Global Assembly Cache (GAC)

You want to access your custom control from any application on a server by registering its assembly in the Global Assembly Cache, or GAC.

Technique

The Global Assembly Cache in the .NET Framework provides a central place for registering assemblies. Registered assemblies are then available to all applications, including the development environments like Visual Studio.NET and Web Matrix. The process of adding an assembly to the Global Assembly Cache can be compared to the process of registering COM components in the server, as is done in the case of Windows DNA applications.

The first step involved in adding an assembly is to *strong-name* the assembly. A strong name is basically assigned to an assembly or a component to distinguish it from other assemblies and components existing in the GAC. A strong name consists of an assembly identity (name, version, and so on), a public key, and a digital signature.

Assigning a strong name to an assembly ensures that it is unique, has version protection, and has code integrity. Assigning a strong name to an assembly is not a difficult task. You can use the `sn.exe` utility to generate strong names, which are then added to the code of the assembly. For example, to create a strong name for an assembly named sample.dll, you would write the following in the command prompt:

```
c:\MyAssembly>sn -k sample.snk
```

This would generate a strong name keypair and store it in a file named sample.snk. The file extension can be anything, but.SNK is normally used as a convention. The -k option creates a strong name keypair. There are other options that you can search for in MSDN.

The second step is to associate the generated strong name file with the assembly. Add the following code to your assembly to associate the strong name. By default, Visual Studio .NET projects include skeleton declarations of these attributes in the `AssemblyInfo` file.

```
Imports System.Reflection

<assembly: AssemblyKeyFile("sample.snk")>
```

Note here that the information regarding the file containing the strong name keypair is placed in the code file before any namespace declaration. Also, you must import the `System.Reflection` namespace in order for the statement to work, otherwise the compiler will not recognize the `<assembly: AssemblyKeyFile("sample.snk")>` statement.

After compiling the assembly with the statements containing the strong name information being added to it, you now have to place the assembly into the GAC. You can do this manually by simply copying and pasting the assembly into the GAC, which is located at `C:\WINNT\ASSEMBLY\`.

You can also use the gacutil.exe utility, installed with the .NET Framework. In order to add an assembly, you write the following on the command prompt:

```
gacutil /i sample.dll
```

The `/i` option is for installation. In order to remove an assembly from the GAC, you can use the same utility, as follows:

```
gacutil /u sample.dll
```

The `/u` option is for uninstalling or removing an assembly from the cache. Typing `gacutil /?` lists all of its options.

See Also

Section 3.1, "Declaring a Simple Custom Control"

Section 3.2, "Creating a Composite Control"

Command-Line Compilation—`http://aspalliance.com/hrmalik/articles/2002/200211/20021101.aspx`, Haroon Rasheed Malik

The .NET Assemblies—`http://aspalliance.com/hrmalik/articles/2002/200202/20020201.aspx`, Haroon Rasheed Malik

4

Caching

4.0. Introduction

Caching can provide huge performance benefits to almost any Web application if it is used correctly. The caching support in ASP.NET is top notch and provides users with the perfect combination of simple one-line page-level caching and a powerful and flexible caching API with tight control over how and when data should be cached. In this chapter, you learn how to use caching on pages, User Controls, and in your code to improve the performance of your ASP.NET applications.

4.1. Page Output Caching

You want to cache the output from an ASP.NET page and reuse it on subsequent requests.

Technique

Page output caching can be accomplished declaratively using a page @OutputCache directive or programmatically using the Response.Cache API. The following code samples are equivalent:

```
<script runat="server">
 Sub Page_Load (sender As object, e As EventArgs)
   Response.Cache.SetExpires(DateTime.Now.AddSeconds(100))
   Response.Cache.SetCacheability(HttpCacheability.Public)
   Response.Cache.SetValidUntilExpires(true)

   ' Set the timestamp
   timestamp.Text = DateTime.Now.ToString()
 End Sub
</script>
<asp:Label id="timestamp" runat="server" />
```

Or

```
<%@ OutputCache Duration="100" VaryByParam="none" %>
<script runat="server">
  Sub Page_Load(sender As Object, e As EventArgs)
   timestamp.Text = DateTime.Now.ToString()
  End Sub
</script>
<asp:Label id="timestamp" runat="server" />
```

Comments

As you can clearly see in the code sample, the page `@OutputCache` directive is much easier to implement. However, the lower-level `Response.Cache` API provides more flexibility when necessary. In either case, the content for the response is generated once and stored in memory before being sent back to the client. The contents are never written to disk, but instead are kept in memory within the application using the Cache API.

In the `@OutputCache` directive example, the `Duration` and `VaryByParam` attributes are required (if they are not specified, an exception is thrown detailing the requirements of these attributes). The `Duration` attribute is a time dependency, in seconds, used to control the lifetime of the cached response in memory. The `VaryByParam` attribute specifies which parameters (in the `Request.Params` collection) should cause separate versions of the page to be stored in the cache.

The `SetValidUntilExpires()` method on `Response.Cache` is used to control a nuance of HTTP caching. By default, this method is set to `true` when using the `@OutputCache` directive. Conversely, the default is `false` when using the `Response.Cache API`. `SetValidUntilExpires()` controls how ASP.NET honors cache invalidation headers sent by browsers. When users click the Refresh button in the browser, the browser sends an HTTP header to the server specifying that the requested content cannot come from a cache. When `SetValidUntilExpires()` is `true`, the HTTP cache invalidation request sent by the browser is ignored and the request can be served from the cache; when `false`, the HTTP cache invalidation request is honored and the request is removed from the cache. It's recommended to always set this to `true` to guarantee that the server can respond from the cache, otherwise a simple refresh in the browser can remove the item from the cache.

4.2. Partial Page Output Caching Using VaryByControl

> You want to cache the output of a User Control based on values of a contained server control.

Technique

The `VaryByControl` directive provides a helpful shortcut to vary the User Controls output by a contained control.

```
<%@ Imports Namespace="System.Data.SqlClient" %>

<%@ OutputCache Duration="60" VaryByControl="SortBy" %>

<script runat="server">
 Sub Page_Load (sender As object, e As EventArgs)
  Dim connection As New SqlConnection([your connection string])
  Dim command As New SqlCommand("BookSelection", connection)

  ' Mark as a stored procedure
  command.CommandType = CommandType.StoredProcedure

  ' Set up a SQL parameter for the book type selected
  command.Parameters.Add("@BookType",
      ➥SqlDbType.NVarChar, 25).Value =
      ➥SortBy.SelectedItem.Value

  ' Execute
  connection.Open()
  BookListing.DataSource = command.ExecuteReader()
  BookListing.DataBind()
  connection.Close()

 End Sub
</script>
<form runat="server">
Please select the types of books you are interested in:
 <asp:DropDownList AutoPostBack="true" id="SortBy" runat="server" >
  <asp:listitem >Technology</asp:listitem>
  <asp:listitem >Fiction</asp:listitem>
  <asp:listitem >Non-Fiction</asp:listitem>
 </asp:DropDownList>
<br>
<asp:DataGrid runat="server" id="BookListing" />
</form>
```

Comments

Consider a User Control that displays a list of the top 10 books with a SortBy
DropDownList containing Technology, Fiction, and Non-Fiction. Whenever a user
changes a value in the DropDownList the server returns data filtered by the value of
SortBy.

The content generated by the User Control can be varied just as you can vary page output cached responses. However, within a User Control, the name of the control, SortBy, is namespaced to the name of the containing control—UserControl1:SortBy. This allows multiple Top10 User Controls to be hosted in the same page without experiencing naming collisions.

For example, if you had two of these User Controls on your page, they might have the IDs Top10Books1 and Top10Books2. Top10Books1:SortBy and Top10Books2:SortBy are treated as separate drop-down controls. The VaryByControl option simply allows you to avoid typing VaryByParam="Top10Books2:SortBy"—instead simply type VaryByControl="SortBy".

4.3. Inserting Data into the Cache

You want to insert some arbitrary data into the cache using the ASP.NET Cache API.

Technique

There are several ways to add items into the Cache API:

- Dictionary style—Similar to the way the Session or Application API is used.
- Insert method—Inserts the named item into the cache and allows for additional parameters that specify other cache behavior, such as when the item should be removed from the cache.
- Add method—Same as insert, but adds the item only if it did not already exist.

In the following examples, products is assumed to be a dataset. However, it could be any .NET class.

```
' Add an item using the dictionary style API
Cache("MyProducts") = products

' Insert an item using the overloaded Insert method
Cache.Insert("MyProducts", products)

' Insert an item and specify a cache dependency
Cache.Insert("MyProducts", products, cacheDependency)

' Insert an item and specify that the item exists for only 60 minutes
Cache.Insert("MyProducts", products, Nothing,
        DateTime.Now.AddMinutes(60), TimeSpan.Zero)

' Insert an item and specify that the item exists for only 60 minutes, has a
' high priority and specify a callback function called when the item is
' removed from the cache
```

```
Cache.Insert("MyProducts", products, Nothing, DateTime.Now.AddMinutes(60),
        TimeSpan.Zero, CacheItemPriority.High, cacheCallBack)

' Add an item using the Add method
Cache.Add("MyProducts", products, cacheDependency,
        DateTime.Now.AddMinutes(60), TimeSpan.Zero,
        CacheItemPriority.High, cacheCallBack)
```

Comments

The Cache API, accessible simply as the Cache property within an ASP.NET page, is the underlying data store used by page output caching, partial page caching, and Web service caching. There are many cases when caching the output of the page is not desirable, but data can still be reused. One example is a listing of products or reports. The data is stored in memory, but options within the page determine how the data is displayed.

Something to keep in mind when using the cache is that it is *scavenging*. As memory is needed, items are removed from the cache using an LRU (least recently used) algorithm. Therefore, before using an item from the cache it is always wise to verify that the item exists and is not Nothing:

```
If (Cache("MyProducts") Is Not Nothing)
 … Insert into the cache
End If
```

The various parameters accepted by `Insert()` and `Add()` provide control over how the cache stores data. You can provide a `CacheDependency`, which then enforces a relationship between the item stored within the cache and either a file or cache key. When the file or cache key changes, the related entry within the cache is removed. It is also possible to specify time-based constraints using a fixed point in time or a sliding window of time. It's possible to control the priority of items stored within the cache using the `CacheItemPriority` enumeration—this affects how the scavenging algorithm removes items. Finally, you can specify a callback function that the cache will call when an item is removed.

4.4. Retrieving Data from the Cache

You want to ensure that data from the cache exists, retrieve the data, and regenerate it if necessary.

Technique

Retrieving objects stored within the cache is simple; there are two options for doing so:

- Dictionary style—Using patterns similar to that of Session and Application.
- `Cache.Get()` API—The `Get()` method accepts a single parameter that fetches the value of the named key.

Given the example used in Section 4.3 that added a dataset into the cache using the key
`MyProducts`, you could retrieve this value from the Cache:

```
' Get a value from the cache
<script runat="server">
Sub Page_Load(object As Sender, e As EventArgs)
 Dim ds As DataSet
 If (Cache("MyProducts") Is Not Nothing) Then ' Uses Dictionary style API
  ds = CType(Cache.Get("MyProducts"), DataSet) ' Uses Get() method
 End If
End Sub
</script>
```

Comments

Getting items stored within the cache is very simple. Although both techniques—dictionary style and `Get()`—are used in this example, the dictionary style access is the one most frequently used.

4.5. Creating a Cache Dependency

You want to create an entry within the cache and have it removed when a dependency changes.

Technique

As discussed in Section 4.3, the cache allows for items to be inserted or added to the Cache along with several other parameters, such as time-based constraints or an instance of `CacheDependency`.

```
<script runat="server">
Sub Page_Load(object As Sender, e As EventArgs)
 Dim stringArray As string {"Rob", "Steve", "Mike", "Anne"}


 ' Time based dependency for 60 minutes
 Cache.Insert("myArray-Time", stringArray, Nothing,
         DateTime.Now.AddMinutes(60), TimeSpan.Zero)

 ' File based dependency
 Dim fileDep = New CacheDependency(Server.MapPath("Products.xml"))
 Cache.Insert("myArray-File", stringArray, fileDep)

 ' Key based dependency
 Cache.Insert("myKey", "key for dependencies")
```

```
Dim keyDep = New CacheDependency(Nothing, "myKey")
Cache.Insert("myArray-Key", stringArray, fileDep)

End Sub
</script>
```

Comments

In the previous examples, three types of dependencies are created:

- Time—Time-based dependencies specify that an item is to remain in the cache for the specified duration of time. This is the same functionality found when using the @OutputCache directive and setting the Duration attribute.
- File—File-based dependencies specify that an item is to remain in the cache until the named file changes. Any output cached page is automatically made dependent upon itself. However, it's possible—as demonstrated in this example—to use this same functionality for entries within the Cache API.
- Key—Key-based dependencies specify that an item is to remain in the cache until a related cache key changes. This is very powerful because any running ASP.NET code can affect the cache key to enforce this relationship. For example, cascading relationships can be established whereby one cache entry is changed or removed and multiple other cache entries are affected.

Dependencies provide a simple but powerful programming model for controlling removal of resources from the cache when other resources change.

4.6. Varying Output Caching by Parameter(s)

You want to control when a page or User Control's output is placed in the cache based on parameters passed to the page via the QueryString or Post body.

Technique

There are two techniques for varying by parameters in pages; partial page caching only supports the @OutputCache directive.

```
<%@OutputCache Duration="60" VaryByParam="productId" %>
[content specific to the product id value]
```

or

```
<script runat="server">
 ' Note, this only works for pages and not user controls
 Sub Page_Load(object As Sender, e As EventArgs)
```

```
    Response.Cache.SetExpires(DateTime.Now.AddSeconds(100))
    Response.Cache.SetCacheability(HttpCacheability.Public)
    Response.Cache.SetValidUntilExpires(true)
    Response.Cache.VaryByParams("productId") = True
End Sub
</script>
```
[content specific to the product id value]

Dynamic pages usually accept parameters and potentially display different output determined by these parameters. A common example is a page used to display product information, such as `products.aspx?productId=10`.

The page is passed a single parameter, the product ID, and the content is retrieved for that particular product. Output caching allows you to cache the results of a dynamically generated page so you don't need to execute the page on each request. Varying the output cache by parameters allows you to cache multiple views of the page based on parameters that affect the output, such as a products.aspx page that accepts a `productId` parameter.

Multiple parameters can be specified using the `@OutputCache` directive by using a semicolon to separate items. For example, if you were generating output based on the `productId` and the `salesId`, you could specify the following:

```
<%@OutputCache Duration="60" VaryByParam="productId;salesId" %>
```

Using the `@OutputCache` directive, it is also possible to vary all parameters. This isn't a recommended approach, but if you're not sure how many parameters you depend upon, using `VaryByParam = "*"` will vary by all parameters. Conversely, using `VaryByParam = "none"` will vary by no parameters.

4.7. Varying Output Caching by Browser

You want to determine whether the output of a Web Form or User Control should be cached based on the user's browser (or agent).

Technique

You can vary by browser the output cache for pages using two techniques; only the `@OutputCache` directive is supported for User Control caching:

```
<%@OutputCache Duration="60" VaryByParam="none"
         VaryByCustom="browser" %>
[content]
```

or

```
<script runat="server">
 ' Note, this only works for pages and not user controls
 Sub Page_Load(object As Sender, e As EventArgs)
```

```
    Response.Cache.SetExpires(DateTime.Now.AddSeconds(100))
    Response.Cache.SetCacheability(HttpCacheability.Public)
    Response.Cache.SetValidUntilExpires(true)
    Response.Cache.SetVaryByCustom("browser")
  End Sub
</script>
[content]
```

Comments

ASP.NET server controls can render different content depending upon the user/agent presented to the server during the request. All browsers present a user/agent that allows the server addressing the request to know the capabilities of the browser. This is regardless of whether the browsers are desktop browsers such as IE, Netscape, or Opera, or mobile/device browsers, such as the browser found in a RIM device, cellular phone, or handhelds.

Many ASP.NET server controls can render different content that is better suited to the browser type making the request. A great example of this capability is existence of IE Web Controls and ASP.NET Mobile controls (both available at www.asp.net). These controls intelligently detect the browser type. When desktop browsers are used, HTML is rendered. When mobile browsers are used, WML is rendered.

Varying the cache by browser allows for the ASP.NET cache to store different versions of the requested page in the cache based on the type of browser making the request. The only caveat is that only the browser type and major version number—IE 6.0, for example—are tracked. For example, versions 4.0, 4.1, and 4.5, of Netscape browsers would all resolve to one entry within the cache.

4.8. Varying Output Caching by HTTP Headers

You want to vary how output caching is implemented for Web Forms and User Controls based on certain headers in the client's HTTP request.

Technique

As demonstrated in Sections 4.6 and 4.7, it is possible to be very explicit about how pages can be output cached. The last technique for controlling how pages can be cached involves varying by HTTP headers presented by the client browser:

```
<%@OutputCache Duration="60" VaryByParam="none"
          VaryByHeader="Accept-Language" %>
[content]
```

or

```
<script runat="server">
```

```
' Note, this only works for pages and not user controls
Sub Page_Load(object As Sender, e As EventArgs)
   Response.Cache.SetExpires(DateTime.Now.AddSeconds(100))
   Response.Cache.SetCacheability(HttpCacheability.Public)
   Response.Cache.SetValidUntilExpires(true)
   Response.Cache.VaryByHeaders("Accept-Language") = true;
End Sub
</script>
[content]
```

Comments

All browsers send over headers that provide information about the browser, or other relevant information pertinent to the request. As discussed in Section 4.7, browsers provide a user/agent header that allows ASP.NET to generate different content based on the browser type. In addition to the user/agent header, several other headers are sent over that you can vary by. The most common is the `Accept-Language` header.

The `Accept-Language` header provides information about the language the client prefers. For example, for United States English, the value is EN-US, whereas a request from the United Kingdom might be EN-EN, France is FR-FR, and Japan is JP-JP.

When the output cache is varied by the `Accept-Language` header, different localized versions of the page can be stored and served from the cache—assuming you've written the code to do so.

4.9. Using HttpContext for Per-Request Caching

You want to cache some information that is needed only for the current request in the most efficient manner possible.

Technique

Storing data within `HttpContext.Current.Items` allows for data to exist for the duration of the request and to be automatically discarded when the request is complete.

```
Public Function GetUserInfo(string username) As User
   ' Let's not go to the database each time we need the user's info
   ' the userKey is a unique value that identifies the user, such as the
   ' username
 If (HttpContext.Current.Items(username) Is Nothing) Then
   // Hang on to the data for this request only
   HttpContext.Current.Items(username) = Provider.GetUserInfo(username);
 End If

   Return CType(HttpContext.Current.Items(username), User);
End Function
```

To see this code in action, see `Users.cs` class in the ASP.NET forums source code.

Comments

In some specialized cases, you want to cache some data only for the duration of the request. A great example of this is in the ASP.NET forums (source code available at `www.asp.net`).

The forums make use of personalization within each server control. A single page may be composed of 10-12 server controls. Rather than each server control retrieving its own set of data from the database, the code can reliably call the `GetUserInfo()` function repeatedly. If the item is not found in the `HttpContext.Items` collection—a special dictionary that exists for the duration of the request—it is created from the database and added to `HttpContext.Items`.

This technique is very powerful because it allows your code to remain modular and to take advantage of a caching technique to improve performance.

4.10. Implementing a CallBack when a Cached Item Expires

You want to execute a function whenever a particular item in the cache expires.

Technique

The capability to call a method whenever an item expires from the cache allows you to build systems that can intelligently add data back into the cache.

```
<Script runat=server>
  Shared reason As CacheItemRemovedReason
  Dim onRemove As CacheItemRemovedCallback

  Public Shared Sub ItemRemovedCallback(key As String,
                value As Object,
                removedReason As CacheItemRemovedReason)
    ' Reason why the item was removed
    reason = removedReason

    ' Reinsert the item into the Cache, but change the value
    Cache.Insert(key, "Item re-inserted")
  End Sub

  Public Sub Page_Load(sender As Object, e As EventArgs)
    onRemove = New CacheItemRemovedCallback(
            AddressOf Me.ItemRemovedCallback)
```

```
' Add an item to the Cache with the callback
If Is Nothing(Cache("Key1")) Then
  Cache.Insert("Key1", "In the Cache", Nothing,
        DateTime.Now.AddSeconds(10),
        TimeSpan.Zero, CacheItemPriority.Low, onRemove)
End If

' Set the label value
Label1.Text = Cache("Key1")
End Sub
</Script>
Value of the Cache: <asp:label id="Label1" runat="server" />
```

Comments

The capability of a function to be called when an item is removed from the cache is very powerful. It allows you to reinsert the item or to report a reason as to why the item was removed.

The only caveat is that during the time between when the item is removed from the cache, yet before the callback function is called, another request might ask for the item from the cache and would not find it. Regardless, it's still a very powerful technique for controlling how items are removed from the cache.

5

Mobile Controls

5.0. Introduction

In addition to standard Web controls, ASP.NET also provides a suite of controls for
working with mobile devices. Although these controls render in an ordinary PC's browser, their behavior is customized to work with the small form factor of most PDA and
Internet-enabled cellular phone devices. This chapter covers several of the most common
tasks that face a mobile forms developer. These controls are built into the 1.1 version of
the ASP.NET framework; for 1.0 they are available as a separate download from
Microsoft's Web site.

See Also

LearnMobile.Net by Anil John—`http://LearnMobile.Net/`

Mobile Web Development with ASP.NET—`http://msdn.microsoft.com/vstudio/device/`
`mobilecontrols/default.asp`

5.1. Creating a Mobile Web Form

You want to create a mobile ASP.NET Web Form.

Technique

To declare an ASP.NET mobile page (a mobile Web Form), simply create a file with an
.ASPX extension and place it in a Web folder. The ASPX page must contain the following directives and at least one `form` element:

```
<%@ Page Inherits="System.Web.UI.MobileControls.MobilePage" %>
<%@ Register TagPrefix="mobile" Namespace="System.Web.UI.MobileControls"
```

```
Assembly="System.Web.Mobile" %>
<mobile:Form id="Form1" runat="server">Hello</mobile:Form>
<mobile:Form id="Form2" runat="server">World</mobile:Form>
```

Comments

ASP.NET pages that use mobile controls must inherit from `System.Web.UI.`
`MobileControls.MobilePage`. Just like with a regular Web Form, you can also set
optional parameters such as `Language` in the `Page` directive. The second directive associ-
ates the `mobile` prefix with the mobile control namespace.

Note that HTML constructs such as `<HTML>` and `<BODY>` are not present, as these tags
do not render properly in a mobile device that does not support HTML. One key difference between a regular Web Form and a mobile Web Form is that you can have more
than one form control in a mobile Web Form. This allows a single Web Form to display
multiple screens in a mobile device using form elements.

Finally, note that mobile controls support are built into ASP.NET v1.1, which should
make the @ Register directive unnecessary.

See Also

@ Page–http://msdn.microsoft.com/library/en-us/cpgenref/html/
cpconpage.asp

Section 1.1, "Declaring an ASP.NET Page"

5.2. Navigation in a Mobile Web Form

You want to navigate within a mobile Web Form.

Technique

The ASPX page is as follows:

```
<mobile:Form id="Form1" runat="server">
    <mobile:Label id="Label1" runat="server">This is Form1</mobile:Label>
    <mobile:Link id="Link1" runat="server"
    NavigateUrl="#Form2">Go To Form2</mobile:Link>
    <mobile:Link id="Link2" runat="server"
    NavigateUrl="#Form3">Go To Form3</mobile:Link>
</mobile:Form>
<mobile:Form id="Form2" runat="server">
    <mobile:Label id="Label2" runat="server">This is Form2</mobile:Label>
    <mobile:Link id="Link3" runat="server"
    NavigateUrl="#Form1">Go To Form1</mobile:Link>
    <mobile:Link id="Link4" runat="server"
```

```
            NavigateUrl="#Form3">Go To Form3</mobile:Link>
</mobile:Form>
<mobile:Form id="Form3" runat="server">
    <mobile:Label id="Label3" runat="server">This is Form3</mobile:Label>
    <mobile:Command id="Command1" onclick="Command1_Click"
    runat="server">Go To Form1</mobile:Command>
    <mobile:Command id="Command2" onclick="Command2_Click"
    runat="server">Go To Form2</mobile:Command>
</mobile:Form>
```

In `<script runat="server" />` block or codebehind:

```
void Command1_Click(Object sender, EventArgs e) {
  ActiveForm = Form1;
}

void Command2_Click(Object sender, EventArgs e) {
  ActiveForm = Form2;
}
```

Comments

Mobile ASP.NET Web Forms, unlike ASP.NET Web Forms, can have multiple form elements. By default, the first form on a mobile page becomes the active form. The `<mobile:Link>` control allows you to navigate from one form to another within a page. The target of the link is set by the `NavigateUrl` property and takes the form of `#FormID`, where `FormID` is the ID of the form that you want to navigate to.

You can also programmatically make a form active by using the `ActiveForm` property as shown in `Form3`.

See Also
Section 5.1, "Creating a Mobile Web Form"

5.3. Configuring Automatic Paging of Content

You want to automatically split your page content across multiple screens.

Technique

The ASPX page is as follows:

```
<mobile:Form id="Form1" Paginate="true" runat="server">
<mobile:List id="List1" runat="server"></mobile:List>
</mobile:Form>
```

In `<script runat="server" />` block or codebehind:

```
Sub Page_Load(ByVal sender As Object, ByVal e As EventArgs)
  If Not IsPostBack
    Dim count AS Integer
      For count = 1 To 100
      Dim listItem = New MobileListItem(count.ToString())
      List1.Items.Add(listItem)
    Next
  End If
End Sub
```

Comments

Because the screens of mobile devices are typically small and cannot display large amounts of data, ASP.NET mobile controls provide the capability to automatically paginate across large amounts of data by splitting them into multiple screens. The `form` control is an example of a mobile control that contains this functionality.

By setting the `Paginate` property of the form control, you enable this capability. The control automatically inserts navigation constructs that are appropriate for the device in question. This enables the users to page back and forth between multiple screens of data.

The TextView, List, and the ObjectList controls also support internal pagination.

See Also

Paginate Property—`http://msdn.microsoft.com/library/en-us/mwsdk/html/ mwlrfpaginateproperty.asp`

5.4. Displaying ObjectList Information in a Table

You want to display the initial screen of the ObjectList control in a tabular format.

Technique

The ASPX page is as follows:

```
<mobile:Form id="Form1" runat="server">
    <mobile:ObjectList id="ObjectList1" runat="server"
    LabelStyle-StyleReference="title"
    CommandStyle-StyleReference="subcommand" >
    </mobile:ObjectList>
</mobile:Form>
```

In `<script runat="server" />` block or codebehind:

```
Sub Page_Load

        ' Code here to retrieve Book Listing
        ' Fields returned are
        ' - BookName
        ' - BookCategory
        ' - BookISBN

        ObjectList1.DataSource = myBookList
        ObjectList1.LabelField =   "BookName"
        ObjectList1.TableFields= "BookName;BookCategory;BookISBN"
        ObjectList1.DataBind()
End Sub
```

Comments

The ObjectList control is the mobile control equivalent to the ASP.NET DataGrid. The default display of the ObjectList in all devices is a single column listing of links. You designate the field to be displayed as the link using the `LabelField` property. Clicking on the link takes you to another screen that displays all fields for that item.

On mobile devices that have browsers that support HTML markup, it is possible to display the initial listing in a tabular format by using the `TableFields` property. As shown in this example, you need to separate each field that is to be displayed by a semicolon. The first item in the TableField list is designated as the LabelField. Note that on devices that do not support HTML markup, the ObjectList provides the default display.

See Also
ObjectList Control—`http://msdn.microsoft.com/library/en-us/mwdesign/html/mwconIntroductiontotheObjectListControl.asp`

5.5. Customizing Output for a Device

You want to customize the output sent to a specific device.

Technique

The web.config file is as follows:

```
<deviceFilters>
  <filter name="isHTML32" compare="PreferredRenderingType" argument="html32" />
  <filter name="isWML11" compare="PreferredRenderingType" argument="wml11" />
</deviceFilters>
```

The ASPX page is as follows:

```
<mobile:Form id="Form1" runat="server">
  <DeviceSpecific>
    <Choice Filter="isHTML32">
      <HeaderTemplate>
        Header visible only in HTML Browsers
        <BR>
        <img Src="poweredbyaspnet.gif" border="0">
        <HR>
      </HeaderTemplate>
      <FooterTemplate>
        <HR>
        Footer visible only in HTML Browsers
      </FooterTemplate>
    </Choice>
    <Choice>
      <mobile:Label id="Lable1" runat="server" >Powered by
      ASP.NET Visible on non-HTML browsers</mobile:Label>
    </Choice>
  </DeviceSpecific>
  <mobile:Label id="Label1" runat="server">Content of Mobile
    Form visible in all devices</mobile:Label>
</mobile:Form>
```

Comments

It want is possible to provide a richer user experience by optimizing the output of a specific device. You can do this by configuring device filters in your application's web.config file. Using the results of that filter test, you can enable content to be rendered on a device-specific basis. As shown in the previous web.config file, the first device filter provides HTML 3.2 support and the second provides WML 1.1 support.

All mobile controls support the capability to use a DeviceSpecific/Choice filter to customize the output. The mobile:Form control (which is a *templated* control) supports header and footer templates as well. Combining these two features in the previous example allows you to include a header and footer on browsers that support HTML. The device that passes the isHTML32 test will be sent HTML content, and all other devices are sent the content in the default <Choice> filter.

See Also

Using Device Filters—http://msdn.microsoft.com/library/en-us/mwdesign/html/mwconUsingDeviceFilters.asp

Customizing for want Specific Devices—http://msdn.microsoft.com/library/en-us/mwdesign/html/mwwlkcustomizingforspecificdevices.asp

ASP.NET Applications

6

ASP.NET Application Configuration

6.0. Introduction

ASP.NET moves away from the registry and IIS metabase settings that were the methods of configuring ASP applications by placing most of the setup information into *.CONFIG files. Among other things, this allows applications in most cases to be deployed simply by copying all of the files from one location to another. Each server has a *machine.config* configuration that serves as the default for all applications on that server, and each ASP.NET application can define one or more *web.config* files to customize these settings for that application. This chapter covers the most common configurations sections you need for your ASP.NET applications. Remember that these files are all in XML format, which means that they must be well-formed and that they are case-sensitive.

6.1. Storing and Reading Custom Settings from the web.config File

You want to store application settings in the web.config file and retrieve these settings in your ASP.NET application.

Technique

ASP.NET provides two ways to store information within the configuration file. The first is to store simple name/value settings within an `<appSettings />` section, as discussed in Section 6.2. The second is to create a custom configuration section that can store data in any format.

In order to implement a custom configuration section handler, you must implement a custom class that implements IConfigurationSectionHandler. The following is a partial code sample for the new configuration section handler used for the ASP.NET forums:

```
Imports System
Imports System.Collections
Imports System.Collections.Specialized
Imports System.Xml
Imports System.Configuration
Imports System.Web.Configuration

Namespace AspNetForums.Configuration

    ' ********************************************************************
    ' ForumsConfigurationHandler
    '
    ' Class used by ASP.NET Configuration to load ASP.NET Forums configuration.
    ' ********************************************************************/
    Class ForumsConfigurationHandler
        Implements IConfigurationSectionHandler

        Public Overridable Overloads Function Create(ByVal parent As Object,
➥ ByVal configContext As Object, ByVal node As XmlNode) As Object
➥Implements IConfigurationSectionHandler.Create
            Dim config As New ForumConfiguration(CType(parent,
ForumConfiguration))
            config.LoadValuesFromConfigurationXml(node)
            Return config
        End Function
    End Class



    ' ********************************************************************
    ' ForumConfiguration
    '
    ' Class used to represent the configuration data for the ASP.NET Forums
    ' ********************************************************************/
    Public Class ForumConfiguration

        Dim _pageSize As Integer = 25

        ' ********************************************************************
        ' ForumConfiguration
        '
        ' Internal constructor for creating a new instance.
        ' ********************************************************************/
```

```
        Public Sub New(ByVal parent As ForumConfiguration)

            ' Place holder for future work

        End Sub

        ' ******************************************************************
        ' LoadValuesFromConfigurationXml
        '
        ' Loads the forums configuration values.
        ' ******************************************************************/
        Sub LoadValuesFromConfigurationXml(ByVal node As XmlNode)
            Dim attributeCollection As XmlAttributeCollection = node.Attributes

            ' Get the attributes of the <forums> element
            _pageSize =
                Int32.Parse(attributeCollection("defaultPageSize").Value)

        End Sub

        ' Properties
        Public ReadOnly Property PageSize() As Integer
            Get
                Return _pageSize
            End Get
        End Property
    End Class

End Namespace
```

This configuration section handler is compiled and then registered within an application. It can then be used within web.config:

```
<configuration>

  <configSections>
    <sectionGroup name="system.web">
      <section name="forums"
  type="AspNetForums.Configuration.ForumsConfigurationHandler, AspNetForums" />
    </sectionGroup>
  </configSections>


  <system.web>
    <forums defaultPageSize = "25" />
  </system.web>
</configuration>
```

Comments

This code example shows how you can create a custom configuration section. It's obviously not a simple task. However, for controlling exactly how the configuration information represents the data stored in the configuration file, it is the only option. If having a custom configuration section seems to you like too much work just to store application items, you're not alone. In Section 6.2, you'll learn how to use the `<appSettings/>` section of configuration to store name-value pairs that are more easily retrieved.

6.2. Creating Custom Application Settings in the web.config File

You want to create a custom section of the web.config file for storing application configuration settings.

Technique

The web.config file has a predefined section for application settings, called `appSettings`. This section can be placed in any .config file, and must reside with the `<configuration>` section. The following is an example of a simple web.config file:

```
<configuration>
  <appSettings>
    <add key="PageSize" value="25" />
  </appSettings>
</configuration>
```

Values can be retrieved using the Configuration API. However, all values are returned as string types:

```
Dim pageSize As Integer
pageSize = CType(ConfigurationSettings.ApplicationSettings("PageSize"),
                    Integer)
```

Comments

Storing common values within configuration, such as database connection strings, is a common feature that many applications take advantage of. Requiring developers to write customer configuration section handlers to store simple values is overkill; hence the existence of the `<appSettings/>` section.

Any simple data that you need stored in a central location and that must be available anywhere within your Web application is a good candidate for the `<appSettings/>` section. For other more complicated configuration data structures, you'll probably want to create a custom configuration section handler—see Section 6.1 for more information.

6.3. Configuring Application Tracing

You want to set up application tracing for your ASP.NET application using the web.config file.

Technique

The web.config file includes a `<trace ...>` section that is used to set up tracing options for an ASP.NET application. A typical trace section follows:

```
<trace
    enabled="false"
    requestLimit="10"
    pageOutput="false"
    traceMode="SortByTime"
  localOnly="true"
/>
```

This example demonstrates all of the fields available to modify application tracing. The first field controls whether tracing is enabled. This defaults to `false` and can be overridden at the individual page level. The second item, `requestLimit`, controls how many requests' trace results should be stored on the server. Once filled, this queue will not accept new entries until the queue is deleted (which can be done from the trace.axd page). The third attribute, `pageOutput`, controls whether trace output should be displayed on every page in the application. When set to `false`, trace output is available only from the trace.axd URL (for example, `http://mydomain/myapplication/trace.axd`). Individual pages can override this setting by explicitly setting `trace="true"` or `trace="false"` in their page directive.

The fourth attribute, `traceMode`, simply controls the ordering of the trace messages in the Trace Information section of the trace output. The allowable options are `SortByTime` (the default) and `SortByCategory`. Finally, the last attribute, `localOnly`, enables application tracing only for requests originating from the local machine when set to `true`. Note that these items are case-sensitive.

Comments

Tracing can provide a powerful way to debug applications. By using the trace.axd URL for trace output, developers can pull important details about a production ASP.NET application without interfering with current users. However, be careful that you do not place sensitive information in trace statements or collections that are exposed by the trace output (Application, Session, Forms, Cookies, QueryString, and so on), because by default anybody can access the trace.axd URL and access this data. Note that you can change the name of the trace.axd file by changing its name in the machine.config file, and you can protect access to the file using the technique described in Section 8.3, "Requiring Authentication to Access Files and Folders."

See Also
Section 8.3, "Requiring Authentication to Access Files and Folders"

6.4. Configuring Application Debugging

You want to configure application-level debugging for your ASP.NET application using the web.config file.

Technique

The web.config file includes a `<compilation ...>` section that sets whether debug mode is set for an ASP.NET application. A typical compilation section follows:

```
<compilation
        defaultLanguage="vb"
        debug="true"
/>
```

Setting `debug="true"` (which is case-sensitive) enables debug mode for your application. This means the .PDB file for your assembly will be copied to the application's `/bin` folder, which means detailed debug information (stack trace, line numbers, and so on) will be provided in response to exceptions. Note that there is a significant performance penalty to application running in debug mode. Individual pages can also be set up to run in debug mode by setting `debug="true"` in the individual page directive.

See Also
Debug Mode in ASP.NET Applications—`http://msdn.microsoft.com/library/en-us/vsdebug/html/vxtskDebugModeInASPNETApplications.asp`

6.5. Configuring Application Error Handling

You want to configure your ASP.NET application's default error-handling behavior in the web.config file.

Technique

The web.config file includes a `<customErrors ...>` section that controls how the application responds to errors on its pages. A typical `customErrors` section follows:

```
<customErrors mode="RemoteOnly" defaultRedirect="/Maintenance.aspx" >
  <error statusCode="404" redirect="/NotFound.aspx" />
</customErrors>
```

The settings are case-sensitive. The first attribute, `mode`, can be `On`, `Off`, or `RemoteOnly`. The first two are self-explanatory; the third redirects errors only for non-local users, so that a local developer can still debug problems without being routed to the "friendly" error page. The second attribute, `defaultRedirect`, specifies the page to which any request that results in an unhandled exception is sent. If it is not set but custom errors are on, users will see a generic error message (instead of the detailed exception information). Optionally, specific redirects can be set up for individual error codes by adding `<error ...>` elements within the `customErrors` element. Each of these can specify a `statusCode`, such as 404, that maps to a file not found error code, or 500, for a generic application error. Each error code can be mapped to its own specific error page by setting the path to the page in the redirect attribute.

Comments

Setting up friendly default error pages for ASP.NET applications and their common errors is fairly straightforward. It is useful to have the default error page write to a log with details of the request or URL that caused the problem. It can also be useful to log which files users are requesting that are resulting in 404s, and ideally to have the 404 error page automatically redirect users to new locations of old resources.

Note, however, that these error pages handle requests only for resources that the ASP.NET engine is registered to handle. So a request for a missing .ASPX file would result in the 404 page being called, but by default a request for a nonexistent .HTM or .GIF file would not. Additional file types can be associated with the ASP.NET process in IIS, but this imposes a performance penalty. Note that most of this functionality is also available within IIS.

See Also

`customErrors` Element—`http://msdn.microsoft.com/library/en-us/cpgenref/html/gngrfcustomerrorssection.asp`

6.6. Configuring Application Security

You want to configure application-level security for your ASP.NET application using the web.config file.

Technique

You can easily limit access to your application to specified groups by modifying the `<authorization>` section in the web.config file. The rules are processed from the top down, so in the following example, the `<deny users="*" />` rule will not apply to users of the Admins group or Jack and Jill, who have already been granted access. You can use the special characters * to specify all users and ? to specify anonymous users. You can also grant or deny access to a particular action such as Get or Post, by adding the VERB attribute. For more detailed information on setting up application security, see Chapter 8.

The web.config file:

```xml
<?xml version="1.0" encoding="utf-8" ?>
<configuration>
  <system.web>
    <authorization>
      <allow roles="Admins" />
      <deny VERB="Post" users="Jack" />
      <allow users="Jack, Jill" />
      <deny users="*" />
    </authorization>
  </system.web>
</configuration>
```

Comments

The `<authorization>` section is created automatically for you in a VB.NET Web application, but for a C# Web application you need to create it yourself. A useful technique is to place a web.config file in each folder whose access you want to control, and simply specify the authorization information in this web.config file.

See Also

Section 8.1, "Configuring Forms Authentication"

Section 8.2, "Configuring Windows Authentication"

Section 8.3, "Requiring Authentication to Access Files and Folders"

6.7. Configuring Sessions in your ASP.NET Application

You want to configure user sessions for your ASP.NET application using the web.config file.

Technique

All of the configuration is provided by the `<sessionState>` element in the web.config file; all you have to do is alter the appropriate attributes.

There are several ways to store session information; these are described next. To disable `Session` state, add this to web.config:

```
<configuration>
   <system.web>
      <sessionState mode="Off"/>
   </system.web>
</configuration>
```

To enable local storage of `Session` state, add this to web.config:

```
<configuration>
   <system.web>
      <sessionState mode="InProc"
   cookieless="true"
   timeout="10" />
      </system.web>
</configuration>
```

The `InProc` setting sets it so that the information is stored locally (the default). `Cookieless` can be set to `true` or `false` and tells ASP.NET whether to use cookies when storing session information. `Timeout` sets the time in minutes that sessions will expire if they remain unused.

To enable storage of `Sessions` on a state server add this to web.config:

```
<configuration>
   <system.web>
      <sessionState mode="StateServer"
   stateConnectionString="tcpip=127.0.0.1:42424" />
      </system.web>
</configuration>
```

This tells ASP.NET to use a state server at the specified address (`stateConnectionString`). The state server is found at `%SYSTEMROOT%\Microsoft.NET\Framework\`*version*`\` `aspnet_state.exe`. This server then listens on port 42424 over TCP/IP; you can use this port to store your session information.

To enable storage of `Sessions` on a SQL Server, add this to web.config:

```
<configuration>
   <system.web>
      <sessionState mode="SQLServer"
   sqlConnectionString="data source=localhost;user id=sa;
➥password=securepassword;" />
      </system.web>
</configuration>
```

This method tells ASP.NET to use SQL Server to store the information. To set up a SQL Server to store session information, you must run the InstallSqlState.sql file located in `%SYSTEMROOT%\Microsoft.NET\Framework\`*`version`*`\` on the SQL Server (there is an UninstallSqlState.sql file to uninstall it as well).

See Also

ASP.NET Settings Schema (`<sessionState>` Element)—`http://msdn.microsoft.com/library/en-us/cpgenref/html/gngrfsessionstatesection.asp`

Store Session Information in SQL Server—`http://aspalliance.com/wisemonk/view.aspx?id=AN061702`

Section 8.1, "Configuring Forms Authentication"

Section 8.2, "Configuring Windows Authentication"

7

State Management

7.0. Introduction

ASP.NET provides many ways to maintain state, or information, about users and their activity on the site, between and within requests. Some of these techniques can be used to persist information about a user for months or years, whereas others can be used to hold data simply between postbacks as the user interacts with a Web Form. This chapter covers recipes for maintaining state information in the Application, Session, and ViewState collections, as well as how to store information in browser cookies.

7.1. Reading and Writing Values to the Application Object

You want to read or store some information that will be available to all pages in your application by using the Application object.

Technique

You can store the name of the server in application state using `Application("ServerName") ="WebFarm1"`. You can retrieve it and display its value by using `MyLabel.Text=Application("ServerName").ToString()`. Because it returns the server name as an object, you need to convert it to a string using the `.ToString()` method before assigning it to `MyLabel.Text`. The ASPX page is as follows:

```
<html>
  <body>
    <form id="Recipe0701vb" method="post" runat="server">
      <asp:Label ID="MyLabel" Runat="server"/>
    </form>
  </body>
</html>
```

In `<script runat="server" />` block or codebehind:

```
Sub Page_Load(sender As Object, e As EventArgs)
    Application.Lock()
    Application("ServerName")="WebFarm1"
    Application.UnLock()
    MyLabel.Text=Application("ServerName").ToString()
End Sub
```

Comments

Application state is useful for storing values that you need to access throughout your application. Once a value is added to application state, it exists for the life of the application. Because multiple pages can attempt to write to the Application collection simultaneously, it must be locked using `Application.Lock` prior to any writes. The lock is released using `Application.UnLock`. The only time locking isn't necessary is in code that isn't executed by multiple page requests, such as in `Application_Start` in the global.asax.

See Also

Section 7.2, "Reading and Writing Values to the Session Object"

Section 7.3, "Reading and Storing Data in Cookies"

7.2. Reading and Writing Values to the Session Object

> You want to read or store some information that will be available for this user's session, using the Session object.

Technique

You can store user-specific information, such as a user's name, in the Session collection. Because the Session collection is user specific, it should not be written to by multiple threads concurrently. Therefore, you do not need to use locks around your writes, as you must with the Application collection (see Section 7.1). Otherwise, the syntax is similar:

```
Session("UserName")=UserNameTextBox.Text
UserNameLabel.Text = Session("UserName")
```

Comments

By default, the Session collection holds data for 20 minutes after the last request to an application by a particular user. You can adjust this time period in the application's configuration (see Section 6.7). Because data stored in sessions can grow linearly with the number of users, and because it persists for quite some time after each user leaves, it can quickly impede scalability if it is used to store large amounts of data. It should therefore be used sparingly.

See Also

Section 6.7, "Configuring Sessions in Your ASP.NET Application"

Section 7.1, "Reading and Writing Values to the Application Object"

Section 7.3, "Reading and Storing Data in Cookies"

7.3. Reading and Storing Data in Cookies

You want to read or store some information in a user's Cookies collection.

Technique

You can store small pieces of user-specific information in the user's Cookies collection on the user's local machine, assuming the local browser supports cookies and the user has not disabled this feature. You can use cookies to hold data for as long as the current browser window is open, or you can give them an expiration date some time in the future. The first variety is called an in-memory cookie, because they are never written to the user's hard drive. The second variety is referred to as a persistent cookie, because these cookies persist across browser and even machine restarts.

There are several ways to work with cookies in ASP.NET. The simplest uses syntax very similar to that used for the Application and Session collections:

```
'write a cookie
Response.Cookies("UserName").Value = UserNameTextBox.Text


'read a cookie
UserNameLabel.Text = Request.Cookies("UserName").Value
```

In addition, you can give the cookies an expiration date, which will cause them to be persisted to the user's hard drive. To delete these (and other) cookies, simply set their expire date to any past date, as shown:

```
'persist a cookie
Response.Cookies("UserName").Expires =
➥System.DateTime.Now.AddDays(1) ' persist for 1 day


'delete a cookie
Response.Cookies("UserName").Expires = System.DateTime.Now.AddDays(-1)
```

Comments

Cookies can be a great place to store small pieces of data that are needed from page to page. They do not have the overhead of sessions, and they can span multiple user visits over large time periods. They can also span applications within the same domain (for example, yahoo.com). Not all users will accept cookies, however. It's best to test for this by writing a test cookie and attempting to read it back on a subsequent request. Cookies can store only small amounts of text data, with an upper limit of less than 4KB, which includes the data and the keys used to extract the data (for example, UserName in the previous example).

See Also

Section 7.1, "Reading and Writing Values to the Application Object"

Section 7.2, "Reading and Writing Values to the Session Object"

7.4. Reading and Storing Data in ViewState

You want to store or access some information related to a particular Web Form across one or more postbacks.

Technique

The ViewState collection provides an easy way to maintain values on a particular Web Form across postbacks. This collection is stored as a hidden form field, and thus all data stored in ViewState is passed to and from the client on every request. You access it using syntax similar to what you have seen for the Session and Application collections:

```
ViewState("UserName")="UserNameTextBox.Text"
UserNameLabel.Text = ViewState("UserName")
```

Comments

By default, Web controls that do not post back values will maintain their state automatically using ViewState. This can be controlled individually for each control or globally for each page by setting EnableViewState to true or false as desired (either for a given control or in the page directive). The amount of space a control occupies in ViewState can easily be determined from the control tree section of the trace output (see Section 6.3 for more on tracing).

See Also

Section 3.3, "Creating ViewState-Enabled Control Properties"

Section 6.3, "Configuring Application Tracing"

Section 7.3, "Reading and Storing Data in Cookies"

8

Security

8.0. Introduction

ASP.NET provides support for several authentication mechanisms, which are set up in the web.config file. These settings enable you to specify which users or which roles should have access to various Web Forms and other resources in your application. Note that these security settings apply only to files that the ASP.NET engine is set up to handle in IIS. Therefore, by default, file formats such as .XML, .HTM, and .GIF are not covered by the ASP.NET security policies. This chapter contains recipes that describe how to configure ASP.NET security using several options, as well as how to properly construct login and logout features for your application.

8.1. Configuring Forms Authentication

You want to set up forms authentication for your Web application.

Technique

The forms authentication setup process is done in the `<authentication>` part of your web.config file. As with all XML documents, the web.config file's contents are case sensitive.

Here's the application's web.config file:

```
<configuration>
  <system.web>
   <authentication mode="Forms">
     <forms name="CookBookForm"
          loginUrl="login.aspx"
          protection="All"
          timeout="30"
```

```
        path="/" />
    </authentication>
  </system.web>
</configuration>
```

Comments

The `<forms>` tag in web.config provides all the configuration necessary to provide forms authentication for your application.

This tag includes the following options:

- `name`—This sets the name of the HTTP cookie that will be sent. If you have multiple applications on the same server with forms authentication set up, you must make this value unique in each one of them.

- `loginUrl`—This sets the location where the users are redirected for login (or any other action) if they are not authenticated and try to access a secure page.

- `protection`—This specifies the level of protection to place on the cookie. You can set this to All, None, Encryption or Validation, the default (and recommended) is All.

- `timeout`—This sets the amount of time (in minutes) that a cookie remains valid, after it was last requested, before it expires.

- `path`—This sets the path for the cookies to use; default is a backslash. This provides additional protection because the client browser will not send the cookie if there is a path mismatch. This value is case-sensitive to some browsers.

See Also

Section 6.6, "Configuring Application Security,"—You want to configure application level security for your ASP.NET application using the web.config file.

Section 8.4, " Creating a Simple Forms Authentication Login Page"—You want to create a login form for your Web application using Forms Authentication.

8.2. Configuring Windows Authentication

You want to set up Windows authentication for your Web application.

Technique

Open the web.config file. Find the authentication tag under `system.web` and set the mode to `Windows`. This is the default setting if you created the web.config file in Visual Studio.

The web.config file is as follows:

```
<system.web>
 <authentication mode="Windows">
<system.web>
```

You must also configure IIS to require authentication. To do this, follow these steps:

1. Open Administrative Tools from either the Start menu or the Control Panel (depending on the OS).

2. Open Internet Information Services.

3. Branch out the tree to find your Web application folder.

4. Right-click your Web application folder and choose Properties.

5. Click the Director Security tab.

6. Click the Edit button in the Authentication Control section.

7. Uncheck the Anonymous Access box and make sure Integrated Authentication (Challenge Response) option is checked.

8. If you want to allow the users to type their passwords if IIS Challenge Response fails, check Basic Authentication.

9. Click both OK buttons and close IIS.

Comments

Your application is now set up to use Windows authentication. For more information on granting and checking access, see Section 8.3, "Requiring Authentication to Access Files and Folders."

See Also

Section 8.1, "Configuring Forms Authentication"

Section 8.3, "Requiring Authentication to Access Files and Folders"

8.3. Requiring Authentication to Access Files and Folders

You want to configure certain files and folders in your application to require authentication.

Technique

Define separate location sections in the web.config file with unique authorization settings:

- `<location path="file">`
- `<location path="folder">`

In the web.config file in Web application's root folder:

```
<?xml version="1.0" encoding="utf-8" ?>
<configuration>
  <system.web>
    <authentication mode="Forms">
      <forms name=".FormsCookie" loginUrl="Login.aspx" />
    </authentication>
    <authorization>
      <allow users="?,*" />
    </authorization>
    <compilation defaultLanguage="VB" debug="true" />
  </system.web>
  <location path="SpecialFile.aspx">
    <system.web>
      <authorization>
        <deny users="?" />
        <allow users="*" />
      </authorization>
    </system.web>
  </location>
  <location path="SpecialFolder">
    <system.web>
      <authorization>
        <deny users="?" />
        <allow users="*" />
      </authorization>
    </system.web>
  </location>
</configuration>
```

Comments

Each sub-folder of the Web application can have its own web.config file that specifies its authorization settings. Individual files however can only have unique authorization settings specified with the use of the location section. Note that authentication, unlike authorization, is an application-wide setting that cannot be overridden for files or folders.

See the other topics in this chapter for more information on setting up forms authentication and defining users. It is also possible to use roles, in addition to users, for authorization, but that implementation is not discussed here. Note that the order of the deny and allow elements in the authorization section of the web.config file can make a big difference.

See Also

`<forms>` Element—http://msdn.microsoft.com/library/en-us/cpgenref/html/gngrfforms.asp, MSDN Library

`<authorization>` Element—http://msdn.microsoft.com/library/en-us/cpgenref/html/gngrfauthorizationsection.asp, MSDN Library

8.4. Creating a Simple Forms Authentication Login Page

You want to create a login form for your Web application using forms authentication.

Technique

Place two TextBox controls for the username and password on the page. Set the TextMode property of the password TextBox control to `Password`. Add a Button control to perform the login, and a Label control to provide feedback to the users.

The ASPX page is as follows:

```
<p align="center">
  <table cellpadding="2" cellspacing="0" bgcolor="#fafade">
  <tr>
    <th colspan="2" bgcolor="#baba99">
    Login</th>
  </tr>
  <tr>
    <td>User Name:</td>
    <td><asp:TextBox ID="UserName" Runat="server" /></td>
  </tr>
  <tr>
    <td>Password:</td>
    <td><asp:TextBox ID="Password" Runat="server"
      TextMode="Password" /></td>
  </tr>
  <tr>
    <td colspan="2" align="center"><asp:Button ID="Login"
      Text="Login" Runat="server" OnClick="Login_Click"/></td>
  </tr>
  </table>
  <br>
  <asp:Label ID="Message" Runat="server" ForeColor="#FF0000"></asp:Label>
</p>
```

In `<script runat="server" />` block or codebehind:

```
Private Sub Login_Click(sender as Object, e as System.EventArgs)
  If UserName.Text="johndoe" AND Password.Text="password" Then
  System.Web.Security.FormsAuthentication.RedirectFromLoginPage(
➡UserName.Text, False)
  Else
  Message.Text="Invalid Username/Password combination"
  End If
End Sub
```

Comments

On the Login button `Click` event, you simply add code to verify the user ID and password are correct. You will most likely want to query a database or check another source to verify the password instead of hard coding the logins in your code. If the password is correct, you call `System.Web.Security.FormsAuthentication.` `RedirectFromLoginPage` to send the users to the page they had originally requested. Pass this function the name of the user who has logged in for use later in your application, and pass it a boolean of whether to persist the cookie across browser sessions (many login forms use a check box to determine which value to use for this). If the password is not correct, you display an error to the users.

See Also

Section 8.1, "Configuring Forms Authentication"

Section 8.3, "Requiring Authentication to Access Files and Folders"

Section 8.5, "Creating a Simple Forms Authentication Logout Page"

8.5. Creating a Simple Forms Authentication Logout Page

You want to provide a way for your users to log out of your Web application using forms authentication.

Technique

Place a LinkButton control on the page and assign it the text of `Logout`. Place a Literal control on your page and title it message. This will be populated with a message telling the users they have logged out and including the code to redirect them to another page. The ASPX page is as follows:

```
<p align="center"><asp:LinkButton ID="Logout" Runat="server" OnClick="Logout_
➥Click">Logout</asp:LinkButton></p>
<p align="center"><asp:Literal ID="Message" Runat="server" /></p>
```

In `<script runat="server" />` block or codebehind:

```
private void Logout_Click(object sender, System.EventArgs e)
{
  System.Web.Security.FormsAuthentication.SignOut();
  Message.Text="You have been logged out.";
  Message.Text+="<meta http-equiv=\"Refresh\"
➥content=\"3;URL=http://aspalliance.com\" />";
}
```

Comments

On the Logout button `Click` event, do the following:

- Call `System.Web.Security.FormsAuthentication.SignOut()`. This method forces a log out by removing the authentication ticket and session cookies.
- Add text to the Message literal control to let the users know they have been logged out.
- Add a Meta tag to the Message literal control to redirect the users to another page. If you want to send the users back to the login page, you can redirect them to any page in the application. Forms authentication will force the users to log in first (assuming the page requires an authenticated user).

See Also

Section 8.1, "Configuring Forms Authentication"

Section 8.3, "Requiring Authentication to Access Files and Folders"

Section 8.4, "Creating a Simple Forms Authentication Login Page"

8.6. Perform Custom Authentication on Each Request

You need to perform some custom authentication activity for each user request.

Technique

The application event, `Application_AuthenticateRequest`, which is defined in global.asax, is used to perform custom authentication on every request to an application.

It is the perfect place to add custom checks to determine whether the users should be given access to a particular resource, or to determine which resources the user should be able to access. In the following example, the list of roles the user belongs to is retrieved and stored in the HttpContext collection, which is available for the life of each request. Individual resources can then use the list to determine whether the users should have access to them.

In global.asax (or its codebehind), do the following:

```
Sub Application_AuthenticateRequest(ByVal sender As Object sender,
➡ByVal e As EventArgs)
  If Request.IsAuthenticated = True Then
  Dim roles() As String

  ' get this user's roles (left out)

  ' store roles in Context for the rest of this request
  Context.Items.Add("SecurityRoles", roles)
  End If
End Sub
```

Comments

The IBuySpy portal makes good use of this technique; study it if you're using this approach.

See Also

Section 4.9, "Using HttpContext for Per-Request Caching"

IBuySpy Portal Sample Application—http://ibuyspyportal.com/

Data Access

Error Handling and Debugging

9.0. Introduction

I would love to be able to tell you that ASP.NET doesn't break, have bugs, or crash, but unfortunately sometimes it does. Usually, at least when I'm the one writing the code, it's the programmer's fault. At times like these, the debugging and error-handling features of ASP.NET make your job much easier. In this chapter, you'll learn how to debug your ASP.NET pages, handle errors gracefully without showing them to your users, and log problem details for later analysis. I hope you never need to use any of these techniques in your application, but I'm pretty sure you'll find at least a few of these recipes useful.

9.1. Configuring a Default Error Page

You want to have your users redirected to a friendly error-handler page whenever an application error occurs.

Technique

In the web.config file, locate the `customErrors` section. Set the mode to on and set the URL for the default redirect.

The web.config file is as follows:

```
<customErrors mode="On" defaultRedirect="Recipe0901bvb.aspx"/>
```

In `<script runat="server" />` block or codebehind:

```
Sub Page_Load(sender As Object, e As EventArgs)
  Dim a as Integer=1/0
End Sub
```

The error handler page is as follows:

```html
<html>
 <body>
  <form id="Recipe0901bvb" method="post" runat="server">
  An error has occurred in this application.
  </form>
 </body>
</html>
```

Comments

Whenever an unhandled error occurs anywhere in your application, the users are direct-
ed to your custom error screen. This is an important part of creating a professional and
secure Web site. Note that the contents of the web.config file are case sensitive.

See Also
Section 9.2, "Logging Error Details"

9.2. Logging Error Details

You need to store the details of any exceptions that occur in an event log.

Technique

Create an object of type `System.Diagnostics.EventLog`. Then begin the `try/catch`
block and enter the code you suspect is causing the error. Create a `catch` block to run if
an error occurs and assign the exception to the ex variable. Inside the block, create a
new `EventLog` instance. Set the log to send the error to, and enter your application name
as the source. Finally, write the exception to the event log.

In `<script runat="server" />` block or codebehind:

```vbnet
Sub Page_Load(sender As Object, e As EventArgs)
  Dim a as Integer=0
  Dim myEventLog as System.Diagnostics.EventLog


  Try
   a=1/a
  Catch ex as Exception
   myEventLog=new System.Diagnostics.EventLog()
   myEventLog.Log="Application"
   myEventLog.Source="Recipe0902"
   myEventLog.WriteEntry(ex.ToString())
```

```
   End Try
End Sub
```

You also can handle errors on an application error by modifying the `Application_Error` event handler in the global.asax file. Use `Server.GetLastError()` to get a reference to the exception that was thrown.

In the global.asax file:

```
Sub Application_Error(ByVal sender As Object, ByVal e As EventArgs)
   Dim myEventLog As System.Diagnostics.EventLog
   Dim ex As Exception = Server.GetLastError()
   myEventLog = New System.Diagnostics.EventLog()
   myEventLog.Log = "Application"
   myEventLog.Source = "Recipe0902"
   myEventLog.WriteEntry(ex.ToString())
End Sub
```

Comments

Catching and keeping a log of errors that occur can greatly decrease the amount of time you spend supporting an application. Note: The ASP.NET account does not have access to write to the event log by default. To run this example, you need to do one of the following:

- Modify the `processModel` element in `machine.config` to set ASP.NET to run as the System account.
- Add the ASP.NET account to the local Administrators group.
- Use regedt32 to grant the ASP.NET account write access to the `HKEY_LOCAL_MACHINE\SYSTEM\CurrentControlSet\Services\Eventlog` key.

See Also
Section 9.1, "Configuring a Default Error Page"

9.3. Enabling Page Level Tracing

You want to view detailed trace output for a particular Web Form.

Technique

In order for page level tracing to be enabled, you need to add the `Trace` attribute to the @ Page directive.

```
<%@ Page Language="VB" Trace="true"%>
```

The default value of the `Trace` attribute is `false`, which means that it is disabled. In order to enable it, you simply set its value to `true`. In `<script runat="server" />` block or codebehind:

```
Private Sub Page_Load(Source As Object, E As EventArgs)
 Trace.Write("Page_Load", "Declaring and initializing variables.")
 Dim _A As Integer = 10
 Dim _B As Integer = 20

 Trace.Write("Page_Load", "Applying add operation.")
  _A += _B

 Trace.Write("Page_Load", "Variable values changed.")
 Trace.Write("_A", _A)
 Trace.Write("_B", _B)
End Sub
```

`Trace.Write` can accept up to three arguments—the first one is the category for the message, the second is the actual message to display, and the third is the exception information displayed after the message. The following listing demonstrates all three arguments:

```
   . . .
   . . .
Try
 'code goes here
Catch _Error As Exception
 Trace.Write("Category", "Message", E)
End Try
```

Comments

In order to display `Trace` messages from your code, use either the `Trace.Write()` or the `Trace.Warn()` statement. The difference between the two is that `Trace.Warn` shows the output text in red, indicating a warning, whereas `Trace.Write()` shows output in black text. Both methods accept the same number and type of arguments.

You can also use the `Trace.IsEnabled` Boolean property to test whether tracing is enabled prior to performing an expensive operation, such as looping through all values on the page as part of a `Trace` output operation.

Note that to access tracing outside of a page, such as in a custom control, you must refer to the current Web context by using `System.Web.HttpContext.Current.Trace()` instead of just `Trace()` or `Page.Trace()`.

See Also
Section 6.3, "Configuring Application Tracing"

9.4. Raising Exceptions

You want to raise an exception in the event that something unexpected happens within a certain section of the code.

Technique

In `<script runat="server" />` block or codebehind:

```
Private Sub Page_Load(Source As Object, E As EventArgs)

Dim _Connection As New
SqlConnection("Server=localhost;Database=pubs;uid=sa;pwd=;")
Dim _Command As New SqlCommand("Select * From Authors", _Connection)

Try
 _Connection.Open()
 DG1.DataSource = _Command.ExecuteReader(CommandBehavior.CloseConnection)
 DG1.DataBind()
Catch _Error As Exception
 Throw New Exception("Whoops.... You've got an error in the code!")
Finally
 _Connection.Close()
End Try
End Sub
```

The Throw statement here creates a new exception and raises it, replacing the original exception object. The error message that will appear on the page in this case is the one that has been provided as an argument to the constructor of the Exception object.

The original error message can also be passed to the Throw statement in order to show the details. You can achieve this by passing the Exception object as a second argument to the constructor of the newly raised exception.

```
Catch _Error As Exception
 Throw New Exception("Whoops.... You 've got an error in the code!", _Error)
```

Your exception message has been replaced by the original one, but your exception message still appears. Where? Check out the Stack Trace section.

Comments

The Throw statement can be used to explicitly throw an exception or to rethrow a caught exception. The new exception being raised is provided with a customized statement, so as to hide error details and display a more simplified error message to the viewer. You can also pass along the original exception object to the raised exception. This can be useful because it allows a friendly error message to be displayed to the user, but keeps the detailed information for debugging purposes (perhaps the exception information is logged for later analysis, as Section 9.2 demonstrates).

See Also

MSDN Library: "Throwing Exceptions"

Section 9.2, "Logging Error Details"

Section 9.6 "Catching Exceptions"

9.5. Handling Page Level Errors

You want to handle any error that occurs on a page by implementing the `Page_Error` event handler.

Technique

The `Page_Error()` event, exposed by the Page object, can be used to catch errors on a page level. The following code demonstrates how you can use this event for page level error handling.

In `<script runat="server" />` block or codebehind:

```
Private Sub Page_Load(Source As Object, E As EventArgs)
  Dim _Connection As New
➡SqlConnection("Server=localhost;Database=pubs;uid=sa;pwd=;")
  Dim _Command As New SqlCommand("Select * From Authors", _Connection)

  '_Connection.Open()  causes an exception
  DG1.DataSource = _Command.ExecuteReader(CommandBehavior.CloseConnection)
  DG1.DataBind()
  _Connection.Close()
End Sub

Public Sub Page_Error(Source As Object, E As EventArgs)
  Response.Write(Server.GetLastError.ToString())
  Server.ClearError()
End Sub
```

Comments

The demonstrated code tries to execute a query without having an open connection to the datasource. This raises an exception, which is captured by the `Page_Error()` event of the Page object itself. Within the `Page_Error` event, the code displays the error message by calling the `GetLastError` method of the Server object. This returns an exception object that is generated by the error. Note that the data access technique used in this code is not a good approach for connecting to datasources; it has been adopted here only for demonstrating the `Page_Error` event. You should always use the `Try/Catch/Finally` statements for interacting with datasources.

Errors can also be handled at the application level using the `Application_Error` event found in global.asax. This technique is demonstrated by implementing a logging solution for an application; see Section 9.2, "Logging Error Details."

See Also

Section 9.2, "Logging Error Details"

Section 9.6, "Catching Exceptions"

9.6. Catching Exceptions

You want to handle an exception that occurred within a certain block of code and, based on the nature of the exception, take some action.

Technique

In `<script runat="server" />` block or codebehind:

```
Private Sub Page_Load(Source As Object, E As EventArgs)

  Dim _Connection As New
➡SqlConnection("Server=localhost;Database=pubs;uid=sa;pwd=;")
  Dim _Command As New SqlCommand("Select * From Authors", _Connection)

  Try
  '_Connection.Open commented to cause an exception
    '_Connection.Open()
  DG1.DataSource = _Command.ExecuteReader(CommandBehavior.CloseConnection)
  DG1.DataBind()
  Catch _Error As Exception
   MessageLabel.Text = _Error.Message
  Finally
   _Connection.Close()
  End Try

End Sub
```

You can also provide multiple `Catch` statements, as shown here:

```
  Private Sub Page_Load(Source As Object, E As EventArgs)

  'Error has been produced in the connection
  'string by writing "Server=localhos" (no 't')
```

```
  Dim _Connection As New
➡SqlConnection("Server=localhos;Database=pubs;uid=sa;pwd=;")
  Dim _Command As New SqlCommand("Select * From Authors", _Connection)

  Try
   _Connection.Open()
   DG1.DataSource = _Command.ExecuteReader(CommandBehavior.CloseConnection)
   DG1.DataBind()
  Catch _SqlError As SqlException
   MessageLabel.Text = _SqlError.Message
  Catch _Error As Exception
   MessageLabel.Text= _Error.Message
  Finally
   _Connection.Close()
  End Try

End Sub
```

Comments

The `Try/Catch/Finally` block is the best approach towards error handling. It provides a structured error-handling technique that was not available in previous versions of Visual Basic. The `Try` block is provided with the code that is to be run. The `Catch` block is for catching the exceptions raised by any line of code in the `Try` block. The `Finally` block is executed under both conditions—either when the `Try` section successfully executes or when an error occurs and is passed to the `Catch` block. It is for this reason that the `Close()` method of the connection object has been coded in the `Finally` block, so as to ensure that under both cases (whether successful or unsuccessful), the connection to the data store is closed.

Multiple `Catch` statements can also be provided to capture different types of errors raised by objects. In the second code listing, the exceptions that would be related to `SqlClient` objects are going to be captured by the `Catch` statement having an object of the `SqlException` class. All other exceptions are caught by the second catch statement provided in the `Try` block.

The order of the `Catch` statements is very important. Make sure you put the more generalized `Catch` exceptions after the more specific exceptions. For example, in the second code listing, `SqlException` is a subclass of `Exception`, and so is more specific. Thus, its `Catch` block occurs above the more generic exception's `Catch` block. If the order were reversed, the `SqlException` `Catch` block would never be reached, because the exception block would always catch a `SqlException` that was thrown.

See Also

MSDN Library: "SqlException class"

MSDN Library: "Structured Exception Handling"

Section 9.4, "Raising Exceptions"

Basic Data Operations with ADO.NET

10.0. Introduction

ADO.NET provides a huge upgrade from ADO, while maintaining many of the same objects to allow ADO users a relatively painless transition. This chapter describes some of the simpler ADO.NET operations, including how to open a connection to several kinds of datasources and how to use Microsoft's data access application block, which provides helper functions for accessing SQL Server data. The procedures for calling stored procedures using a few different techniques and for using Access Query objects, which are quite similar, are described here as well. Although quite powerful, the syntax required for working with databases can still be quite verbose and tedious to remember. This chapter, therefore, can serve as a reference when you find that you need to perform some common data-related task and can't quite remember the exact code needed.

10.1. Connecting to SQL Server

You need to connect to a SQL Server database.

Technique

Use the SQL Server .NET data provider in the `System.Data.SqlClient` namespace to connect to a Microsoft SQL Server 7.0 or 2000 database (for example, the Northwind sample database). Your connection strings can take advantage of integrated security or connect using a given SQL login and password.

First, you need to reference the `SqlClient` namespace. Add the following statement to the top of your data access client source file to reference the `System.Data.SqlClient` namespace:

```
Imports System.Data.SqlClient
```

Next, you need to create the connection, use it, and clean up inside a method. For example, you can place the following in `Page_Load`:

```
Dim connectString As string =
➥"Integrated Security=yes;Initial Catalog=Northwind;Data Source=(local)"
Dim sqlConn As SqlConnection = New SqlConnection( connectString )
Try
  sqlConn.Open()
  'do something and then be sure to close the connection...
Finally
  If Not sqlConn Is Nothing Then
   sqlConn.Close()
  End If
End Try
```

Here's an alternative version of an integrated security connection string. This will look familiar if you build your connection strings using Universal Data Link (.UDL) files. This VB.NET example explicitly references the Security Support Provider Interface (SSPI) for the integrated security string and sets the connection string via the `ConnectionString` property:

```
Dim sqlConn As SqlConnection = New SqlConnection()
sqlConn.ConnectionString = "Integrated Security=SSPI;Initial
➥Catalog=Northwind;Data Source=(local)"
Try
  sqlConn.Open()
  'do something and then be sure to close the connection...
Finally
  If Not sqlConn Is Nothing Then
   sqlConn.Close()
  End If
End Try
```

As mentioned, you might also define a connection string that uses a specific SQL Server logon ID. Using the first example, only the connection string changes:

```
connectString =
 "User ID=user;Password=pass;Initial Catalog=Northwind;Data Source=(local)"
```

Now, let's say you want to create a connection to a remote database server. In this case, you need to specify the SQL Server logon ID and password again. Using the `ConnectionString` property, the connection string will look similar to this:

```
sqlConn.ConnectionString = "User ID=user;Password=pass;
➥Network Library=DBMSSOCN;Data Source=192.168.1.1,1433"
```

Of course, you have to change the IP address to match your configuration.

Comments

The most important point to remember is this: if you open a connection you must
remember to close it. You cannot rely on ADO.NET's garbage collector to do it for you
in a timely manner. If you neglect to close your connections, you will likely run out of
available connections in short order! The best way to ensure that connections are properly closed is to wrap their usage in `Try/Catch/Finally` blocks. Also, in addition to the
techniques you've just seen, `SqlConnection` can also be created implicitly by certain
ADO.NET objects like the dataset.

See Also

SqlConnection Class—`http://msdn.microsoft.com/library/en-us/cpref/html/`
`frlrfsystemdatasqlclientsqlconnectionclasstopic.asp`

Creating and Configuring Universal Data Link (.UDL) Files—
`http://msdn.microsoft.com/library/en-us/vsintro7/html/`
`vxtskcreatingconfiguringuniversaldatalinkfiles.asp`

INFO: Accessing SQL Server with Integrated Security from ASP—
`http://support.microsoft.com/default.aspx?scid=KB;EN-US;Q176377`

The Security Support Provider Interface—`http://www.microsoft.com/windows2000/`
`techinfo/howitworks/security/sspi2000.asp`

Setting the SQL Server Network Library in an ADO Connection String—`http://msdn.microsoft.com/`
`library/enus/vbcon/html/vburfIntroductionToADOConnectionDesignTools.asp`

10.2. Connecting to Oracle

You need to connect to an Oracle database.

Technique

Use the .NET data provider for Oracle, which is in the `System.Data.OracleClient`
namespace. This data provider does not come with .NET 1.0, but must be downloaded
separately. Working with Oracle connections is similar to working with SQL Server connections, as the following code demonstrates:

```
Dim connectString As string =
  "Data Source=Oracle-Test;User ID=user;Password=pass"
Dim myConn As OracleConnection = New OracleConnection( connectString )
```

```
Try
  myConn.Open()
  //do something and then be sure to close the connection...
Finally
  If Not myConn Is Nothing Then
    myConn.Close()
End Try
```

Comments

As with the `SqlClient` data provider, the Oracle data provider offers significant per-formance benefits over the OleDB connection method.

> ### See Also
>
> Download the Oracle Data Provider—`http://msdn.microsoft.com/downloads/default.asp`
>
> Using the Data Provider for Oracle to Improve .NET Application Performance—`http://msdn.microsoft.com/library/library/en-us/dndotnet/html/manprooracperf.asp`

10.3. Connecting to a Microsoft Access Database

You want to connect to a Microsoft Access database.

Technique

To connect to a Microsoft Access database, you must include the `System.Data.OleDb` namespace because all the ASP.NET classes that are required to connect to datasources through an OleDB connection are located in this namespace. The ASPX page looks as follows:

```
<html>
<head>
 <title>Connecting to a Microsoft Access Database<title>
</head>
<body>
 <form runat="server">
 <h3>Connecting to a Microsoft Access Database</h3>
 <p>
   <asp:DataGrid id="dg1" runat="server"></asp:DataGrid>
 </p>
 <p>
   <asp:Literal id="ltlError" runat="server"></asp:Literal>
 </p>
 </form>
```

```
</body>
</html>
```

Add the following code within the `<script>` tags:

```
Public Sub Page_Load(Source As Object, E As EventArgs)

  Dim ConnectionString As String
   ConnectionString =
"Provider=Microsoft.Jet.OleDb.4.0;Data Source=" & _
Server.MapPath("Northwind.mdb") & ";"

  Dim QuerySQL As String
   QuerySQL = "SELECT * FROM Shippers"

   Dim objConn As New OleDbConnection(ConnectionString)
   Dim objCmd As OleDbCommand

  objCmd = New OleDbCommand
   objCmd.CommandText = QuerySQL
   objCmd.Connection = objConn

  Try
     objConn.Open()

     dg1.DataSource = objCmd.ExecuteReader()
     dg1.DataBind()

  Catch Err As Exception
     ltlError.Text = Err.ToString()

  Finally
     objConn.Close()

  End Try

 End Sub
```

Comments

First, you must create a connection string that includes the driver and the source path of the source database. In this example, this has been assigned to the string type variable named `ConnectionString`. Remember that if you are using Microsoft Access 97, the connection string is going to be as follows:

```
"Provider=Microsoft.Jet.OleDb.3.75;Data Source=" & _
  Server.MapPath("Northwind.mdb") & ";"
```

Whereas when using Microsoft Access 2000 and XP, the string is as demonstrated in the code. You must create the `Connection` and `Command` objects as well. The Connection object's constructor is provided with `ConnectionString`, which contains the connection string. The Command object's instance is assigned the query and the connection that it will use to access the datasource.

Having established the basic settings for the Connection and the Command objects, you enclose the rest of the code within a `Try/Catch/Finally` block to capture any type of errors that arise. Afterwards, within the `Try/Catch` block, you open the connection and call the `ExecuteReader` method of the command object. This method executes the specified query text and returns the results to the DataGrid control that has been assigned to it.

When you view the page in the browser, you will see all the records from the database table specified in the query.

See Also

Retrieving Records without a Dataset—`http://aspalliance.com/hrmalik/articles/2002/200209/20020901.aspx`, by Haroon Rasheed Malik

SQL Direct—`http://aspalliance.com/hrmalik/articles/2002/200208/20020801.aspx`, by Haroon Rasheed Malik

10.4. Connecting to MySQL

You need to connect to a MySQL database.

Technique

You can use the OleDB provider that ships with the .NET Framework. In this case, your code would look something like this:

```
Dim connectString As string = _
  "Provider=MySQLProv;Data Source=mydb;User Id=user;Password=pass"
Dim myConn As System.Data.OleDb.OleDbConnection = _
  New System.Data.OleDb.OleDbConnection( connectString )
Try
  myConn.Open()
  'do something and then be sure to close the connection...
Finally
  If Not myConn Is Nothing Then
   myConn.Close()
  End If
End Try
```

Another option is to use the MySQL data provider by eInfoDesigns (which I have only minimally examined). In which case, your code would look like so:

```
Dim connectString As string = _
  "Data Source=server;Database=mydb;User ID=user;
➥Password=pass;Command Logging=false"
Dim myConn As eInfoDesigns.dbProvider.MySqlClient.MySqlConnection = _
  New eInfoDesigns.dbProvider.MySqlClient.MySqlConnection( connectString )
Try
  myConn.Open()
  'do something and then be sure to close the connection...
Finally
  If Not myConn Is Nothing Then
   myConn.Close()
  End If
End Try
```

Comments

You can access most datasources with the OleDB data provider, although it's not the most efficient way to do so. You get better performance using a custom data provider dedicated to that particular datasource. Although Microsoft does not support a custom MySQL data provider, third-party software vendors are beginning to supply these, as listed in the following "See Also" section.

See Also

Connection String Information—http://www.connectionstrings.com/

eInfoDesigns (producers of MySQL data provider)—http://www.einfodesigns.com/

10.5. Connecting to an ODBC Datasource

You need to connect to an ODBC datasource.

Technique

Download the ODBC .NET data provider from the link mentioned in the "See Also" section that follows. Its use is similar to other data providers covered in this chapter.

```
Dim connectString As string = "DSN=myDSN;Uid=user;Pwd=pass"
Dim myConn As Microsoft.Data.Odbc.OdbcConnection = _
  New Microsoft.Data.Odbc.OdbcConnection( connectString )
Try
  myConn.Open()
```

```
    'do something and then be sure to close the connection...
Finally
  If Not myConn Is Nothing Then
    myConn.Close()
  End If
End Try
```

Comments

According to Carsten Thomsen, author of *Database Programming in C#*:

> *The OdbcConnection class, which uses the Platform Invoke feature, is roughly twice as fast for standard applications than the OleDbConnection. The latter uses COM, which is chatty, and hence has more server round-trips. So unless your application is shipping large amounts of data (hundreds of thousands of rows or more) per data request, you should at least consider using the* OdbcConnection *class.* SqlConnection *is roughly 20 percent faster than* OdbcConnection.

See Also

Section 10.1, "Connecting to SQL Server"

ODBC .NET Data Provider–http://msdn.microsoft.com/downloads/default.asp

Database Programming in C#–by Carsten Thomsen (Apress, ISBN 1-59059-010-4)

10.6. Using Microsoft's Data Access Application Block

You want to use Microsoft's data access application block to simplify your data access.

Technique

The first step is to reference the data, SQLClient, and data access application block namespaces. Add the following statements to the top of your data access client source file:

```
<%@ Page Language="VB" ClassName="Recipe1001vb" %>
<%@ import Namespace="System.Data" %>
<%@ import Namespace="System.Data.SqlClient" %>
<%@ import Namespace="Microsoft.ApplicationBlocks.Data" %>
<script runat="server">
```

Next, you have to place the following code inside a method. `Page_Load` will do fine for this example:

```
Sub Page_Load(sender As Object, e As EventArgs)
  Dim dataSet As DataSet
  'parameter value variables
  Dim beginningDate As string = "1/1/1996"
  Dim endingDate As string = "12/31/1996"

  Try
    Dim connectionString As string = _
  "Integrated Security=yes;Initial Catalog=Northwind;Data Source=(local)"
    Dim arParams(1) As SqlParameter

    arParams(0) = New SqlParameter("@Beginning_Date", beginningDate)
    arParams(1) = New SqlParameter("@Ending_Date", endingDate)

    dataSet = SqlHelper.ExecuteDataset(connectionString, _
  CommandType.StoredProcedure, "Employee Sales by Country", arParams)

    'bind dataSet to a WebControl and call Page.DataBind()
  Catch exception As Exception
    'An error occurred - were your connection string,
    'stored procedure name and parameters correct?
    'you could display the error via a WebControl or throw an exception here
  End Try
End Sub 'Page_Load
```

Comments

This is a simple example—it barely scratches the surface of data access application block functionality. There's support for performing transactional updates and fetching XML as well as data-readers and caching parameters for multiple calls to a given stored procedure.

The `SqlHelper` object manages just about everything for you. In order to achieve the same result in ADO.NET, you would need `SqlConnection`, `SqlCommand`, and `SqlDataAdapter` objects in addition to what you've declared here. Connection management is improved as well because the `SqlConnection` is created internally to the object. There is no need you for to close the connection—the object handles closing the connection as it goes out of scope.

Finally, take the opportunity to examine the source code for the application block. There are many examples of best practices in the source code that you might want to apply to your own projects!

See Also

Section 11.3, "Executing a Stored Procedure and Returning the Results in a Dataset"

Microsoft Application Blocks for .NET Data Access Application Block Overview—
`http://msdn.microsoft.com/library/default.asp?url=/library/en-us/`
`dnbda/html/daab-rm.asp`

10.7. Using a Tool to Create a Data Access Layer

You want to automate the creation of your data access layer using a tool.

Technique

There are quite a few data access code generators available for .NET, with widely varying costs and feature sets. This example demonstrates LLBLGen, an open source data tier
generator that supports a wide array of options for the created files. It generates stored
procedures for insert, update, select, and delete for the tables selected, and then creates
VB or C# classes to call these procedures. It is available at `http://www.sd.nl/`
`software/`. This section uses version 1.2, released in November 2002.

To use LLBLGen, simply start the program and provide the connection information
for your database, as Figure 10.1 shows.

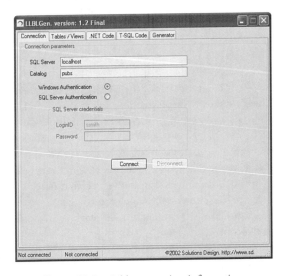

Figure 10.1   Add connection information.

Next, choose the tables and views for which you want to generate data access classes, as shown in Figure 10.2.

Figure 10.2   Choose tables and views desired.

Now, choose the options you want for your .NET classes, including naming conventions, namespaces, language, and method of storing the connection string. Figure 10.3 shows the available options.

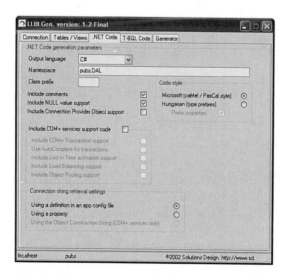

Figure 10.3   Use .NET Code tab to choose options.

Do the same thing for the SQL procedures—pick which ones you want to generate, choose a common name prefix for them, and pick other options as described in Figure 10.4.

Figure 10.4   Use T-SQL Code tab to pick SQL procedures.

Finally, generate the code! Choose the output paths for the .NET source files and the T-SQL script file, and watch as it generates your code for you. Figure 10.5 concludes this example, showing how a successful code generation should end.

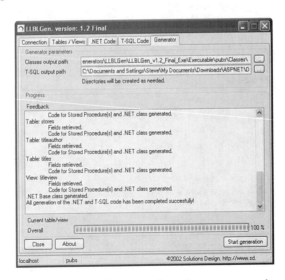

Figure 10.5   Use Generator tab to choose output paths.

See Also

LLBLGen—http://www.sd.nl/software/default.asp

ProcBlaster—http://www.lockwoodtech.com/
index.asp?PageId=proc-blaster&TitleID=products

nTierGen—http://www.gavinjoyce.com/nTierGen/

DataHand—http://dotnetdan.com/utilities/

10.8. Executing a Stored Procedure with No Results Returned

You need to execute a stored procedure that doesn't return any results, or that returns a single scalar value.

Technique

```
' Set up the connection / command
Dim connectionString as String = "server=.;database=Northwind;
                        Trusted_Connection=true"
Dim connection As New SqlConnection(connectionString)
Dim command As New SqlCommand("IncrementDownloads", connection)
command.CommandType = CommandType.StoredProcedure

' Execute, but don't return any results
connection.Open()
command.ExecuteNonQuery()
connection.Close()
```

Comments

There are many cases, especially when using stored procedures, where it is unnecessary to return a result set from the database. In those cases, the SqlCommand provides a simple ExecuteNonQuery() method that can be used to run the results on the database. This method doesn't return a result set—if one is returned it's simply ignored.

This technique is also useful when executing non-SELECT SQL scripts, such as UPDATE, INSERT, and DELETE, where returning a result set serves no purpose.

When working with a datareader, make sure to close the connection. Unlike a dataset, the connection stays open until you close it.

10.9. Inserting an Image into SQL Server

You want to upload an image and store it in a SQL Server database.

Technique

You must properly set up the SQL Server database table to accept images, as well as provide a way on your Web Form to upload an image and send it to the SQL Server.

The table that will store the image must utilize the image data type on a column that will store the image. In the following examples, the name of this column is called Image. In the .ASPX file:

```
<form enctype="multipart/form-data" runat="server">
  <input id="ImageFile" runat="server" type="file" /><p />
  <asp:button runat="server" id="UploadButton" OnClick="UploadImage" />
</form>
```

In <script runat="server" /> block or codebehind:

```
Sub UploadImage(sender As Object, e As EventArgs)
    Dim connectionString As String = "Enter your Connection String"
    Dim imageStream As Stream = ImageFile.PostedFile.InputStream
    Dim byteData(ImageFile.PostedFile.ContentLength) As Byte
    Dim objConn As New SqlClient.SqlConnection(ConnectionString)
    Dim cmdText As String = "INSERT INTO sql_images(Image) VALUES(@image)"
    Dim objCommand As New SqlClient.SqlCommand(cmdText, objConn)
    Dim objParam As New SqlClient.SqlParameter("@image", SqlDbType.Image)

    imageStream.Read(byteData, 0, imageFile.PostedFile.ContentLength)
    objParam.Value = byteData
    objCommand.Parameters.Add(objParam)

    Try
      objConn.Open()
      objCommand.ExecuteNonQuery()
    Catch exc as System.Exception
      ErrorLabel.Text = exc.ToString()
    Finally
      objConn.Close()
      imageStream.Close()
    End Try
End Sub
```

Note that you must include the System.Data namespace for this code to compile.

Comments

The <form> tag has an additional attribute called enctype. This attribute allows binary data to be passed through the form (which is needed for the image).

In the code, the submitted image file is broken into a byte array (imgdata) and then used as the value of the SqlParameter that is passed in as the image (imgparam, @image).

See Also

Section 10.10, "Displaying an Image from SQL Server"

Storing Images in SQL Server—

http://aspalliance.com/wisemonk/view.aspx?id=AN062302, by Philip Quinn

10.10. Displaying an Image from SQL Server

You want to display an image that is stored in a SQL Server database.

Technique

You can stream the binary data returned by SQL Server directly using the Response.BinaryWrite method. Do this after retrieving the data from the database.

In <script runat="server" /> block or codebehind:

```
Sub Page_Load(sender As Object, e As EventArgs)
  Dim connectionString as String = "Your connection string"
  Dim objConnection as New SqlConnection(connectionString)
  Dim commandText as String = "SELECT Image FROM imageTable"
  Dim objCommand as New SqlCommand(commandText, objConnection)
  Dim objReader as SqlDataReader

  Try
   objConnection.Open()
   objReader = objCommand.ExecuteReader()

   If objReader.Read() Then
     Response.ContentType = "image/jpeg"
     Response.BinaryWrite( CType(objReader("Image"), Byte()) )
   End If
  Catch exc as Exception
   Response.Write( exc.ToString() )
  Finally
   If Not objConnection Is Nothing Then
     If objConnection.State = ConnectionState.Open Then
      objConnection.Close()
     End If
```

```
    End If
    If Not objReader Is Nothing Then
      objReader.Close()
    End If
  End Try
End Sub
```

Comments

This code will display the contents of the first record in the `imageTable`. In the example code, the `Image` field in the SQL Server contains the binary data that is written out with the `Response.BinaryWrite` method.

`Response.ContentType` should be set to the appropriate MIME-type of the image that you are trying to display. This can be stored in the database as well and retrieved along with the image data.

See Also

Section 10.9, "Inserting an Image into SQL Server"

Retrieving Images Stored in SQL Server—
`http://aspalliance.com/wisemonk/view.aspx?id=AN062322`

10.11. Invoking a Simple Query Object in Microsoft Access

You want to execute a SQL statement in a `Query` object in Microsoft Access.

Technique

The Query object in Microsoft Access acts as stored procedures do in SQL Server. These can therefore be thought of as the stored procedures of Microsoft Access. Just as the performance of a Web application increases when used with stored procedures, so to does it improve when using Query objects in Microsoft Access. A simple Query object containing a `SELECT` query can easily be invoked in ASP.NET using the classes provided in the `System.Data.OleDb` namespace. In fact, the procedure is similar to invoking stored procedures from SQL Server using the managed drivers in the `System.Data.SqlClient` namespace.

You are required to import the `System.Data` and the `System.Data.OleDb` namespaces for the following example. The following example has been implemented using the Northwind database; make sure you have a copy of it in the root directory containing this file.

The ASPX page is as follows:

```
<html>
<head>
<title>Recipe1011</title>
</head>
<body style="FONT-FAMILY: arial">
  <h2>Simple Query Object in Microsoft Access
  </h2>
  <hr size="1" />
  <form runat="server">
    <p>
      <asp:datagrid id="DataGrid1" runat="server"
EnableViewState="False"
   ForeColor="Black" BackColor="White" CellPadding="3"
➥GridLines="None"
CellSpacing="1">
        <HeaderStyle font-bold="True" forecolor="white"
 backcolor="#4A3C8C"></HeaderStyle>
        <ItemStyle backcolor="#DEDFDE"></ItemStyle>
      </asp:datagrid>
    </p>
    <p>
     <asp:Literal id="ErrorLiteralControl" runat="server"
 EnableViewState="false"></asp:Literal>
    </p>
  </form>
</body>
</html>
```

In `<script runat="server" />` block or codebehind:

```
Sub Page_Load(Sender As Object, E As EventArgs)


    Dim ConnectionString As String =
  "Provider=Microsoft.Jet.OleDb.4.0;Data Source=" & _
  Server.MapPath("Northwind.mdb") & ";"

    'Name of the query object in Microsoft Access
    Dim CommandText As String = "[Current Product List]"

    Dim _Connection As New OleDbConnection(ConnectionString)
    Dim _Command As New OleDbCommand(CommandText, _Connection)

    'Set the command type property to stored procedure
    _Command.CommandType = CommandType.StoredProcedure
```

```
    Try
      _Connection.Open()
      DataGrid1.DataSource =
  _Command.ExecuteReader(CommandBehavior.CloseConnection)
      DataGrid1.DataBind()

    Catch Err As Exception
      ErrorLiteralControl.Text = Err.ToString()

  Finally
    _Connection.Close()

    End Try

  End Sub
```

Comments

Like other data access techniques, first you must create Connection and Command objects. After you create these two objects, you need to set two properties for the Command object. The `CommandType` property of the Command object is set to `StoredProcedure` and the `CommandText` property is set to the name of the Query object that is to be invoked. This example passes the name of the Query object to the constructor of the Command object, thus setting the `Connection` and the `CommandText` properties. Note that the mentioned Query object must exist in the database. If the name of the Query object contains spaces, it is to be enclosed in braces([]); otherwise you aren't required to enclose the name within braces ([]). You simply bind it to any control and execute the page. The results of the Query object are displayed on the ASP.NET page.

See Also

Section 10.0, "Introduction to Basic Operations with ADO.NET"

Section 10.3, "Connecting to a Microsoft Access Database"

Section 10.8, "Executing a Stored Procedure with No Results Returned"

Section 11.1, "Executing a Stored Procedure and Returning the Results in a Datareader"

10.12. Invoking Parameterized Query Objects in Microsoft Access

You want to invoke parameterized Query objects in Microsoft Access.

Technique

Import `System.Data` and `System.Data.OleDb` namespaces and be sure to have the Northwind.mdb database in the application's root folder. The interface consists of two

TextBox controls, a Button, and a DataGrid control. The TextBox controls are for taking the parameters required for invoking the Sales By Year Query object. In <script runat="server" /> block or codebehind:

```
Sub GetRecords_Click(sender As Object, e As EventArgs)

  Dim ConnectionString As String =
  "Provider=Microsoft.Jet.OleDb.4.0;Data Source=" & _
  Server.MapPath("Northwind.mdb") & ";"

  'The name of the Stored Procedure for your application
  Dim CommandText As String = "[Sales By Year]"

  Dim _Connection As New OleDbConnection(ConnectionString)
  Dim _Command As New OleDbCommand(CommandText, _Connection)

  'OleDbParameter objects for passing in Query parameters.
  Dim _BeginingDate As New OleDbParameter()
  Dim _EndingDate As New OleDbParameter()

  _Command.CommandType = CommandType.StoredProcedure

  ' Set the input parameter, for your application
  _Command.Parameters.Add("@BeginningDate", DbType.Date).Value =
  BeginingDateTextBox.Text
  _Command.Parameters.Add("@EndingDate", DbType.Date).Value =
  EndingDateTextBox.Text

  Try

    _Connection.Open()

    DataGrid1.DataSource =
    _Command.ExecuteReader(CommandBehavior.CloseConnection)
    DataGrid1.DataBind()

  Catch Err As Exception
    ErrLiteralControl.Text = Err.ToString()

  Finally
    _Connection.Close()
  End Try

End Sub
```

Comments

This recipe uses the `Sales By Year` Query object from the Northwind database, which requires two parameters, the `BeginningDate` and the `EndingDate`, in order to display the results of the query. These two parameters are passed to the Query object through the `OleDbParameter` objects, by adding them to the Command object's `Parameters` collection.

See Also

Section 10.0, "Introduction to Basic Operations with ADO.NET"

Section 10.3, "Connecting to a Microsoft Access Database"

Section 10.8, "Executing a Stored Procedure with No Results Returned"

Section 11.1, "Executing a Stored Procedure and Returning the Results in a Datareader"

10.13. Using ADO.NET Transactions

You need to execute several ADO.NET commands within a transaction, so that either all succeed or all fail.

Technique

The two namespaces in ADO.NET for connecting to datasource are `System.Data.OleDb` and `System.Data.SqlClient`. Both these namespaces contain the `Transaction` class (`OleDbTransaction` or `SqlTransaction`, respectively). Depending upon your needs or the data store that you are using, you can create an object of either the SQL type or the OleDB type. The following example uses the `SqlTransaction` object of the `System.Data.SqlClient` namespace.

A `SqlTransaction` object is generally created by a `SqlConnection` object, using its `BeginTransaction` method. This method starts a new transaction. It requires an open connection. The method utilizes the open connection and changes made to the data are tracked as a transaction, until the changes are committed or rolled back.

The `SqlTransaction` object provides two methods:

- `Commit` (`Transaction`)—Saves all the changes that have been made to the data store. The method is called in case of a successful transaction.

- `Rollback` (`Transaction`)—Returns the source to its previous state by abandoning the changes that were made. This method is normally called in case of an unsuccessful transaction.

Note that the following example uses the `pubs` database in SQL Server. SQL installs this database by default.

In `<script runat="server" />` block or codebehind:

```
Sub Page_Load(Sender As Object, E As EventArgs)


  Dim ConnectionString As String = _
  "Server=localhost; Database=pubs; uid=sa; pwd=;"
  Dim CommandText As String = _
  "UPDATE authors SET state='PU' WHERE state='UT'"
  Dim CommandText2 As String = _
  "UPDATE authors SET au_id='172-32-1177' WHERE au_lname='white'"

  Dim _Connection As New SqlConnection(ConnectionString)
  Dim _Command As New SqlCommand()

  'Create a transaction object
  Dim _Transact As SqlTransaction
  Try
   'Open connection and begin the transaction
   _Connection.Open()
   _Transact = _Connection.BeginTransaction()

   'Set up the command and execute the statements
   _Command.Connection = _Connection
   _Command.Transaction = _Transact

   'Execute the first sql statement
   _Command.CommandText = CommandText
   _Command.ExecuteNonQuery

   'Execute the second sql statement
   _Command.CommandText = CommandText2
   _Command.ExecuteNonQuery

   'Commit if we got this far
   _Transact.Commit()

  MessageLabel.Text = "Transaction Successful!"

  Catch Err As Exception
   'Rollback transaction and report problem
   MessageLabel.Text = "Transaction Failed! <br/>" & Err.Message
   _Transact.Rollback()

  Finally
   'Clean up resources
   _Connection.Close()
  End Try

End Sub
```

Comments

This example sends two update statements using the same Connection and Command objects to update some values in the pubs database. The first SQL statement updates the state field's value to PU, where its value is UT. The au_id of the author White also changes. If both queries are executed separately, the first one will execute successfully and the second one will fail. The update fails because au_id is related to another table, so its value cannot be altered without updating the related records in the other table.

In transactions SQL statements are sent as a unit, and either all the statements execute successfully or none of the statements in the block do. To combine several commands into a transaction using ADO.NET, use the Transaction class, as demonstrated previously. The Commit() method allows all commands in the transaction to complete; the Rollback() method cancels all commands.

See Also

The Transaction Object in ADO.NET—http://aspalliance.com/hrmalik/2002/200216/20021601.aspx, by Haroon Rasheed Malik

Transactions in SQL Server 2000—http://aspalliance.com/hrmalik/2002/200217/20021701.aspx, by Haroon Rasheed Malik

11

Working with Datareaders and Datasets

11.0. Introduction

In ADO, the recordset object could represent a collection of in-memory data, like an advanced array, or it could represent a single row of data from a datasource, with an open connection to that source to navigate and fetch more data. This dual nature of the recordset led to some confusion and many bugs, or at least poor practices, when developers treated a recordset as if it were connected when in fact it was not (and vice versa).

To combat this problem, ADO.NET separates its two primary data-retrieval objects into the always-connected datareader and the never-connected dataset. The datareader provides a "firehose" of data—fast, forward-only, read-only. It is usually the fastest way to access data and uses few resources on the server, because only one row of data needs to be held in memory at any given time. However, the disadvantage is that the datareader holds open a connection to the datasource as long as it is in use, so you must be careful to open the datareader as late as possible and close it as soon as possible once you are finished with it. Proper error handling is a must for datareaders to avoid resource leaks.

Datasets are disconnected recordsets from the ADO world, on steroids. Unlike recordsets, datasets can hold multiple tables' worth of data. In addition, the dataset can specify the types and constraints and keys of those tables, as well as their relationships to one another. In concert with the dataview, this data can be queried and sorted and filtered in a variety of ways. Essentially, each instance of a dataset is a full-fledged database, kept in memory. Unlike datareaders, datasets can be serialized, which means they can be passed to and from Web services, as well as cached. This chapter demonstrates the commonly used functionality of datasets.

11.1. Executing a Stored Procedure and Returning the Results in a Datareader

You want to execute a stored procedure and return the results in a datareader.

Technique

```
' Set up the connection / command
Dim connectionString as String = "server=.;database=Northwind;
                                      Trusted_Connection=true"
Dim connection As New SqlConnection(connectionString)
Dim command As New SqlCommand("GetDownloads", connection)
command.CommandType = CommandType.StoredProcedure

' Create the DataReader
Dim reader As SqlDataReader()

' Execute and get a single result set
connection.Open()
reader = command.ExecuteReader()

… do some work with the reader …

' Close the reader and connection
reader.Close()
connection.Close()
```

Stored procedures provide a clean abstraction layer allowing business logic that is closely tied to the database to be managed by the database. Executing a stored procedure and then populating a datareader—which can then be bound to a server control or used to read the result set row by row—is a common and recommended approach for accessing data.

When working with a datareader, make sure to close the connection. Unlike a dataset, the connection stays open until you close it.

11.2. Using a Datareader to Return Multiple Result Sets

You want to return multiple result sets from a stored procedure using a datareader.

Technique

```
' Set up the connection / command
Dim connectionString as String = "server=.;database=Northwind;
                                      Trusted_Connection=true"
```

```
Dim connection As New SqlConnection(connectionString)
Dim command As New SqlCommand("GetStatistics", connection)
command.CommandType = CommandType.StoredProcedure

' Create the DataReader
Dim reader As SqlDataReader()

' Execute - expect that two result sets are returned
connection.Open()
reader = command.ExecuteReader()

If (reader.Read()) Then
  … do some work with the reader on the current result set …
End If

' Move to the next result set in the reader
reader.NextResult()

If (reader.Read()) Then
  … do some work with the reader on the current result set …
End If

'

' Close the reader and connection
reader.Close()
connection.Close()
```

It's very easy to write a stored procedure that returns multiple result sets. The stored procedure simply has to execute two SELECT statements when the procedure is executing. This can be as simple as:

```
SELECT * FROM Products
SELECT * FROM Customers
```

The ADO.NET classes can easily handle this and allow you to navigate (forward only) through the result sets returned. It's a handy trick; especially in more advanced stored procedures where all the data manipulation can't take place within the stored procedure.

```
        lblErrorMsg.Text = exception.ToString()

    End Try
End Sub
```

Comments

This is a great way to optimize your data access, by performing several queries in a single call to the database. The key method to note here is `reader.NextResult()`, which is responsible for moving the reader to the next resultset coming back from the database.

See Also

Section 11.3, "Executing a Stored Procedure and Returning the Results in a Dataset"

11.3. Executing a Stored Procedure and Returning the Results in a Dataset

You want to execute a stored procedure and return the results in a dataset.

Technique

Use the `SqlConnection`, `SqlDataAdapter`, `SqlCommand`, `SqlParameter`, and `DataSet` objects in the `System.Data.SqlClient` namespace to execute a stored procedure and return the results in a Microsoft SQL Server 7.0 or 2000 database. This example uses the `[Employee Sales by Country]` stored procedure from the Northwind sample database and an integrated security connection string.

First you import the `SqlClient` namespace:

```
<%@ Page Language="VB" ClassName="Recipe1001vb" %>
<%@ import Namespace="System.Data" %>
<%@ import Namespace="System.Data.SqlClient" %>
<script runat="server">
```

Then you place the following code inside a method. `Page_Load` will do fine for this example.

```
Sub Page_Load(sender As Object, e As EventArgs)

 'object vars
 Dim sqlConnection As SqlConnection
 Dim sqlDataAdapter As SqlDataAdapter
 Dim sqlCommand As SqlCommand
 Dim sqlParameter As SqlParameter
 Dim dataSet As DataSet

 'parameter value variables
 Dim beginningDate As string = "1/1/1996"
 Dim endingDate As string = "12/31/1996"
```

```
Try
  sqlConnection = New SqlConnection("Integrated Security=yes;Initial
➡ Catalog=Northwind;Data Source=(local)")

  sqlCommand = New SqlCommand("Employee Sales by Country", sqlConnection)
  sqlCommand.CommandType = CommandType.StoredProcedure

  'we can do this several different ways.  here's one way:
  sqlParameter = New SqlParameter("@Beginning_Date", SqlDbType.DateTime, 8)
  sqlParameter.Direction = ParameterDirection.Input
  sqlParameter.Value = beginningDate
  sqlCommand.Parameters.Add(sqlParameter)

  'here's another - this works if you know the parameter value when
  'you add the parameter and this doesn't work for output parameters
  sqlCommand.Parameters.Add("@Ending_Date", SqlDbType.DateTime, 8).
➡Value = endingDate

  sqlDataAdapter = New SqlDataAdapter(sqlCommand)
  dataSet = New DataSet()

  sqlDataAdapter.Fill(dataSet)

  'bind to a WebControl or manipulate dataSet

Catch exception As Exception
  'handle the exception here
End Try
End Sub
```

Comments

There are two areas of special interest in the example code. First, you must set
`sqlCommand.CommandType` equal to `CommandType.StoredProcedure`, because
`CommandType.StoredProcedure` is not the default value for `CommandType`. Second,
you can create SQL parameters several ways. A common way is to instantiate a
`SqlParameter` variable. The second form uses a more compact technique to assign the
`endingDate` value. This variation works if you know the parameter value when you add
the parameter but doesn't work for stored procedure output parameters.

It's important to note that in this example, the `SqlConnection` is managed by the
`SqlDataAdapter`. There is no need to explicitly open or close the `SqlConnection`. The
`Fill` method does this for you on a just-in-time basis and is closed immediately after it
populates the dataset. This definitely qualifies as a best practice!

> **See Also**
>
> Calling SQL Server Stored Procedures in ASP.NET by Using Visual C# .NET—
>
> http://support.microsoft.com/default.aspx?scid=kb;en-us;Q320916
>
> Calling SQL Server Stored Procedures in ASP.NET by Using Visual Basic .NET—
>
> http://support.microsoft.com/default.aspx?scid=kb;en-us;Q306574

11.4. Creating a Dataset Consisting of Several DataTables Using a Stored Procedure

You want to create a dataset consisting of several DataTables using a stored procedure.

Technique

Use the `SqlConnection`, `SqlDataAdapter`, `SqlCommand`, `DataSet`, and `DataTable` objects in the `System.Data.SqlClient` namespace to execute a stored procedure and return the results from a Microsoft SQL Server 7.0 or 2000 database. This example uses the `[SelectCustomersAndOrders]` stored procedure, which you can add to the Northwind sample database, as well as an integrated security connection string.

You add a stored procedure to the database with one or more SELECT statements:

```
CREATE PROCEDURE SelectCustomersAndOrders  AS
SELECT TOP 10 *
FROM   Customers;

SELECT TOP 10 *
FROM   Orders
```

then you import the namespaces:

```
<%@ Page Language="VB" ClassName="Recipe1202vb" %>
<%@ import Namespace="System.Data" %>
<%@ import Namespace="System.Data.SqlClient" %>
<script runat="server">
```

You then place the following code inside a method. This example uses `Page_Load`.

```
Sub Page_Load(sender As Object, e As EventArgs)

  'object vars
  Dim sqlConnection As SqlConnection
  Dim sqlDataAdapter As SqlDataAdapter
  Dim sqlCommand As SqlCommand
  Dim dataSet As DataSet

  Try
    sqlConnection = New SqlConnection("Integrated Security=yes;Initial
➥ Catalog=Northwind;Data Source=(local)")
```

```
    sqlCommand = New SqlCommand("SelectCustomersAndOrders", sqlConnection)
    sqlCommand.CommandType = CommandType.StoredProcedure

    sqlDataAdapter.Fill(dataSet, "MyTable")

    dataGrid1.DataSource = dataSet.Tables(0)

    dataGrid2.DataSource = dataSet.Tables("MyTable1")

    DataBind()

  Catch exception As Exception

    lblErrorMsg.Text = exception.ToString()

  End Try
End Sub
```

Comments

Most of the work in this example happens when you call the `SqlDataAdapter.Fill` method. Notice that the string `"MyTable"` is passed as the second argument of the `Fill` method. This argument, `srcTable`, establishes a basis for all the DataTable objects that ADO.NET generates. As a result, the first DataTable is named `MyTable` in the first SQL statement in the stored procedure and `MyTable1` in the second statement. If you leave the `srcTable` argument off, `SqlDataAdapter` would simply name the tables `Table`, `Table1`, `Table2`, and so on.

To access the data, you can choose from several techniques to bind a control to the dataset's DataTables. This example binds `dataGrid1` to the first DataTable using its zero-based ordinal number, 0. A second technique is demonstrated when binding `dataGrid2` to the second DataTable by name, `MyTable1`.

See Also
Section 11.3, "Executing a Stored Procedure and Returning the Results in a Dataset"

11.5. Filtering the Contents of a Dataset

You want to access a filtered view of the contents of a dataset (or datatable).

Technique

Use a dataview to filter the contents of a datatable (within a dataset). The following example includes a datatable with three columns: `JediID`, `MasterJediID`, and `Name`. You want to be able to view all of the Jedi with the same Master Jedi, using a filter specified in `DropDownList1`. The complete code for this page is available from this book's Web site—the relevant code for the filter is listed here:

```
' Get filtered view from datatable dt
Dim dv As New DataView(dt)
If Int32.Parse(DropDownList1.SelectedItem.Value) > 0 Then
    dv.RowFilter = "masterjediID = " + DropDownList1.SelectedItem.Value
End If

DataGrid1.DataSource = dv
DataGrid1.DataBind()
```

The `RowFilter` property takes string syntax similar to syntax used in a `WHERE` statement in SQL. In this case, it is returning only those rows in which a column has a particular value. You can also use other comparison operators and the `LIKE` statement with the `%` wildcard (* also serves as a wildcard), just like in SQL.

Comments

Dataviews provide a powerful way to work with data in ADO.NET. You can create many views of the same data without having to store the data in memory multiple times and without having to go back and re-query the database.

See Also

`DataView.RowFilter` Property—
`http://aspalliance.com/aspxtreme/sys/Data/DataViewClassRowFilter.aspx`

11.6. Sorting the Contents of a Dataset

You want to sort the contents of a dataset.

Technique

Use the `Sort` property of the `DataView` class to sort the data. `DataView` is part of the `System.Data` namespace. This example executes a SQL string via the `SqlCommand` object. It accesses the `Customers` table in the Northwind sample database using an integrated security connection string.

First you must import the namespaces:

```
<%@ Page Language="VB" ClassName="Recipe1204vb" %>
<%@ import Namespace="System.Data" %>
<%@ import Namespace="System.Data.SqlClient" %>
<script runat="server">
```

Then you place the following code inside a method. `Page_Load` will suffice for this example.

```
Sub Page_Load(sender As Object, e As EventArgs)

    'object vars
    Dim sqlConnection As SqlConnection
    Dim sqlDataAdapter As SqlDataAdapter
    Dim sqlCommand As SqlCommand
    Dim dataSet As DataSet

    Try
        sqlConnection = _
New SqlConnection("Integrated Security=yes;Initial Catalog=Northwind;
➥Data Source=(local)")

        'instantiate SqlAdapter and DataSet
        sqlDataAdapter = New SqlDataAdapter(sqlCommand)
        dataSet = New DataSet()
        sqlCommand = New SqlCommand("Select * From Customers", sqlConnection)
        sqlDataAdapter.Fill(dataSet, "Customers")
        dataSet.Tables(0).DefaultView.Sort = "City DESC"

        dataGrid1.DataSource = dataSet.Tables("Customers").DefaultView
        DataBind()

    Catch exception As Exception
        lblErrorMsg.Text = exception.ToString()
    End Try
End Sub
```

Comments

A dataview is a customized view of a datatable. The `DataView` class is based on the *document-view* pattern where the `DataTable` class represents the document and the `DataView` class represents the view. The idea here is that for a given set of data, you can view that data in many ways. The default view of the data is returned in an arbitrary order related to the way the data is stored in the database. You must specify an order in the SQL statement.

In the previous example, there isn't a sorting order in the SQL statement. The data is returned via a single datatable in the dataset. Note that the example accesses the datatable ordinally when it sets the `Sort` property and by name (`Customers`) when binding to `dataGrid1`. In both cases, the example accesses the one and only datatable in the dataset. The `Sort` method of the `DefaultView` object then returns the data, sorted in descending order on the `City` column.

Note that you can use a stored procedure to retrieve the data that you want to sort as well. Simply use the techniques listed next to fill your dataset and use the `DataView.Sort` property. Also note that you can instantiate new dataviews and keep several of them, each with different sort properties, available at the same time.

See Also

Section 11.3, "Executing a Stored Procedure and Returning the Results in a Dataset"

11.7. Finding a Particular Row in a Dataset

You want to find a particular row in a dataset and access its contents.

Technique

ADO.NET provides three ways to find an arbitrary row in a dataset: the `DataRowCollection.Find` and `DataRowCollection.Contains` methods and the `DefaultView.Find` method. All three techniques require you to set up a primary key against the datatable in the dataset. This example uses the `DataRowCollection.Find` method. It accesses the Northwind sample database's `Customers` table using a SQL statement and an integrated security connection string. The `CustomerID` field is the primary key for the `Customers` table.

First you must import the namespaces:

```
<%@ Page Language="VB" ClassName="Recipe1205vb" %>
<%@ import Namespace="System.Data" %>
<%@ import Namespace="System.Data.SqlClient" %>
<script runat="server">
```

Then you place the following code inside a method. `Page_Load` will suffice for this example.

```
Sub Page_Load(sender As Object, e As EventArgs)

    'object vars
    Dim sqlConnection As SqlConnection
    Dim sqlDataAdapter As SqlDataAdapter
    Dim sqlCommand As SqlCommand
    Dim dataSet As DataSet

    If IsPostback Then
```

```
    Try
        sqlConnection = New
SqlConnection("Integrated Security=yes;Initial Catalog=Northwind;
➥Data Source=(local)")
        sqlCommand = New SqlCommand("Select * From Customers", sqlConnection)

        sqlDataAdapter = New SqlDataAdapter(sqlCommand)
        dataSet = New DataSet()

        sqlDataAdapter.Fill(dataSet, "Customers")

        Dim pkColumn(1) as DataColumn
        pkColumn(0) = dataSet.Tables(0).Columns("CustomerID")

        dataSet.Tables(0).PrimaryKey = pkColumn

      'This is the key line of code
        Dim rowFound as DataRow = _
    dataSet.Tables(0).Rows.Find(customerIdTextBox.Text)

        If rowFound Is Nothing Then
            msgLabel.Text = "The Customer ID entered was not found."
        Else
            Dim stringBuilder as New StringBuilder("Contact ")

            stringBuilder.Append(rowFound("ContactName").ToString())
            stringBuilder.Append(", ")
            stringBuilder.Append(rowFound("ContactTitle").ToString())
            stringBuilder.Append(" at ")
            stringBuilder.Append(rowFound("CompanyName").ToString())

            msgLabel.Text = stringBuilder.ToString()
        End If

    Catch exception As Exception
        msgLabel.Text = exception.ToString()

    End Try
      End If
End Sub
```

Comments

In order to use the Find method, you have to set the datatable's primary key. First, you allocate a DataColumn array object that will serve to hold the primary key information for the CustomerID column in the Customers table. After assigning a value to the first element in the array, you set the DataTable.PrimaryKey property.

You are then ready to find a row from the dataset. The `DataRowCollection.Find` method returns a `DataRow` object and takes a key value of type `Object`. This example is looking for a string. After executing the `Find` method, the `rowFound` variable will either be null (Nothing) or contain a `DataRow` object. The rest of the example deals with displaying a message based on these two object states. It uses a `StringBuilder` object to build up the display string because it handles memory more efficiently than using string concatenation.

See Also

`DataRowCollection.Contains` Method—http://www.aspalliance.com/
aspxtreme/sys/Data/datarowcollectionclasscontains.aspx

`DefaultView.Find` Method—
http://www.aspalliance.com/aspxtreme/sys/Data/DataViewClassFind.aspx

11.8. Persisting Changes in a Dataset to the Database

You want to modify the contents of a dataset and have your changes persisted in the database.

Technique

Thanks to ADO.NET, manipulating data has become extremely easy in ASP.NET. In this example, you're going to pull two authors from the `pubs` database, which comes with the default installation of SQL. You'll modify one record, delete the other, and add a new record while disconnected from the database. You'll then publish the changes back to the database.

First create a `SqlConnection` pointing to your copy of the `pubs` database. Then create a new `SqlDataAdapter` and select all the authors whose name begins with `Green`. This should return two authors. Use this `Fill` method of the adapter to populate the `myTable` datatable.

You can change the first name of the first author by using `myTable.Rows(0)` `("au_fname")="Newname"`. To delete an author, use the `DataRow.Delete` method. The following code deletes the second author: `myTable.Rows(1).Delete()`. To add a new author, you need to first create a new row from `myTable`. Next, you set the required fields by using the syntax `myRow("fieldname")="value"`. Once you have set all the properties for the row, you add it to `myTable` by using `myTable.Rows.Add(myRow)`. So far all the changes have been made in memory and have not been sent to the database.

Before you can send them to the database, you must first supply the command syntax for performing inserts, updates, and deletes. You can use a `SqlCommandBuilder` to write

these for you in most cases. In some situations, such as when you want to use stored procedures to retrieve and modify data, you might want to write these manually. See
http://msdn.microsoft.com/library/en-us/dnsmart01/html/sa01k9.asp for more
information on how to manually write insert, update, and delete commands.

For this example, you'll create a SqlCommandBuilder to write them for you. Finally,
you call myAdapter.Update(myTable) to publish the changes to the database.

In <script runat="server" /> block or codebehind:

```
Sub Page_Load(sender As Object, e As EventArgs)
    Dim myConn As New SqlConnection
➡ ("Server=localhost;Database=Pubs;UID=sa;PWD=")
    Dim myAdapter As New SqlDataAdapter
➡ ("SELECT au_id, au_lname, au_fname, contract
➡ FROM Authors WHERE au_lname LIKE 'Green%' ORDER BY au_lname", myConn)
    Dim myTable As New DataTable()
    Dim myRow As DataRow
    Dim myBuilder As SqlCommandBuilder

    myAdapter.Fill(myTable)

    myTable.Rows(0)("au_fname")="Newname"
    myTable.Rows(1).Delete()

    myRow=myTable.NewRow()
    myRow("au_id")="123-45-6789"
    myRow("au_fname")="Jeremy"
    myRow("au_lname")="Green"
    myRow("contract")=0
    myTable.Rows.Add(myRow)

    myBuilder=new SqlCommandBuilder(myAdapter)
    myAdapter.Update(myTable)
End Sub
```

See Also

Section 10.1, "Connecting to SQL Server"

ADO.NET Revolution—http://msdn.microsoft.com/library/en-us/dnsmart01/html/
sa01k9.asp

12

XML

12.0. Introduction

Extensible Markup Language, XML, has been a great success as a standard and is now prevalent throughout the information industry on all major platforms. Microsoft has thoroughly embraced XML, and provides a great deal of support for it in the .NET Framework. In fact, I'm composing this chapter within an XML document, which I am editing with Visual Studio .NET. You've already seen in Chapter 6, "ASP.NET Application Configuration," that ASP.NET configuration files are all XML formatted. In this chapter, you learn how to open, read, manipulate, transform, and save XML data. The `System.Xml` namespace holds the relevant classes that you will use to work with XML data, and the most commonly used ones are covered in this chapter.

12.1. Opening an XML File

You want to access an XML file on the server or at a particular URL.

Technique

You first create a generic reusable method that will take any sort XML string input, and return an appropriate `System.IO.Stream` with that XML properly loaded. The XML input can be in the following formats:

- Raw XML
- File system location
- HTTP URL

You must first determine whether the input received is raw XML. You can attempt to decide this by first determining whether the XML document provided starts with `<?xml` or `<schema`. If this is true, you simply load the raw XML using the `System.IO.MemoryStream` class; if not true, you move to step two. The code is as follows:

```
Public Shared Function GetXmlDoc(ByVal xmlsource As String) _
As System.IO.Stream
    'first determine if xml source is actual raw xml
    'or if it is a url or file path
    Dim stream As System.IO.Stream = Nothing
    If xmlsource.StartsWith("<?xml") Or xmlsource.StartsWith("<schema") Then
      'raw xml
      stream = New System.IO.MemoryStream(
        System.Text.ASCIIEncoding.ASCII.GetBytes(xmlsource))
    End If
```

Now that you know the input is not raw XML, you still have one more decision to make. Is it a file system location or an actual HTTP URL? To determine this, you can take advantage of the `System.Uri` namespace provided by the framework. If you determine that it is a file system location, you can use the `System.IO.FileStream` class to load up the XML stream.

```
Dim xmluri As New System.Uri(xmlsource)
If xmluri.IsFile Then
  'file
  stream = New System.IO.FileStream(xmlsource, System.IO.FileMode.Open)
End If
```

You know that it is an HTTP URL (`xmluri.IsFile` returns `false`), so you need to first create an `HttpWebRequest` to download the stream off of the remote server.

```
Dim request As System.Net.HttpWebRequest =
CType(System.Net.WebRequest.Create(xmluri), System.Net.HttpWebRequest)
Dim response As System.Net.WebResponse = request.GetResponse()
stream = response.GetResponseStream()
```

The next step is to load the "stream" object into something you can work with for your XML needs. The object used here is `System.Xml.XmlDocument`.

```
Dim xmlDocStream As System.IO.Stream = GetXmlDoc(XmlSourceTextBox.Text)
Dim xmlSource As New System.Xml.XmlDocument()
xmlSource.Load(xmlDocStream)
ResultText.Text = xmlSource.InnerXml
```

Comments

These four steps describe the process flow of loading an XML document when the source location and type are unknown. It's a good idea to place the method in its own project (class library), so that you can reuse it in any of your projects in the future.

12.2. Finding a Particular Node in an XML Document

> You want to locate a particular node in an XML document.

Technique

This example builds on the previous one by enabling the ASP.NET application to select a node or a set of nodes from the XML document. Notice that this new ASP.NET Web Form has a few more TextBoxes and a new Query button. The first TextBox enables you to enter any XPath expression. The result appears in the second TextBox. You place the logic within the Query button.

The code is as follows:

```
Private Sub QueryButton_Click(ByVal sender As System.Object, _
    ByVal e As System.EventArgs)
  Dim s as new System.Text.StringBuilder()

  If xmlSource Is Nothing Or xmlSource.InnerText = "" Then
      xmlSource.LoadXml(ResultText.Text)
  End If
  Try
      Dim nl As System.Xml.XmlNodeList = xmlSource.SelectNodes(XPathText.Text)
      Dim counter As Integer = 1
      Dim node As System.Xml.XmlNode
      For Each node In nl
          s.Append(Convert.ToString(counter) + "]" & node.InnerText & _
              System.Environment.NewLine)
          counter += 1
      Next node
      QueryResult.Text=s.ToString()
  Catch selectNodesError As Exception
      QueryResult.Text = selectNodesError.ToString()
  End Try
End Sub
```

Comments

Test the form using these steps:

1. For the XML source, use `http://aspalliance.com/cookbook/samples/cdcatalog.xml`.

2. Press the Load Xml Document button.

3. Now use the following XPath expression: `/catalog/cd[title='Hide your heart']`.

4. Press the Query button.

5. You will notice that the expression resulted in the single node, which is placed in the last TextBox on the form.

6. Test different XPath expressions using this same procedure.

See Also

XPath Examples—`http://www.w3schools.com/xpath/xpath_examples.asp`

12.3. Storing an XML File

You want to store an XML file on the file system.

Technique

This example builds on Section 12.1 and enables the ASP.NET application to save the XML to the local file system. The code is as follows:

```
Private Sub SaveButton_Click(ByVal sender As System.Object, _
ByVal e As System.EventArgs) Handles SaveButton.Click
    If xmlSource Is Nothing Or xmlSource.InnerText = "" Then
        xmlSource.LoadXml(ResultText.Text)
    End If
    Try
        Dim path As String = FilePathText.Text.Substring(0, _
FilePathText.Text.LastIndexOf("\"))
        If System.IO.Directory.Exists(path) Then
            Try
                xmlSource.Save(FilePathText.Text)
                SaveResultsText.Text = FilePathText.Text & _
" was saved successfully."
            Catch saveErr As Exception
                SaveResultsText.Text = saveErr.ToString()
            End Try
        Else
            SaveResultsText.Text =
"Directory Does Not Exist, Try a different path."
            FilePathText.Text = ""
        End If

    Catch saveError As Exception
        SaveResultsText.Text = saveError.ToString()
    End Try
End Sub
```

Comments

Test the form using these steps:

1. For the XML source, use `http://aspalliance.com/cookbook/samples/cdcatalog.xml`.

2. Press the Load Xml Document button.

3. Now enter a valid path in your file system.

4. Press the Save button.

5. You will notice that the result of the save is outputted to the bottom TextBox.

6. Navigate to the path you gave in your file system to ensure the file was saved successfully.

See Also

Section 12.1, "Opening an XML File"

12.4. Transforming an XML Document Using XSLT

You want to transform an XML document using XSLT.

Technique

This example builds on Section 12.1 and enables the ASP.NET application to ask for a URL to an XSLT document, which it will then transform and output the result. You need to add a few new elements to the form. The first is a TextBox to allow the users to enter the URL of the XSLT document they want to use during transformation. Next, you need a literal control to hold the output of the XSLT transformation. Lastly, you'll add a Transform button, which will trigger the event handler to transform the XML and XSLT documents.

You need to create a method that will handle the transformation. The `Button` event handler will call this method.

The code is as follows:

```
    Public Function Transform(ByVal docXml As System.Xml.XmlDocument, _
ByVal xslUrl As String, ByVal xslParamNames() As String, _
ByVal xslParamValues() As String) As String
        Dim xslTransform As New System.Xml.Xsl.XslTransform()
        Dim sResult As New System.IO.StringWriter()
        'load xsl to a xsltransform object
        Try
          xslTransform.Load(xslUrl)
```

```
      Catch exc As Exception
      End Try

      'load up the xsl parameters, if any
      Dim xslArgs As New System.Xml.Xsl.XsltArgumentList()
      If Not (xslParamNames Is Nothing) Then
        Dim counter As Integer = 0
        Dim paramname As String
        For Each paramname In xslParamNames
          xslArgs.AddParam(paramname, Nothing, xslParamValues(counter))
        Next paramname
      End If

      'try to transform it
      Try
        ' call transform
        If Not (xslParamNames Is Nothing) Then
          xslTransform.Transform(docXml, xslArgs, sResult)
        Else
          xslTransform.Transform(docXml, Nothing, sResult)
        End If
      Catch exc As Exception
      End Try
      Return sResult.ToString()
    End Function 'Transform
```

Next, you call this method with the inputs from the ASP.NET Web Form with the Button event handler.

The Button event handler code is as follows:

```
  If xmlSource Is Nothing Or xmlSource.InnerText = "" Then
    xmlSource.LoadXml(ResultText.Text)
  End If
  Try
    ResultsLiteral.Text = Transform(xmlSource, XslUrlTextBox.Text, _
        Nothing, Nothing)
    ResultsPanel.Visible = True
  Catch transformError As Exception
    ResultsLiteral.Text = transformError.ToString()
  End Try
```

Comments

Test the form following these steps:

1. For the XML source, use http://aspalliance.com/cookbook/samples/
   cdcatalog.xml.

2. Press the Load Xml Document button.

3. For the XSLT source, use `http://aspalliance.com/cookbook/samples/cdcatalog.xsl`.

4. Press the Transform button.

5. The result of the transformation is displayed at the bottom `LiteralControl`.

See Also
Section 12.1, "Opening an XML File"

12.5. Converting Between XML Documents and Datasets

You want to convert an XML document into a dataset, or convert a dataset into an XML document.

Technique

The recipe is divided into three parts.

- Converting the XML document into a dataset
- Modifying data in the dataset
- Writing data in the dataset into an XML file

The work is done in the `Page_Load` event handler:

```
Private Sub Page_Load(ByVal sender As System.Object, _
ByVal e As System.EventArgs)
    Try
        Response.Write("STEPS: <br>")
        Dim Ds As New DataSet
        ' Reading DSRead.XML file into DataSet Ds

        Ds.ReadXml(Server.MapPath("DSRead.XML"))
        Response.Write("1. DSRead.XML file is loaded
➥ into DataSet DS successfully.<br>")

        ' Modifying the data in Ds DataSet

        Ds.AcceptChanges()
        Ds.Tables(0).Rows(0).Item("LastModified") = DateTime.Now.ToString()
        Response.Write("2. Data is modified successfully
➥ in Ds DataSet.<br>")
```

```
            ' Writing Ds into XML DSWrite.XML file
            Dim dsChanges As DataSet
            dsChanges = Ds.GetChanges()
            dsChanges.WriteXml(Server.MapPath("") & "\DSWrite.xml")
            Response.Write("3. Ds DataSet changes are successfully
➡ written into DSWrite.XML file.<br>")
        Catch ex As Exception
            lblvalue.text = ex.Message
        End Try
    End Sub
```

Comments

Working with simple XML files can be easy using ADO.NET's dataset. Its `ReadXml` and `WriteXml` methods allow quick conversion from XML to datasets and back again. Note that in order for this example to work, the users must have permission to write to the file specified.

See Also

For the `DataSet.ReadXml` method—`http://msdn.microsoft.com/library/en-us/cpref/html/frlrfSystemDataDataSetClassReadXmlTopic.asp`

For the `DataSet.WriteXML` method—`http://msdn.microsoft.com/library/en-us/cpref/html/frlrfSystemDataDataSetClassWriteXmlTopic.asp`

Managing XML Data Using a Dataset in ADO .NET—
`http://www.msdnaa.net/Resources/Display.aspx?ResID=1489`

12.6. Creating a Class from an XML Document

You want to create a class from an XML document using the XSD.EXE tool, and use the created class in your Visual Studio .NET project.

Technique

The XSD.EXE tool, which ships with the .NET Framework SDK, allows you to take an XML document and convert it into an XSD (an XML schema). After you have this XSD, you can use it along with the XSD1.EXE tool to generate a sub-classed dataset or a set of classes. This is handy when you only have the XML document, and do not want to parse it using XSLT.

This tool is a command line tool, so you must first dump to DOS. The easiest way in Visual Studio .NET to do this is to go to the Start menu, and then choose Programs, Microsoft Visual Studio .NET, Visual Studio .NET Tools. Then choose Visual Studio .NET Command Prompt.

If you do not have Visual Studio .NET, the location of the program on my machine is `C:\Program Files\Microsoft Visual Studio .NET\FrameworkSDK\Bin\xsd.exe`. If you do not have the path in the `PATH` environment variable, make sure you add that first.

Next take a look at the syntax of the command. Pay close attention to the `/c` and `/d` switches.

This example uses the XML document found at `http://aspalliance.com/cookbook/samples/cdcatalog.xml`.

First, issue the following command:

```
xsd.exe http://aspalliance.com/cookbook/samples/cdcatalog.xml
```

This should produce something similar to:

```
Microsoft (R) Xml Schemas/DataTypes support utility
[Microsoft (R) .NET Framework, Version 1.0.3705.0]
Copyright (C) Microsoft Corporation 1998-2001. All rights reserved.

Writing file 'C:\Inetpub\wwwroot\CookBook\Recipe1206\cdcatalog.xsd'.
```

Now that you have the XSD, you can generate a class file for this schema as follows:

```
xsd.exe cdcatalog.xsd /c
```

Produces:

```
Writing file 'C:\Inetpub\wwwroot\CookBook\Recipe1206\cdcatalog.cs'.
```

If you want to do this using VB.NET, simply add the `/l:vb` switch to the command.

Now that you have generated a class file, you can use it to load the XML document and then use that class file to manipulate the XML document. If you are not familiar with the XML serialization process, read up on it and continue reading after you feel comfortable with the topic.

The first thing you need to do is create a function that will load the XML document, and deserialize it into an instance of the catalog class. This project uses a new class created just to handle the serialization needs. Here it is:

```
Imports System
Imports System.Runtime.Serialization

Namespace Recipe1206vb
    Public Class Serialization
        Public Shared Function SerializeXML(ByVal request As Object, _
ByVal type As System.Type) As System.IO.MemoryStream
            Try
                Dim serializer As New System.Xml.Serialization.XmlSerializer(type)
                Dim stm As New System.IO.MemoryStream()
                serializer.Serialize(stm, request)
                Return stm
```

```
            Catch e As Exception
                Return Nothing      '
            End Try
        End Function        'SerializeXML


        Public Shared Function DeSerializeXML(ByVal envelope As String, _
ByVal type As System.Type) As Object
            Try
                Dim serializer As New System.Xml.Serialization.XmlSerializer(type)
                Dim stm As New System.IO.MemoryStream( _
System.Text.Encoding.ASCII.GetBytes(envelope))
                Dim ud As Object = serializer.Deserialize(stm)
                stm.Close()
                Return ud
            Catch e As Exception
                Return Nothing
            End Try
        End Function        'DeSerializeXML
    End Class     'Serialization
End Namespace 'Recipe1206vb
```

Next you need to define the `Catalog` class:

```
<System.Xml.Serialization.XmlRootAttribute("catalog",
➥[Namespace]:="", IsNullable:=False)> _
Public Class catalog
    <System.Xml.Serialization.XmlElementAttribute("cd")> _
    Public Items() As catalogCD
End Class


Public Class catalogCD
    Public title As String
    Public artist As String
    Public country As String
    Public company As String
    Public price As String
    Public year As String
End Class
```

Now you can use that class to deserialize the catalog class:

```
Private Function LoadData(ByVal path As String) As catalog
    Try
        Dim fs As System.IO.FileStream = System.IO.File.OpenRead(path)
        Dim buff(fs.Length) As Byte
        fs.Read(buff, 0, CInt(fs.Length))
        fs.Close()
        cat = CType(Serialization.DeSerializeXML(
➥System.Text.ASCIIEncoding.ASCII.GetString(buff), GetType(catalog)), catalog)
```

```
      Return cat
   Catch
   End Try
End Function    'LoadData
```

The last major portion of the puzzle involves the process of saving the catalog class, with data that has been changed. This example includes enough functionality to enable you to edit any node and then press the Save button. This Save button consists of:

```
Private Sub SaveButton_Click(ByVal sender As System.Object, _
ByVal e As System.EventArgs) Handles SaveButton.Click
   Dim findvalue As String = titleDropDownList.SelectedItem.Text
   Dim foundcd As catalogCD = Nothing
   Dim cd As catalogCD
   For Each cd In cat.Items
      If cd.title = findvalue Then
         foundcd = cd
         Exit For
      End If
   Next cd
   If Not (foundcd Is Nothing) Then
      foundcd.artist = artistTextBox.Text
      foundcd.country = countryTextBox.Text
      foundcd.company = companyTextBox.Text
      foundcd.price = priceTextBox.Text
      foundcd.year = yearTextBox.Text
      Dim data As System.IO.MemoryStream = _
Serialization.SerializeXML(cat, GetType(catalog))
      Dim databytes As Byte() = data.ToArray()
      If System.IO.File.Exists(xmlPath) Then
         System.IO.File.Delete(xmlPath)
      End If
      Dim f As System.IO.FileStream = System.IO.File.OpenWrite(xmlPath)
      f.Write(databytes, 0, databytes.Length)
      f.Close()
   End If
End Sub
```

First you find the currently selected item from the catalog, and then set its members equal to the values provided on the form. Then, you take advantage of the serialization class again, this time to serialize the content into a `MemoryStream`. This enables you to easily save it using the `FileStream`, as shown previously. Note that this example requires the users to have write permission for the file being saved.

See Also

XML Serialization—`http://msdn.microsoft.com/library/en-us/cpguide/html/ cpconintroducingxmlserialization.asp`

12.7. Reading an XML Document Using an XmlTextReader

You want to read through an XML document using the `XmlTextReader` class.

Technique

This example uses the `System.Xml` namespace. In `<script runat="server" />` block or codebehind:

```
Public Sub Page_Load(Source As Object, E As EventArgs)
     Dim _Reader As XmlTextReader
     Try
         _Reader = New XmlTextReader(Server.MapPath("users.xml"))
         Call ReadDocument(_Reader)
     Catch _Error As Exception
         ErrorLabel.Text = _Error.Message
     Finally
         _Reader.Close()
     End Try
End Sub
```

When the load event of the Web Form is raised, an object of the `XmlTextReader` class is created. This object is initiated with a reference to an XML document. The `Try/Catch` block is implemented to capture any errors that occur due to an improper reference or insufficient permissions.

```
Sub ReadDocument(ByRef _XmlReader As XmlTextReader)
   Dim sb As New System.Text.StringBuilder(100)
   Dim space As String = " "
   Dim space3 As String = "   "

   While _XmlReader.Read()

      Select Case _XmlReader.NodeType

      Case XmlNodeType.Element
            sb.Append("<B>Element: </B>")
            sb.Append(_XmlReader.Name)
            sb.Append("<BR/>")

         'Print attributes for current node, if any available...
         If _XmlReader.AttributeCount > 0 Then
            While _XmlReader.MoveToNextAttribute()
```

```
                    sb.Append(space3)
                    sb.Append("<B>Attribute Name: </B>")
                    sb.Append(_XmlReader.Name)
                    sb.Append(space)
                    sb.Append("<B>Attribute Value: </B>")
                    sb.Append(_XmlReader.Value)
                    sb.Append("<BR/>")
            End While
        End If

    Case XmlNodeType.Text
            sb.Append(space3)
            sb.Append("<B>Value: </B>")
            sb.Append(_XmlReader.Value)
            sb.Append("<BR/>")

    End Select

    End While
    OutputLiteral.Text = sb.ToString()
End Sub
```

The `ReadDocument()` method is responsible for printing the contents of the XML document. `Read()` property keeps the external `while` loop moving until the last node. Through the `NodeType` property, the current node type of the reader object is compared. If the current node happens to be an element, its name or attributes are displayed; if it happens to be text, the value of the text is displayed.

Comments

The `XmlTextReader` class provides methods and properties to read through an XML document. However, you cannot navigate within the document freely. The object of the `XmlTextReader` class can only move forward. It works similar to the Datareader object in the .NET Framework. This means that after you have read a node you can only move forward, to the next node, and cannot move back unless you re-initialize the object (starting at the beginning).

To simply reformat some XML, XSLT provides a much cleaner and more efficient method.

See Also

Section 12.8, "Writing an XML Document Using an XmlTextWriter"

MSDN—search for `System.Xml.XmlTextReader`

12.8. Writing an XML Document Using an XmlTextWriter

You want to write an XML document using the **XmlTextWriter** class.

Technique

Import **System.Xml** namespace for this example. In `<script runat="server" />` block or codebehind:

```
Public Sub Page_Load(Source As Object, E As EventArgs)
    Dim _Writer As New XmlTextWriter(Server.MapPath("users.xml"), Nothing)
    'Nothing means use default UTF-8 format

    'Default formatting property is None
    _Writer.Formatting = Formatting.Indented

    Try
        _Writer.WriteStartDocument(True)
        _Writer.WriteStartElement("users")

        Call WriteUsers(_Writer)

        _Writer.WriteEndElement()
        MessageLabel.Text = "File successfully created..."

    Catch _Error As Exception
        MessageLabel.Text = _Error.Message

    Finally
        _Writer.Flush()
        _Writer.Close()
    End Try
End Sub
```

Next, set the formatting property for the `writer` object. This will write the elements in the target file in an indented format. The `WriteStartDocument()` method writes the first line of the XML document, and encloses the XML document declaration within the (?) delimiters. The `WriteStartElement()` writes an element of the specified name that's provided to it. In order to write the closing tag of an element, its name need not be specified. The object itself checks for the last opened tag and automatically writes the closing tag for the related element. The `Flush()` and `Close()` calls ensure that the XML is correctly written to the file and the output stream is closed after the task is completed.

```
Public Sub WriteUsers(ByRef _output As XmlTextWriter)
```

```
With _output

    'First user...
    .WriteStartElement("user")
    .WriteAttributeString("role", "admin")

    .WriteStartElement("username")
    .WriteString("jsmith")
    .WriteEndElement()
    .WriteStartElement("password")
    .WriteString("john")
    .WriteEndElement()

    .WriteEndElement()

    'Second user...
    .WriteStartElement("user")
    .WriteAttributeString("role", "operator")

    .WriteStartElement("username")
    .WriteString("tcruise")
    .WriteEndElement()
    .WriteStartElement("password")
    .WriteString("tom")
    .WriteEndElement()

    .WriteEndElement()

End With

End Sub
```

This method writes the user data into the XML file. The WriteUsers method is passed a reference to the XmlTextWriter object. The various methods of the object are then called to write elements, attributes, and their values to the XML document being produced. The WriteAttributeString() accepts two arguments. The first is the name of the attribute itself and the second is the value of the attribute. The WriteString() method accepts a single argument of string type. This method is used for writing the content of an element. Here, you can also see that the WriteEndElement is called without being passed any parameters. This is because the object checks out the last opened element tag and writes the appropriate closing element tag.

Comments

The XmlTextWriter class provides a serialized, forward-only way to write XML to a file. The class exposes various methods and properties to create components of an XML document. It requires that you know the precise schema of the XML being output. `XmlTextWriter` provides no methods to make changes to the content after it is written to the output file.

See Also

Section 12.7, "Reading an XML Document Using an XmlTextReader"

MSDN—`System.Xml.XmlTextWriter`

12.9. Navigating an XML Document Using XPathNavigator

You want to navigate an XML document using the `XPathNavigator` class.

Technique

Import the `System.Xml` and `System.Xml.XPathNavigator` namespaces.

In `<script runat="server" />` block or codebehind:

```
Private Sub Page_Load(Source As Object, E As EventArgs)

        Dim sb As New StringBuilder
        Dim space2 As String = "  "
        Dim space3 As String = "   "

        'Create an XmlDocument object and load the xml file...
        Dim _XmlDoc As New XmlDocument()
        _XmlDoc.Load(Server.MapPath("users.xml"))

        'Create an XPathNavigator object for the loaded document...
        Dim _Nav As XPathNavigator
        _Nav = _XmlDoc.CreateNavigator()

        'Move to the root element...
        _Nav.MoveToRoot()
        sb.Append("<B>Root: </B>")
        sb.Append("name=" & _Nav.Name & ", type=" & _
 _Nav.NodeType.ToString())
        sb.Append("<BR/><BR/>")

        'Move to first child element :: Users...
        _Nav.MoveToFirstChild()
        sb.Append("name=" & _Nav.Name & ", type=" & _
 _Nav.NodeType.ToString())
```

```
            sb.Append("<BR/>")

            'Move to first child element :: User...
            _Nav.MoveToFirstChild()

        Do
            sb.Append(space2)
            sb.Append("name=" & _Nav.Name & ", type=" & _
_Nav.NodeType.ToString())
            sb.Append("<BR/>")

            'Get Attributes...
            _Nav.MoveToFirstAttribute
            sb.Append(space2)
            sb.Append("Attribute: " & _Nav.Name & "=" & _Nav.Value)
            sb.Append("<BR/>")

            'Bring the navigator back to attribute parent
            _Nav.MoveToParent()

            'Move to first child element :: Username...
            _Nav.MoveToFirstChild()

            Do
                sb.Append(space3)
                sb.Append("name=" & _Nav.Name & ", type=" & _
_Nav.NodeType.ToString() & ", value=" & _Nav.Value)
                sb.Append("<BR/>")
            Loop While _Nav.MoveToNext()

            _Nav.MoveToParent()

        Loop While _Nav.MoveToNext()

        OutputLiteral.Text = sb.ToString()

    End Sub
```

Comments

The XPathNavigator object cannot be created directly. You must first create the XmlDocument or XPathDocument in order to create one. These classes provide a CreateNavigator() method that returns an XPathNavigator. The XPathNavigator class exposes methods for navigating within an XML document. Some of these methods are MoveToNext(), MoveToPrevious(), MoveToRoot(), MoveToFirstChild(), and MoveToParent(). Using the XPathNavigator to navigate XML documents is fairly straightforward. All you have to do is call a property or a method of the class to move to a particular node in the document or display a node's name, type, value, and so on, as demonstrated in the previous example.

See Also

MSDN Library—`System.Xml.XPath.XPathNavigator`

Rendering Data with ASP.NET Web Controls

13.0. Introduction

ASP.NET provides several Web controls that make displaying data on a Web page easier than ever before. This chapter shows you how to take advantage of a process called data-binding to easily display data in a variety of formats using very little code. This chapter covers many of the most commonly used features of the Repeater, DataList, and DataGrid, including some fairly advanced DataGrid features. Using these data-bound Web controls, it is very easy to write data-driven Web Forms by just dragging and dropping a few controls onto a form and writing a few lines of code.

13.1. Rendering Data Directly on a Web Form

You want to display a piece of data on a Web Form using data-binding.

Technique

You can use the `<%#%>` syntax to easily bind data to a control. Simply create a variable, assign it a value, and call `Page.DataBind` to bind it to the page. The ASPX page is as follows:

```
<html>
  <body>
    <form id="Recipe1401vb" method="post" runat="server">
      <asp:Label ID="MyLabel" Runat="server">Hello <%#FirstName%>!</asp:Label>
    </form>
  </body>
</html>
```

In `<script runat="server" />` block or codebehind:

```
Protected FirstName as string

Sub Page_Load(sender As Object, e As EventArgs)
    FirstName="Jeremy"
    Page.DataBind()
End Sub
```

Comments

If you are using codebehind, it is important to declare the variable with `Protected` access level so the page can access it. It is also important to realize that calling `Page.DataBind()` will result in all controls on the page being data-bound, because any time a control container calls its `DataBind()` method, it recursively calls the `DataBind()` method of all of its child controls.

See Also

Section 13.2, "Data-binding to a DropDownList"

Section 13.3, "Data-binding to a Repeater"

Section 13.4, "Data-binding to a DataList"

Section 13.7, "Data-binding to a DataGrid"

13.2. Data-binding to a DropDownList

You want to create a DropDownList that is populated from a database.

Technique

To data-bind a DropDownList to a data container such as a dataset or datareader, you must set three properties and call one method. The following example demonstrates this.

In `<script runat="server" />` block or codebehind:

```
Sub Page_Load(sender As Object, e As EventArgs)
    'object vars
    Dim sqlConnection As SqlConnection
    Dim sqlDataAdapter As SqlDataAdapter
    Dim sqlCommand As SqlCommand
    Dim dataSet As DataSet
    Dim dataTable As DataTable

    Try
        sqlConnection = New SqlConnection("Integrated Security=yes;
```

```
➥Initial Catalog=Northwind;Data Source=(local)")

        'pass the stored proc name and SqlConnection
        sqlCommand = New SqlCommand("Select * From Customers", _
            sqlConnection)

        'instantiate SqlAdapter and DataSet
        sqlDataAdapter = New SqlDataAdapter(sqlCommand)
        dataSet = New DataSet()

        'populate the DataSet
        sqlDataAdapter.Fill(dataSet, "Customers")

    'apply sort to the DefaultView to sort by CompanyName
        dataSet.Tables(0).DefaultView.Sort = "CompanyName"

        DropDownList1.DataSource = dataSet.Tables("Customers").DefaultView
    DropDownList1.DataTextField = "CompanyName" ' what to display
    DropDownList1.DataValueField = "CustomerID" ' what to set as value
    DropDownList1.DataBind()

    Catch exception As Exception
        errorMsgLabel.Text = exception.ToString()

    End Try
End Sub
```

Comments

As a general rule, you can perform this kind of data-binding only when the form first
loads, as opposed to on every postback. To do this, simply place the data access and
data-binding code within an If statement so that they are only performed when
Page.IsPostback is false (for example, on the first load of the page). You can manipulate the Items collection after calling DataBind() if you need to set a particular item as
Selected (use Items.FindByText or Items.FindByValue to find the item you want) or
insert a default entry for the first item (use Items.Insert() with an index of 0 for the
first item).

See Also

ASP.NET DropDownList I—http://aspalliance.com/stevesmith/articles/
dotnetlistbox1.asp

ASP.NET DropDownList II—http://aspalliance.com/stevesmith/articles/
dotnetlistbox2.asp

Dynamically Set Text and Value of DropDownList—http://aspalliance.com/aldotnet/
examples/dynamicdatasource.aspx

13.3. Data-binding to a Repeater

You want to use a repeater to output the results of a data query.

Technique

The Repeater control is the simplest of three templated data-bound controls provided with ASP.NET (the others being the DataList and DataGrid). It supports templates for Header, Item, AlternatingItem, Separator, and Footer, which can each contain static and dynamic (data-bound) content. The following example demonstrates how to set up a Repeater's templates and how to data-bind the Repeater to a dataset.

The ASPX page is as follows:

```
<asp:Repeater id="Repeater1" runat="server">
    <HeaderTemplate>Customers:<br/><ul></HeaderTemplate>
    <ItemTemplate>
        <li><%#DataBinder.Eval(Container.DataItem, "CompanyName")%>,
            <%#DataBinder.Eval(Container.DataItem, "ContactName")%></li>
    </ItemTemplate>
    <AlternatingItemTemplate>
        <li><font color="red">
<%#DataBinder.Eval(Container.DataItem, "CompanyName")%>,
<%#DataBinder.Eval(Container.DataItem, "ContactName")%></font></li>
    </AlternatingItemTemplate>
    <FooterTemplate><hr/>Data Retrieved at:
<%# System.DateTime.Now.ToString() %></FooterTemplate>
</asp:Repeater>
            <br>
            <br>
            <asp:Label id="errorMsgLabel" runat="server"
Width="327px" Height="111px"></asp:Label>
```

In `<script runat="server" />` block or codebehind:

```
Sub BindRepeater()
    'object vars
    Dim sqlConnection As SqlConnection
    Dim sqlDataAdapter As SqlDataAdapter
    Dim sqlCommand As SqlCommand
    Dim dataSet As DataSet
    Dim dataTable As DataTable

    Try
        sqlConnection = New SqlConnection("Integrated Security=yes;
➡Initial Catalog=Northwind;Data Source=(local)")

        'pass the stored proc name and SqlConnection
```

```
    sqlCommand = New SqlCommand("Select * From Customers", sqlConnection)

    'instantiate SqlAdapter and DataSet
    sqlDataAdapter = New SqlDataAdapter(sqlCommand)
    dataSet = New DataSet()

    'populate the DataSet
    sqlDataAdapter.Fill(dataSet, "Customers")

  'apply sort to the DefaultView to sort by CompanyName
    dataSet.Tables(0).DefaultView.Sort = "CompanyName"

    Repeater1.DataSource = dataSet.Tables("Customers").DefaultView
  Repeater1.DataBind()

Catch exception As Exception
    errorMsgLabel.Text = exception.ToString()

  End Try
End Sub
```

Comments

`BindRepeater()` is called by `Page_Load` only when it is first loaded (not after a post-back). It will automatically retain its state between postbacks using ViewState, thus avoiding additional requests to the database.

See Also

Repeater Class—`http://msdn.microsoft.com/library/en-us/cpref/html/`
`frlrfsystemwebuiwebcontrolsrepeaterclasstopic.asp`

13.4. Data-binding to a DataList

You want to use a DataList control to output the results of a data query.

Technique

Create a DataList and set the layout and visual formatting the way you want. Inside the DataList, add an `ItemTemplate` tag. Inside this tag, you can set static HTML code to display along with pieces of data. To insert a piece of data, use the following syntax:

`<%#DataBinder.Eval(Container.DataItem, "FieldName")%>`.

After you have the DataList set up, populate a DataTable (or any class that implements the `System.Collections.IEnumerable` interface). Then set the `DataSource` property of the DataList to point to your DataTable, and call the `DataBind()` method of the DataList.

The ASPX page is as follows:

```
<%@Import namespace="System.Data" %>
<%@Import namespace="System.Data.SqlClient" %>
<html>
  <body>
    <form id="Recipe1404vb" method="post" runat="server">
    <asp:DataList id="MyDataList" Runat=server
RepeatDirection=Horizontal RepeatColumns=2 ItemStyle-BorderWidth=1>
        <ItemTemplate>
          Name: <%#DataBinder.Eval(Container.DataItem, "CategoryName")%><br>
          Description: <%#DataBinder.Eval(Container.DataItem, "Description")%>
        </ItemTemplate>
    </asp:DataList>
    </form>
  </body>
</html>
```

In `<script runat="server" />` block or codebehind:

```
Sub Page_Load(sender As Object, e As EventArgs)
   Dim myTable As New DataTable()
   Dim myConn As _
   New SqlConnection("Server=localhost;Database=Northwind;UID=sa;PWD=")
   Dim myAdapter As New SqlDataAdapter(
➥"Select CategoryName, Description FROM Categories", myConn)
   myAdapter.Fill(myTable)
   MyDataList.DataSource=myTable
   MyDataList.DataBind()
End Sub
```

Comments

This code uses the Northwind database that comes with the default installation of Microsoft SQL Server.

> **See Also**
>
> Section 10.1, "Connecting to SQL Server"
>
> Section 11.1, "Executing a Stored Procedure and Returning the Results in a Datareader"
>
> Section 13.2, "Data-binding to a DropDownList"
>
> Section 13.3, "Data-binding to a Repeater"
>
> Section 13.7, "Data-binding to a DataGrid"

13.5. Implementing Sorting in a DataList

You want to implement sorting in your DataList.

Technique

Create a DataList and set the data items to display in the `ItemTemplate` as outlined in example 13.4. Add a header template with link buttons `SortByName` and `SortByDescription`. `OnClick` events should be wired to the `SortByName_OnClick` and `SortByDescription_OnClick` methods.

Create the `PullCategories()` method to query the categories table and populate `myView` and the `PopulateCategories()` method to bind `myView` to `MyDataList`. In the `Page_Load` event, determine whether this is the first load of the page and, if so, populate the DataList with the default sort. In the `SortByName_Click` event, call `PullCategories()`, set the `Sort` property of `myView` to `CategoryName` and call the `PopulateCategories()` method. Do the same for `SortByDescription_Click`, setting the sort to `Description`.

The ASPX page is as follows:

```
<%@Import namespace="System.Data.SqlClient" %>
<%@Import namespace="System.Data" %>

<HTML>
    <body>
        <form id="Recipe1405vb" method="post" runat="server">
          <asp:DataList id="MyDataList" Runat="server" ItemStyle-BorderWidth="1">
              <HeaderTemplate>
                Sort By
                <asp:LinkButton ID="SortByName" Runat="server"
 OnClick="SortByName_Click">Name</asp:LinkButton> /
                <asp:LinkButton ID="SortByDescription" Runat="server"
OnClick="SortByDescription_Click">Description</asp:LinkButton>
              </HeaderTemplate>
              <ItemTemplate>
                <%#DataBinder.Eval(Container.DataItem, "CategoryName")%>
                <br>
                <%#DataBinder.Eval(Container.DataItem, "Description")%>
              </ItemTemplate>
          </asp:DataList>
        </form>
    </body>
</HTML>
```

In `<script runat="server" />` block or codebehind:

```
private myView AS DataView
```

```
Private Sub Page_Load(sender As Object, e As EventArgs)
   If Not IsPostBack Then
      PullCategories()
      myView.Sort="CategoryName"
      PopulateCategories()
   End If
End Sub

Protected Sub SortByName_Click(sender As Object, e As EventArgs)
   PullCategories()
   myView.Sort="CategoryName"
   PopulateCategories()
End Sub

Protected Sub SortByDescription_Click(sender As Object, e As EventArgs)
   PullCategories()
   myView.Sort="Description"
   PopulateCategories()
End Sub

Private Sub PullCategories()
   Dim myTable As New DataTable()
   Dim myConn As New SqlConnection("Server=localhost;
➡Database=Northwind;UID=sa;PWD=")
   Dim myAdapter As New SqlDataAdapter(
➡"Select CategoryName, Description FROM Categories", myConn)
   myAdapter.Fill(myTable)
   myView=New DataView(myTable)
End Sub

Private Sub PopulateCategories()
   MyDataList.DataSource=myView
   MyDataList.DataBind()
End Sub
```

Comments

This code uses the Northwind database that comes with the default installation of
Microsoft SQL Server.

See Also

Section 13.4, "Data-binding to a DataList"

Section 13.6, "Implementing Paging in a DataList"

Section 13.11, "Enabling Sorting in a DataGrid"

Section 13.12, "Enabling Bi-Directional Sorting in a DataGrid"

13.6. Implementing Paging in a DataList

You want to implement paging in your DataList.

Technique

By default, the DataList control does not support paging—only the DataGrid has that functionality built in. However, you can implement your own custom paging solution with the DataList by following these steps:

1. Add paging controls (Next/Prev at a minimum, but perhaps also First, Last, Next 5, Prev 5, and so on).

2. Set and maintain a PageSize variable.

3. Modify DataSource prior to data-binding to ensure the records for the appropriate page are the only ones bound.

For Step 1, consider the following pager construct within the FooterTemplate of the following DataList:

```
<asp:DataList id="DataList1" runat="server"
RepeatDirection="Horizontal" RepeatColumns="3">
   <HeaderTemplate>
      Customers
   </HeaderTemplate>
   <FooterTemplate>
      <!— Pager Construct —>
      <table width="100%" align="right">
         <tr>
            <td width="76%" align="left">
               <asp:Label ID="StatusLabel" Runat="server"
Font-Name="verdana" Font-Size="10pt" />
            </td>
            <td width="6%">
               <a href="datalistpaging.aspx#this"
ID="hrefFirst" onserverclick="ShowFirst" runat="server">
                  <<</a>
            </td>
            <td width="6%">
               <a href="datalistpaging.aspx#this"
ID="hrefPrevious" onserverclick="ShowPrevious" runat="server">
                  <<</a>
            </td>
            <td width="6%">
               <a href="datalistpaging.aspx#this"
ID="hrefNext" onserverclick="ShowNext" runat="server">
                  >></a>
```

```
                   </td>
                   <td width="6%">
                       <a href="datalistpaging.aspx#this"
ID="hrefLast" onserverclick="ShowLast" runat="server">
                          >>></a>
                   </td>
              </tr>
          </table>
     </FooterTemplate>
     <ItemTemplate>
          <table border="1" cellpadding="0" cellspacing="0">
              <tr>
                  <td>
                      Company:
                      <%#DataBinder.Eval(Container.DataItem, "CompanyName")%>
                      <br />
                      Contact:
                      <%#DataBinder.Eval(Container.DataItem, "ContactName")%>
                  </td>
              </tr>
          </table>
     </ItemTemplate>
     <AlternatingItemTemplate>
          <table border="1" cellpadding="0" cellspacing="0" bgcolor="#CCCCCC">
              <tr>
                  <td>
                      Company:
                      <%#DataBinder.Eval(Container.DataItem, "CompanyName")%>
                      <br />
                      Contact:
                      <%#DataBinder.Eval(Container.DataItem, "ContactName")%>
                  </td>
              </tr>
          </table>
     </AlternatingItemTemplate>
</asp:DataList>
```

The pager code includes a label to display the current position in the records, a first page link, a last page link, and next and previous links. Each of the links is wired to an event through the use of the `onserverclick` attribute. In the code, the page retrieves the data from the database as a DataTable and stores it in ViewState so that subsequent requests do not require further data access. Then each event handler adjusts the `currentPage` variable that is also maintained in ViewState. Using the current page index and the page size, the `ShowPage()` method pulls out just the records that should be displayed on that page and places them into a new DataTable, which is then bound to the DataList.

In `<script runat="server" />` block or codebehind:

```
Dim dataTable As DataTable = Nothing
Dim pageSize As Integer = 5
Dim currentPage As Integer

Sub Page_Load(sender As Object, e As EventArgs)
    If Not IsPostBack Then
        ShowFirst(Me, System.EventArgs.Empty)
    End If
End Sub

Sub GetData()
    If ViewState("Data") Is Nothing Then
        'object vars
        Dim sqlConnection As SqlConnection
        Dim sqlDataAdapter As SqlDataAdapter
        Dim sqlCommand As SqlCommand

        Try
            Trace.Write("GetData","Getting data from database.")
            sqlConnection = New SqlConnection("Integrated Security=yes;
➥Initial Catalog=Northwind;Data Source=(local)")

            'pass the stored proc name and SqlConnection
            sqlCommand = New SqlCommand(
➥"Select * From Customers Order By CompanyName", sqlConnection)

            'instantiate SqlAdapter and DataTable
            sqlDataAdapter = New SqlDataAdapter(sqlCommand)
            dataTable = New DataTable()

            'populate the DataTable
            sqlDataAdapter.Fill(dataTable)

                ViewState("Data") = dataTable

        Catch exception As Exception
            ErrorLabel.Text = exception.ToString()
        End Try
    Else
        Trace.Write("GetData","Getting data from ViewState.")
        dataTable = CType(ViewState("Data"), DataTable)
    End If
End Sub

Sub ShowFirst(sender As Object, e As EventArgs)
    currentPage = 1
```

```
      ShowPage()
   End Sub

   Sub ShowLast(sender As Object, e As EventArgs)
      GetData()
      currentPage = CType(System.Math.Ceiling(CType(
➥dataTable.Rows.Count,Double) / pageSize), Integer)
      ShowPage()
   End Sub

   Sub ShowNext(sender As Object, e As EventArgs)
      GetData()
      currentPage = CType(ViewState("CurrentPage"), Integer)
      If  currentPage <= CType(System.Math.Ceiling(CType(
➥dataTable.Rows.Count,Double) / pageSize), Integer) Then
         currentPage += 1
      End If
      ShowPage()
   End Sub

   Sub ShowPrevious(sender As Object, e As EventArgs)
      currentPage = CType(ViewState("CurrentPage"), Integer)
      If currentPage > 1 Then
         currentPage -= 1
      End If
      ShowPage()
   End Sub

   Sub ShowPage()
      Dim I As Integer
      If dataTable Is Nothing Then
         GetData()
      End If
      If dataTable Is Nothing Then
         Throw New ApplicationException("Data failed to load.")
      End If

      Dim dt2 As DataTable = dataTable.Clone()
   'Copy the structure of the data to a new container

      For I = ((currentPage-1)*pageSize) To (currentPage*pageSize) -1
         If I >= dataTable.Rows.Count Then Exit For
         dt2.ImportRow(dataTable.Rows(I))
      Next

      DataList1.DataSource = dt2
      DataList1.DataBind()
```

```
    'Display status line
    CType(DataList1.Controls(DataList1.Controls.Count-1).
➥FindControl("StatusLabel"), Label).Text = _
        "Total Records: " & _
dataTable.Rows.Count & ".  Page " & currentPage & " of " & _
        CType(System.Math.Ceiling(CType(
➥dataTable.Rows.Count,Double) / pageSize), Integer) & "."
    ' Store current page
    ViewState("CurrentPage") = currentPage
End Sub
```

Comments

This example uses the same kind of paging as the default behavior of the DataGrid. That is, the records are retrieved once from the database and from then on they are passed back and forth with each request in the page's ViewState. This design choice has advantages and disadvantages, which you must consider before you choose to implement paging in this fashion in your solutions.

The advantage is that it greatly reduces the number of requests that must be made to the database server, which is important because the database is typically one of the most difficult pieces of an application to scale upward if it becomes the bottleneck.

The disadvantage is that all of the data is being passed to and from the client with each request. Obviously for extremely large result sets, this is not ideal. Even for relatively small result sets, this can be a problem when the client is not using a high-speed network connection.

An alternative approach is to write a query or stored procedure that takes a page index and page size and returns only those records needed for the specified page. This results in more database resources being consumed, but fewer network and Web server resources and less dependence on the client's connection speed. For more on this approach, see section 13.10, "Enabling Custom Paging in a DataGrid."

See Also
Section 13.10, "Enabling Custom Paging in a DataGrid"

13.7. Data-binding to a DataGrid

You want to use a DataGrid control to display the results of a data query.

Technique

Use `System.Data.SqlClient.SqlDataAdapter` to retrieve data from a SQL Server database as a `System.Data.DataSet` and bind the results to `System.Web.UI.WebControls.DataGrid` in a Web page.

Import the following namespaces into your page:

```
<%@ Import Namespace="System.Data" %>
<%@ Import Namespace="System.Data.SqlClient" %>
```

In `<script runat="server" />` block:

```
Sub Page_Load(sender As Object, e As EventArgs)
    Dim PubsDataSet As DataSet
    Dim PubsConnection As SqlConnection
    Dim PubsAdapter As SqlDataAdapter
    PubsConnection = New _
SqlConnection("server=localhost;database=pubs;Trusted_Connection=yes")
    PubsAdapter = New SqlDataAdapter(
➥"SELECT * FROM Publishers", PubsConnection)
    PubsDataSet = New DataSet()
  Try
      PubsConnection.Open()
      PubsAdapter.Fill(PubsDataSet, "Publishers")
      PublisherDataGrid.DataSource = PubsDataSet
      PublisherDataGrid.DataMember = "Publishers"
      PublisherDataGrid.DataBind()
    Catch PubsException As SqlException
      PubsExceptionLabel.Text = PubsException.Message
    Finally
      PubsConnection.Close()
    End Try
  End Sub
```

The ASPX page is as follows:

```
<html>
  <body>
    <asp:DataGrid id="PublisherDataGrid" EnableViewState="false"
        runat="server" />
    <asp:Label id="PubsExceptionLabel" EnableViewState="false"
        runat="server" />
  </body>
</html>
```

Comments

The SQL SELECT statement determines which rows and columns are displayed in the DataGrid. You can change the appearance (border, color, font) of the DataGrid by setting the DataGrid's style properties. It's best to store the connection string information in the application settings of the web.config file. In addition to `System.Data.SqlClient.SqlDataAdapter`, `System.Data.Oledb.OledbDataAdapter` allows you to display data from Access, Oracle and other OleDb databases.

See Also

Section 6.2, "Creating Custom Application Settings in the web.config File"

Section 10.1, "Connecting to SQL Server"

Section 11.3, "Filtering the Contents of a Dataset"

Populating a Dataset from a DataAdapter—`http://msdn.microsoft.com/library/en-us/cpguide/html/cpconpopulatingdatasetfromdataadapter.asp`

13.8. Using Different Column Types in a DataGrid

> You want to display data, buttons, or custom formatted output within a DataGrid using its various column types.

Technique

The DataGrid has five types of columns—Bound, Button, EditCommand, HyperLink, and Template. Each one of these provides a different functionality, as you will see in this example.

The `BoundColumn` directly binds a column from the datasource to the DataGrid. In the .ASPX file:

```
<asp:DataGrid ...>
<Columns>
<asp:BoundColumn
    HeaderText="Phone Number"
    DataField="PhoneNo"
    ReadOnly="False"
    DataFormatString="{0:N}" />
</Columns>
</asp:DataGrid>
```

The `HeaderText` specifies the text for the column header, `DataField` specifies the field in the datasource to bind to the column, `ReadOnly` specifies whether the column can be edited in edit mode, and `DataFormatString` specifies how to format the column (in the example, as a number).

The `ButtonColumn` displays a command button in each row of the DataGrid. In the .ASPX file:

```
<asp:DataGrid ...>
<Columns>
<asp:ButtonColumn
    HeaderText="Remove Contact"
    ButtonType="LinkButton"
    Text="Remove"
```

```
    CommandName="RemoveContact" />
</Columns>
</asp:DataGrid>
```

The `ButtonType` specifies the type of command button to use; this can be set to `PushButton` or `LinkButton`. You can specify `DataTextField` and `DataTextFormatString` instead of `Text` in the tag. This would set the text value from a field in the datasource (`DataTextField`), and format it according to the `DataTextFormatString` specified.

The `EditCommandColumn` displays a column with command buttons for editing the data in each row. In the .ASPX file:

```
<asp:DataGrid ...>
<Columns>
<asp:EditCommandColumn
    ButtonType="LinkButton"
    UpdateText="Save"
    CancelText="Cancel"
    EditText="Edit" />
</Columns>
</asp:DataGrid>
```

`HyperLinkColumn` displays a hyperlink in each row of the DataGrid. In the .ASPX file:

```
<asp:DataGrid ...>
<Columns>
<asp:HyperLinkColumn
    Text="View Contact Details"
    DataNavigateUrlField="UserID"
    DataNavigateUrlFormatString="userdetails.aspx?userid={0}"
    Target="_new" />
</Columns>
</asp:DataGrid>
```

The `DataNavigateUrlField` and `DataNavifateUrlFormatString` properties determine the field and formatting string to use when setting the link. You can also use `DataTextField` and `DataTextFormatString` instead of the `Text` field (as you can with `ButtonColumn`). Finally, you can use the `NavigateUrl` property instead of the `DataNavigateUrl` and `DataNavigateUrlFormatString` properties to set a static URL.

The `TemplateColumn` provides the most functionality, because it allows you to specify a customized column layout. In the .ASPX page:

```
<asp:DataGrid ...>
<Columns>
<asp:TemplateColumn>
<HeaderTemplate>
Name
</HeaderTemplate>
<ItemTemplate>
```

```
<asp:Label runat="server"
   Text='<%# Container.DataItem("FirstName") & " " & _
Container.DataItem("LastName") %>' />
</ItemTemplate>
<EditItemTemplate>
First Name : <asp:TextBox runat="server"
     Text='<%# Container.DataItem("FirstName") %>' />
<br>
Last Name : <asp:TextBox runat="server"
     Text='<%# Container.DataItem("LastName") %>' />
</EditItemTemplate>
<FooterTemplate>
<asp:HyperLink runat="server"
   Text="Go Home"
   NavigateUrl="default.aspx"  />
</FooterTemplate>
</asp:TemplateColumn>
</Columns>
</asp:DataGrid>
```

Comments

The different types of DataGrid columns provide a great deal of functionality when developing a DataGrid, as you can see in these examples. Each of the column types inherit from the `DataGridColumn` class and therefore provide some basic functionality within all of them, such as visibility and styles.

See Also

The DataGridColumn Class—`http://msdn.microsoft.com/library/en-us/cpref/html/frlrfsystemwebuiwebcontrolsdatagridcolumnclasstopic.asp`

The DataGrid Class—`http://msdn.microsoft.com/library/en-us/cpref/html/frlrfsystemwebuiwebcontrolsdatagridclasstopic.asp`

Section 15.12, "Formatting Strings"

13.9. Enabling Default Paging in a DataGrid

You want to enable paging in your DataGrid.

Technique

Use the `System.Web.UI.WebControls.DataGrid.OnPageIndexChanged` event to set the `System.Web.UI.WebControls.DataGrid.CurrentPageIndex` property equal to `System.Web.UI.WebControls.DataGridSortCommandEventArgs.NewPageIndex`.

Import the following namespaces into your page:

```
<%@ Import Namespace="System.Data" %>
<%@ Import Namespace="System.Data.SqlClient" %>
```

In `<script runat="server" />` block or codebehind:

```
Sub Page_Load(Sender As Object, E As EventArgs)
  If Not Page.IsPostBack Then
    BindGrid()
  End If
End Sub


Sub BindGrid()
  Dim PubsDataSet As DataSet
  Dim PubsConnection As SqlConnection
  Dim PubsAdapter As SqlDataAdapter
  PubsConnection = New _
SqlConnection("server=localhost;database=pubs;Trusted_Connection=yes")
  PubsAdapter = New SqlDataAdapter(
➥"select * from Publishers", PubsConnection)
  PubsDataSet = new DataSet()
 Try
      PubsConnection.Open()
      PubsAdapter.Fill(PubsDataSet, "Publishers")
      PublisherDataGrid.DataSource = PubsDataSet
      PublisherDataGrid.DataMember = "Publishers"
      PublisherDataGrid.DataBind()
    Catch PubsException As SqlException
      PubsExceptionLabel.Text = PubsException.Message
    Finally
      PubsConnection.Close()
    End Try
  End Sub


  Sub PublisherDataGrid_Page(Sender As Object, _
E As DataGridPageChangedEventArgs)
    PublisherDataGrid.CurrentPageIndex = e.NewPageIndex
    BindGrid()
  End Sub
```

The ASPX page:

```
<html>
  <body>
    <form runat="server">
      <asp:DataGrid id="PublisherDataGrid" runat="server"
        OnPageIndexChanged="PublisherDataGrid_Page"
```

```
              PageSize="3"
              AllowPaging="True"/>
          <asp:Label id="PubsExceptionLabel" EnableViewState="false"
runat="server" />
        </form>
      </body>
    </html>
```

Comments

The `System.Web.UI.WebControls.DataGrid.PageSize` property has a default of 10. The `System.Web.UI.WebControls.DataGrid.PagerStyle-Mode` property default is `NextPrev`. For numeric page links, you should use `NumericPages`.

See Also

DataGrid Paging in a Web Form—`http://msdn.microsoft.com/library/en-us/dnvssamp/html/vbcs_PagingThroughQueryResults.asp`

Specifying Paging Behavior in a DataGrid Web Server Control—`http://msdn.microsoft.com/library/en-us/vbcon/html/vbtskspecifyingpagingbehaviorindatagridwebcontrol.asp`

13.10. Enabling Custom Paging in a DataGrid

You want to configure a custom paging solution for a DataGrid.

Technique

Using custom paging in the DataGrid control, you can retrieve and display only those records needed for the current request. In order to implement the custom paging feature of DataGrid, you have to adjust four properties first—`PageSize`, `AllowPaging`, `AllowCustomPaging`, and `VirtualItemCount`.

The `PageSize` property determines the number of records displayed per page on the DataGrid. The `AllowPaging` property enables pagination of the DataGrid. `AllowCustomPaging` determines whether the default paging behavior should be used. In this example, you are replacing the default paging behavior with your own. The `VirtualItemCount` determines the total number of items in the DataGrid control when custom paging is used.

The ASPX page:

```
<asp:datagrid id="myDataGrid" runat="server"
  width="100%"
  OnPageIndexChanged="myDataGrid_Page"
```

```
        PageSize="6"
        AllowCustomPaging="True"
        AllowPaging="True">

            <PagerStyle mode="NumericPages"/>

    </asp:datagrid>
```

You have to retrieve the total number of records in the database table first—that number is used for the `VirtualItemCount`. After that, the `OnPageIndexChanged` event handler will be executed if the page number link was clicked. In this event handler, you have to change the current page index of the DataGrid as usual, but you also have to calculate the starting and ending index for the record. This is calculated by multiplying the index of the selected page by the page size.

In `<script runat="server" />` block or codebehind:

```
Sub myDataGrid_Page(Sender As Object, _
e As DataGridPageChangedEventArgs)

    myDataGrid.CurrentPageIndex = e.NewPageIndex
    BindGrid(e.NewPageIndex * myDataGrid.PageSize)

End Sub
```

In the BindGrid procedure, you have to calculate the starting index of the record by multiplying the index of the selected page by the page size. The ending index of the records is the sum of the starting index and the page size of DataGrid. Using these starting and ending indexes, you can retrieve the records within this range.

```
Sub BindGrid(StartingIndex As Integer)

    Dim startingID As Integer = StartingIndex
    Dim endingID As Integer = startingID + myDataGrid.PageSize

    Dim ConnectionString As String = _
"server=(local);database=Northwind;trusted_connection=true"
    Dim CommandText As String = "select ProductID, " & _
                        "ProductName, " & _
                        "UnitPrice, " & _
                        "UnitsInStock " & _
                        "from Products " & _
                        "where ProductID > @StartingID and " & _
                        "ProductID <= @EndingID"

    Dim objConnection As New SqlConnection(ConnectionString)
    Dim objCommand As New SqlDataAdapter(CommandText, objConnection)
```

```
    Try

        objCommand.SelectCommand.Parameters.Add("@StartingID", startingID)
        objCommand.SelectCommand.Parameters.Add("@EndingID", endingID)

        Dim objDataSet As New DataSet()
        objCommand.Fill(objDataSet)

        myDataGrid.DataSource = objDataSet.Tables(0).DefaultView
        myDataGrid.VirtualItemCount = GetVirtualItemCount()
        myDataGrid.DataBind()

    Catch SqlEx As SqlException
        MessageLabel.Text = SqlEx.Message

    Catch Ex As Exception
        MessageLabel.Text = Ex.Message

    Finally
        objConnection.Close()

    End Try

End Sub
    Function GetVirtualItemCount As Integer

        If ViewState("GetVirtualItemCount") Is Nothing Then
            Dim ConnectionString As String = _
"server=(local);database=Northwind;trusted_connection=true"
            Dim CommandText As String = "select count(*) from Products"
            Dim objConnection As New SqlConnection(ConnectionString)
            Dim objCommand As New SqlCommand(CommandText, objConnection)
            Try
                objConnection.Open()
                ViewState("GetVirtualItemCount") = _
CType(objCommand.ExecuteScalar(), Integer)
            Catch SqlEx As SqlException
                MessageLabel.Text = SqlEx.Message
            Catch Ex As Exception
                MessageLabel.Text = Ex.Message
            Finally
                objConnection.Close()
            End Try
        End If
        Return CInt(ViewState("GetVirtualItemCount"))
    End Function
```

Comments

Even though there is built-in pagination capability in the DataGrid control, custom paging gives you better performance. When you enable the built-in paging, all the records must be retrieved from the datasource in your first page load or page index changed. Then all of these records must be passed to and from the browser in ViewState on each subsequent page request.

Using custom paging, only the rows needed for each page are retrieved. This will make a huge difference in a paged DataGrid with 1,000,000 records.

One important assumption made here is that the database table has a unique column that can be used by the data retrieval procedure for its starting and ending points.

See Also

Section 13.9, "Enabling Default Paging in a DataGrid"

13.11. Enabling Sorting in a DataGrid

You want to enable sorting in certain columns of your DataGrid.

Technique

Use the `System.Web.UI.WebControls.DataGrid.SortCommand` event to set the `System.Data.DataView.Sort` property equal to the `System.Web.UI.WebControls.DataGridColumn.SortExpression` property.

Import the following namespaces into your page:

```
<%@ Import Namespace="System.Data" %>
<%@ Import Namespace="System.Data.SqlClient" %>
```

In `<script runat="server" />` block:

```
Sub Page_Load(Sender As Object, E As EventArgs)
If Not Page.IsPostBack Then
    BindGrid("pub_id")
End If
End Sub


Sub BindGrid(SortColumn As String)
Dim PubsDataSet As DataSet
Dim PubsConnection As SqlConnection
Dim PubsAdapter As SqlDataAdapter
Dim PublishersDataView As DataView
PubsConnection = New SqlConnection("server=localhost
➥;database=pubs;Trusted_Connection=yes")
PubsAdapter = New SqlDataAdapter("select * from Publishers", PubsConnection)
```

```
PubsDataSet = new DataSet()
Try
    PubsConnection.Open()
    PubsAdapter.Fill(PubsDataSet, "Publishers")
    PublishersDataView = PubsDataSet.Tables(0).DefaultView
    PublishersDataView.Sort = SortColumn
    PublisherDataGrid.DataSource = PublishersDataView
    PublisherDataGrid.DataBind()
Catch PubsException As SqlException
    PubsExceptionLabel.Text = PubsException.Message
Finally
    PubsConnection.Close()
End Try
End Sub

Sub PublisherDataGrid_Sort(Sender As Object, E As DataGridSortCommandEventArgs)
    BindGrid(E.SortExpression)
End Sub
```

The ASPX page:

```
<html>
  <body>
    <form runat="server">
      <asp:DataGrid id="PublisherDataGrid" runat="server"
        OnSortCommand="PublisherDataGrid_Sort"
        AllowSorting="True"/>
      <asp:Label id="PubsExceptionLabel"
EnableViewState="false" runat="server" />
    </form>
  </body>
</html>
```

Comments

You can set the System.Web.UI.WebControls.DataGridColumn.SortExpression property for each column that you want to sort. When using System.Web.UI.WebControls.DataGrid.AutoGenerateColumns, the default used for System.Web.UI.WebControls.DataGridColumn.SortExpression is the System.Web.UI.WebControls.DataGridColumn.DataColumn.DataField property.

See Also

Adding Sorting to a DataGrid Web Server Control—http://msdn.microsoft.com/en-us/vbcon/html/vbtskspecifyingpagingbehaviorindatagridwebcontrol.asp

Sorting Data in a SQL Database—http://msdn.microsoft.com/library/en-us/cpguide/html/cpconsortingdatainsqldatabase.asp

13.12. Enabling Bi-Directional Sorting in a DataGrid

> You want to allow users to click column headers in your DataGrid to sort that column, and to click the columns once again to reverse the order of the sort.

Technique

First you read an XML file into a dataset, and then bind the dataset to a DataGrid. Keep track of two attributes of the DataGrid—SortExpression and SortDirection. When a column is clicked, the SortDataGrid method is called. The grid is sorted by that column using e.SortExpession. If a column is clicked a second time, the sort direction is reversed.

The ASPX page:

```
<asp:DataGrid id="SortGrid" runat="server"
CellPadding="5" AllowSorting="true" OnSortCommand="SortDataGrid">
    <AlternatingItemStyle BackColor="#ccffcc" />
    <HeaderStyle HorizontalAlign="center"
BackColor="#cccccc" Font-Bold="true" />
    </asp:DataGrid>
```

In <script runat="server" /> block or codebehind:

```
Protected Sub Page_Load([Source] As Object, e As EventArgs)
    If Not IsPostBack Then
        If SortGrid.Attributes("SortExpression") Is Nothing Then
            SortGrid.Attributes("SortExpression") = "HDate"
            SortGrid.Attributes("SortDirection") = "ASC"
        End If
        BindData()
    End If
End Sub


Private Sub BindData()
    Dim ds As New DataSet()
    Dim path As String = MapPath("BUD_WEN.xml")
    ds.ReadXml(path)
    Dim dv As DataView = ds.Tables(0).DefaultView

    Dim sortExpression As String = _
SortGrid.Attributes("SortExpression").ToString()
    Dim sortDirection As String = _
SortGrid.Attributes("SortDirection").ToString()
    dv.Sort = sortExpression + " " + sortDirection
```

```
        SortGrid.DataSource = dv
        SortGrid.DataBind()
    End Sub


    Public Sub SortDataGrid(sender As [Object], _
e As DataGridSortCommandEventArgs)
        Dim sortExpression As String = e.SortExpression
        Dim sortDirection As String = "ASC"
        If sortExpression.Equals(_
SortGrid.Attributes("SortExpression").ToString()) Then
            If SortGrid.Attributes("SortDirection").
➥ToString().StartsWith("ASC") Then
                sortDirection = "DESC"
            Else
                sortDirection = "ASC"
            End If
        End If
        SortGrid.Attributes("SortExpression") = sortExpression
        SortGrid.Attributes("SortDirection") = sortDirection

        BindData()
    End Sub
```

Comments

The DataGrid attributes should be set when the page first loads so that they do not have null values when you need to use them later. Set SortExpression to the default data field by which the grid is sorted.

The BindData method reads the XML data into a dataset. The sort expression and sort direction values are retrieved from the DataGrid attributes SortExpression and SortDirection and are used to sort the data. The data is then bound to the DataGrid.

The SortDataGrid method is called whenever one of the column headings is clicked. If the column that is clicked is the same as the value of the SortExpression attribute of the DataGrid, the sort direction is set to the opposite direction of SortDirection's value.

See Also

Effective Sorting in ASP.Net DataGrids—
http://msdn.microsoft.com/msdnnews/2001/sept/Sorting/Sorting.asp

Sorting XML Data using the .NET DataGrid—
http://www.codeproject.com/aspnet/XmlDataGrid.asp

Bi-directional Sorting Without ViewState Enabled—http://aspalliance.com/olson/
articles/Bisort.aspx

13.13. Editing Items in a DataGrid

You want to edit the contents of your DataGrid.

Technique

This example uses the Northwind database. Begin by inserting the DataGrid along with its attributes associated with making it editable.

Insert this as your HTML block:

```
<%@ Page Language="VB" %>
<%@ Import Namespace="System.Data" %>
<%@ Import Namespace="System.Data.SqlClient" %>
<script Runat="server" >

</script>
<html>
<head>
    <title>The Editable DataGrid</title>
</head>
<body>
    <h1>The Editable DataGrid
    </h1>
    <form runat="server">
        <asp:Label ID="ErrorLabel" ForeColor="#FF0000"
Font-Bold="True" Runat="server" />
        <asp:DataGrid id="myDataGrid" Runat="server"
AutoGenerateColumns="False" OnEditCommand="myDataGrid_Edit"
OnCancelCommand="myDataGrid_Cancel" OnUpdateCommand="myDataGrid_Update">
            <Columns>
                <asp:BoundColumn HeaderText="Customer ID"
                    HeaderStyle-Font-Size="12pt"
                    HeaderStyle-HorizontalAlign="Center"
                    HeaderStyle-BackColor="#FFCC00"
                    DataField="CustomerID" ReadOnly="True" />
                <asp:BoundColumn HeaderText="Company"
                    HeaderStyle-Font-Size="12pt"
                    HeaderStyle-HorizontalAlign="Center"
                    HeaderStyle-BackColor="#FFCC00"
                    DataField="CompanyName" />
                <asp:BoundColumn HeaderText="Name"
                    HeaderStyle-Font-Size="12pt"
                    HeaderStyle-HorizontalAlign="Center"
                    HeaderStyle-BackColor="#FFCC00"
                    DataField="ContactName" />
```

```
                <asp:BoundColumn HeaderText="Title"
                    HeaderStyle-Font-Size="12pt"
                    HeaderStyle-HorizontalAlign="Center"
                    HeaderStyle-BackColor="#FFCC00"
                    DataField="ContactTitle" />
                <asp:BoundColumn HeaderText="Phone No."
                    HeaderStyle-Font-Size="12pt"
                    HeaderStyle-HorizontalAlign="Center"
                    HeaderStyle-BackColor="#FFCC00"
                    DataField="Phone" />
                <asp:BoundColumn HeaderText="Fax No."
                    HeaderStyle-Font-Size="12pt"
                    HeaderStyle-HorizontalAlign="Center"
                    HeaderStyle-BackColor="#FFCC00"
                    DataField="Fax" />
                <asp:EditCommandColumn ButtonType="LinkButton"
                    CancelText="Cancel" EditText="Edit"
                    UpdateText="Save" />
            </Columns>
        </asp:DataGrid>
    </form>
</body>
</html>
```

The following code will be inserted within your script block. If you plan to use this tool with codebehind, make sure that you make all of your DataGrid functions `Protected`. The reason for this is because you have a DataGrid control within your HTML block that is trying to access a function within your codebehind. Whenever you have a Web control within your HTML that is accessing any variable or function within your codebehind, that function or variable must be protected. For example, the `UpdateCommand` in this DataGrid would look like this if you were using codebehind:

```
Public ConnString As String = "SERVER=(local);
➥Database=Northwind;uid=user;pwd=password"

Sub BindData()
    '— Using the Try statement, we attempt to connect to our
    '— database, execute a SqlDataAdapter to store our data,
    '— populate a dataset and then bind that dataset
    '— to our DataGrid.
    Try
        Dim SqlConn As New SqlConnection(ConnString)
        Dim SqlString As String = & _
"SELECT CustomerID, CompanyName, ContactName, ContactTitle,
➥ Phone, Fax FROM Customers"
        Dim SqlComm As New SqlDataAdapter(SqlString, SqlConn)
        Dim customerData As New DataSet()
```

```vb
        SqlComm.Fill(customerData, "Customers")

        myDataGrid.DataSource = customerData
        myDataGrid.DataBind()

        SqlConn.Close()
        SqlComm.Dispose()
        SqlConn.Dispose()


    '— If we are not able to connect, display a friendly error
    Catch e As Exception
        ErrorLabel.Text = _
"Not able to connect to database. See description below: "
        ErrorLabel.Text += e.ToString()
    End Try
End Sub



Sub myDataGrid_Update(Sender As Object, e As DataGridCommandEventArgs)
    '— Take the data from each textbox in our editable item
    '— and assign that text to a string variable
    Dim CustomerID As String = Convert.ToString(e.Item.Cells(0).Text)
    Dim Company As String = CType(e.Item.Cells(1).Controls(0), TextBox).Text
    Dim Name As String = CType(e.Item.Cells(2).Controls(0), TextBox).Text
    Dim Title As String = CType(e.Item.Cells(3).Controls(0), TextBox).Text
    Dim Phone As String = CType(e.Item.Cells(4).Controls(0), TextBox).Text
    Dim Fax As String = CType(e.Item.Cells(5).Controls(0), TextBox).Text
    '— Again, using the Try statement, attempt to connect to our database
    '— and make an update with the data from our datagrid
    Dim SqlConn As New SqlConnection(ConnString)
    Try
        SqlConn.Open()
        Dim SqlString As String = "UPDATE Customers "
        SqlString &= "SET CompanyName = '" & _
Company.Replace("'", "''") & "', "
        SqlString &= "ContactName = '" + Name.Replace("'", "''") & "', "
        SqlString &= "ContactTitle = '" + Title.Replace("'", "''") & "', "
        SqlString &= "Phone = '" + Phone.Replace("'", "''") & "', "
        SqlString &= "Fax = '" + Fax.Replace("'", "''") & "'"
        SqlString &= " WHERE CustomerID = '" & CustomerID + "'"
        Dim SqlComm As New SqlCommand(SqlString, SqlConn)
        SqlComm.ExecuteNonQuery()
        SqlConn.Close()
        SqlComm.Dispose()
        SqlConn.Dispose()
    '— If for some reason we cannot connect, display a friendly error.
    Catch exc As Exception
```

```
        ErrorLabel.Text = _
"Not able to connect to database. See description below: "
        ErrorLabel.Text += exc.ToString()
    End Try
    '— Remove the edit focus
    myDataGrid.EditItemIndex = - 1
    '— Rebind our datagrid
    BindData()
End Sub


Sub myDataGrid_Cancel(Sender As Object, e As DataGridCommandEventArgs)
    '— Remove the edit focus
    myDataGrid.EditItemIndex = - 1
    '— Rebind our datagrid
    BindData()
End Sub


Sub myDataGrid_Edit(Sender As Object, e As DataGridCommandEventArgs)
    '— Set the edit focus to the item that was selected
    myDataGrid.EditItemIndex = CInt(e.Item.ItemIndex)
    '— Rebind our datagrid
    BindData()
End Sub


Sub Page_Load(Sender As Object, e As EventArgs)
    '— If this is not a postback event, bind the data to our datagrid
    If Not Page.IsPostBack Then
        BindData()
    End If
End Sub
```

Comments

Probably one of the simplest yet most efficient features of the DataGrid is its editing capability. Developers who have worked with classic ASP will probably remember how the editable DataGrid functionality worked. To code the functionality that the .NET DataGrid gives you today in classic ASP would take more than triple the time it takes for developers to create and present a fully functional editable .NET DataGrid.

See Also

http://aspalliance.com/Colt/Articles/Article3.aspx

http://aspalliance.com/andrewmooney/default.aspx?page=5

http://aspalliance.com/aldotnet/examples/dgautoscroll.aspx

13.14. Manipulating Individual Rows in a DataGrid

You want to manipulate or hide certain rows in a DataGrid.

Technique

A DataTable with four columns—Color, ColorName, Hexadecimal, and TurnedOn—is bound to a DataGrid. The ItemDataBound event looks at the ColorName column and makes the background of the Color column that color. The ItemDataBound event also looks at the TurnedOn column to determine whether the row is visible.

The ASPX page:

```
<asp:DataGrid id="ColorGrid" runat="server" CellPadding="5"
OnItemDataBound="ColorGrid_ItemDataBound">
    <HeaderStyle HorizontalAlign="center" BackColor="#cccccc"
Font-Bold="true" />
    </asp:DataGrid>
    <br>
    <asp:Button id="RedButton" runat="server" Text="Red"
onclick="RedButton_Click" />
    <asp:Button id="GreenButton" runat="server" Text="Green"
onclick="GreenButton_Click" />
    <asp:Button id="BlueButton" runat="server" Text="Blue"
onclick="BlueButton_Click" />
    <asp:Button id="AllButton" runat="server" Text=" All "

onclick="AllButton_Click" />
```

In `<script runat="server" />` block or codebehind:

```
Protected Sub Page_Load([Source] As Object, e As EventArgs)
   If Not IsPostBack Then
      BindData(True, True, True)
   End If
End Sub


   Private  Sub BindData(ByVal RedOn As Boolean, _
ByVal GreenOn As Boolean, ByVal BlueOn As Boolean)
   Dim Colors As DataTable = New DataTable()
   Colors.Columns.Add("Color", Type.GetType("System.String"))
   Colors.Columns.Add("ColorName", Type.GetType("System.String"))
   Colors.Columns.Add("Hexadecimal", Type.GetType("System.String"))
   Colors.Columns.Add("TurnedOn", Type.GetType("System.Boolean"))

   Dim Row1 As DataRow =  Colors.NewRow()
   Row1("Color") = " "
```

```
        Row1("ColorName") = "Red"
        Row1("Hexadecimal") = "#ff0000"
        Row1("TurnedOn") = RedOn
        Colors.Rows.Add(Row1)

        Dim Row2 As DataRow =  Colors.NewRow()
        Row2("Color") = " "
        Row2("ColorName") = "Green"
        Row2("Hexadecimal") = "#00ff00"
        Row2("TurnedOn") = GreenOn
        Colors.Rows.Add(Row2)

        Dim Row3 As DataRow =  Colors.NewRow()
        Row3("Color") = " "
        Row3("ColorName") = "Blue"
        Row3("Hexadecimal") = "#0000ff"
        Row3("TurnedOn") = BlueOn
        Colors.Rows.Add(Row3)

        ColorGrid.DataSource = Colors
        ColorGrid.DataBind()
    End Sub


    Protected  Sub ColorGrid_ItemDataBound(ByVal sender As Object, ByVal e As
System.Web.UI.WebControls.DataGridItemEventArgs)
        If e.Item.ItemType = ListItemType.Item Or e.Item.ItemType =
ListItemType.AlternatingItem Then
            e.Item.Cells(0).BackColor = Color.FromName(e.Item.Cells(1).Text)
            e.Item.Visible = Convert.ToBoolean(e.Item.Cells(3).Text)
        End If
    End Sub

    Protected  Sub RedButton_Click(ByVal Source As Object,
      ByVal e As EventArgs)
        BindData(True, False, False)
    End Sub

    Protected  Sub GreenButton_Click(ByVal Source As Object,
      ByVal e As EventArgs)
        BindData(False, True, False)
    End Sub

    Protected  Sub BlueButton_Click(ByVal Source As Object,
      ByVal e As EventArgs)
        BindData(False, False, True)
    End Sub
```

```
Protected  Sub AllButton_Click(ByVal Source As Object,
   ByVal e As EventArgs)
      BindData(True, True, True)
End Sub
```

Comments

As the DataGrid binds the data from the DataTable, the `ItemDataBound` event is fired for each row of the DataTable. If the row in the `ItemDataBound` event is a `ListItemType` or an `AlternatingItem` type, two things happen:

- The `BackColor` of the Color column changes to the color indicated in the ColorName column.
- The TurnedOn column shows or hides the row depending on whether the property `visible` is set to `true` or `false`.

Note that if your DataGrid allows the users to select certain rows, you should also check for the `SelectedItemType`.

The `Click` event for each of the buttons calls the BindData method with the parameters telling which rows to show or hide. Changing the content of the DataTable causes the DataGrid to appear different by manipulating the rows in the `ItemDataBound` event.

See Also

Section 13.7, "Data-binding to a DataGrid"

ItemDataBound Event—`http://msdn.microsoft.com/library/en-us/cpref/html/frlrfsystemwebuiwebcontrolsdatagridclassitemdataboundtopic.asp`

13.15. Implementing a Master-Detail Report Using Two DataGrids

You want to create a master-detail view of some data using two DataGrid controls.

Technique

There are two master and details DataGrid controls, in which the master DataGrid lists the information of authors, whereas the details DataGrid lists the information of titles of the author. When you select an author from the master DataGrid, the information corresponding to the selected author is displayed in the details DataGrid.

The ASPX page:

```
        <asp:datagrid id="MasterDataGrid" runat="server"
OnPageIndexChanged="MasterDataGrid_PageIndexChanged" PageSize="6"
```

```
AllowPaging="True" OnSelectedIndexChanged="MasterDataGrid_SelectedIndexChanged"
 DataKeyField="Last Name" Width="100%">
                <Columns>
                    <asp:ButtonColumn Text="Show details"
CommandName="Select" />
                </Columns>
            </asp:datagrid>
            <br />
            <asp:datagrid id="DetailsDataGrid" runat="server"
EnableViewState="False" Width="100%"/>
        </p>



        <p/>
            <asp:Label id="ErrorLabel" runat="server"/>
```

In `<script runat="server" />` block or codebehind:

Both of the master and details DataGrid must be databound during `Page_Load`, as demonstrated here:

```
Sub Page_Load(Sender As Object, E As EventArgs)

    If Not IsPostBack Then

        MasterDataGrid.SelectedIndex = 0
        BindMasterDataGrid()
        BindDetailDataGrid()

    End If

End Sub
```

When you click the Show Details Button on the master DataGrid, its `SelectedIndexChanged` event handler will be fired:

```
Protected Sub MasterDataGrid_SelectedIndexChanged(Sender As Object, E As
EventArgs)
    BindDetailDataGrid()
End Sub
```

The `SelectedIndexChanged` event handler will then fire the data-binding of the details DataGrid, based on the primary key of the selected grid item row. That primary key is retrieved from the DataKeys collection of the master DataGrid.

```
Sub BindDetailDataGrid()

    If MasterDataGrid.SelectedIndex <> -1 Then

        Dim ConnectionString As String = _
```

```
"server=Localhost;database=pubs;trusted_connection=true"


        Dim FilterValue As String
        Try
            FilterValue = CStr(MasterDataGrid.DataKeys( _
                        MasterDataGrid.SelectedIndex)).Replace("'", "''")
        Catch
            FilterValue = ""
        End Try



        Dim CommandText As String = "select title as Title, price as Price,
➥ ytd_sales as [YTD Sales] from titleview where au_lname = '"
➥ & FilterValue & "'"

        Try
            Dim objConnection As New SqlConnection(ConnectionString)
            Dim objCommand As New SqlCommand(CommandText, objConnection)

            objConnection.Open()

            DetailsDataGrid.DataSource = _
                objCommand.ExecuteReader(CommandBehavior.CloseConnection)
            DetailsDataGrid.DataBind()

        Catch SqlEx As SqlException
            ErrorLabel.Text = SqlEx.Message
        Catch Ex As Exception
            ErrorLabel.Text = Ex.Message
        Finally
            objConnection.Close()


        End Try

    End If

End Sub
```

After passing the primary key to the `BindDetailDataGrid` procedure, the example binds and displays the author's title information on the detail DataGrid.

Comments

Using two DataGrids to display data with a master-detail relationship is very useful, especially when you're showing some nested or hierarchical data, such as menu and submenus.

13.16. Rendering Images in a DataGrid

You want to display an image in each row of a DataGrid.

Technique

You can add images to a DataGrid by using a template column. This example uses the template column to display the photos of the top five authors of this book. You start off by creating a new DataGrid and adding two columns to it. You then set the first column to `TemplateColumn` and begin to set up the `ItemTemplate`. You create the first half of the HTML `<img>` tag. When setting the source attribute, be sure to use single quotes to encapsulate the image URL so that you can use double quotes within the data-binding syntax.

Add the following code to data-bind the Photo column to the `source` attribute:

```
<%#DataBinder.Eval(Container.DataItem, "Photo")%>
```

Then you close the `<img>` tag. Finally, you set the second column to a `BoundColumn` and bind it to the Name column.

The ASPX page is as follows:

```
<%@Import namespace="System.Data"%>
<HTML>
    <body>
        <form id="form1" method="post" runat="server">
            <asp:DataGrid ID="Authors" Runat="server" AutoGenerateColumns="False">
                <Columns>
                    <asp:TemplateColumn HeaderText="Picture">
                        <ItemTemplate>
                            <img
                             src='<%#DataBinder.Eval(Container.DataItem, "Photo")%>' >
                        </ItemTemplate>
                    </asp:TemplateColumn>
                    <asp:BoundColumn DataField="Name" HeaderText="Name" />
                </Columns>
            </asp:DataGrid>
        </form>
    </body>
</HTML>
```

The technique for populating a DataTable and data-binding it isn't relevant to this example, so it's not covered in a lot of detail. In short, you create a new DataTable and add a photo and a name column to it. Then, you call the `AddRow` function to add the authors to the table and data-bind the DataTable to the DataGrid.

In `<script runat="server" />` block or codebehind:

```
Sub Page_Load(sender As Object, e As EventArgs)
    Dim authorsTable As DataTable
    authorsTable=new DataTable()
    authorsTable.Columns.Add("Photo")
    authorsTable.Columns.Add("Name")
    AddRow(authorsTable, "recipe1316a.jpg", "Steven Smith")
    AddRow(authorsTable, "recipe1316b.jpg", "Jeremy Zongker")
    AddRow(authorsTable, "recipe1316c.jpg", "Haroon Malik")
    AddRow(authorsTable, "recipe1316d.jpg", "Rob Howard")
    AddRow(authorsTable, "recipe1316e.jpg", "Daniel Olson")
    Authors.DataSource=authorsTable
    Authors.DataBind()
End Sub

Sub AddRow(AuthorsTable As DataTable, Photo As String, Name As String)
    Dim row As DataRow
    row=AuthorsTable.NewRow()
    row("Photo")=Photo
    row("Name")=Name
    AuthorsTable.Rows.Add(row)
End Sub
```

See Also

Section 10.10, "Displaying an Image from SQL Server"

Section 13.7, "Data-binding to a DataGrid"

Section 13.8, "Using Different Column Types in a DataGrid"

13.17. Adding a Confirmation Box to a DataGrid Button

You want to add a confirmation dialog box to a button in a DataGrid.

Technique

Consider a Delete button in a DataGrid. Whenever you want to delete a record in the DataGrid, you want to trigger an `onclick` event and ask for your confirmation before actual deletion. This would avoid accidental data loss. You can use two approaches to display a button in a DataGrid for deletion—using the built-in Button column or using a Template column with a Button control.

The ASPX page is as follows:

```
<asp:datagrid id="myDataGrid" runat="server"
    OnItemDataBound="DataGrid_ItemDataBound"
    DataKeyField="au_id"
    OnDeleteCommand="DataGrid_Delete"
    AllowPaging="True"
    PageSize="6"
    OnPageIndexChanged="DataGrid_Page"
    AutoGenerateColumns="False">

    <PagerStyle mode="NumericPages"/>
    <Columns>
        <asp:ButtonColumn Text="Delete" CommandName="Delete"/>
        <asp:BoundColumn DataField="au_id" HeaderText="Author ID"/>
        <asp:BoundColumn DataField="au_fname" HeaderText="Last Name"/>
        <asp:BoundColumn DataField="au_lname" HeaderText="First Name"/>
        <asp:TemplateColumn>
           <ItemTemplate>
              <asp:Button id="DeleteButton" Runat="Server"
                 Text="Delete"
                 OnCommand="DeleteButton_Click"
                 CommandArgument='<%# Container.ItemIndex %>'/>
           </ItemTemplate>
        </asp:TemplateColumn>
    </Columns>
</asp:datagrid>
```

You can locate the button by finding and casting it for each item of the DataGrid, and then add a JavaScript method to the attributes collection of the button in the `ItemDataBound` event of the DataGrid.

In `<script runat="server" />` block or codebehind:

```
Sub DataGrid_ItemDataBound(Sender As Object, e As DataGridItemEventArgs)

    If e.Item.ItemType = ListItemType.Item Or _
        e.Item.ItemType = ListItemType.AlternatingItem Then

        Dim LinkButtonControl As LinkButton = _
CType(e.Item.Cells(0).Controls(0), LinkButton)
        LinkButtonControl.Attributes.Add("onclick", _
"Javascript:return confirm('Are you sure?');")

        Dim ButtonControl As Button = _
CType(e.Item.FindControl("DeleteButton"), Button)
        ButtonControl.Attributes.Add("onclick", _
"Javascript:return confirm('Are you sure?');")
    End If
End Sub
```

Comments

When an item is data-bound to the DataGrid control, you can add a JavaScript method to ask for confirmation. This will display a confirmation dialog box, which means the click is processed and the event is executed only when the users confirm that they are sure they want to do so.

In the `ItemDataBound` event, you can explicitly locate the Button control from its cell and control index, or you can use the `FindControl` method to do this. However, no matter which approach you use to locate the Button control, you have to cast it into the correct type so that the `OnClick` client script can be added to it successfully.

See Also

Section 13.18, "Implementing Support for Double-Clicks in a DataGrid"

13.18. Implementing Support for Double-Clicks in a DataGrid

You want to select an item by double-clicking anywhere in the DataGrid row.

Technique

Start with an existing DataGrid that is populated from a data source (see example 13.7), or download the full example for this recipe from the book's Web site. In the `ItemDataBound` event handler of DataGrid, you assign a JavaScript `ondblclick` method to the DataGrid item.

The ASPX page is as follows:

```
    <asp:DataGrid id="DblClickDataGrid"
OnItemDataBound="DblClickDataGrid_ItemDataBound" Runat="Server">
        <SelectedItemStyle backcolor="Yellow" />
        <Columns>
            <asp:ButtonColumn Text="Select" HeaderText="Select"
CommandName="Select"/>
        </Columns>
    </asp:DataGrid>
```

You add a JavaScript method to the DataGrid item in the `ItemDataBound` event handler of the DataGrid.

In `<script runat="server" />` block or codebehind:

```
Sub DblClickDataGrid_ItemDataBound(Sender As Object, _
e As DataGridItemEventArgs)
    If e.Item.ItemType = ListItemType.Item Or e.Item.ItemType = _
ListItemType.AlternatingItem Then
        e.Item.Attributes.Add("ondblclick", _
```

```
"Javascript:__doPostBack('myDblClick','" & e.Item.ItemIndex & "');")
    End If
End Sub
```

If the page is being posted back, check and parse the index from __EventTarget, and then set the corresponding SelectedIndex of DataGrid.

```
Sub Page_Load(Sender As Object, E As EventArgs)
    If Not IsPostBack Then
        BindGrid()
    Else
        If Not Request.Form("__EventTarget") Is Nothing And _
            Request.Form("__EventTarget") = "myDblClick" Then
            DblClickDataGrid.SelectedIndex = _
CInt(Request.Form("__EVENTARGUMENT"))
        End If
    End If
End Sub
```

Comments

In addition to the classic Select button of a DataGrid, users can select an item by double-clicking any object on the DataGrid. A client-side double-click method was added to the attributes collection of the DataGridItem. Because this page uses a postback event, ASP.NET generates the __doPostBack JavaScript method to the page automatically, which consists merely of a form submission.

A DataGrid is basically an HTML table, whereby each cell per DataGridItem is equivalent to a <td> and each grid row is equivalent to a <tr> element. By assigning the JavaScript ondblclick method to the table row, you can select an item by double-clicking anywhere on a grid item row. This is similar to selecting a row by clicking the Select button column in a DataGrid.

See Also

Selecting Rows by Clicking Anywhere—http://msdn.microsoft.com/library/en-us/dv_vstechart/html/vbtchTopQuestionsAboutASPNETDataGridServerControl.asp

13.19. Implementing a Check Box Column in a DataGrid

You want to implement a check box column in a DataGrid.

Technique

If you add a Template column with a CheckBox control to a DataGrid, your users can select multiple items in a DataGrid for a bulk operation.

The ASPX page is as follows:

```
<asp:datagrid id="myDataGrid" runat="server" AutoGenerateColumns="False">
   <Columns>
      <asp:TemplateColumn>
         <HeaderTemplate>
            <input type="CheckBox" name="SelectAllCheckBox"
onclick="SelectAll(this)">
         </HeaderTemplate>
         <ItemTemplate>
            <asp:CheckBox id="SelectCheckBox" Runat="Server" />
         </ItemTemplate>
      </asp:TemplateColumn>
      <asp:BoundColumn DataField="pub_id" HeaderText="ID"/>
      <asp:BoundColumn DataField="pub_name" HeaderText="Name"/>
      <asp:BoundColumn DataField="city" HeaderText="City"/>
      <asp:BoundColumn DataField="state" HeaderText="State"/>
      <asp:BoundColumn DataField="country" HeaderText="Country"/>
   </Columns>
</asp:datagrid>
```

Using the `TemplateColumn` with the CheckBox control, you can select multiple items in the DataGrid, or click the check box in the `HeaderTemplate` of this CheckBox column to (de)select all items in one click.

After selecting the items, you can click a button and then walk through the items in the DataGrid. You can find and cast the CheckBox control from the appropriate column to determine whether the check box is checked.

In `<script runat="server" />` block or codebehind:

```
Function GetSelectedPublishers() As String
   Dim i As Integer

   For i = 0 To myDataGrid.Items.Count - 1
      If CType(myDataGrid.Items(i).FindControl("SelectCheckBox"), _
CheckBox).Checked Then
         If PublisherIDs <> "" Then PublisherIDs &= ","
         PublisherIDs &= myDataGrid.DataKeys(i)
      End If
   Next
   GetSelectedPublishers = PublisherIDs
End Function
```

In the previous function, the items in the DataGrid are looped through and the CheckBox control is found by using `FindControl` method. Therefore, the `DataKeyField` of the current `DataGridItem`, which is normally the primary key of the working table, is distinguished and appended to form a collection. This concatenated string will be used for the later bulk operation (such as a delete or copy opration).

For example, using the `GetSelectedPublishers()` method, you could implement a delete event as follows:

```
Sub DeleteButton_Click(sender As Object, e As EventArgs)
    Dim PublisherIDs As String = GetSelectedPublishers()
    Dim ConnectionString As String = _
"server=(local);database=pubs;uid=user;pwd=password"
    Dim CommandText As String = _
"delete from Publishers where pub_id in (" & PublisherIDs & ")"
    Dim objConnection As New SqlConnection(ConnectionString)
    Dim objCommand As New SqlCommand(CommandText, objConnection)

    Try
        objConnection.Open()
        objCommand.ExecuteNonQuery()
    Catch SqlEx As SqlException
        MessageLabel.Text = SqlEx.Message & "<br>" & CommandText
    Catch Ex As Exception
        MessageLabel.Text = Ex.Message
    Finally
        objConnection.Close()
    End Try
    BindGrid()
End Sub
```

The `BindGrid()` method:

```
Sub BindGrid()
    Dim ConnectionString As String = _
"server=(local);database=pubs;uid=user;pwd=password"
    Dim CommandText As String = "select * from Publishers"
    Dim objConnection As New SqlConnection(ConnectionString)
    Dim objCommand As New SqlCommand(CommandText, objConnection)

    Try
        objConnection.Open()
        myDataGrid.DataSource = _
objCommand.ExecuteReader(CommandBehavior.CloseConnection)
        myDataGrid.DataBind()
    Catch SqlEx As SqlException
        MessageLabel.Text = SqlEx.Message
    Catch Ex As Exception
        MessageLabel.Text = Ex.Message
        Finally
          objConnection.Close()
    End Try
End Sub
```

Comments

You can use the `FindControl` method to locate the CheckBox control in the `TemplateColumn` of DataGrid, whereas you can also use the standard approach—getting a control by specifying its column and control index. If you are getting a CheckBox control via its control index, bear in mind that the CheckBox control is usually the second control in the `TemplateColumn` (index 1) because a literal control precedes it.

In the `HeaderTemplate` of the CheckBox column, you can put a check box HTML control and fire a simple client-side method to fill in the check boxes all at once.

See Also

Andy Smith's RowSelectorColumn control—
`http://www.metabuilders.com/Tools/RowSelectorColumn.aspx`

13.20. Implementing a DropDownList in Edit Mode in a DataGrid

You want to use a DropDownList for one of the fields in your DataGrid when in Edit mode, and then retrieve the value of this DropDownList when the user saves the item.

Technique

To provide a DropDownList when a user edits a record, you can put it in the `EditItemTemplate` of a TemplateColumn in a DataGrid.

The ASPX page is as follows:

```
<asp:TemplateColumn HeaderText="Region">
  <ItemTemplate>
    <asp:Label id="regionDescriptionLabel" runat="server"
   Text='<%# DataBinder.Eval(Container.DataItem, "RegionDescription") %>'/>
  </ItemTemplate>
  <EditItemTemplate>
    <asp:DropDownList id="regionDropDownList" Runat="Server"
       DataSource="<%# GetRegionDataTable() %>"
       DataTextField="RegionDescription"
       DataValueField="RegionID" />
  </EditItemTemplate>
</asp:TemplateColumn>
```

After adding a DropDownList to the EditItemTemplate of a DataGrid, you have to bind some data to this control, and set its display text and corresponding values. For the data-binding process, you can retrieve the data from a database and construct a DataTable, and then you can return this DataTable and bind it to the DropDownList. This data-binding takes place in the `ItemDataBound` event of the DataGrid, shown here:

```
Sub myDataGrid_ItemDataBound(ByVal sender As Object, _
ByVal e As DataGridItemEventArgs)
    If e.Item.ItemType = ListItemType.EditItem Then
        Dim objDataRowView As DataRowView = CType(e.Item.DataItem, DataRowView)
        Dim currentgenre As String = CType(objDataRowView(2), String)
        Dim ctlDropDownList As DropDownList = _
CType(e.Item.FindControl("regionDropDownList"), DropDownList)
        ctlDropDownList.SelectedIndex =
ctlDropDownList.Items.IndexOf(ctlDropDownList.items.findbytext(currentgenre))
    End If
End Sub
```

Comments

In `EditItemTemplate` of the DataGrid, the datasource of the DropDownList is set to a function, which returns a DataTable. In this function, the data can be retrieved from the database once, and then the DataTable can be inserted into the cache to reduce the number of database hits required. The complete source for this is available online.

See Also

DataGrid In-place Editing—`http://msdn.microsoft.com/msdnmag/issues/01/06/cutting/default.aspx`

13.21. Editing Items in a DataList

You want to edit an item from within a DataList.

Technique

Import the `System.Data` and `System.Data.SqlClient` namespaces for this example.
    The ASPX page is as follows:

```
<asp:DataList id="DL1" runat="server" OnCancelCommand="CancelItem"
OnDeleteCommand="DeleteItem" OnUpdateCommand="UpdateItem"
OnEditCommand="EditItem" DataKeyField="au_id" EditItemStyle-BackColor="yellow"
CellSpacing="2">
    <HeaderTemplate>
        <h1>List of Authors
        </h1>
    </HeaderTemplate>
    <ItemTemplate>
```

```
      <%# Container.DataItem("au_fname") %>  
<%# Container.DataItem("au_lname") %>
      <br />
      <%# Container.DataItem("Address") %>
      <br />
      <asp:Button CommandName="Edit" Text="Edit Record" runat="server" />
  </ItemTemplate>
  <SeparatorTemplate>
      <hr width="20%" />
  </SeparatorTemplate>
  <AlternatingItemStyle backcolor="Lime"></AlternatingItemStyle>
  <EditItemTemplate>
      <b>First Name</b>
      <asp:TextBox id="FNameTextBox"
Text='<%# Container.DataItem("au_fname") %>' runat="server" />
      <br />
      <b>Last Name</b>
      <asp:TextBox id="LNameTextBox"
Text='<%# Container.DataItem("au_lname") %>' runat="server" />
      <br />
      <b>Address</b>
      <asp:TextBox id="AddressTextBox"
Text='<%# Container.DataItem("Address") %>' runat="server" />
      <br />
      <asp:Button CommandName="Update" Text="Update" runat="server" />
       
      <asp:Button CommandName="Delete" Text="Delete" runat="server" />
       
      <asp:Button CommandName="Cancel" Text="Cancel" runat="server" />
  </EditItemTemplate>
  <FooterTemplate>
      <hr width="100%" />
  </FooterTemplate>
</asp:DataList>
```

In order to use a DataList for editing, certain properties must be set. The
EditItemTemplate setting specifies the appearance of the list when the selected record
in the DataList switches it to editing mode. Other attributes of the DataList control, such
as the OnEditCommand, OnUpdateCommand, OnDeleteCommand, and OnCancelCommand
controls, are passed the name of the events that are to be raised. These events are defined
within the <script> blocks or the codebehind file.

The second important property is the DataKeyField, which should be set to the
name of the primary key column in the datasource.

In <script runat="server" /> block or codebehind:

```
Private Sub Page_Load(Source As Object, E As EventArgs)
      If Not Page.IsPostback Then
```

```vb
                BindToList()
        End If
        'Clear any previous messages...
        MessageLabel.Text = ""
End Sub


Public Sub BindToList()
        Dim _Connection As New SqlConnection( _
"Server=localhost; Database=pubs; uid=user; pwd=password;")
        Dim _Command As New SqlCommand( _
"Select au_id, au_fname, au_lname, address From authors", _Connection)

        Try
            _Connection.Open()
            DL1.DataSource = _Command.ExecuteReader
            DL1.DataBind()
        Catch _Error As Exception
            MessageLabel.Text = _Error.Message
        Finally
            _Connection.Close()
        End Try
End Sub


Private Sub EditItem(Source As Object, E As DataListCommandEventArgs)
        'Set EditItemIndex property to the index of the record raising the event
        DL1.EditItemIndex = E.Item.ItemIndex
        BindToList()
End Sub


Private Sub UpdateItem(Source As Object, E As DataListCommandEventArgs)
        'Get References to the Textboxes...
        Dim _FName, _LName, _Address As TextBox

        _FName = CType(E.Item.FindControl("FNameTextBox"), TextBox)
        _LName = CType(E.Item.FindControl("LNameTextBox"), TextBox)
        _Address = CType(E.Item.FindControl("AddressTextBox"), TextBox)

        'Create the query...
        Dim _Query As String
        _Query = "Update authors Set au_fname='" & _FName.Text & _
"', au_lname='" & _LName.Text & "', address='" & _Address.Text & _
"' Where au_id='" & DL1.DataKeys(E.Item.ItemIndex) & "'"

        'Update the data source...
        Dim _Connection As New SqlConnection( _
"Server=localhost; Database=pubs; uid=user; pwd=password;")
        Dim _Command As New SqlCommand(_Query, _Connection)
```

```
        Try
            _Connection.Open()
            _Command.ExecuteNonQuery
                'Switch off the Edit mode
            DL1.EditItemIndex = -1
            BindToList()
        Catch _Error As Exception
            MessageLabel.Text = _Error.Message
        Finally
            _Connection.Close()
        End Try
End Sub

Private sub DeleteItem(Source As Object, E As DataListCommandEventArgs)
        'Create the query...
        Dim _Query As String
        _Query = "Delete From authors Where au_id='" & _
DL1.DataKeys(E.Item.ItemIndex) & "'"

        'Update the data source...
        Dim _Connection As New SqlConnection( _
"Server=localhost; Database=pubs; uid=user; pwd=password;")
        Dim _Command As New SqlCommand(_Query, _Connection)

        Try
            _Connection.Open()
            _Command.ExecuteNonQuery
            'Switch off the Edit mode
            DL1.EditItemIndex = -1
            BindToList()
        Catch _Error As Exception
            MessageLabel.Text = _Error.Message
        Finally
            _Connection.Close()
        End Try
End Sub

Private Sub CancelItem(Source As Object, E As DataListCommandEventArgs)
        'Switch off the Edit mode...
        DL1.EditItemIndex = -1
        BindToList()
End Sub
```

Comments

All the events and methods defined in this section are self-explanatory. The `EditItem()` method is responsible for enabling the editing mode of the DataList control. The `Update` and `Delete` event methods update or delete the currently selected record, whose index is stored in the `Index` property of the `DataListEventArgs` object.

The `UpdateItem()`, `DeleteItem()`, and `CancelItem()` events, when raised, also disable the editing mode of the DataList control and refresh it by calling the `BindToList()` method. The `BindToList()` method queries the datasource for records and then displays them in the control.

See Also

Section 13.4, "Data-binding to a DataList"

Section 13.5, "Implementing Sorting in a DataList"

Section 13.6, "Implementing Paging in a DataList"

IV

Common Tasks

14

Working with Classes

14.0. Introduction

Unlike ASP, ASP.NET's languages are full-fledged object-oriented compiled languages, not just scripting languages. Thus, as an ASP.NET developer, it is important that you be familiar with object-oriented programming features like classes, inheritance, methods, properties, and events. This chapter is by no means meant to provide a foundation in OOP, but it does demonstrate the syntax used for many of the more common features related to classes, which make up the foundation for all object-oriented programs. Although these features are not directly related to programming ASP.NET Web Forms, as an ASP.NET developer you will find that these features of classes are especially useful as you write more advanced and reusable applications.

14.1. Working with Namespaces

You want to define a namespace to help organize a group of classes.

Technique

Namespaces allow you to organize your classes into a hierarchical structure. All classes with a similar functionality can be grouped into one namespace. They also prevent naming conflicts. You can give two classes the same name, as long as they don't exist in the same namespace.

Namespaces are defined by the `namespace` keyword.

```
Namespace Shapes
    Class Rectangle
    ' Rectangle members
    End Class
End Namespace
```

Namespaces can also be nested, as this example illustrates:

```
Namespace Shapes
    Namespace Circular
        Class Circle
        ' Circle members
        End Class
        Class Ellipse
        ' Ellipse members
        End Class
    End Namespace

    Namespace Angular
        Class Rectangle
        ' Rectangle members
        End Class
        Class Square
        ' Square Members
        End Class
    End Namespace
End Namespace
```

Unlike other entities, namespaces are open-ended. You can declare them multiple times within the same program, or even across many programs, as illustrated here:

```
Namespace Shapes
    Class Rectangle
    ' Rectangle members
    End Class
End Namespace
Namespace Shapes
    Class Circle
    ' Circle members
    End Class
End Namespace
```

Using namespaces is as easy as declaring them. Here's an example:

```
Imports System
Class NamespaceExample
    Public Shared Sub Main()
        Dim c As Shapes.Circle = New Shapes.Circle()
        c.MyMethod
    End Sub
End Class
```

Classes that are declared in a namespace can be used by adding the appropriate namespace declaration before the class name. An alternative solution is to add the namespace of the classes to the namespace collection. You can do this by using the Import (VB.NET) or using (C#) statement.

```
            Imports System
            Imports Shapes
            Class NamespaceExample
                Public Shared Sub Main()
                    Dim c As Circle = New Circle()
                    c.MyMethod
                End Sub
            End Class
```

Beware that you can only use namespace names, so this example is invalid:

```
            Imports Shapes.Circle
```

Comments

In Visual Studio .NET, there is a small difference between the default root namespace for VB.NET projects and the default root namespace for C# projects. In a VB.NET project, the default root namespace is part of the project's properties. By default it will have the same name as the project. When a namespace is declared, it is actually added to this root namespace. Its real name is `MyProject.MyNameSpace`. In C# projects, the default root namespace is actually included in each class file, so it is clear what namespace the class resides within, and the namespace does not change when the class is copied from one project to another.

14.2. Using Access Modifiers

You want to control which classes have access to your class's members.

Technique

In general, there are three accessibility levels for class members:

- Public
- Private
- Protected

When you use the `public` keyword, it means that the member declaration that immediately follows `public` is available to everyone (in particular to the client programmer who uses the class).

```
        Class MyObject
            Public Sub MyFunction()
                ' function data
            End Sub
        End Class
```

When the programmer wants to use the class, he or she can access the `MyFunction()` member like this:

```
Dim o As MyObject = new MyObject()
o.MyFunction()
```

The `private` keyword means that no one can access that member, except that particular class inside methods of that class.

```
Class MyObject
    Private Sub MyFunction()
        ' function data
    End Sub
End Class
```

When you want to use the class and you try to use the `MyFunction()` member, you will get a compiler error. This code is invalid:

```
Dim o As MyObject = new MyObject()
o.MyFunction()  ' INVALID -> causes a compiler error !
```

However, this code is valid:

```
Class MyObject
    Private Sub MyFunction()
        ' function data
    End Sub
    Private Sub MyInternalFunction()
      ' The private declaration can be replaced by
      ' public or protected
        MyFunction()
        ' This is valid: MyFunction is called
        ' from within another member function of MyObject
    End Sub
End Class
```

To understand the protected access specifier, a little extra knowledge is required. The `protected` keyword deals with a concept called *inheritance*, which takes an existing class and adds new members to that class without touching the existing class. The original class is referred to as the *base class*. You can also change the behavior of existing members of the class. To inherit from an existing class, you say that your new class extends an existing class. Inheritance is discussed in Section 10.4. When you declare a member with the `protected` keyword, you say that no one can access that member, except that particular class inside methods of that class, and all members from an extended class, derived from that class. `Protected` has the same restrictions as `private`, but allows access from derived classes as well. This is illustrated by the next few examples:

```
Class MyObject
    Protected Sub MyFunction()
```

```
         ' function data
       End Sub
    End Class
```

The next example causes an error:

```
    Dim o As MyObject = new MyObject()
    o.MyFunction()  ' INVALID -> causes a compiler error !
```

But these examples work perfectly:

```
 Class MyObject
 Private Sub MyFunction()
   ' function data
 End Sub
 Private Sub MyInternalFunction()
➡' The private declaration can be replaced by public or protected
   MyFunction()
     ➡' This is valid: MyFunction is called from
     ➡' within another member function of MyObject
 End Sub
  End Class
```


```
 Class MyExtendedClass
 Inherits MyObject       ' MyObject is the base class for this inherited class

 Public Sub ExtraFunction()
➡' The public declaration can be replaced by private or protected
   MyFunction()
➡' This is valid: MyExtendedClass is an extended class from
➡' MyObject and has access to MyObject's protected members
  End Sub
   End Class
```

Besides these three, there are two additional access methods:

- `Friend` (internal in C#)
- `Protected Friend` (protected internal in C#)

When you declare a member as `friend`, it can be accessed from anywhere in the current project, but it is inaccessible from outside of the project. A `protected friend` member can be accessed from anywhere in the current project, and from all derived classes of that class. `Protected` is the only keyword that can be combined with the `friend` keyword.

Comments

The access specification for members is optional. If it is omitted from a class member, that member is treated as a private member.

14.3. Creating Properties

You want to create properties for your class to control access to its data members.

Technique

Create a private string called _firstName to store the value from your property. In the constructor for the class, initialize _firstName with a default value. Then create a public property called FirstName. Set the Get property to return the value of the _firstName variable, and the Set property to store the incoming value in _firstName.

The class is as follows:

```
Public Class recipe1503class
    Private _firstName As String

    Public Sub New()
        _firstName = ""
    End Sub

    Public Property FirstName() As String
        Get
            Return _firstName
        End Get
        Set(ByVal Value As String)
            _firstName = Value
        End Set
    End Property
End Class
```

In <script runat="server" /> block or codebehind:

```
Sub Page_Load(sender As Object, e As EventArgs)
    Dim myFirstClass As recipe1503class = New recipe1503class()
    myFirstClass.FirstName="Jeremy"
    Response.Write(myFirstClass.FirstName)
End Sub
```

Comments

To make the property read-only in VB.NET, simply add the ReadOnly keyword to the Property definition, just before the Property keyword. Similarly, you can use the WriteOnly keyword to make a property write-only. To make the property read-only or write-only in C#, just remove the code for the undesired action. If your class is in a *different* namespace you will need to import the name space using the Imports statement.

See Also

Section 14.1, "Working with Namespaces"

Section 14.2, "Using Access Modifiers"

14.4. Using Inheritance

You want your class as a subclass of another class, or you want to create a class specifically so that other classes can inherit from it.

Technique

Inheritance is an object-oriented programming technique that allows you to reuse existing functionality by placing it in generic classes (which you then inherit from) or subclass, with more specific classes. It is useful sometimes to create generic classes that can be used only to define child classes, and that cannot be instantiated themselves. These are called *abstract* classes, and are created with the abstract keyword in C languages like C#, and with the MustInherit keyword in VB. The following demonstrates the syntax used for inheritance by creating an abstract base class BankAccount and its child (or derived) class, CheckingAccount:

```
Namespace AspNetCookbook.Recipe1404vb
    Public MustInherit Class BankAccount
        Private _balance As Decimal = 0
        Public Property Balance() As Decimal
            Get
                Return _balance
            End Get
            Set(ByVal Value As Decimal)
                _balance = Value
            End Set
        End Property
        Protected Overridable Sub DepositFunds(ByVal Amount As Decimal)
            _balance += Amount
        End Sub
        Protected Overridable Sub WithdrawFunds(ByVal Amount As Decimal)
            _balance -= Amount
        End Sub
    End Class

    Public Class CheckingAccount
        Inherits BankAccount
        Public Const CheckFee As Decimal = 0.25
```

```
        Public Sub ProcessCheck(ByVal Amount As Decimal)
            MyBase.WithdrawFunds(Amount + CheckFee)
        End Sub
        Public Sub Deposit(ByVal Amount As Decimal)
            MyBase.DepositFunds(Amount)
        End Sub
    End Class
End Namespace
```

Note the use of the `Overridable` keyword on the `Subs`—this is necessary to allow child classes to override a class member. The C# equivalent is `virtual`. To specify that a class inherits from another class in VB, use the `Inherits` keyword and specify the class on the line following the class definition. In C#, simply follow the class name with a colon (`:`) and the name of the base or parent class. You can refer to a base class's members by using `MyBase` (or `base` in C#) just as you use `Me` (or `this` in C#) to refer to your class's own members.

Comments

Inheritance is an advanced programming technique that typically takes a long time to master. This recipe merely demonstrates some of the syntax required to implement inheritance in the .NET Framework. You will find examples of inheritance everywhere in .NET. For more on object-oriented programming, see the following references.

See Also

OOP with MS VB.NET and MS C# Step By Step, Microsoft Press

Review of OOP with MS VB.NET and MS C# Step By Step—
http://aspalliance.com/stevesmith/articles/ViewArticle.aspx?id=45

Design Patterns Explained, Shalloway/Trott, Addison-Wesley

Design Patterns, Gang of Four, Addison-Wesley

Refactoring, Fowler, Addison-Wesley

14.5. Using Interfaces

> You want your class to implement an interface, or you want to define an interface for other classes to implement.

Technique

Interfaces define contracts that classes must support. They allow code to refer to many kinds of classes in a similar fashion, because all of them must support the same interface. There are many interfaces defined in the .NET Framework that you will encounter as you write solutions for ASP.NET. In the following example, a simple interface is defined and two classes are shown that implement the interface.

```
Namespace AspNetCookbook.Recipe1405vb
    Public Interface IPrintable
        Function Print() As String
    End Interface

    Public Class User
        Implements IPrintable
        Private _username As String = "Default user"

        Public Property Username() As String
            Get
                Return _username
            End Get
            Set(ByVal Value As String)
                _username = Value
            End Set
        End Property

        Public Function Print() As String Implements IPrintable.Print
            Return Username
        End Function
    End Class

    Public Class Widget
        Implements IPrintable

        Public Function Print() As String Implements IPrintable.Print
            Return Me.ToString()
        End Function
    End Class
End Namespace
```

To define an interface, simply use the Interface keyword. By convention, interfaces are always named with a prefix of I and should typically be adjectives, because they usually describe a class (typically a noun). For instance, the interface in the previous example, after the two classes implement it, describes User and Widget in that it says that they are Printable. To add support for an interface to a class, simply use the Implements [InterfaceName] syntax, on a line following the class definition. In C#, the syntax for implementing interfaces is identical to the syntax for inheritance, simply follow the class name with a colon (:) and add supported interfaces there, separated by commas.

Note that when implementing interface-defined methods and properties in Visual Basic, it is necessary to add the Implements [Interface].[Member] syntax after each member definition. This is not necessary in C#.

Interfaces allow groups of disparate objects to be treated like one type of object, which is known as *polymorphism*. The following example demonstrates how the `User` and `Widget` classes can be referenced polymorphically using the `IPrintable` interface:

```
Private Sub Page_Load(ByVal sender As System.Object, _
   ByVal e As System.EventArgs)
   ' create an array of printable objects
   Dim arr() As AspNetCookbook.Recipe1405vb.IPrintable = _
   {New AspNetCookbook.Recipe1405vb.User(), _
   New AspNetCookbook.Recipe1405vb.Widget()}

   ' print each object
   Dim p As AspNetCookbook.Recipe1405vb.IPrintable
   For Each p In arr
      Response.Write(p.Print() + "<br>")
   Next
End Sub
```

Comments

Some of the most important .NET interfaces include:

- `IDisposable`—Resource cleanup
- `IEnumerable` and `IEnumerator`—Iteration through collections
- `IList`—Data-binding

See Also

Section 14.4, "Using Inheritance"

14.6. Overloading Methods

You want to create several different signatures (sets of parameters) for a given method. You want to allow optional parameters.

Technique

Both Visual Basic and C# support method overloading; only Visual Basic supports optional and named parameters and default values for optional parameters. The following code demonstrates method overloading with the `PrintLine()` method, and shows optional parameters with the `Filter()` method.

```
Private Sub Page_Load(ByVal sender As System.Object, _
   ByVal e As System.EventArgs)
   'Method Overloading
```

```
    PrintLine("This is some default text.")
    PrintLine("This is some red text.","Red")
    Response.Write("<hr>")

    ' Optional Parameters
    Filter(1)
    Response.Write("<hr>")
    Filter(ModelId := 2, ManufacturerId := 3)
    Response.Write("<hr>")
    Filter(ManufacturerId := 4)

End Sub


Private Sub PrintLine(ByVal Text As String)
    PrintLine(Text, "Black")
End Sub

Private Sub PrintLine(ByVal Text As String, ByVal Color As String)
    Response.Write("<font color=""" & Color & """>" & Text & "</font><br/>")
End Sub

Private Sub Filter(Optional ByVal MakeId As Integer = -9999, _
    Optional ByVal ModelId As Integer = -9999, _
    Optional ByVal ManufacturerId As Integer = -9999)
    Response.Write("Filtering by ")
    If MakeId <> -9999 Then
        Response.Write(" make " & MakeId)
    End If
    If ModelId <> -9999 Then
        Response.Write(" model " & ModelId)
    End If
    If ManufacturerId <> -9999 Then
        Response.Write(" manufacturer " & ManufacturerId)
    End If
End Sub
```

The Optional keyword defines your optional parameters, which must not be followed by any non-optional parameters. In VB, you cannot overload methods with variations that differ only by optional parameters, because these would be ambiguous. To specify a particular optional parameter, the parameter name is named and followed by := and the value (such as ModelId := 2). Named parameters and optional parameters are not supported in C#. Note that the Filter() method is not ideal because you have to set some kind of default value for the unset parameters, thus setting you up for errors if the default you choose later becomes a valid value for the parameter.

Method overloading is easily accomplished; simply redefine the method. Overloads must differ by signature, not just by return type.

Because C# does not support optional parameters, a workaround can be used, which takes advantage of the SqlTypes namespace provided in the .NET Framework. This technique is also useful in VB because it eliminates the need to hard-code a particular default value for unset parameters. The trick is to use a SqlType equivalent to the required parameter. Because all SqlTypes can be set to Null, the unset value is easily represented.

```csharp
<%@ Import Namespace="System.Data.SqlTypes" %>
<script Language="c#" runat="server">
void Page_Load(object sender, EventArgs e)
{
   // Method Overloading
   PrintLine("This is some default text.");
   PrintLine("This is some red text.","Red");
   Response.Write("<hr>");

   // Optional Parameters
   Filter(1, SqlInt32.Null, SqlInt32.Null);
   Response.Write("<hr>");
   Filter(SqlInt32.Null, 2, 3);
   Response.Write("<hr>");
   Filter(SqlInt32.Null, SqlInt32.Null, 4);
}

void Filter(SqlInt32 ModelId, SqlInt32 MakeId, _
   SqlInt32 ManufacturerId)
{
   Response.Write("Filtering by ");
   if(!ModelId.IsNull)
      Response.Write(" model " + ModelId);
   if(!MakeId.IsNull)
      Response.Write(" make " + MakeId);
   if(!ManufacturerId.IsNull)
      Response.Write(" manufacturer " + ManufacturerId);
}

void PrintLine(String Text)
{
   PrintLine(Text, "Black");
}

void PrintLine(String Text, String Color)
{
   Response.Write("<font color=\"" + Color + "\">" + Text + "</font><br/>");
}
</script>
```

Comments

See Also

Optional Parameters in C#—

http://aspalliance.com/stevesmith/articles/ViewArticle.aspx?id=33

14.7. Creating Multiple Constructors for a Class

You want to create several constructors for a class.

Technique

A constructor is a method that is called when an instance of a class is instantiated. You can overload constructors the same way you overload methods—by using different parameter lists. In the following code snippet, three constructors are created.

```
Public Class Recipe1407Class
   Private _Title As String
   Private _Chapter As Integer
   Private _SubTitle As String

   Public Sub New()
     _Chapter = 15
   End Sub
   Public Sub New(ByVal ttl As String)
     MyClass.New()
     _Title = ttl
   End Sub
   Public Sub New(ByVal ttl As String, ByVal subTtl As String)
     MyClass.New()
     _Title = ttl
     _SubTitle = subTtl
   End Sub


End Class
```

Comments

When overloading, it is a good idea to cascade constructors. In the previous code snippet, for example, the second constructor calls the default constructor. The logic implemented in the default constructor does not have to be re-implemented in the other constructor.

See Also

Section 14.2, "Using Access Modifiers"

Section 14.3, "Creating Properties"

Section 14.6, "Overloading Methods"

14.8. Using Shared Class Members

You want to create methods and/or properties that are available to all instances of your class, or outside of your class without requiring an instance of the class.

Technique

Classes are about encapsulating data. In most cases, each instance of a class (object) has its specific dataset that is independent from other instances. On some occasions, however, data items are common to all objects. Such members are referred to as *shared* (or static). As opposed to instance members, shared (static) members belong to the type rather than to a specific instance of that type.

To mark fields, methods, properties, operators, or constructors as shared, use the Shared (or static in C#) keyword. The following code snippet illustrates how to declare shared methods and properties.

```
Public Class Recipe1408Class
   Private Shared _InstanceCount As Integer = 0
   Public Sub New()
      Recipe1408Class._InstanceCount += 1
   End Sub
   Public Shared ReadOnly Property InstanceCount() As Integer
      Get
          Return Recipe1408Class._InstanceCount
      End Get
   End Property
   Public Shared Sub ResetCounter()
      Recipe1408Class._InstanceCount = 0
   End Sub
End Class
```

Comments

The InstanceCount property reflects the number of instances of the Recipe1408Class. Whenever an instance of the class is created, the InstanceCount property is incremented by means of the constructor (for brevity, no decrement is implemented).

Note that it is impossible to access instance members inside of a static member. Also, there is a difference between VB.NET and C# in how shared members are used. In VB.NET, you can access shared members by using both the class name and the instance name. In C#, only the former is allowed.

See Also

Section 14.2, "Using Access Modifiers"

Section 14.3, "Creating Properties"

14.9. Handling Events

You want to handle an event raised by a control used by your class.

Technique

Objects can signal that an action occurred by means of events. A Button object, for example, can signal when—as a result of user interaction—it is clicked. You can connect (wire/handle) your own method to an event for it to be executed when the event is raised.

In order to work with events in VB.NET, you will use the keywords `WithEvents` and `Handles`. The former is used for declaring a variable that refers to an object that can raise events. With the latter, you can specify a procedure that should be executed when a given event is triggered. In C#, there is no equivalent to `WithEvents`. In order to hook up to an event, use the `+=` operator. In the following code snippet, a `myButton` object of `Button` type is declared with event handling enabled:

```
    Protected WithEvents myButton As _
New System.Web.UI.WebControls.Button()
```

In order to assign an event handler to an object, you need to declare a method with the `Handles` modifier. In the following code snippet, the method `myButton_Click` is declared as the handler of the `Click` event of `myButton`:

```
    Protected Sub myButton_Click(ByVal sender As System.Object,
➥ ByVal e As System.EventArgs) Handles myButton.Click
        Response.Write(CType(sender, System.Web.UI.WebControls.Button).
➥Id & " was clicked")
    End Sub
```

When working with events in ASP.NET, you can wire events by using an appropriate attribute. In the following example, the `onClick` attribute of the `asp:Button` control is used to wire the `myButton_Click` method to the `Click` event.

```
    <asp:Button runat="server" id="myButton" onClick="myButton_Click"
Text="Click Me" />
```

Note that if you use more than one of these techniques, such as the attribute *and* the `Handles` keyword, your event handler will be invoked multiple times for each event.

Comments

The name of the event handler is up to the programmer's discretion. However, using the convention `[Object Name]_[Event]` yields code that is easier to read.

The signature of the `Button_OnClick` method is important. The number of parameters it has and their types are both determined by the delegate used by the `Click` event. A *delegate* is a class that can hold a reference to a method. In the .NET Framework, delegates are used to implement the event-handling functionality.

It is possible to wire more than one method to an event. Also, you can assign the same method to multiple events.

In ASP.NET, you can instruct the page framework to automatically wire the `Init` and `Load` events of the `Page` object. To that end, you need to define methods with appropriate signatures named `Page_Init` or `Page_Load`, respectively, and set the `AutoEventsWireup` attribute of the `Page` directive to `true`.

See Also
Section 2.6, "Raising Events from a User Control"

Manipulating Strings

15.0. Introduction

Strings of text make up the primary content of almost any Web page, so understanding how to work with this data type is critical for any Web developer. This chapter covers many of the techniques available in the .NET Framework for manipulating string data, and although it is not specifically part of ASP.NET, it is definitely something that ASP.NET developers need to understand. Most of these techniques are simple to implement once you know which method to call or which framework class to use, and it is primarily this latter knowledge that you will gain by referring to the examples in this chapter when you find yourself needing to perform some string manipulation.

15.1. Dissecting Strings

You want to access or change a portion of a string, but not the entire string.

Technique

Visual Basic .NET supports many of the VB6 legacy string operations like `Left()`, `Right()`, `Mid()`, `Trim()`, and so on. However, these require the use of the `Microsoft.VisualBasic` namespace and are not necessary because these operations can easily be performed by the built-in methods of any string variable. The primary method that you will use when dissecting strings in .NET is `.Substring()`, which returns a substring of the current string given a starting position and a length. The following example demonstrates how to use `.Substring()` and other `System.String` properties to manipulate a string in a variety of ways.

```
Private Sub Page_Load(ByVal sender As System.Object, _
    ByVal e As System.EventArgs)
```

```
    Dim source as String = "Try not.  Do.  Or do not.  There is no try."
    Response.Write("Source String: " & source & "<hr>")

    Dim firstEight As String = Left(source,8) 'Or use .Substring(0,8)
    Response.Write("First eight characters: " & firstEight & "<hr>")

  Dim last16 As String = source.Substring(source.Length-16, 16)
  Response.Write("Last sixteen characters: " & last16 & "<hr>")

  Dim capitalizeNot As String = source.Replace("not", "NOT")
  Response.Write("Capitalize NOT: " & capitalizeNot & "<hr>")

  Dim capitalizeFirstNot As String = _
    source.Substring(0, source.IndexOf("not")) & _
              source.Substring(source.IndexOf("not"), 3).ToUpper() & _
              source.Substring(source.IndexOf("not") + 3, _
    source.Length - (source.IndexOf("not") + 3))
  Response.Write("Capitalize first NOT: " & capitalizeFirstNot & "<hr>")

  Dim capitalizeLastNot As String = _
    source.Substring(0, source.LastIndexOf("not")) & _
     source.Substring(source.LastIndexOf("not"), 3).ToUpper() & _
     source.Substring(source.LastIndexOf("not") + 3, _
     source.Length - (source.LastIndexOf("not") + 3))
  Response.Write("Capitalize last NOT: " & capitalizeLastNot & "<hr>")
End Sub
```

The Left() method demonstrates that it is still supported.

See Also

String Class—http://msdn.microsoft.com/library/en-us/cpref/html/
frlrfsystemstringclasstopic.asp

15.2. Converting ASCII Codes into Characters

You want to convert ASCII numeric codes into characters, or vice versa.

Technique

With ASP.NET you can quickly convert an entire string into an array of ASCII bytes and back into a string. To go from a string to an ASCII byte array, use the System.Text.Encoding.ASCII.GetBytes() method. To display the bytes, create a For/Next loop to write out each byte. To convert the ASCII byte array back into a string, you must first convert it to a character array using the

`System.Text.Encoding.ASCII.GetChars()` method, and then convert the character array into a string by passing it into the constructor of a new string object.

In `<script runat="server" />` block or codebehind:

```
Sub Page_Load(sender As Object, e As EventArgs)
  Dim i As Integer
  Dim myBytes As Byte() = System.Text.Encoding.ASCII.GetBytes("Hello World")
  For i=0 to myBytes.Length-1
    Response.Write(myBytes(i).ToString() & " ")
  Next i
  Dim myChars as Char() = System.Text.Encoding.ASCII.GetChars(myBytes)
  Dim myString as String = New String(myChars)
  Response.Write("<BR>" & myString)
End Sub
```

See Also

Section 15.3, "Converting Unicode Codes into Characters"

15.3. Converting Unicode Codes into Characters

You want to convert Unicode numeric codes into their character equivalents, or vice versa.

Technique

With ASP.NET, you can quickly convert an entire string into an array of Unicode bytes and back into a string. To go from a string to a Unicode byte array, you use the `System.Text.Encoding.Unicode.GetBytes()` method. To display the bytes, create a `For/Next` loop to write out each byte. To convert the Unicode byte array back into a string, you must first convert it to a character array using the `System.Text.Encoding.Unicode.GetChars()` method, and then convert the character array into a string by passing it into the constructor of a new string object.

In `<script runat="server" />` block or codebehind:

```
Sub Page_Load(sender As Object, e As EventArgs)
  Dim i As Integer
  Dim myBytes As Byte() = System.Text.Encoding.Unicode.GetBytes("Hello World")
  For i=0 to myBytes.Length-1
    Response.Write(myBytes(i).ToString() & " ")
  Next i
  Dim myChars as Char() = System.Text.Encoding.Unicode.GetChars(myBytes)
  Dim myString as String = New String(myChars)
  Response.Write("<BR>" & myString)
End Sub
```

See Also

Section 15.2, "Converting ASCII Codes into Characters"

15.4. Looping Through Each Character of a String

You need to process a string one character at a time.

Technique

All strings in .NET support the `ToCharArray()` method, which provides easy access to the string's contents as an array of characters. The following code demonstrates how to convert to a character array and then loop through each character.

```
<%@ Page Language="vb" %>
<script runat="server">
Private Sub Page_Load(ByVal sender As System.Object, _
   ByVal e As System.EventArgs)
    Dim input As String = "ASPAlliance.com"
    Dim chArray As Char()
    chArray = input.ToCharArray()
    Dim I As Integer
    For I = 0 To chArray.GetLength(0) - 1
        Response.Write(chArray(I) & "<br>")
    Next
End Sub
</script>
```

15.5. Reversing a String

You want to reverse all the words or characters in a given string.

Technique

The key to reversing a string is to convert it into an array of characters (or words), and then reverse the order of those characters (words).

```
<%@ Page Language="vb" %>
<script runat="server">
Private Sub Page_Load(ByVal sender As System.Object, _
```

```
        ByVal e As System.EventArgs)
        Dim input As String = "ASPAlliance.com - The #1 ASP.NET Community"
        Response.Write(Reverse(input) & "<br>")
        Response.Write(ReverseWords(input))
End Sub
Private Function Reverse(ByVal input As String) As String
        Dim chArray As Char() = input.ToCharArray()
        Dim swap As Char
        Dim length As Integer = chArray.GetLength(0)
        Dim I As Integer
        For I = 0 To (length / 2) - 1
            swap = chArray(I)
            chArray(I) = chArray(length - I - 1)
            chArray(length - I - 1) = swap
        Next
        Return New String(chArray)
End Function

Private Function ReverseWords(ByVal input As String) As String
        Dim strArray As String() = input.Split(" ")
        Dim swap As String
        Dim length As Integer = strArray.GetLength(0)
        Dim I As Integer
        For I = 0 To (length / 2) - 1
            swap = strArray(I)
            strArray(I) = strArray(length - I - 1)
            strArray(length - I - 1) = swap
        Next
        Return String.Join(" ", strArray)
End Function
</script>
```

Comments

For the maximum efficiency, these loops don't touch any one character (or word) twice.

See Also

Splitting—http://msdn.microsoft.com/library/en-us/cpref/html/
frlrfsystemstringclasssplittopic.asp

Joining—http://msdn.microsoft.com/library/en-us/cpref/html/
frlrfsystemstringclassjointopic.asp

15.6. Converting the Case of a String

You need to convert the case of a string.

Technique

All strings in .NET support the `ToUpper()` and `ToLower()` methods, the preferred methods to use for converting strings between upper- and lowercase, because they work across any .NET language. VB.NET also supports the `UCase()` and `LCase()` functions.

```
<%@ Page Language="vb" %>
<script runat="server">
Private Sub Page_Load(ByVal sender As System.Object, _
    ByVal e As System.EventArgs)
    Dim input As String = "ASPAlliance.com"
    Dim UPPER, lower As String
    UPPER = input.ToUpper()
    lower = input.ToLower()
    Response.Write(input & "<br>" & UPPER & "<br>" & lower)
End Sub
</script>
```

15.7. Removing Whitespace from a String

You want to trim spaces, tabs, or other whitespace from the beginning or end of your string.

Technique

The `System.String` class provides several methods for dealing with whitespace, including options that support removing whitespace from the beginning, end or both sides of a string. It also supports padding a string with whitespace so that it is a certain length of characters.

```
<%@ Page Language="vb" %>
<script runat="server">
Private Sub Page_Load(ByVal sender As System.Object, _
    ByVal e As System.EventArgs)
    Dim input As String = " ASPAlliance.com "
    OutputTextBox.Text = "[" & input & "]" & System.Environment.NewLine
    ' Trim Left
    OutputTextBox.Text &= "[" & input.TrimStart() & "]" & _
    System.Environment.NewLine
    ' Trim Right
    OutputTextBox.Text &= "[" & input.TrimEnd() & "]" & _
```

```
    System.Environment.NewLine
     ' Trim All
     OutputTextBox.Text &= "[" & input.Trim() & "]" & _
    System.Environment.NewLine
     ' Pad Left
     OutputTextBox.Text &= "[" & input.PadLeft(30) & "]" & _
    System.Environment.NewLine
     ' Pad Right
     OutputTextBox.Text &= "[" & input.PadRight(30) & "]" & _
    System.Environment.NewLine
End Sub
</script>
<html>
<body>
<form id="Test" method="post" runat="server">
  <asp:TextBox id="OutputTextBox" runat="server" TextMode="MultiLine"
  Height="157px" Width="306px"></asp:TextBox>
</form>
</body>
</html>
```

See Also

Manipulating Strings—http://msdn.microsoft.com/library/en-us/cpguide/html/
cpconmanipulatingstrings.asp

15.8. Encoding Special Characters in a String

You want to encode certain special characters in a string, such as for use in a
SQL statement or a URL.

Technique

Certain characters must be encoded for use by various languages like SQL or HTML.
For SQL statements, it is generally sufficient to replace single quotes with two single
quotes anywhere they are encountered within string parameters. Note that ideally you
should be using stored procedures and parameter lists, which eliminates the need for this.
URLs require special encoding as well, so anytime you create a URL with a query
string that includes parameter data, it should be UrlEncoded. Similarly, in order for
HTML or XML to display data that includes special characters properly, it should be
HtmlEncoded. The following example demonstrates each of these techniques.

```
Private Sub Page_Load(ByVal sender As System.Object, _
    ByVal e As System.EventArgs)
```

```
    Response.Write("View Source to see the actual HTML
➥ used for these strings.<br><br>")

    Dim name As String = "Ray's"
    Dim sql As String = "SELECT * FROM Restaraunts
➥WHERE Name = '" & name.Replace("'","''") & "'"
    Response.Write("SQL: " & sql & "<hr>")

    Dim sentence As String = "Jay&Bob's Great Adventure"
    Dim url As String = "http://aspalliance.com/cookbook/default.aspx?" & _
    Server.UrlEncode(sentence)
    Response.Write("Encoded Querystring: " & url & "<hr>")

    Dim input As String = "If x < y Then Print x & <y>"
    Response.Write("HTML Encoded input: " & Server.HtmlEncode(input))
End Sub
```

Comments

The `UrlEncode` and `HtmlEncode` methods reside in the `Server` class, which is only accessible from a valid `HttpContext`. To use these methods outside of ASP.NET pages and controls, use `System.Web.HttpContext.Current`'s `Server` class to access the properties.

15.9. Encrypting a String

You want to encrypt or decrypt a string.

Technique

Encryption and description classes are found in the `System.Security.Cryptography` namespace. This example performs symmetric (reversible with the same key) encryption on a string given a particular password. This can be a useful way to protect user information in a database. This example uses the TripleDES algorithm, with a key length of 192 bits (24 bytes).

The following code includes two functions: `EncryptData()`, which takes a string and a password and returns a `Byte` array, and `DecryptData`, which takes a `Byte` array and a password and returns a string. The IV Byte array in each method is an eight-byte initialization vector required for the algorithm, which can be set to whatever values you like (keep it the same for encryption and decryption). The comments in the example describe the process step-by-step.

```
Private Sub Page_Load(sender As Object, e As System.EventArgs)
    Dim clearText As String = "Try not.  Do.  Or do not.  There is no try."
    Dim passPhrase As String = "Password"
    Dim encoder As New System.Text.UTF8Encoding()
```

```
    Response.Write(("Clear Text: " + clearText))
    Response.Write("<hr>")

    Dim cypherText As Byte() = EncryptData(clearText, passPhrase)

    Response.Write(("Encrypted Text: " + encoder.GetString(cypherText)))
    Response.Write("<hr>")
    Response.Write(("Decrypted Text: " + DecryptData(cypherText, passPhrase)))
    Response.Write("<hr>")
End Sub 'Page_Load


Private Function EncryptData(ClearText As String, password As String) As Byte()
    Dim keySize As Integer = 24 ' 192 bit
    Dim hash() As Byte
    Dim passwordArray() As Byte = New [Byte](password.Length) {}
    Dim tdeskey(keySize-1) As Byte
    Dim IV As Byte() = {1, 2, 3, 4, 5, 6, 7, 8}
    Dim encoder As New System.Text.UTF8Encoding()
    encoder.GetBytes(password, 0, password.Length, passwordArray, 0)


    ' hash the password into the key byte array
    Dim SHA As New System.Security.Cryptography.SHA1CryptoServiceProvider()
    hash = SHA.ComputeHash(passwordArray)

    Dim i As Integer
    For i = 0 To keySize - 1
        tdeskey(i) = hash((i Mod hash.Length))
    Next i
    ' Encrypt the string data
    ' Create a service provider
    Dim tdes As
    New System.Security.Cryptography.TripleDESCryptoServiceProvider()
    ' Create an ICryptTransform using the key and initialization vector
    Dim cryptoTransform As System.Security.Cryptography.ICryptoTransform = _
    tdes.CreateEncryptor(tdeskey, IV)
    ' Create an output stream to hold the encrypted data
    Dim EncryptedStream As New System.IO.MemoryStream()
    ' Get the input string into a byte array
    Dim input As Byte() = encoder.GetBytes(ClearText)
    ' Create a CryptoStream to perform the encryption
    Dim crStream As New System.Security.Cryptography.CryptoStream( _
    EncryptedStream, cryptoTransform, _
    System.Security.Cryptography.CryptoStreamMode.Write)
    ' Write the input data to the output stream via the cryptoStream
    crStream.Write(input, 0, input.Length)
    crStream.FlushFinalBlock()
```

```
    ' Reset the output stream to its beginning
    EncryptedStream.Position = 0
    ' Read the encrypted stream back into a string
    Dim output(EncryptedStream.Length) As Byte
    EncryptedStream.Read(output, 0, CInt(EncryptedStream.Length))
    crStream.Close()
    EncryptedStream.Close()
    ' Return the result as a string
    Return output
End Function 'EncryptData


Private Function DecryptData(CypherText() As Byte, password As String) _
➡As String
    Dim keySize As Integer = 24 ' 192 bit
    Dim hash() As Byte
    Dim passwordArray() As Byte = New [Byte](password.Length) {}
    Dim tdeskey(keySize-1) As Byte
    Dim IV As Byte() = {1, 2, 3, 4, 5, 6, 7, 8}
    Dim encoder As New System.Text.UTF8Encoding()
    encoder.GetBytes(password, 0, password.Length, passwordArray, 0)

    ' hash the password into the key byte array
    Dim SHA As New System.Security.Cryptography.SHA1CryptoServiceProvider()
    hash = SHA.ComputeHash(passwordArray)

    Dim i As Integer
    For i = 0 To keySize - 1
        tdeskey(i) = hash((i Mod hash.Length))
    Next i
    ' Decrypt the string data
    ' Create a service provider
    Dim tdes As New _
    System.Security.Cryptography.TripleDESCryptoServiceProvider()
    ' Create an ICryptTransform using the key and initialization vector
    Dim cryptoTransform As System.Security.Cryptography.ICryptoTransform = _
    tdes.CreateDecryptor(tdeskey, IV)
    ' Create an output stream to hold the encrypted data
    Dim DecryptedStream As New System.IO.MemoryStream()
    ' Create a CryptoStream to perform the encryption
    Dim crStream As New System.Security.Cryptography.CryptoStream(_
    DecryptedStream, _
    cryptoTransform, System.Security.Cryptography.CryptoStreamMode.Write)
    ' Write the input data to the output stream via the cryptoStream
    crStream.Write(CypherText, 0, CypherText.Length - 1)
    crStream.FlushFinalBlock()
    ' Reset the output stream to its beginning
```

```
    DecryptedStream.Position = 0
    ' Read the encrypted stream back into a string
    Dim output(DecryptedStream.Length) As Byte
    DecryptedStream.Read(output, 0, CInt(DecryptedStream.Length))
    crStream.Close()
    DecryptedStream.Close()
    ' Return the result as a string
    Return encoder.GetString(output)
End Function 'DecryptData
```

Comments

The cryptographic providers are designed to operate with streams, which can make them difficult to comprehend at first. The I/O article mentioned below provides a useful introduction to streams from Microsoft.

See Also

I/O, I/O, It's Off to Work I Go—http://msdn.microsoft.com/library/default.asp?url=/library/en-us/dncscol/html/csharp01162003.asp

SymmetricAlgorithm Class—http://msdn.microsoft.com/library/en-us/cpref/html/frlrfSystemSecurityCryptographySymmetricAlgorithmClassTopic.asp

Keeping Secrets: A Guide to VB.NET Cryptography—http://www.devx.com/security/Article/7019/0/page/4

Encrypting passwords with SHA1 in .NET and Java—http://aspalliance.com/thycotic/articles/view.aspx?id=2

String Encryption with VB.NET—http://www.devarticles.com/art/1/249/4

15.10. Hashing a String

You want to create a one-way hash of a string.

Technique

Hashing a string creates a hash that is specific to the original string, but which cannot be converted back into the source string. Several hashing algorithms exist, and they are frequently used to store passwords securely. Stealing the hashed passwords does a hacker no good, because these cannot be used to access the system. When each user logs in, whatever the user enters is hashed using the same algorithm that was used to store the passwords, and then the hashes are compared to see whether they match. In .NET, the System.Security.Cryptography namespace contains classes for performing hashes. In the following example, the SHA1 algorithm is used.

```
Private Sub Page_Load(sender As Object, e As System.EventArgs)
    Dim clearText As String = "Try not.  Do.  Or do not.  There is no try."
    Dim encoder As New System.Text.UTF8Encoding()

    Response.Write(("Clear Text: " + clearText))
    Response.Write("<hr>")

    Dim sha As New System.Security.Cryptography.SHA1Managed()
    Dim input As Byte() = encoder.GetBytes(clearText)
    Dim output As Byte() = sha.ComputeHash(input)
    Response.Write(("Hash Value: " + encoder.GetString(output)))
End Sub
```

Comments

SHA1 stands for US Secure Hash Algorithm 1.

> **See Also**
>
> RFC3174 (SHA1)—`http://www.faqs.org/rfcs/rfc3174.html`
>
> Encrypting Passwords with SHA1 in .NET and Java—`http://aspalliance.com/thycotic/`
> `articles/view.aspx?id=2`

15.11. Appending Several Strings

You want to create one string from many smaller strings in the most efficient way possible.

Technique

Concatenating strings is extremely expensive because they are *immutable*—that is, they cannot be altered once created. To change a string by adding another string to it, the two source strings are both copied into a new string, and then the two original strings are (eventually) cleaned up by the garbage collector. Doing this over and over is very inefficient and uses a great deal of memory. Any time you need to concatenate strings more than a couple of times, you should use the `System.Text.StringBuilder` class. The following example demonstrates the benefits this can have:

```
Private Sub Page_Load(sender As Object, e As System.EventArgs)
    Dim startTime, endTime As DateTime
    Dim output As String = ""
    Dim span As TimeSpan
    Dim i As Integer

    ' build a string using concatenation
```

```
   startTime = DateTime.Now
   For i = 1 To 9999
      output += i.ToString() + " "
   Next i
   'Response.Write(output);
   endTime = DateTime.Now
   span = New TimeSpan(endTime.Ticks - startTime.Ticks)
   Response.Write(("<hr>Time Using Concatenation: " & _
   span.TotalSeconds.ToString() & "<hr>"))

   ' build a string using stringbuilder
   startTime = DateTime.Now
   Dim sb As New System.Text.StringBuilder(10000)
   For i = 1 To 9999
      sb.Append(i.ToString())
      sb.Append(" ")
   Next i
   'Response.Write(sb.ToString());
   endTime = DateTime.Now
   span = New TimeSpan(endTime.Ticks - startTime.Ticks)
   Response.Write(("<hr>Time Using StringBuilder: " & _
   span.TotalSeconds.ToString() & "<hr>"))
End Sub 'Page_Load
```

Comments

If you are simply going to be streaming the result to Response (via Response.Write(), for instance) or another stream, you gain nothing by using a StringBuilder. Instead just Write() each substring directly to the output stream as you come to it.

See Also

StringBuilder Class—http://msdn.microsoft.com/library/en-us/cpref/html/ frlrfSystemTextStringBuilderClassTopic.asp

Section 16.13, "Benchmarking a Section of Code"

15.12. Formatting Strings

You want to format a date or number in a particular string format.

Technique

The ToString() methods of a double and datetime are overloaded to provide formatting options. For a complete list of formatting options, see

```
http://msdn.microsoft.com/library/en-us/cpref/html/
frlrfsystemdoubleclasstostringtopic2.asp and
http://msdn.microsoft.com/library/en-us/cpref/html/
frlrfsystemdatetimeclasstostringtopic.asp.
```

The ASPX page is as follows:

```
<html>
  <body>
    <form id="Recipe1612vb" method="post" runat="server">
    <asp:Label ID="MyNumberLabel" Runat="server"></asp:Label><br>
    <asp:Label ID="MyDateLabel" Runat="server"></asp:Label>
     </form>
  </body>
</html>
```

In `<script runat="server" />` block or codebehind:

```
Sub Page_Load(sender As Object, e As EventArgs)
  Dim myNumber As Double=12345678.9
  MyNumberLabel.Text=myNumber.ToString("$###,###,###.00")
  MyDateLabel.Text=DateTime.Now.ToString("MMMM dd, yyyy")
End Sub
```

See Also

Section 16.5, "Formatting Numbers"

Section 16.12, "Formatting Dates and Times"

Double.ToString() method—http://msdn.microsoft.com/library/en-us/cpref/
html/frlrfsystemdoubleclasstostringtopic2.asp

DateTime.ToString() method—http://msdn.microsoft.com/library/en-us/
cpref/html/frlrfsystemdatetimeclasstostringtopic.asp

DateTime Format Strings—http://msdn.microsoft.com/library/en-us/cpguide/html/
cpcondatetimeformatstrings.asp

Numeric Format Strings—http://msdn.microsoft.com/library/en-us/cpguide/html/
cpconstandardnumericformatstrings.asp

15.13. Counting the Total Number of Words in a String

You want to determine the number of words in a string.

Technique

Using the `String` class's `Split()` method, it is easy to create an array of strings from another string based on a delimiter. To find the number of words in a string, simply choose a single space as the delimiter. This simple technique is fairly accurate, but returns inaccurate results if there are multispace substrings (these will each appear to be a word).

```
Private Sub Page_Load(sender As Object, e As System.EventArgs)
    Dim inputString As String = "Try not. Do. Or do not. There is no try."
    Response.Write(("Input: " + inputString))
    Response.Write("<hr>")
    Response.Write(("Word Count: " + WordCount(inputString).ToString()))
End Sub 'Page_Load

Private Function WordCount(input As String) As Integer
    ' note that " " will appear as a word using this method.
    Dim separators As Char() = {" "c}
    Dim words As String() = input.Split(separators)

    ' remove this loop for production code
    Dim i As Integer
    For i = 0 To words.Length - 1
        Response.Write(("[" + words(i) + "]<br>"))
    Next i

    Return words.Length
End Function 'WordCount
```

Comments

A more accurate word count algorithm might be achieved using the `System.Text.RegularExpressions` library and the \w or \s expressions, which match word characters and space characters, respectively.

See Also

Section 15.14, "Converting a String into an Array of Strings"

15.14. Converting a String into an Array of Strings

You want to convert a string into an array of substrings.

Technique

Using the `String` class's `Split()` method, it is easy to create an array of strings from another string based on a delimiter. This recipe is essentially the same as the previous one. Note that the \n character in C# or the `System.Environment.NewLine` character in VB can be used as a delimiter if you're interested in counting the number of lines in a string.

```
Private Sub Page_Load(sender As Object, e As System.EventArgs)
    Dim inputString As String = "Try not. Do. Or do not. There is no try."
    Response.Write(("Input: " + inputString))
    Response.Write("<hr>")
    Response.Write(("Sentence Count: " + SentenceCount(inputString).ToString()))
End Sub 'Page_Load


Private Function SentenceCount(input As String) As Integer
    ' note that "  " will appear as a word using this method.
    Dim separators As Char() = {"."c}
    Dim sentences As String() = input.Split(separators)

    ' remove this loop for production code
    Dim i As Integer
    For i = 0 To sentences.Length - 1
        Response.Write(("[" + sentences(i) + "]<br>"))
    Next i

    Return sentences.Length - 1
    ' subtract one to get 1 sentence per instance of a period
End Function 'SentenceCount
```

See Also

Section 15.13, "Counting the Total Number of Words in a String"

15.15. Counting the Occurrences of One String Within Another String

You want to count how many occurrences of a particular string occur within another string.

Technique

Create a `Regex` object using the string you want to count. Pass the string you want to search to the `Matches(string searchString)` method of the `Regex` object. The `Matches` method returns a `MatchCollection`. The `Count` property of the `MatchCollection` will have the number of strings that matched the search.

The ASPX page is as follows:

```
<table id="Table1" cellSpacing="1" cellPadding="1">
  <tr>
    <td>
      <p>
        <asp:TextBox id="SearchString" width="550" rows="3"
TextMode="MultiLine" wrap="true" runat="server">
Any intelligent fool can make things bigger, more complex, and
more violent. It takes a touch of genius to move in the opposite
direction. E. F. Schumacher</asp:TextBox><br />
        <asp:TextBox id="FindString" runat="server">more</asp:TextBox>
      </p>
      <p>
        <asp:Button id="CountString" runat="server"
Text="Count Occurances of String"
OnClick="CountString_Click"></asp:Button></p>
    </td>
  </tr>
  <tr>
    <td colspan="2"> </td>
  </tr>
  <tr>
    <td>
      <p>
        <asp:Label id="Output" runat="server"></asp:Label></p>
    </td>
  </tr>
</table>
```

In `<script runat="server" />` block or codebehind:

```
Private Function CountStrings(ByVal searchString As String, _
ByVal regexString As String) As Integer
```

```
    Dim regex As New Regex(regexString)
    Return regex.Matches(searchString).Count
  End Function


  Private Sub CountString_Click(ByVal sender As System.Object, _
ByVal e As System.EventArgs)
    Output.Text = CountStrings(SearchString.Text, _
FindString.Text).ToString()
  End Sub
```

Comments

The `Matches(String searchString)` method of the `Regex` object searches through the `searchString` looking for any occurrences of the `regexString`. The `regexString`, which is used when creating the `Regex` object, is a regular expression string or pattern. Any alphanumeric string can be used, but a regular expression results in much more powerful searches.

See Also

Regex Constructor (String)—`http://msdn.microsoft.com/library/en-us/cpref/html/ frlrfSystemTextRegularExpressionsRegexClassctorTopic2.asp in .Net Framework Class Library`

Regex.`Matches` Method (String)—`http://msdn.microsoft.com/library/en-us/cpref/ html/frlrfsystemtextregularexpressionsregexclassmatchestopic1.asp` in the .NET Framework Class Library

`MatchCollection.Count` Property—`http://msdn.microsoft.com/library/en-us/ cpref/html/frlrfsystemtextregularexpressionsmatchcollectionclasscount- topic.asp` in the .NET Framework Class Library

16

Working with Numbers, Dates, and Times

16.0. Introduction

One of the most common sources of questions in online forums and communities like `ASPAlliance.com` involves working with and formatting numbers, dates, and times. Naturally most non-trivial applications require some code to access, modify, or present numeric and/or date-time data, so it makes sense that this common requirement is a frequent source of confusion. In this chapter, you will find examples describing how to perform many of the most common operations on numbers, dates, and times using the .NET Framework. Although presented in VB.NET, wherever possible the .NET routines used in this chapter are available to C# and any other .NET language, and are not VB-specific.

16.1. Converting a String to a Number

You want to convert a string into a numeric type.

Technique

Each of the numeric types supports a `Parse()` method that accepts a string. You should use this for your conversions from strings to numeric types, because it relies on the .NET Framework rather than any language-specific feature of VB or C#.

```
Private Sub Page_Load(sender As Object, e As System.EventArgs)
  ' converting strings to numeric types
  Dim myByte As Byte = [Byte].Parse("5")
```

```
  Dim myInt As Integer = Int32.Parse("3")
  Dim myDouble As Double = [Double].Parse("123.456")
  Dim myDecimal As Decimal = [Decimal].Parse("5.35")
End Sub 'Page_Load
```

Comments

Note that if the string is not in the proper format, an exception will be thrown, so provide proper exception handling and/or format checking whenever you use this technique.

16.2. Working on a Range of Numbers

You want to perform some work on each number within a given range.

Technique

You can retrieve a range of numbers in ASP.NET much like many other programming languages, by using a `for/next` loop. You create a `for` statement that sets a variable (`i`) to your initial value and specify a number to which it should run (`100`). You also have the option of setting the incremental or decremental amount for each loop by setting the `Step` value. The following example populates a drop-down list with all even numbers between 2 and 100.

The ASPX page is as follows:

```
<html>
  <body>
    <form id="Recipe1702vb" method="post" runat="server">
      <asp:DropDownList ID="MyDropDownList" Runat="server" />
    </form>
  </body>
</html>
```

In `<script runat="server" />` block or codebehind:

```
Sub Page_Load(sender As Object, e As EventArgs)
  Dim i As Integer
  Dim li As ListItem
  For i=2 To 100 Step 2
    li=new ListItem(i.ToString())
    MyDropDownList.Items.Add(li)
  Next
End Sub
```

16.3. Converting Numbers Between Different Bases

> You want to convert a number from one base to another, such as from decimal to binary or hexadecimal.

Technique

Use the `System.Convert.ToInt32(string input, int base)` method to convert a number from binary, octal, or hexadecimal to decimal. Use the `System.Convert.ToString(int decimalValue, int base)` method to convert from decimal to binary, octal, or hexadecimal.

The ASPX page is as follows:

```
<body>
  <form id="ConvertBases" method="post" runat="server">
    <p>
      <table id="Table1" cellSpacing="1" cellPadding="1">
        <tr>
          <td>
            <p>
              <asp:TextBox id="Input" runat="server"></asp:TextBox></p>
            <p>
              <asp:Button id="ConvertNumber" runat="server"
Text="Convert" OnClick="ConvertNumber_Click"></asp:Button></p>
          </td>
          <td valign="top">
            <asp:RadioButton id="BinaryRadioButton" Text="Binary"
GroupName="Bases" runat="server"></asp:RadioButton><br />
            <asp:RadioButton id="OctalRadioButton" Text="Octal"
GroupName="Bases" runat="server"></asp:RadioButton><br />
            <asp:RadioButton id="DecimalRadioButton" Text="Decimal"
Checked="True" GroupName="Bases" runat="server"></asp:RadioButton><br />
            <asp:RadioButton id="HexadecimalRadioButton"
➥Text="Hexadecimal"
GroupName="Bases" runat="server"></asp:RadioButton>
          </td>
        </tr>
        <tr>
          <td colspan="2"> </td>
        </tr>
        <tr>
          <td colspan="2">
            <p>
              <asp:Label id="Output" runat="server"></asp:Label></p>
```

```
        </td>
       </tr>
      </table>
     </p>
    </form>
   </body>
```

In `<script runat="server" />` block or codebehind:

```
Public Function ConvertBase(ByVal Dec As Int32) As String
   Dim sb As New System.Text.StringBuilder()
   sb.Append("Binary: " & Convert.ToString(Dec, 2) & "<br />")
   sb.Append("Octal: " & Convert.ToString(Dec, 8) & "<br />")
   sb.Append("Decimal: " & Convert.ToString(Dec, 10) & "<br />")
   sb.Append("Hexadecimal: " & Convert.ToString(Dec, 16) & "<br />")
   Return sb.ToString()
End Function

Protected Sub ConvertNumber_Click(ByVal sender As System.Object,
➡ ByVal e As System.EventArgs)
   Dim InputText As String = Input.Text
   Dim Dec As Int32 = 0

   Try
     If (BinaryRadioButton.Checked) Then
       Dec = Convert.ToInt32(InputText, 2)
     End If
     If (OctalRadioButton.Checked) Then
       Dec = Convert.ToInt32(InputText, 8)
     End If
     If (DecimalRadioButton.Checked) Then
       Dec = Convert.ToInt32(InputText)
     End If
     If (HexadecimalRadioButton.Checked) Then
       Dec = Convert.ToInt32(InputText, 16)
     End If
     Output.Text = ConvertBase(Dec)
   Catch ex As Exception
     Output.Text = "Error: " & ex.Message
   End Try

End Sub
```

Comments

Converting numbers between bases is a two-step process. First, use the
`Convert.ToInt32(string input, int base)` method to convert the input number to

decimal. Second, you use the `System.Convert.ToString(int decimalValue, int base)` method to convert the decimal number to the other bases.

See Also

Convert.ToUInt32 Method (String, Int32)—`http://msdn.microsoft.com/library/en-us/ cpref/html/frlrfSystemConvertClassToUInt32Topic19.asp` in .NET Framework Class Library

Convert.ToString Method (Int32, Int32)—`http://msdn.microsoft.com/library/en-us/ cpref/html/frlrfSystemConvertClassToStringTopic27.asp` in .NET Framework Class Library

16.4. Finding the Log of a Number

You want to find the log (natural, base 10, or other) of a number.

Technique

Logarithmic functions are part of the `System.Math` class. The following code demonstrates how to use these functions:

```vb
<%@ Import Namespace="System" %>
<%@ Import Namespace="System.Math" %>

<script language="vb" runat="server">
      Sub GetLogButton_click(ByVal sender As Object, _
ByVal e As System.EventArgs)
          Try
              If Log10RadioButton.Checked Then
                  ResultLabel.Text="Log10("& numberTextBox.Text & _
")=" &Math.Log10(CDbl(numberTextBox.Text))
              ElseIf LogRadioButton.Checked Then
                  ResultLabel.Text="Log("& numberTextBox.Text & _
")=" &Math.Log(CDbl(numberTextBox.Text))
              ElseIf LoganyBaseRadioButton.Checked Then
                  ResultLabel.Text="Log"& baseTextBox.Text & _
_"("&numberTextBox.Text &")=" & _
Math.Log(CDbl(numberTextBox.Text),CDbl(baseTextBox.Text))
              End If
          Catch ex As Exception
              ResultLabel.Text = ex.message
          End Try
      End Sub
  </script>
```

```
<form runat="server">
    <h3>Finding Log of Number</h3>
    Enter Number For value :
    <asp:TextBox id="numberTextBox" runat="server" /></br>
Enter Number For Base:
    <asp:TextBox id="baseTextBox" runat="server" /></br>
    <asp:RadioButton id="Log10RadioButton" Text="Log10" checked="true"
GroupName="RadioLog" runat="server" /><br />
    <asp:RadioButton id="LogRadioButton" Text="Log" GroupName="RadioLog"
runat="server" /><br />
    <asp:RadioButton id="LoganyBaseRadioButton" Text="Log for base in TextBox2"
GroupName="RadioLog" runat="server" /><br />
    <asp:Button id="GetLogButton" onclick="GetLogButton_click" runat="server"
Text="Click" /></br>
    <asp:Label id="ResultLabel" runat="server" />
</form>
```

Comments

Input parameters for all logarithmic functions must be of type `Double`. `Math.Log` returns the natural (base e) logarithm of a specified number by default, but it supports method overloads that allow any base to be specified. The `Log10` method can be used for base-10 logarithms. If input value is equal to `NaN`, logarithmic functions will return `NaN`. If input value is negative, logarithmic functions will return `NaN`. If input value is equal to `PositiveInfinity`, logarithmic functions will return `PositiveInfinity`.

See Also

Logarithmic functions—`http://msdn.microsoft.com/library/en-us/cpref/html/frlrfSystemMathClassLogTopic.asp`

16.5. Formatting Numbers

You want to format a number in a particular fashion.

Technique

The .NET Framework provides extensive support for formatting numbers using built-in formatting codes. Some of the more common ones are demonstrated here.

```
Private Sub Page_Load(sender As Object, e As System.EventArgs)
    ' formatting numbers
    Dim myDouble As Double = 123.456
    Dim myInt As Integer = 4567
```

```
  Response.Write((myDouble.ToString("C") & "<br>")) ' currency
  ' decimal - use with int types
  Response.Write((myInt.ToString("D") & "<br>"))

' decimal - zero padded to 6 digits
  Response.Write((myInt.ToString("D6") & "<br>"))
  Response.Write((myDouble.ToString("E") & "<br>")) ' scientific
  Response.Write((myDouble.ToString("F") & "<br>")) ' fixed-point
  Response.Write((myDouble.ToString("G") & "<br>")) ' general
' general - 4 digits of accuracy
  Response.Write((myDouble.ToString("G4") & "<br>"))

  Response.Write((myDouble.ToString("P") & "<br>")) ' percent
  Response.Write((myDouble.ToString("N") & "<br>")) ' number
' round-trip (re-castable back to a number)
  Response.Write((myDouble.ToString("R") & "<br>"))
  Response.Write((myInt.ToString("X") & "<br>")) ' hexadecimal - use with int
types
End Sub 'Page_Load
```

Comments

The results of these format strings vary with the culture settings of the server.

> **See Also**
>
> Section 15.12, "Formatting Strings"
>
> Standard Numeric Formatting Strings—http://msdn.microsoft.com/library/en-us/
> cpguide/html/cpconstandardnumericformatstrings.asp

16.6. Validating Credit Card Numbers

You want to validate a user's credit card number, using the *Luhn* algorithm.

Technique

This example validates a credit card number using the Luhn algorithm. The Luhn algorithm is a mathematical equation used to validate credit card numbers before they are processed. The formula for this is actually quite simple.

You begin by taking the credit card number entered and doubling every other digit within the number beginning with the right most digit. If the digit that you doubled is equal to or greater than 10, you take the sum of the two digits. For instance, you have the number 7. Double it to get 14. Then, instead of adding 14 to your equation, you add 1 and 4 to get 5. You would then continue until you have your equation. At that point, you will then add all of those numbers together. If the sum of that equation is divisible by 10, the credit card is valid, otherwise it is invalid. Now that you hopefully understand how the Luhn algorithm works, you can dig into some code.

Begin by entering the following HTML interface:

```
<form runat="server">
    <asp:TextBox id="CreditNo" Runat="server"></asp:TextBox>
    <asp:Button id="Button1" onclick="ValidateCC" Runat="server"
Text="Validate"></asp:Button>
    <br />
    <asp:Label id="Result" Runat="server"></asp:Label>

</form>
```

Now enter this code within the `<script>` tags:

```
Sub ValidateCC(Sender As Object, E As EventArgs)
    '-- the credit card number that the user entered
    Dim ccText As String = CreditNo.Text
    '-- will be indicator for every other number
    Dim indicator As Integer = 1        '-- will be used to store sum of first
set of numbers
    Dim firstNumToAdd As Integer = 0
    '-- will be used to store second set of numbers
    Dim secondNumToAdd As Integer = 0
    '-- will be used if every other number added is greater than 10,
    'store the left-most integer here
    Dim num1 As String
    '-- will be used if ever yother number added is greater than 10,
    'store the right-most integer here
    Dim num2 As String

    Dim ccArr As Char() = ccText.ToCharArray()

    Dim i As Integer
    For i = ccArr.Length - 1 To 0 Step -1
        Dim ccNoAdd As Char = ccArr(i)
        Dim ccAdd As Integer = Int32.Parse(ccNoAdd.ToString())

        If indicator = 1 Then
            '-- If we are on the odd number of numbers, add
            'that number to our total
            firstNumToAdd += ccAdd
            '-- set our indicator to 0 so that our code will
            'know to skip to the next piece
            indicator = 0
        Else
            '-- if the current integer doubled is greater than 10
            '-- split the sum in to two integers and add them together
            '-- we then add it to our total here
            If ccAdd + ccAdd >= 10 Then
```

```
        Dim temporary As Integer = ccAdd + ccAdd
        num1 = temporary.ToString().Substring(0, 1)
        num2 = temporary.ToString().Substring(1, 1)
        secondNumToAdd += Convert.ToInt32(num1) + Convert.ToInt32(num2)
    Else
        '-- otherwise, just add them together and add them to our total
        secondNumToAdd += ccAdd + ccAdd
    End If
    '-- set our indicator to 1 so for the next integer we will
    'perform a different set of code
    indicator = 1
    End If
Next i

'-- If the sum of our 2 numbers is divisible by 10, then the card
'is valid. Otherwise, it is not
If(firstNumToAdd + secondNumToAdd) Mod 10 = 0 Then
    Result.Text = "This Card Is Valid"
Else
    Result.Text = "This Card Is Invalid"
End If
End Sub
```

Comments

This piece of code is useful when taking credit card information via the Web for order placements.

See Also

Section 16.1, "Converting a String to a Number"

Section 16.2, "Working on a Range of Numbers"

Section 16.5, "Formatting Numbers"

Section 16.7, "Performing Trigonometric Functions"

```
http://www.beachnet.com/~hstiles/cardtype.html
```

16.7. Performing Trigonometric Functions

You want to perform trigonometry functions such as sine, cosine, and tangent on a number.

Technique

Trigonometric functions are part of the `System.Math` class. This example illustrates how you can use the sin, cosine, and tangent functions using this `Math` class. The `recipe1707vb.aspx` page is shown here:

```
<%@ Page Language="vb" %>
<%@ Import Namespace="System.Math" %>

<html>
<title>Trigonometric Functions</title>
<head>
   <script language="VB" runat="server">
       Sub Button1_Click(sender As Object, e As EventArgs)
  Try
    If RadSin.Checked Then
      LblValue.Text = "Sin " & TxtInput.Text & " = "
           LblValue.Text &= _
Math.Round(Math.Sin(Ctype(TxtInput.Text,Double) * (Math.PI/180)),3)
    Else if RadCos.Checked Then
      LblValue.Text = "Cos " & TxtInput.Text & " = "
      LblValue.Text &= _
Math.Round(Math.Cos(Ctype(TxtInput.Text,Double) * (Math.PI/180)),3)
    Else if RadTan.Checked Then
      LblValue.Text = "Tan " & TxtInput.Text & " = "
      LblValue.Text &= _
Math.Round(Math.Tan(Ctype(TxtInput.Text,Double) * (Math.PI/180)),3)
    End if
  Catch Ex as Exception
    LblValue.Text= "<font color=red>Error:" & Ex.Message
  End Try
       End Sub
   </script>
</head>
<body>
    <h3><font face="Verdana">Trigonometric Functions Recipe</font></h3>
    <form runat=server>
Please enter angle:
<asp:TextBox id=TxtInput runat="server"/><br/>
<asp:RadioButton id=RadSin Text="Sin" Checked="True"
GroupName="RadioTrigo" runat="server" />
<br/>
<asp:RadioButton id=RadCos Text="Cosine" GroupName="RadioTrigo"
runat="server"/><br/>
<asp:RadioButton id=RadTan runat="server" Text="Tangent"
GroupName="RadioTrigo" /><br/>
<asp:Button id=BtnCheck Text="Click Me" onclick="Button1_Click"
runat="server" /><br/><br/>
```

```
<asp:Label id=LblValue runat=server />
    </form>
</body>
</html>
```

Comments

The input parameter (the angle) for all trigonometric functions must be in radians. If you are taking input in degrees, you must convert degrees into radians. This example starts with degrees, so it multiplies the input value by pi/180. If input value is equal to NaN, NegativeInfinity, or PositiveInfinity, the trigonometric functions will return NaN.

See Also

MSDN Math Functions—http://msdn.microsoft.com/library/en-us/vblr7/html/valrfMathFunctions.asp

16.8. Generating Random Numbers

You want to generate a random number.

Technique

Generating random numbers is easy with ASP.NET. This example first declares an integer (randomInt) and a double (randomDouble) in order to store the random numbers it generates. Next, it creates an object of type System.Random. To generate a random integer, you call myRandom.Next and pass in the maximum value (optionally, you can pass in a minimum value and a maximum value to generate a number within a given range). To generate a random double, call myRandom.NextDouble() to generate a random number between 0 and 1. Then multiple that value by the maximum value to get the desired number. Finally, write out the values.

The default minimum value is 0. Also note that the maximum value is a non-inclusive upper bound—the number generated will be less than the maximum value, not equal to it. In the following example, which passes in a max value of 100, the number generated will be between 0 and 99, inclusive.

In <script runat="server" /> block or codebehind:

```
Sub Page_Load(sender As Object, e As EventArgs)
  Dim randomInt As Integer
  Dim randomDouble As Double
  Dim myRandom As New Random()

  randomInt=myRandom.Next(100)
```

```
  randomDouble=myRandom.NextDouble()*100
  Response.Write(randomInt.ToString() & "<BR>")
  Response.Write(randomDouble.ToString())
End Sub
```

16.9. Accessing Today's Date and Time

You want to access today's date and/or time.

Technique

Accessing today's date and/or time is easily accomplished using the `System.DateTime` class's static property, `Now`.

```
Sub Page_Load(sender As Object, e As System.EventArgs)
  Response.Write("The current date and time is: " & System.DateTime.Now)
End Sub 'Page_Load
```

Comments

The `DateTime` type in the .NET Framework provides many methods that can be used to add or subtract from the date and time, as well as formatting options.

> **See Also**
>
> Section 16.12, "Formatting Dates and Times"
>
> Section 16.15, "Adding to a Date or Time"

16.10. Converting a String to a Date or Time

You need to convert a string variable into a **DateTime** variable.

Technique

You can convert a string into a `DateTime` by calling the `Convert.ToDateTime()` method and passing in the string value of the date, formatted correctly for your region. An example of a valid format for the United States is `"12/25/2003 05:30:00"`. You can also specify a format provider for custom date/time format. For the following example, create a format provider object of type `DateTimeFormatInfo`. Specify the `DateSeparator` and `TimeSeparator` values. You can now pass the `ToDateTime()` method a string in your new format along with the format provider.

You can also create a `DateTime` directly with its constructor, which takes parameters for year, month, day, and so on.

In `<script runat="server" />` block or codebehind:

```
Sub Page_Load(sender As Object, e As EventArgs)
  Dim date1, date2 As DateTime
  date1=Convert.ToDateTime("12/25/2003 05:30:00")

  Dim formatInfo As New System.Globalization.DateTimeFormatInfo()
  formatInfo.DateSeparator="~"
  formatInfo.TimeSeparator="."
  date2=Convert.ToDateTime("12~25~2003 05.30.00", formatInfo)

  Response.Write(date1.ToString() & "<BR>")
  Response.Write(date2.ToString())
End Sub
```

See Also

Section 16.12, "Formatting Dates and Times"

`ToDateTime` method— `http://msdn.microsoft.com/library/en-us/cpref/html/frlrfsystemconvertclasstodatetimetopic.asp`

16.11. Determining Date or Time Intervals

You want to determine the time between two given dates or times.

Technique

Create a new Web Form and add labels for the hours, minutes, and seconds. Use `DateTime.Now.Ticks` and subtract from it `DateTime.Today.Ticks` to get the number of ticks representing the amount of time that has past since the start of the day and now. Create a new `TimeSpan` object and pass in the ticks variable. Once you have this `TimeSpan` object, you can call properties such as hours, minutes, and seconds to get the amount of time that has passed.

In addition to `Ticks`, the `TimeSpan` class's constructor also has overloads that take milliseconds, seconds, minutes, hours, and days. Visual Basic also continues to support the `DateDiff` method.

The ASPX page is as follows:

```
<html>
  <body>
    <form method="post" runat="server">
      Since the start of the day <asp:Label ID="Hours" Runat="server" /> hours,
```

```
    <asp:Label ID="Minutes" Runat="server" /> minutes and
    <asp:Label ID="Seconds" Runat="server" /> seconds have passed.
  </form>
</body>
</html>
```

In `<script runat="server" />` block or codebehind:

```
Sub Page_Load(sender As Object, e As EventArgs)
  Dim ticks As Long
  ticks=DateTime.Now.Ticks-DateTime.Today.Ticks
  Dim ts As New TimeSpan(ticks)
  Hours.Text=ts.Hours.ToString()
  Minutes.Text=ts.Minutes.ToString()
  Seconds.Text=ts.Seconds.ToString()
End Sub
```

See Also

Section 16.13, "Benchmarking a Section of Code"

Section 16.15, "Adding to a Date or Time"

16.12. Formatting Dates and Times

You want to format a date and/or time variable in a particular fashion.

Technique

The .NET Framework provides extensive support for formatting dates and times using built-in formatting codes. Some of the more common ones are demonstrated here.

```
Sub Page_Load(sender As Object, e As System.EventArgs)
  ' Formatting DateTime variables
  ' Using DateTime methods
  Response.Write("Default: " & System.DateTime.Now & "<br>")
  Response.Write("Local Time: " & _
System.DateTime.Now.ToLocalTime() & "<br>")
  Response.Write("Long Date: " & _
System.DateTime.Now.ToLongDateString() & "<br>")
  Response.Write("Long Time: " & _
System.DateTime.Now.ToLongTimeString() & "<br>")
  Response.Write("Short Date: " & _
System.DateTime.Now.ToShortDateString() & "<br>")
  Response.Write("Short Time: " & _
System.DateTime.Now.ToShortTimeString() & "<br>")
  Response.Write("ToString Default: " & _
```

```
System.DateTime.Now.ToString() & "<br>")
  Response.Write("Universal Time: " & _
System.DateTime.Now.ToUniversalTime() & "<br>")
' returns a datetime, which can still be formatted

  ' Using Format Strings
  Response.Write("d - Short Date: " & _
System.DateTime.Now.ToString("d") & "<br>")
  Response.Write("D - Long Date: " & _
System.DateTime.Now.ToString("D") & "<br>")
  Response.Write("t - Short Time: " & _
System.DateTime.Now.ToString("t") & "<br>")
  Response.Write("T - Long Time: " & _
System.DateTime.Now.ToString("T") & "<br>")
  Response.Write("f - Full date/time (short time): " & _
System.DateTime.Now.ToString("f") & "<br>")
  Response.Write("F - Full date/time (long time): " & _
System.DateTime.Now.ToString("F") & "<br>")
  Response.Write("g - General: " & System.DateTime.Now.ToString("g") & _
"<br>")
  Response.Write("G - General: " & System.DateTime.Now.ToString("G") & _
"<br>")
  Response.Write("M/m - Month day: " & System.DateTime.Now.ToString("M") & _
"<br>")
  Response.Write("u - Universal Sortable: " & _
System.DateTime.Now.ToString("u") & "<br>")
  Response.Write("Y/y - Year month: " & _
System.DateTime.Now.ToString("y") & "<br>")

  ' Custom Format Strings
  Response.Write("d, day of month: " & _
System.DateTime.Now.ToString(" d") & "<br>") ' can't use just "d"
  Response.Write("dd, zero-padded day of month: " & _
System.DateTime.Now.ToString("dd") & "<br>")
  Response.Write("ddd, abbreviated day of week: " & _
System.DateTime.Now.ToString("ddd") & "<br>")
  Response.Write("dddd, full day of week: " & _
System.DateTime.Now.ToString("dddd") & "<br>")

  Response.Write("h, hour: " & System.DateTime.Now.ToString(" h") & _
"<br>") ' can't use just "h"
  Response.Write("hh, hour, zero padded " & _
System.DateTime.Now.ToString("hh") & "<br>")
  Response.Write("H, hour, 24-hr " & System.DateTime.Now.ToString(" H") & _
"<br>") ' can't use just "H"
  Response.Write("H, hour, 24-hr, zero padded " & _
System.DateTime.Now.ToString("HH") & "<br>")
```

```
  Response.Write("m, minute: " & System.DateTime.Now.ToString(" m") & _
"<br>") ' can't use just "m"
  Response.Write("M, month: " & System.DateTime.Now.ToString(" M") & _
"<br>") ' can't use just "M"
  Response.Write("MM, month, zero padded: " & _
System.DateTime.Now.ToString("MM") & "<br>")
  Response.Write("MMM, month abbreviated: " & _
System.DateTime.Now.ToString("MMM") & "<br>")
  Response.Write("MMMM, month full name: " & _
System.DateTime.Now.ToString("MMMM") & "<br>")

  Response.Write("y, year (omits century): " & _
System.DateTime.Now.ToString(" y") & "<br>") ' can't use just "y"
  Response.Write("yy, 2-digit year, zero padded: " & _
System.DateTime.Now.ToString("yy") & "<br>")
  Response.Write("yyyy, 4-digit year, zero padded: " & _
System.DateTime.Now.ToString("yyyy") & "<br>")
End Sub 'Page_Load
```

Comments

Note that custom format strings cannot consist of just a single character, because these are reserved for standard format characters. You can use the custom format strings to build your own format, such as formatting 1/1/03 as Jan 01: 2003 by using a string like this: "MMM dd: yyyy".

See Also

Section 15.12, "Formatting Strings"

```
http://msdn.microsoft.com/library/en-us/cpguide/html/
cpcondatetimeformatstrings.asp
```

16.13. Benchmarking a Section of Code

You want to measure the amount of time it takes for a certain section of your program to execute.

Technique

Create a new Web Form and add a label to store the amount of time it takes for your code to execute. Before running the block of code you want to measure, set startTime equal to DateTime.Now(). Run the block or code you want to test. This example runs a simple equation one billion times. Next, you set endDate to DateTime.Now(). Create a new timespan by passing it the number of ticks between startTime and endTime. Finally, you set the Text property of the Seconds label to span.TotalSeconds.ToString() in order to display the number of seconds that have passed.

The ASPX page is as follows:

```
<html>
  <body>
    <form method="post" runat="server">
      Your code took <asp:Label ID="Seconds" Runat="server" /> seconds to run.
    </form>
  </body>
</html>
```

In <script runat="server" /> block or codebehind:

```
Sub Page_Load(sender As Object, e As EventArgs)
  Dim i, a As Integer
  Dim startTime, endTime As DateTime
  Dim span As TimeSpan
  startTime=DateTime.Now
  For i=0 to 1000000000
    a=i+1
  Next i
  endTime=DateTime.Now
  span=new TimeSpan(endTime.Ticks-startTime.Ticks)
  Seconds.Text=span.TotalSeconds.ToString()
End Sub
```

Comments

Notice this example only takes a few seconds to run on most computers. To see the performance gain, ASP.NET offers over ASP, try running a similar test in ASP.

See Also

Section 16.11, "Determining Date or Time Intervals"

Benchmarking Asp code—http://www.4guysfromrolla.com/webtech/122799-1.shtml

16.14. Pausing Your Program

You want your application to pause or sleep for a given amount of time.

Technique

Create a new Web Form and add two labels to it. Set the value of Label1 to the current time by using DateTime.Now.ToString("hh:mm:ss"). You then call the

`System.Threading.Thread.Sleep` method to pause the current thread for the specified number of milliseconds. This example uses `5000` milliseconds (or five seconds). You then set `Label2` to the current time. The times of the two labels should be five seconds apart.

The ASPX page is as follows:

```
<html>
  <body>
    <form method="post" runat="server">
    <asp:Label ID="Label1" Runat="server" /><br>
    <asp:Label ID="Label2" Runat="server" />
     </form>
  </body>
</html>
```

In `<script runat="server" />` block or codebehind:

```
Sub Page_Load(sender As Object, e As EventArgs)
  Label1.Text=DateTime.Now.ToString("hh:mm:ss")
  System.Threading.Thread.Sleep(5000)
  Label2.Text=DateTime.Now.ToString("hh:mm:ss")
End Sub
```

Comments

The `Thread.Sleep` method will only pause the current thread in a multithreaded application. Further, it does not use CPU resources like a long `For` or `While` loop would, but rather lets the CPU process other threads until the sleep period expires.

See Also

Section 16.13, "Benchmarking a Section of Code"

16.15. Adding to a Date or Time

You want to take a given `DateTime` variable and add a period of time to it.

Technique

You can use any of the following methods of a `DateTime` object to add or subtract a period of time from it:

- `AddDays`
- `AddHours`
- `AddMilliseconds`
- `AddMinutes`

- AddMonths
- AddSeconds
- AddTicks
- AddYears
- Subtract

The follow example creates a new `DateTime` object called `currentDate`. You then set the value of the `Text` property `TodaysDate` to the string value of `currentDate`. There isn't an `AddWeeks` method because the same functionality can be achieved using the `AddDays` method, so you use `AddDays(14)` to calculate two weeks. You can also pass negative numbers to the `AddX` methods to subtract the given amount of time. This example uses `AddYears(-1)` to get the date one year ago.

The ASPX page is as follows:

```
<html>
  <body>
    <form method="post" runat="server">
      Right now is: <asp:Label ID="TodaysDateTime" Runat="server" /><br>
      Two weeks from now is: <asp:Label ID="TwoWeeks" Runat="server" /><br>
      Three months from now is: <asp:Label ID="ThreeMonths"
         Runat="server" /><br>
      One year ago was: <asp:Label ID="OneYearAgo" Runat="server" />
    </form>
  </body>
</html>
```

In `<script runat="server" />` block or codebehind:

```
Sub Page_Load(sender As Object, e As EventArgs)
  Dim currentDate As DateTime
  currentDate=DateTime.Now
  TodaysDateTime.Text=currentDate.ToString()
  TwoWeeks.Text=currentDate.AddDays(14).ToString()
  ThreeMonths.Text=currentDate.AddMonths(3).ToString()
  OneYearAgo.Text=currentDate.AddYears(-1).ToString()
End Sub
```

See Also

Section 16.9, "Accessing Today's Date and Time"

Section 16.11, "Determining Date or Time Intervals"

17

Working with Files and Folders

17.0. Introduction

Working with file system resources is a very common requirement in Web-based applications, which is why this chapter is devoted to common file and folder operations. This chapter describes how to find, open, delete, copy, move, read, write, and otherwise work with files and folders using the .NET Framework's System.IO namespace libraries. For most of these operations, you will need to ensure that the ASP.NET worker process has sufficient permissions, or that the user is logged in with the necessary permissions.

17.1. Opening a File

You want to open a text file and access its contents.

Technique

You'll use the System.IO namespace to deal with files. This example reads the contents of the file test.txt. It assumes that you have a folder called Upload in the current Web application directory. When the user clicks on the specified button, the code will read the file contents in .\Upload\test.txt.

In `<script runat="server" />` block or codebehind:

```
Sub ReadFile(ByVal sender As Object, ByVal e As EventArgs)
Dim FileStreamReader As StreamReader
Try
FileStreamReader = File.OpenText(Server.MapPath(".\Upload\") & "test.txt")
txtTextContent.Text = FileStreamReader.ReadToEnd()
FileStreamReader.Close()
OutputLabel.Text = "File Succesfully Read!"
Catch exc As Exception
```

```
OutputLabel.Text = "Error in Reading file. Error is " & exc.ToString()
Finally
If Not FileStreamReader Is Nothing Then
    FileStreamReader.Close()
End If
End Try
End Sub
```

Comments

You need to use a `StreamReader` object to read files. To open a text file, you have to use the `OpenText` method of the `File` object. Once you determine where the text file is, you can easily read the file content. There are many methods available in the `StreamReader` object to read content from files. To read the entire content of a file, you can use the `ReadToEnd()` method.

When reading text files, unexpected errors can occur. Therefore, the `catch` block is used to catch any unexpected error and display it to the user. After the file operation is complete, the file is closed.

See Also

Section 17.4, "Creating a File"

17.2. Deleting a File

You want to delete a file from the Web server.

Technique

For this example, you include the `System.IO` namespace in your code.

The ASPX page is as follows:

```
<html>
<head>
<title>Deleting a File</title>
</head>
<body>
<form runat="server">
<h4>Type Path/Name of file to delete it</h4>
<p>
    <asp:TextBox id="FileNameTextBox" runat="server"></asp:TextBox>
    <asp:Button id="DeleteFileButton" onclick="DeleteFile"
runat="server" Text="Delete File"></asp:Button>
</p>
```

```
<p>
   <asp:Literal id="MessageLiteral" runat="server"></asp:Literal>
</p>
</form>
</body>
</html>
```

The interface for the example simply consists of a TextBox, a button, and a literal control.

In `<script runat="server" />` block or codebehind:

```
Public Sub Page_Load(Source As Object, E As EventArgs)
 'Initialize value
 MessageLiteral.Text = ""
End Sub


Public Sub DeleteFile(Source As Object, E As EventArgs)
 'Create an instance of FileInfo class
 Dim fileSource As New FileInfo(FileNameTextBox.Text)

 Try   'Delete the file if it exists
  If fileSource.Exists Then
    fileSource.Delete()
    MessageLiteral.Text = "File has been deleted."
  Else
    MessageLiteral.Text = FileNameTextBox.Text & " does not exist."
  End If
 Catch _Error As Exception
  MessageLiteral.Text = _Error.Message
 End Try
End Sub
```

This event gets called on the `click` event of the `Button` control. The example illustrates the deletion procedure of a file implementing the `FileInfo` class. An instance of the class is created, which is then used to delete the specified file, if it exists, by calling the `delete` method of the `FileInfo` class. This can also be implemented using the `File` class, as shown in the following code snippet:

```
Public Sub DeleteFile(Source As Object, E As EventArgs)

  'Delete the file if it exists
  Try
  If File.Exists(FileNameTextBox.Text) Then
    File.Delete(FileNameTextBox.Text)
    MessageLiteral.Text = "File has been deleted."
  Else
    MessageLiteral.Text = FileNameTextBox.Text & " does not exist."
  End If
```

```
Catch _Error As Exception
  MessageLiteral.Text = _Error.Message
End Try
End Sub
```

Comments

Remember that the `FileInfo` class must create an instance of the class, whereas the `File` class is used for directly referencing the files and for performing file operations.

See Also

Section 17.0, "Introduction to Working with Files and Folders"

Section 17.1, "Opening a File"

Section 17.4, "Creating a File"

17.3. Creating a File Search Utility

You want to develop an application that you can use to locate files on the server.

Technique

This example develops an application that can be used to locate files on the server. The application is like Windows' File Search utility.

This example uses the `System.IO` namespace and several of its classes. The ASPX page is as follows:

```
<html>
<head>
<title>File Search Utility</title>
</head>
<body>
  <form runat="server">
    <h4>Type Path/Name of file to search for it</h4>
    <p>
    <asp:TextBox id="CriteriaTextBox" runat="server"></asp:TextBox>
    <asp:Button id="SearchButton" runat="server" Text="Search"
onclick="Search_Click"></asp:Button>
    </p>
    <p>
    <asp:DropDownList id="DriveDisplay" runat="server"></asp:DropDownList>
    </p>
    <p>
```

```
        <hr>
        </p><p></p><p></p><p></p><p></p><p></p><p></p>
        <p><asp:Literal id="SearchResultsLiteral"
runat="server"></asp:Literal></p>
        </form>
    </body>
    </html>
```

The following code goes in the `<script runat="server" />` block.

```
    Public Sub Page_Load(Source As Object, E As EventArgs)

    If Not Page.IsPostback Then
        Dim Drive As String
        Dim Drives() As String

        Drives = Directory.GetLogicalDrives()

        DriveDisplay.DataSource = Drives
        DriveDisplay.DataBind()
    End If

    SearchResultsLiteral.Text = ""


    End Sub
```

Under the `Page_Load()` event, all of the logical drives from the system are obtained through the `GetLogicalDrives()` method of the `Directory` object. The result returned is stored in an array of `string` type, which is then further assigned to the DropDownList control on the page. The following method is called when the Search button is clicked.

```
    Public Sub Search_Click(Source As Object, E As EventArgs)

    If CriteriaTextBox.Text <> "" Then

        'Assign the search criteria to the declared variable
        Dim Criteria As String = CriteriaTextBox.Text

        Dim DriveRoot As String = DriveDisplay.SelectedItem.Text
        Dim Directories  As String(), Files As String()
        Dim iFile As String, iDirectory As String

        Directories  = Directory.GetDirectories(DriveRoot)
        Files = Directory.GetFileSystemEntries(DriveRoot, Criteria)

        BeginTable()

        For Each iDirectory In Directories
```

```
        Search(iDirectory, Criteria)
    Next

    For Each iFile In Files
     ListFiles(iFile)
    Next

    EndTable()

    Else
       SearchResultsLiteral.Text = "Enter a search criteria."
    End If

    End Sub
```

The following method is called from the `Search()` method. This method searches in the sub-directories present in the selected root drive.

```
    'Iteration carried out to search within directories
    Private Sub Search(Dir As String, Cri As String)

     Dim Directories  As String(), Files As String()
     Dim iFile As String, iDirectory As String

     Directories  = Directory.GetDirectories(Dir)
     Files = Directory.GetFileSystemEntries(Dir, Cri)

     For Each iDirectory In Directories
        Search(iDirectory, Cri)
     Next

     For Each iFile In Files
        ListFiles(iFile)
     Next

    End Sub
```

The following methods are used to format the output format of the files.

```
    'Formats the output
    Public Sub ListFiles(FileName As String)

        Dim iFileInfo As New FileInfo(FileName)

        SearchResultsLiteral.Text += "<Tr>"
        SearchResultsLiteral.Text += "<Td>" & iFileInfo.Name & "</Td>"
        SearchResultsLiteral.Text += "<Td><a href='" & _
```

```
Path.GetDirectoryName(iFileInfo.FullName) & "'>" & _
            Path.GetDirectoryName(iFileInfo.FullName) & "</a></Td>"
            If Path.HasExtension(FileName) Then
                SearchResultsLiteral.Text += "<Td>" & _
iFileInfo.Extension & "</Td>"
            Else
                SearchResultsLiteral.Text += "<Td> Dir </Td>"
            End If
            SearchResultsLiteral.Text += "<Td>" & _
iFileInfo.LastWriteTime & "</Td>"
            SearchResultsLiteral.Text += "</Tr>"

        End Sub

        'Method creates the header of the output table
        Public Sub BeginTable()

            SearchResultsLiteral.Text += _
"<Table border='0' cellspacing='1' cellpadding='3'>"
            SearchResultsLiteral.Text += "<Th bgcolor='#C6C6C6'> Name </Th>"
            SearchResultsLiteral.Text += "<Th bgcolor='#C6C6C6'> Path </Th>"
            SearchResultsLiteral.Text += _
"<Th bgcolor='#C6C6C6'> Extension </Th>"
            SearchResultsLiteral.Text += _
"<Th bgcolor='#C6C6C6'> Modified On</Th>"

        End Sub

        'Method creates the closing of the output table
        Public Sub EndTable()

            SearchResultsLiteral.Text += "</Table>"

        End Sub
```

Comments

Note that the account that is running this page, by default the ASPNET user account, must have sufficient privileges to perform this search operation. If it does not have these rights, the page will fail with a System.UnauthorizedAccessException exception.

There are two search methods in the previous code. The first method, Search_Click (Source As Object, E As EventArgs), is raised as a result of the button click event. The second method, Search(Dir As String, Cri As String), is called by the first method.

After the user enters the criteria in the TextBox control and clicks the Search button, the Search_Click event handler is called. This method takes the selected root drive letter from the DropDownList control and searches the root drive for the files matching the criteria. It also collects the sub-directories in the string type array `Directories`. The `For Each` loop within the statement then calls the `Search()` method for each directory collected from the root drive. Afterwards, the `Search()` method calls itself recursively, thus iterating through all subdirectories under the initial subdirectory.

Upon successful match of a criteria with the name of a file or directory, the method `ListFiles( )` is called. The name of the file to format is passed to `ListFiles()` as a parameter, and `ListFiles()` displays that file's information.

See Also

Section 17.0, "Introduction to Working with Files and Folders"

Section 17.6, "Listing All the Files in a Folder"

Section 17.7, "Getting Information About a File"

Working with Directories—`http://aspalliance.com/hrmalik/articles/2002/200219/20021901.aspx`, by Haroon Rasheed Malik

17.4. Creating a File

> You want to create a file and fill it with some text.

Technique

You need to use the `System.IO` namespace when working with files. Assume that you have a folder called Upload under the current Web application directory. You'll create a TextArea in which the user can enter some text. The aim in this example is to create a file called test.txt, given some string data.

```
Sub CreateFile(sender As Object, e As EventArgs)
    If Trim(TextContent.Text).Length > 0 Then
      Dim myFileStream As StreamWriter = Nothing
      Try
        myFileStream = File.CreateText(Server.MapPath(".\Upload\") & _
"test.txt")
        myFileStream.WriteLine(TextContent.Text)
        myFileStream.Close()
        Output.Text = "File Successfully Created!"
      Catch exc As Exception
        Output.Text = "Error in Creating file. Error is " & exc.ToString()
      Finally
      If Not myFileStream Is Nothing Then
        myFileStream.Close()
      End If
```

```
    End Try
  Else
    Output.Text = "File not created, because you didn't enter anything!"
  End If
End Sub
```

Comments

You need a `StreamWriter` object to create text files. To create a text file, you have to use the `CreateText` method of the `File` object. After you determine where the text file is, you can easily create the file. There are two methods available in the `StreamWriter` object to write to files. They are `Write` and `WriteLine`. This example uses the `WriteLine` method.

Unexpected errors can occur when creating text files, such as "permission denied to create text file." The users should have necessary `write` permissions for the folder in which the file is to be created, and of course this folder must exist. The `catch` block catches any unexpected error and displays it to the users. After the file operation is complete, the file should be closed.

See Also

Section 17.1, "Opening a File"

17.5. Working with Binary Data and Files

You want to read and/or write binary data to a file.

Technique

Use the `System.IO.FileStream` class and its `BinaryWriter` and `BinaryReader` methods to manipulate and read/write binary data from/to physical file.

The ASPX page is as follows:

```
<asp:Panel id="WriteBinaryPanel" Runat="Server">
  <p>
      Please enter your Name:
   <asp:TextBox id="NameTextBox" runat="server"></asp:TextBox>
  </p>
  <p>
      Please enter your Age:
      <asp:TextBox id="AgeTextBox" runat="server"></asp:TextBox>
  </p>
  <p>
      Please enter your Sex:
```

```
        <asp:TextBox id="SexTextBox" runat="Server" MaxLength="1"
Columns="1"></asp:TextBox>
        (M/F)
    </p>
    <p>
        <asp:Button id="WriteButton" onclick="WriteButton_Click"
runat="server" Text="Write It!"></asp:Button>
    </p>
</asp:Panel>
```

By using the `BinaryWrite()` method and by creating an instance of `FileStream` object, data entered by the users can be written to a binary file.

In `<script runat="server" />` block or codebehind:

```
Sub WriteButton_Click(sender As Object, e As EventArgs)
    Dim objFileStream As FileStream
    Try
            objFileStream = New FileStream(Server.MapPath( _
".\Upload\myBinaryFileVB.bin", FileMode.Create)
            objBinaryWriter = New BinaryWriter(objFileStream)

            Dim Name As String = NameTextBox.Text
            Dim Age As Integer = Int32.Parse(AgeTextBox.Text)
            Dim Sex As Char = Char.Parse(SexTextBox.Text)

            objBinaryWriter.Write(Name)
            objBinaryWriter.Write(Age)
            objBinaryWriter.Write(Sex)

    Catch FileEx As FileNotFoundException
        MessageLabel.Text = FileEx.Message()
        Exit Sub
    Catch Ex As Exception
        MessageLabel.Text = Ex.Message()
        Exit Sub
    Finally
        objBinaryWriter.Close()
    End Try

    WriteBinaryPanel.Visible = False
    ReadBinaryPanel.Visible = True

End Sub
```

Another panel control will be toggled. The label controls are used to retrieve and display data from the binary file.

```
<asp:Panel id="ReadBinaryPanel" Runat="Server" Visible="False">
    <p>
        <asp:Button id="ReadButton" onclick="ReadButton_Click"
runat="server" Text="Read It!"></asp:Button>
    </p>
    <p>
        <asp:Label id="NameLabel" Runat="Server"></asp:Label>
    </p>
    <p>
        <asp:Label id="AgeLabel" Runat="Server"></asp:Label>
    </p>
    <p>
        <asp:Label id="SexLabel" Runat="Server"></asp:Label>
    </p>
</asp:Panel>
```

This example creates an instance of `FileStream` and the `BinaryReader` object. That way, data stored in the binary file can be retrieved using the several methods from the `BinaryReader` class.

In `<script runat="server" />` block or codebehind:

```
Sub ReadButton_Click(Sender As Object, e As EventArgs)

    Dim objFileStream As FileStream

    Try
            objFileStream = New FileStream(Server.MapPath( _
".\Upload\myBinaryFileVB.bin", FileMode.Open)
            objBinaryReader = New BinaryReader(objFileStream)

            NameLabel.Text = "Your Name: " & objBinaryReader.ReadString()
            AgeLabel.Text = "Your Age: " & objBinaryReader.ReadInt32()
            SexLabel.Text = "Your Sex: " & objBinaryReader.ReadChar()
    Catch FileEx As FileNotFoundException
        MessageLabel.Text = FileEx.Message()
        Exit Sub
    Catch Ex As Exception
        MessageLabel.Text = Ex.Message()
        Exit Sub
    Finally
        objBinaryReader.Close()
    End Try
End Sub
```

Comments

There are many types of files stored in a computer system, including GIF, JPEG, TXT, and BIN. A few of them are stored in binary format, which is the most primitive type of data storage. In order to work with streams of binary data, you can use the `BinaryWriter` and `BinaryReader` classes found in the `System.IO` namespace. Even if you store the same string in a text file and in a binary file, the two strings' content is different and the binary file will not display human readable text in a text editor.

See Also

Designing Reader Classes for .NET Documents—

`http://msdn.microsoft.com/msdnmag/issues/02/08/cuttingedge/default.aspx`

17.6. Listing All the Files in a Folder

You want to display all of the files in a particular folder.

Technique

In order to grab and list files in a particular folder, you'll use the `GetFiles()` method from the `System.IO` namespace. This method provides a function that returns a collection that you can data-bind to a control, thus displaying all the files in a folder.

The ASPX page is as follows:

```
<form runat="server">
    Files in Folder "C:\Program Files\Microsoft Visual Studio .NET":
    <asp:ListBox id="FileListBox" Runat="Server" />
</form>
```

Because the `Directory.GetFiles()` method returns a list of the names of files in a folder, you can assign this collection to an array of `string` object temporarily. The particular folder that you want to search is placed in the first argument of the `GetFiles` method. You can use the wildcard character (*) to search for the second argument.

In `<script runat="server" />` block or codebehind:

```
Sub Page_Load(Sender As Object, E As EventArgs)
    If Not IsPostBack Then

        Dim FileCollection As String()
        Dim myFileInfo As FileInfo
        Dim i As Integer

        FileCollection = Directory.GetFiles( _
"C:\WINNT\Microsoft.NET\Framework\v1.0.3705","*.exe ")
```

```
        For i = 0 To FileCollection.Length - 1
            myFileInfo = New FileInfo(FileCollection(i))
            FileListBox.Items.Add(new ListItem(myFileInfo.Name.ToString()))
        Next
    End If
End Sub
```

Looping through the array of returned filenames, you can add the filename as a ListItem to the ListBox with the use of the `FileInfo` object.

Within the ASP.NET Page, include the following:

```
<form runat="server">
    EXE Files in Folder C:\WINNT\Microsoft.NET\Framework\v1.0.3705:
    <asp:ListBox id="FileListBox" Runat="Server" />
</form>
```

Comments

Using the `GetFiles` method, you can display the name and properties of files in a particular folder. You can also define the search pattern to filter files that have a specific file extension.

See Also

Finding Existing Files and Directories—`http://msdn.microsoft.com/library/en-us/cpguide/html/cpconfindingexistingfilesdirectories.asp`

17.7. Getting Information About a File

You want to create a utility that displays information related to a file when the file's pathname is submitted.

Technique

Most of the classes required for this example are found in the `System.IO` namespace.

In `<script runat="server" />` block or codebehind:

```
Public Sub DisplayFileInfo(Source As Object, Sender As EventArgs)
    Dim iFile As FileInfo
    iFile = New FileInfo(FileTextBox.Text)
    If iFile.Exists Then
        Dim sb As New System.Text.StringBuilder(1000)

        sb.Append("<table border='0' width='50%'>")
        sb.Append("<tr>")
```

```
            sb.Append("<td>Name</td>")
            sb.Append("<td>" & iFile.Name & "</td>")
            sb.Append("</tr><tr>")
            sb.Append("<td>Path\Name</td>")
            sb.Append("<td>" & iFile.FullName & "</td>")
            sb.Append("</tr><tr>")
            sb.Append("<td>Extension</td>")
            sb.Append("<td>" & iFile.Extension & "</td>")
            sb.Append("</tr><tr>")
            sb.Append("<td>Size</td>")
            sb.Append("<td>" & iFile.Length & " bytes</td>")
            sb.Append("</tr><tr>")
            sb.Append("<td>Attributes</td>")
            sb.Append("<td>" & iFile.Attributes.ToString() & "</td>")
            sb.Append("</tr><tr>")
            sb.Append("<td>Creation Time</td>")
            sb.Append("<td>" & iFile.CreationTime & "</td>")
            sb.Append("</tr><tr>")
            sb.Append("<td>Last Accessed</td>")
            sb.Append("<td>" & iFile.LastAccessTime & "</td>")
            sb.Append("</tr><tr>")
            sb.Append("<td>Last Modified</td>")
            sb.Append("<td>" & iFile.LastWriteTime & "</td>")
            sb.Append("</tr></table>")
            ListFileInfoLiteral.Text = sb.ToString()
        Else
            ListFileInfoLiteral.Text = "The file does not exist"
        End If
End Sub
```

Comments

The FileInfo class in the System.IO namespace provides various properties and methods that can be used to obtain information about a file or to manipulate files. The following list shows a list of properties and their descriptions.

- PropertyDescriptionName—Name of the specified file.
- FullName—Full name of the specified file, including its path.
- Extension—Extension of the file, including the period.
- Length—Returns the size of the file in bytes.
- Attributes—Archive, Read Only, and Hidden.
- CreationTime—Date and time the file was created.
- LastAccessTime—Date and time the file was last opened.
- LastWriteTime—Date and time the file was last modified.

The application that has been demonstrated in the example simply makes use of the properties of the `FileInfo` class outlined in the previous list.

See Also

Section 17.0, "Introduction to Working With Files and Folders"

Section 17.1, "Opening a File"

Section 17.2, "Deleting a File"

Section 17.4, "Creating a File"

17.8. Copying or Moving a File

You want to copy or move a file from one folder to another.

Technique

Use the `File.Copy` or `File.Move` methods of the `System.IO` namespace:

- `System.IO.File.Copy(SourceFileName, DestinationFileName)`
- `System.IO.File.Move(SourceFileName, DestinationFileName)`

In `<script runat="server" />` block or codebehind:

```
Sub Page_Load()
  Dim SourceFileName As String = "C:\SourceFolder\OriginalFile.test"
  Dim DestinationFileName As String = "C:\DestinationFolder\NewFile.test"

  System.IO.File.Copy(SourceFileName, DestinationFileName)

  ' and/or

  System.IO.File.Move(SourceFileName, DestinationFileName)
End Sub
```

Comments

`File.Copy` has an alternative overload with a third Boolean parameter that can be set to `true` and used whenever you need to allow file overwrites.

`File.Move` does not require a new filename as long as a new file path is specified. Moving a file is analogous to renaming it.

In both of these cases, the account that is executing the commands (by default the `ASPNET` user account) must have sufficient privileges to perform these operations, or else a `System.UnauthorizedAccessException` exception will occur.

> **See Also**
>
> File.Copy Method—http://msdn.microsoft.com/library/en-us/cpref/html/ frlrfSystemIOFileClassCopyTopic1.asp, MSDN Library
>
> File.Move Method—http://msdn.microsoft.com/library/en-us/cpref/html/ frlrfSystemIOFileClassMoveTopic.asp, MSDN Library

17.9. Parsing a Filename

You want to work with certain parts of a filename, such as its path or extension.

Technique

This recipe uses the `Path` class in the `System.IO` namespace, so make sure you include that namespace.

The ASPX page is as follows:

```
<html>
<head>
<title>Parsing a Filename</title>
</head>
<body>
   <form runat="server">
      <h4>File Path Parser</h4>
      <asp:TextBox id="FileNameTextBox" runat="server"></asp:TextBox>
      <asp:Button id="ParsePathButton" onclick="ParsePath"
runat="server" Text="Parse"></asp:Button>
      <hr />
   <asp:Literal id="PathPropertiesLiteral" runat="server"></asp:Literal>
   </form>


</body>
</html>
```

The interface in this example is composed of a TextBox, a button, and a literal Web control.

In `<script runat="server" />` block or codebehind:

```
Protected Sub Page_Load(Source As Object, E As EventArgs)
        PathPropertiesLiteral.Text = ""
    End Sub
```

The code for the Page_Load( ) event will clear up any existing text in the literal control.

```
Public Sub ParsePath(Source As Object, E As EventArgs)

Dim PropertyContainer As New StringBuilder()
   With PropertyContainer
        .Append("<table border='0' width='100%'>")
        .Append("<tr><td>Full Path</td>")
        .Append( "<td>" &  Path.GetFullPath(FileNameTextBox.Text) & _
           "</td></tr>")
        .Append("<tr><td>Root Drive</td>")
        .Append("<td>" &  Path.GetPathRoot(FileNameTextBox.Text) & _
           "</td></tr>")
        .Append("<tr><td>Directory Path</td>")
        .Append("<td>" &  Path.GetDirectoryName(FileNameTextBox.Text) & _
           "</td></tr>")
        .Append("<tr><td>File Name</td>")
        .Append("<td>" &  Path.GetFileName(FileNameTextBox.Text) & _
           "</td></tr>")
        .Append("<tr><td>File Name (Without Extension)</td>")
        .Append("<td>" &  Path.GetFileNameWithoutExtension
           (FileNameTextBox.Text) & "</td></tr>")
        .Append("<tr><td>File Extension</td>")
        .Append("<td>" &  Path.GetExtension(FileNameTextBox.Text) & _
           "</td></tr>")
        .Append("<tr><td>Temporary Filename</td>")
        .Append("<td>" &  Path.GetTempFileName() &  "</td></tr>")
        .Append("<tr><td>Temprary Filepath</td>")
        .Append("<td>" &  Path.GetTempPath() &  "</td></tr>")
        .Append("<tr><td>Directory Separator</td>")
        .Append("<td>" &  Path.DirectorySeparatorChar &  "</td></tr>")
        .Append("<tr><td>Alt Directory Separator</td>")
        .Append("<td>" &  Path.AltDirectorySeparatorChar &  "</td></tr>")
        .Append("<tr><td>Path Separator</td>")
        .Append("<td>" &  Path.PathSeparator &  "</td></tr>")
        .Append("<tr><td>Volume Separator</td>")
        .Append("<td>" &  Path.VolumeSeparatorChar &  "</td></tr>")
        .Append("<tr><td>Invalid Path Characters</td>")
        .Append("<td>" & Path.InvalidPathChars & "</td></tr>")
        .Append("</table>")
     End With
PathPropertiesLiteral.Text = PropertyContainer.ToString
End Sub
```

Comments

The `Path` class in the `System.IO` namespace contains various properties and methods that return components of the specified path. In this example, you simply call these properties and methods of the `Path` class; each property returns the specified character or path information.

See Also

Section 17.3, "Creating a File Search Utility"

17.10. Reading a File Line-by-Line

You want to read a file and perform an action on each line.

Technique

A `StreamReader` class opens a text file and reads each line of the file. The lines are used to populate a DropDownList Web control.

```
Sub Page_Load (Sender As Object, E As EventArgs)

    Dim MyFileName as String
    Dim ObjectStreamReader as System.IO.StreamReader
    Dim FileLines as New ArrayList()


    MyFileName = Page.MapPath("recipe1710.txt")

    Try
        ObjectStreamReader = new System.IO.StreamReader (MyFileName)
        While ObjectStreamReader.Peek() > -1
          'Do something with each line - in this case add it to our ArrayList
          FileLines.Add(ObjectStreamReader.ReadLine())
        End While
        FileLines.Sort()
        Label1.Text = "Select a title:"
        DropDownList1.DataSource = FileLines
        DropDownList1.DataBind()
        'Bind the drop-down list to the FileLines ArrayList

    Catch ObjectError as Exception
        Label1.Text = ObjectError.Message
        DropDownList1.Visible = False
    Finally
```

```
        If Not ObjectStreamReader Is nothing Then
                    ObjectStreamReader.Close()
        End If
    End Try
End Sub
```

Comments

Each line of the text file is read using the ReadLine() method of the StreamReader class. The line is placed in an ArrayList called FileLines. The Sort() method is then invoked on the ArrayList to sort the text lines alphabetically. Finally, each element of the ArrayList is added as an item to a DropDownList control by making the DropDownList data-bind to the ArrayList.

There are a number of errors that might occur when using text files—these are usually caused by file- or directory-not-found exceptions. The exception handling routine in this example will display any error messages in Label1 and hide the DropDownList.

See Also

Section 1.9, "Working with DropDownLists"

Section 17.1, "Opening a File"

Section 17.16, "Extracting a Random Line from a File"

17.11. Reading a File Word-by-Word

You want to read a file and perform some action on each word.

Technique

This code opens a file and for each line that it reads, it splits the line into words and determines whether each word ends in *r*. If a word ends in r, the code adds the word and a <br> tag to a StringBuilder. After all the lines are read, the StringBuilder contains all the words that end in r. The contents of the StringBuilder are displayed on the page using a label.

The ASPX page is as follows:

```
    <asp:Label id=" WordsLabel" runat="server" />
<hr>
<a href="starwarquotes.txt">Quotes File</a>
```

In <script runat="server" /> block or codebehind:

```
    Protected  Sub Page_Load(ByVal Source As Object, ByVal e As EventArgs)
      WordsLabel.Text = GetWordsFromFile("starwarquotes.txt")
    End Sub
```

```
Private Function GetWordsFromFile(ByVal filename As String) As String
  Dim sr As StreamReader = Nothing
  Dim delimiter() As Char = {"\u0009"," "} 'tab and space

  Dim sb As StringBuilder = New StringBuilder()
  Try
    sr = File.OpenText(filename)
    Dim line As String = sr.ReadLine()
    While Not line Is Nothing
      'split the line into words
      Dim words() As String = line.Split(delimiter)
      Dim word As String
      For Each word In words
        If word.EndsWith("r") Then
          sb.Append(word)
          sb.Append("<br>")
        End If
      Next
      line = sr.ReadLine()
    End While
  Catch ex As Exception
    If sb.Length > 0 Then
      sb.Remove(0,sb.Length-1)
    End If
    sb.Append(ex.Message)
  Finally
    If Not sr Is Nothing Then
      sr.Close()
    End If
  End Try

  Return sb.ToString()
End Function
```

Comments

Each line is split into words using the `String.Split()` method. This method divides the
string using a character array and places the divided string into a string array.

See Also

Section 17.1, "Opening a File"

ReadFromFile—http://www.aspalliance.com/olson/methods/ReadFromFile.aspx

String.Split Method—http://msdn.microsoft.com/library/en-us/cpref/html/
frlrfsystemstringclasssplittopic.asp in the .NET Framework Class Library

StreamReader Class—`http://msdn.microsoft.com/library/en-us/cpref/html/`
`frlrfSystemIOStreamReaderClassTopic.asp` in the .NET Framework Class Library

17.12. Parsing a File Using Delimiters

> You want to process a file with data separated by some kind of delimiter character, such as a comma (,).

Technique

The example reads each line using a stream reader and parses the line using the
`String.Split()` method.

```
Sub Page_Load (Sender As Object, E As EventArgs)
   If Not IsPostBack Then
      Dim MyFileName as String
      Dim ObjectStreamReader as System.IO.StreamReader
      Dim ColorTable As New System.Data.DataTable("Colors")
      Dim fileRow() As String
      Dim dc As System.Data.DataColumn
      Dim dr As System.Data.DataRow

      ' Create Columns
      dc = new System.Data.DataColumn("Hex",GetType(String))
      ColorTable.Columns.Add(dc)
      dc = new System.Data.DataColumn("String",GetType(String))
      ColorTable.Columns.Add(dc)


            MyFileName = Page.MapPath("recipe1712.csv")

      Try
         ObjectStreamReader = new System.IO.StreamReader (MyFileName)
         While ObjectStreamReader.Peek() > -1
            dr = ColorTable.NewRow()
            fileRow = ObjectStreamReader.ReadLine().Split(",")
            dr(0) = fileRow(0)
            dr(1) = fileRow(1)
            ColorTable.Rows.Add(dr)
         End While
         Label1.Text = "Select a color:"
         DropDownList1.DataSource = ColorTable
         DropDownList1.DataTextField = "String"
```

```
        DropDownList1.DataValueField = "Hex"
        DropDownList1.DataBind()

    Catch ObjectError as Exception
        Label1.Text = ObjectError.Message
        DropDownList1.Visible = False
    Finally
        If Not ObjectStreamReader Is nothing Then
            ObjectStreamReader.Close()
        End If
    End Try
  End If
End Sub
```

Comments

A DataTable is created programmatically to hold the data. The file contains data separated by commas. The code provided is fairly fragile in that the data must all be in the correct format or the entire operation will fail—although it would be a simple task to check for blank lines or comment lines. Also note that many standard formats, such as .CSV files, can be read using ODBC drivers for text files.

See Also

Section 15.14, "Converting a String into an Array of Strings"

Section 17.10, "Reading a File Line-By-Line"

17.13. Processing a File in Reverse

You need to process each line of a text file in reverse.

Technique

Be sure to include the System.IO namespace in your code for this example. In <script runat="server" /> block or codebehind:

```
    Sub Page_Load(sender As Object, e As EventArgs)
        ReadReversed()
    End Sub 'Page_Load

    Private Sub ReadReversed()
        Dim sr As StreamReader
        Dim [text] As String
        Dim lines As String()
```

```
    Try
        sr = File.OpenText(Server.MapPath("starwarquotes.txt"))

        [text] = sr.ReadToEnd()
        lines = [text].Split(ControlChars.NewLine)
        sr.Close()

        Dim i As Integer
        For i = lines.Length - 1 To 0 Step -1
            HttpContext.Current.Response.Write(lines(i).ToString())
            HttpContext.Current.Response.Write("<br />")
        Next i

    Catch exc As Exception
        HttpContext.Current.Response.Write(exc.Message)
    Finally
        If Not sr Is Nothing Then
            sr.Close()
        End If
    End Try
End Sub 'ReadReversed
```

Comments

The easiest way to process each line of a text file in reverse order is to read through the entire file and split the file at each new line (`ControlChars.NewLine`). After that it's just a simple matter of looping through the array (lines) from the last to the first element. This can be a useful technique for reading the last few lines of a logfile in which each new log entry is appended to the end of the file.

See Also
Section 17.1, "Opening a File"

17.14. Extracting a Single Line from a File

You want to read a particular line from a text file.

Technique

The example reads a file line-by-line, until the desired line is reached.

The ASPX page is as follows:

```
<asp:Label id="Line" runat="server" />
```

In `<script runat="server" />` block or codebehind:

```
Protected Sub Page_Load(Sender As Object, e As EventArgs)


    Line.Text = GetLineFromFile("starwarquotes.txt", 15)
End Sub

Public Function GetLineFromFile(ByVal filename As String, _
ByVal lineNumber As Integer) As String
    Dim result As String =  String.Empty
    Dim sr As StreamReader =  Nothing
    Try
      Dim lineCount As Integer =  1
      sr = File.OpenText(filename)
      Dim str As String =  sr.ReadLine()
      While Not str Is Nothing
        If lineCount = lineNumber Then
          result = str
          Exit While
        End If
        str = sr.ReadLine()
        lineCount = lineCount + 1
      End While
      If lineNumber > lineCount Then
        result = _
"You entered a line number greater than the number of lines in the file."
      End If
    Catch ex As Exception
      result = ex.Message
    Finally
      If Not sr Is Nothing Then
         sr.Close()
      End If
    End Try

    Return result
  End Function
```

Comments

The file is opened into a stream reader. As the file is read line-by-line, a counter tracks the number of lines read. When the indicated line is reached, that line is retrieved and returned.

See Also

Section 17.1, "Opening a File"

ReadFromFile–http://www.aspalliance.com/olson/methods/ReadFromFile.aspx

StreamReader Class–http://msdn.microsoft.com/library/en-us/cpref/html/
frlrfSystemIOStreamReaderClassTopic.asp in the .NET Framework Class Library

17.15. Counting the Number of Lines in a File

You want to find the number of lines in a file (with the first line indexed as 1).

Technique

The example reads a file line-by-line, incrementing a counter as each line is read.
The ASPX page is as follows:

```
<asp:Label id="LineCounter" runat="server" />
```

In <script runat="server" /> block or codebehind:

```
Protected Sub Page_Load([Source] As Object, e As EventArgs)
  LineCounter.Text =

CountLinesFromFile("starwarquotes.txt
    End Sub


    Private Function CountLinesFromFile(ByVal filename As String) As String
      Dim result As String
      Dim sr As StreamReader = Nothing
      Try
        Dim lineCount As Integer = 1
        sr = File.OpenText(filename)
        While Not sr.ReadLine() Is Nothing
          lineCount = lineCount + 1
        End While
        result = lineCount.ToString()
      Catch ex As Exception
        result = ex.Message
      Finally
        If Not sr Is Nothing Then
          sr.Close()
        End If
      End Try

      Return result
    End Function
```

Comments

A file is opened into a `StreamReader` object. As the file is read line-by-line, a counter keeps track of the number of lines read. After the complete file is read, the counter has the total number of lines.

See Also

Section 17.1, "Opening a File"

ReadFromFile—http://www.aspalliance.com/olson/methods/ReadFromFile.aspx

StreamReader Class—http://msdn.microsoft.com/library/en-us/cpref/html/ frlrfSystemIOStreamReaderClassTopic.asp in the .NET Framework Class Library

17.16. Extracting a Random Line from a File

You want to read a random line from a text file, such as for a random quote or tip of the day.

Technique

Using ASP, this was accomplished through the use of the `Scripting.FileSystemObject` object. With ASP.NET, you use a `System.IO.StreamReader` class.

In `<script runat="server" />` block or codebehind:

```
Function RetrieveRandomLine(FileName as String)
    Dim ObjectStreamReader as System.IO.StreamReader
    Dim FileLines as New ArrayList()
    Dim RandomNumber as Integer
    Randomize
    Try
        ObjectStreamReader = New System.IO.StreamReader(FileName)
        While ObjectStreamReader.Peek() > -1
            FileLines.Add(ObjectStreamReader.ReadLine())
        End While
        RandomNumber = Int(FileLines.Count * Rnd())
        RetrieveRandomLine = FileLines(RandomNumber).ToString()
    Catch ObjectError as Exception
        RetrieveRandomLine = ObjectError.Message
    Finally
        If Not ObjectStreamReader Is nothing Then
            ObjectStreamReader.Close()
            ObjectStreamReader = nothing
        End If
    End Try
End Function
```

```
Sub Page_Load (Sender As Object, E As EventArgs)
    Dim MyFileName as String
    MyFileName = Page.MapPath("starwarquotes.txt")
    RandomQuotation.Text = RetrieveRandomLine(MyFileName)
End Sub
```

Comments

The `RetrieveRandomLine` function will open a text file called recipe1816random.txt and return a random line from that text file. The function has a single argument, `FileName`, that specifies the name of the file from which to retrieve the line of text. Be sure to include the full path to the file (the `MapPath` method of the `System.Web.UI.Page` class can be useful in this situation). Note that this function can also read text files in Unicode format.

When you're using the `StreamReader` object, there are a number of errors that you should trap, including exceptions raised when the text file or the directory in which it resides aren't found. In this example, if an exception is raised, the exception message is displayed instead of the random quotation.

Assuming there are no exceptions raised, the function reads each line of the text file into a `System.Collections.ArrayList`. The `Peek()` method of the `StreamReader` class examines the next character in the text file. A value of -1 indicates that there are no more characters to read, so you can assume that the end of the file has been reached.

The `ReadLine()` method reads a line of the text file up to a line feed or a carriage return immediately followed by a line feed. One of the elements in the `ArrayList` is then selected at random and returned from the function.

See Also

Section 17.1, "Opening a File"

Section 17.10, "Reading a File Line-by-Line"

Section 17.14, "Extracting a Single Line from a File"

Section 17.17, "Randomizing Lines and Words in a File"

17.17. Randomizing Lines and Words in a File

You want to randomize every line, or every word, in a text file.

Technique

This example reads a file word-by-word or line-by-line and places the contents in an ArrayList. It then shuffles the ArrayList and displays the shuffled contents.

The ASPX page is as follows:

```
      <asp:Button id="RandomizeWords" runat="server" Text="Randomize Words"
OnClick="RandomizeWords_Click"></asp:Button> 
      <asp:Button id="RandomizeLines" runat="server" Text="Randomize Lines"
OnClick="RandomizeLines_Click"></asp:Button>
      <br>
      <asp:Label id="Randomized" runat="server" />
```

In `<script runat="server" />` block or codebehind:

```
    Dim fileName As String = Server.MapPath("starwarquotes.txt")
    Private Function GetRandomizedLinesFromFile(filename As String) As String
       Dim sr As StreamReader = Nothing
       Dim result As String = String.Empty
       Dim lines As New ArrayList()
       Try
          sr = File.OpenText(filename)
          Dim line As String = sr.ReadLine()
          While Not (line Is Nothing)
             lines.Add(line)
             line = sr.ReadLine()
          End While
       Catch ex As Exception
          result = ex.Message
       Finally
          If Not (sr Is Nothing) Then
             sr.Close()
          End If
       End Try
       'use GetRandomListOfInts to shuffle the order of lines
       Dim randInts As Integer() = GetRandomListOfInts(lines.Count)
       Dim sb As New StringBuilder()
       Dim i As Integer
       For i = 0 To randInts.Length - 1
          sb.Append((lines(randInts(i)) + "<br>"))
       Next i

       result = sb.ToString()

       Return result
    End Function
    Private Function GetRandomizedWordsFromFile(filename As String) As String
       Dim sr As StreamReader = Nothing
       Dim result As String = String.Empty
       Dim delimiter As Char() = {ControlChars.Tab, " "c} 'tab and space
       Dim words As New ArrayList()
       Try
          sr = File.OpenText(filename)
```

```
        Dim line As String = sr.ReadLine()
        While Not (line Is Nothing)
            'split the line into words
            Dim wordsInLine As String() = line.Split(delimiter)
            Dim word As String
            For Each word In  wordsInLine
                words.Add(word)
            Next word
            line = sr.ReadLine()
        End While
    Catch ex As Exception
        result = ex.Message
    Finally
        If Not (sr Is Nothing) Then
            sr.Close()
        End If
    End Try
    'use GetRandomListOfInts to shuffle the order of words
    Dim randInts As Integer() = GetRandomListOfInts(words.Count)
    Dim sb As New StringBuilder()
    Dim i As Integer
    For i = 0 To randInts.Length - 1
        sb.Append((words(randInts(i)) + " "))
    Next i

    result = sb.ToString()

    Return result
End Function

Private Function GetRandomListOfInts(ListLength As Integer) As Integer()
    'make a list of ints the length of parameter
    Dim listInOrder As New ArrayList()
    Dim i As Integer
    For i = 0 To ListLength - 1
        listInOrder.Add(i)
    Next i

    Dim randomNumbers(ListLength) As Integer
    Dim r As New Random()

    'shuffle the list of numbers
    Dim j As Integer
    For j = 0 To ListLength - 1
        Dim randomIndex As Integer = r.Next(listInOrder.Count)
        randomNumbers(j) = CInt(listInOrder(randomIndex))
```

```
            listInOrder.RemoveAt(randomIndex)
        Next j


        Return randomNumbers
    End Function


    Protected Sub RandomizeWords_Click(ByVal sender As Object, _
ByVal e As System.EventArgs)
        Randomized.Text = GetRandomizedWordsFromFile(fileName)
    End Sub


    Protected Sub RandomizeLines_Click(ByVal sender As Object, _
ByVal e As System.EventArgs)
        Randomized.Text = GetRandomizedLinesFromFile(fileName)
    End Sub
```

Comments

Once the words or lines are in an ArrayList, the contents can be shuffled by shuffling the index. The `GetRandomListOfInts` method creates an ordered list of numbers the same length as the number of words or lines. The code randomizes the ordered list using the `Random.Next` method of the `Random` object. The `Random.Next` method returns a random number between 0 and the number of items in the ordered list.

The random list adds the item from the ordered list that has the index of the generated random number. The ordered list removes that same item from its list so that the number cannot be used again. After looping through the complete list, the ordered list has no items and the random list is filled with the ordered list numbers that are picked out at "random." The following example shows how this works with four items.

Start:

```
random list Empty
ordered list 0, 1, 2, 3
```

Loop 1: `Random.Next` returns 3

```
random list 2
ordered list 0, 1, 3
```

Loop 2: `Random.Next` returns 0

```
random list 2, 0
ordered list 1, 3
```

Loop 3: `Random.Next` returns 1

```
random list 2, 0, 3
ordered list 1
```

Loop 4: Random.Next returns 0

```
random list 2, 0, 3, 1
ordered list Empty
```

See Also

Section 17.1, "Opening a File"

ReadFromFile—http://www.aspalliance.com/olson/methods/ReadFromFile.aspx

Randomize or Shuffle Dataset Contents—http://www.aspalliance.com/stevesmith/articles/RandomizeDataset.aspx

Random.Next Method—http://msdn.microsoft.com/library/en-us/cpref/html/frlrfsystemrandomclassnexttopic.asp in the .NET Framework Class Library

17.18. Creating a File in Isolated Storage

You want to create a file in a user's isolated storage space and fill it with some data.

Technique

You can use the classes available in the System.IO.IsolatedStorage namespace to access a user's isolated store.

In <script runat="server" /> block or codebehind:

```
Sub Page_Load(sender As Object, e As EventArgs)
    Dim stream As System.IO.IsolatedStorage.IsolatedStorageFileStream
    Dim writer As System.IO.StreamWriter
    Dim data As String = "The data you want to store"

    Try
        stream = New System.IO.IsolatedStorage.IsolatedStorageFileStream(_
"datafile.txt", System.IO.FileMode.OpenOrCreate)
        writer = New System.IO.StreamWriter(stream)

        writer.WriteLine(data)
    Catch exc As Exception
        Response.Write(exc.ToString())
    Finally
        If Not writer Is Nothing Then
            writer.Close()
        End If
        If Not stream Is Nothing Then
            stream.Close()
```

```
        End If
    End Try
End Sub
```

Comments

When you need to store data in a file, it is important that you choose a location that doesn't conflict with another file. Isolated storage avoids this risk by using a unique data compartment that is associated with some part of the code's identity (a Web site, publisher, or signature). This example writes a simple file called datafile.txt to a user's isolated storage. The storage area is located on the user's computer (the location depends on the operating system) and enables a Web site or application to store data related to a particular user in a place that's unique to a particular Web page.

This technique requires that the proper permissions be set up for the user account that is running the code. In this case, write access to the server's hard drive is crucial to avoid various exceptions.

See also

Section 17.19, "Reading a File in Isolated Storage"

Introduction to Isolated Storage—`http://msdn.microsoft.com/library/en-us/cpguide/html/cpconintroductiontoisolatedstorage.asp`

17.19. Reading a File in Isolated Storage

You want to open and read a file that is stored in a user's isolated storage.

Technique

You can use the classes available in the `System.IO.IsolatedStorage` namespace to access a user's isolated store.

In `<script runat="server" />` block or codebehind:

```
Sub Page_Load(sender As Object, e As EventArgs)
    Dim stream As System.IO.IsolatedStorage.IsolatedStorageFileStream
    Dim reader As System.IO.StreamReader

    Try

        stream = New System.IO.IsolatedStorage.IsolatedStorageFileStream( _
"datafile.txt", System.IO.FileMode.OpenOrCreate)
        reader = New System.IO.StreamReader(stream)
```

```
      While reader.Peek() > -1
         Response.Write(Server.HtmlEncode(reader.ReadLine()) & "<br>")
      End While
   Catch exc As Exception
      Response.Write(exc.ToString())
   Finally
      If Not reader Is Nothing Then
         reader.Close()
      End If
      If Not stream Is Nothing Then
         stream.Close()
      End If
   End Try
End Sub
```

Comments

The `System.IO.IsolatedStorageFileStream` object can be used to both create and open files in isolated storage. `System.IO.StreamReader` can be used to read the information stored in the file (as demonstrated in this example). Remember when creating or reading files in isolated storage, only the page that created the file can read it. (That is, unless you set the permissions for the file or directory in ASP.NET.) An example of a page that writes to and reads from its isolated storage is included on the book's Web site.

This technique requires that the proper permissions be set up for the user account that is running the code. In this case, `write` access to the server's hard drive is crucial to avoid various exceptions.

See Also

Section 17.18, "Creating a File in Isolated Storage"

Performing Isolated Storage Tasks—`http://msdn.microsoft.com/library/en-us/ cpguide/html/cpconusingisolatedstorage.asp`

18

Working with Collections

18.0. Introduction

Collections play an integral part in any non-trivial application, whether they are simple arrays or more complicated data types. The .NET Framework provides a namespace, `System.Collections`, full of ready-to-use collections of various flavors. In this chapter, you find examples that demonstrate the use of the most common of these built-in collections, as well as examples of how to write your own collections. Once you have that mastered, you'll want to look at some of the references provided, which link to automatic collection code generators that can greatly reduce the amount of grunt work you must go through.

18.1. Declaring Collections

You want to create a collection to hold a number of values or objects.

Technique

The .NET Framework includes a number of commonly used collections. They are found in the `System.Collections` namespace, and can hold any object type, which means they can hold *any* type, because in .NET, all types inherit from object. This example demonstrates this using a simple array list.

```
Sub Page_Load (Sender As Object, E As EventArgs)
  Dim al As New ArrayList(5)

  al.Add("one")
  al.Add(2)
  al.Add(False)
  al.Add(New System.Object())
```

```
   Response.Write("Successfully added " & al.Count & _
" different types of objects to an ArrayList.")
End Sub
```

Comments

Declaring and using collections in .NET is very straightforward. Later in this chapter, you'll learn how to use some of the different collections included in the framework, as well as how to create your own strongly typed collections.

See Also

Section 18.3, "Creating a Custom Collection"

Section 18.9, "Using an ArrayList Collection"

18.2. Looping Through Each Item in an Enumerable Collection

You want to loop through each item in a collection that supports the `IEnumerable` interface.

Technique

`IEnumerable` is an interface that provides simple iteration of items. It is implemented by many of the .NET Framework classes. A few of the more common ones include:

- `Array`
- `ArrayList`
- `ControlCollection`
- `DataGridItemCollection`
- `DataView`
- `HashTable`
- `HttpSessionState`
- `ListItemCollection`
- `Queue`
- `SortedList`
- `SqlDataReader`
- `Stack`
- `StateBag`

To iterate through each item in a collection that implements IEnumerable, you first populate the collection with some data. For this example, you create a new ArrayList called myList and use the Add method to add members. You can loop through the collection by using the For Each statement, and specify the name of the variable (item in this example) to represent each item in the loop. Now just write the value of item on each iteration.

In <script runat="server" /> block or codebehind:

```
Sub Page_Load(sender As Object, e As EventArgs)
  Dim i As Integer
  Dim item As String
  Dim myList As New System.Collections.ArrayList()
  myList.Add("Zero")
  myList.Add("One")
  myList.Add("Two")
  myList.Add("Three")
  myList.Add("Four")
  myList.Add("Five")

  For Each item In myList
    Response.Write(item & "<BR>")
  Next
End Sub
```

See Also

Section 18.5, "Using a HashTable Collection"

Section 18.6, "Using a Queue Collection"

Section 18.7, "Using a Stack Collection"

Section 18.8, "Using a SortedList Collection"

Section 18.9, "Using an ArrayList Collection"

IEnumerable Interface—http://msdn.microsoft.com/library/en-us/cpref/html/frlrfsystemcollectionsienumerableclasstopic.asp

18.3. Creating a Custom Collection

You want to create a custom collection class.

Technique

A custom collection class allows the use of the For Each syntax (foreach in C#) to loop through a set of custom typed items. The custom collection class must internally keep references to the items with an array or other type of collection (ArrayList, HashTable). The .NET Framework then requires the following two interfaces to be implemented in order to support the For Each syntax:

- System.Collections.IEnumerable
- Function GetEnumerator() As IEnumerator
- System.Collections.IEnumerator
- Sub Reset()
- Function MoveNext() As Boolean
- ReadOnly Property Current As Object

In <script runat="server" /> block or codebehind:

```
Sub Page_Load()
   Dim _customCollection As CustomCollection
   Dim _customItem As CustomItem
   Dim _index As Integer

   _customCollection = New CustomCollection(10)
   For Each _customItem In _customCollection
     _index = _customItem.Index
   Next
 End Sub
Custom Collection defined in CustomCollection.vb
   Public Class CustomCollection
     Implements IEnumerable, IEnumerator

     Private customItems() As CustomItem
     Private currentIndex As Integer = -1

     Public Sub New(ByVal Count As Integer)
       Dim index As Integer

       ReDim customItems(Count - 1)
       For index = 0 To Count - 1
         customItems(index) = New CustomItem(index)
       Next
     End Sub

   #Region "Implementation of IEnumerable"
     Public Function GetEnumerator() As Ienumerator
➥Implements IEnumerable.GetEnumerator
       Return CType(Me, IEnumerator)
     End Function
   #End Region
```

```
    #Region "Implementation of IEnumerator"
      Public Sub Reset() Implements IEnumerator.Reset
        currentIndex = -1
      End Sub

      Public Function MoveNext() As Boolean Implements IEnumerator.MoveNext
        If currentIndex < customItems.Length - 1 Then
          currentIndex = currentIndex + 1
          Return True
        Else
          Return False
        End If
      End Function

      Public ReadOnly Property Current() As Object
➥Implements IEnumerator.Current
        Get
          Return customItems(currentIndex)
        End Get
      End Property
    #End Region
    End Class

Custom Item defined in CustomItem.vb
    Public Class CustomItem
      Private _index As Integer

      Public ReadOnly Property Index() As Integer
        Get
          Return _index
        End Get
      End Property

      Public Sub New(ByVal Index As Integer)
        _index = Index
      End Sub
    End Class
```

Comments

This implementation uses a simple array of the CustomItem type and offers nothing beyond the For Each support. It can be easily extended to support additional array or ArrayList methods, such as Count/Length and Item. The base collection type can also be changed to ArrayList or HashTable for further functionality.

This implementation of the CustomItem type is no more than a contrived example with a single property of Index. It should be extended to include the various properties and methods relevant to the actual custom item. The construction of the item, or set of items, can also come from an external data store.

See Also

IEnumerable Members—`http://msdn.microsoft.com/library/en-us/cpref/html/ frlrfSystemCollectionsIEnumerableMembersTopic.asp`, MSDN Library

IEnumerator Members—`http://msdn.microsoft.com/library/en-us/cpref/html/ frlrfSystemCollectionsIEnumeratorMembersTopic.asp`, MSDN Library

Custom Collection Generator add-in for VS.NET—
`http://www.sellsbrothers.com/tools/#collectiongen`

Custom Collection Generator: CodeSmith (beta)—`http://www.ericjsmith.net/ejsmith/ codesmith.htm`

18.4. Passing an Array of Parameters to a Method

> You want to declare a method so that it takes an array of parameters.

Technique

A method can have a `param` array as one of its parameters. The syntax for this varies depending on the language used, but in both C# and VB.NET only one such parameter can exist for a given method, and it must be the last parameter.

The VB.NET code is as follows:

```
Sub Page_Load(sender As Object, e As System.EventArgs)
    PrintParams("a", "b")
    PrintParams("c", "d", "e", "f", "g")
End Sub 'Page_Load

Sub PrintParams(ParamArray list() As String)
    Dim i As Integer
    For i = 0 To list.Length - 1
        Response.Write((list(i) + "<br>"))
    Next i
End Sub 'PrintParams
```

The `PrintParams` method in C# is almost identical, but uses the `params` keyword:

```
void PrintParams(params string[] list)
{
  for(int i=0;i<list.Length;i++)
    Response.Write(list[i] + "<br>");
}
```

Comments

Sometimes it is useful to be able to specify an arbitrary number of parameters for a method. Whenever possible, however, you should try to use method overloading, because this will provide compile-time type checking and allows for enhanced design-time features like code completion.

See Also

Section 14.6, "Overloading Methods"

18.5. Using a HashTable Collection

You want to use a hash table to store a collection of data.

Technique

You create a new object of type System.Collections.HashTable called myHash. Then, you add keys to the hash table by using the add method and passing in the name and value of each key. You can then retrieve the values of each key by using myHash("KeyName"). The value is returned as type of object, so if you need to convert it into a string, as in the following example, you simply call the ToString() method. Otherwise, you'll need to cast it to the type of object that you need.

The ASPX page is as follows:

```
<%@Import namespace="System.Collections"%>
<%@Import namespace="System.Drawing"%>
<HTML>
  <body>
    <form method="post" runat="server">
      <asp:Label ID="MyLabel" Runat="server">Sample Text</asp:Label><br>
    </form>
  </body>
</HTML>
```

In <script runat="server" /> block or codebehind:

```
Sub Page_Load(sender As Object, e As EventArgs)
  Dim myHash As New Hashtable()
  myHash.Add("Red", "#FF0000")
  myHash.Add("Green", "#00FF00")
  myHash.Add("Blue", "#0000FF")

  MyLabel.BackColor=ColorTranslator.FromHtml(myHash("Blue").ToString())
  MyLabel.ForeColor=ColorTranslator.FromHtml(myHash("Red").ToString())
End Sub
```

See Also

HashTable class—http://msdn.microsoft.com/library/en-us/cpref/html/
frlrfSystemCollectionsHashtableClassTopic.asp

18.6. Using a Queue Collection

You want to use a queue to store a collection of data.

Technique

Create a new object of type System.Collections.Queue called myQueue. Add items to
the queue by using the EnQueue method and passing in the object you want to add to
the queue. You can then retrieve items from the front of the queue (remember a queue
is first-in-first-out, or FIFO) by using the DeQueue method. The item is returned as type
of object, so if you need to convert it into a string as in the following example, you simply call the ToString() method. Otherwise, you'll need to cast it to the type of object
that you need.

In <script runat="server" /> block or codebehind:

```
'Make sure System.Collections is imported
Sub Page_Load(sender As Object, e As EventArgs)
  Dim myQueue As New Queue()
  myQueue.Enqueue("One")
  myQueue.Enqueue("Two")
  myQueue.Enqueue("Three")

  While myQueue.Count > 0
    Response.Write(myQueue.Dequeue().ToString() & "<br>")
  End While
End Sub
```

See Also

Queue class—http://msdn.microsoft.com/library/en-us/cpref/html/
frlrfSystemCollectionsQueueClassTopic.asp

18.7. Using a Stack Collection

You want to use a stack to store a collection of data.

Technique

First, you create a new object of type System.Collections.Stack called myStack. You
then add items to the stack by using the Push method and passing in the object you

want to add to the top of the stack. You can then retrieve items from the top of the stack (remember a stack is last-in-first-out, or LIFO) by using the Pop method. The item is returned as type of object, so if you need to convert it into a string, as in the following example, you simply call the ToString() method. Otherwise, you'll need to cast it to the type of object that you need.

In <script runat="server" /> block or codebehind:

```
'Make sure System.Collections is imported
Sub Page_Load(sender As Object, e As EventArgs)
  Dim myStack As New Stack()
  myStack.Push("One")
  myStack.Push("Two")
  myStack.Push("Three")

  While myStack.Count > 0
    Response.Write(myStack.Pop().ToString() & "<br>")
  End While
End Sub
```

See Also

Stack class—http://msdn.microsoft.com/library/en-us/cpref/html/ frlrfSystemCollectionsStackClassTopic.asp

18.8. Using a SortedList Collection

You want to use a sorted list to store a collection of data.

Technique

Create a new object of type System.Collections.SortedList called mySortedList. You can optionally specify an initial capacity for the collection, which will optimize performance if you know in advance how big it will need to be. It will resize as needed if you exceed this initial capacity. You add items to the sorted list by using the Add method and passing in a key value and the object you want to add. You can then retrieve items from the collection by using the key value, just like with a hash table. The objects are stored sorted by the key values (not the value of the objects themselves), and the collection implements the IEnumerable and IEnumerator interfaces, so you can use a For Each loop to output all of its contents in sorted order.

The items are returned as object types, so if you need to convert it into a string, as in the following example, you simply call the ToString() method. Otherwise, you'll need to cast it to the type of object that you need.

In `<script runat="server" />` block or codebehind:

```
'Make sure System.Collections is imported
Sub Page_Load(sender As Object, e As EventArgs)
  Dim mySortedList As New SortedList(10)
  mySortedList.Add("One", 1)
  mySortedList.Add("Two", 2)
  mySortedList.Add("Three", 3)
  mySortedList.Add("Four", 4)
  mySortedList.Add("Five", 5)
  mySortedList.Add("Six", 6)
  mySortedList.Add("Seven", 7)

  ' alternate syntax
  mySortedList("Eight") = 8

  mySortedList.Add("Nine", 9)
  mySortedList.Add("Ten", 10)
  Dim d As DictionaryEntry

  ' Note that results are sorted by Key, not Value
  For Each d In mySortedList
    Response.Write("Key: " & d.Key & " Value: " & d.Value & "<br>")
  Next
End Sub
```

See Also

SortedList class—http://msdn.microsoft.com/library/en-us/cpref/html/
frlrfSystemCollectionsSortedListClassTopic.asp

18.9. Using an ArrayList Collection

You want to use an array list to store a collection of data.

Technique

First, you create a new object of type `System.Collections.ArrayList` called `myArrayList`. You can optionally specify an initial capacity for the collection, which will optimize performance if you know in advance how big it will need to be. It will resize as needed if you exceed this initial capacity. You add items to the array list by using the

Add method and passing in the object you want to add. You can then retrieve items from the collection ordinally, just like an array. This collection implements the IEnumerable and IEnumerator interfaces, so you can use a For Each loop to output all of its contents in order by index.

The items are returned as object types, so if you need to convert it into a string, as in the following example, you simply call the ToString() method. Otherwise, you'll need to cast it to the type of object that you need.

In <script runat="server" /> block or codebehind:

```
'Make sure System.Collections is imported
Sub Page_Load(sender As Object, e As EventArgs)
  Dim myArrayList As New ArrayList(10)
  myArrayList.Add("One")
  myArrayList.Add("Two")
  myArrayList.Add("Three")
  myArrayList.Add("Four")
  myArrayList.Add("Five")
  myArrayList.Add("Six")
  myArrayList.Add("Seven")
  myArrayList.Add("Eight")
  myArrayList.Add("Nine")
  myArrayList.Add("Ten")
  Dim o As Object
  For Each o In myArrayList
    Response.Write(o.ToString() & "<br>")
  Next
End Sub
```

See Also

ArrayList class—http://msdn.microsoft.com/library/en-us/cpref/html/
frlrfSystemCollectionsArrayListClassTopic.asp

V

Network Access

19

Web Services

19.0. Introduction

Web services have received a great deal of press in recent years, and they certainly are useful in many situations. With the .NET Framework, Microsoft has made it incredibly easy to expose and consume Web services in your ASP.NET applications. In this short chapter, you will find everything you need to begin using Web services in your applications.

19.1. Creating a Web Service

You want to create a Web service (an .ASMX file).

Technique

To illustrate creating a Web service, this simple example takes a string and returns a message. To do this, you type in the following code and save it as recipe2001vb.asmx (you can also download this file from the book's Web site).

```
<%@ WebService Language="vb" Class="recipe1901vb" %>
Imports System.Web.Services
Imports System.Text

Public Class recipe1901vb
    <WebMethod()> _
        Public Function GreetCustomer(ByVal person as String) As String
            Dim output As StringBuilder = New StringBuilder()
            output.Append("Welcome to Cook Center Mr/Mrs.")
            output.Append(Person)
            output.Append(" , Hope you are enjoying our recipes!!" )
```

```
            GreetCustomer = output.ToString()

      End Function
End Class
```

Now, you save this file in some Web directory. This is all that is required to create a Web service! To see how it works, open the file in a Web browser. Microsoft provides a default test page feature in the .NET Framework for its Web services. In that page, you will see a `GreetCustomer` function. Click it, and it will take you to another page. There, you enter some text and press Invoke. A new window opens with the output in XML format.

Comments

recipe2001vb is the name of the class in this example. In this class, you create a Web method called `GreetCustomer`. By adding the `<WebMethod()>` attribute to a method within a .ASMX file, you create a Web service. Here, the `Key` attribute is `<WebMethod>`. This `WebMethod` attribute indicates to the .NET Framework that the specified method should be made accessible via standard Internet protocols. These Web service methods should be defined as `public`, which indicates that they can be accessible from outside parent class. This Web method has various attributes. This example uses the `description` attribute. The following properties are defined for the `WebMethod` attribute:

- `BufferResponse`—Specifies whether the response for this Web method should be buffered. By default, it is set to `True`.

- `CacheDuration`—This specifies the number of seconds the Web method response is stored in cache.

- `Description`—Specifies the user-friendly description of the `public` Web method.

- `EnableSession`—Specifies whether session state is enabled for the Web method. Default setting is `false`.

- `MessageName`—Specifies an alias name for a Web method. This `MessageName` attribute allows you to provide different names for overloaded methods.

- `TransactionOption`—Specifies the Enterprise service transaction support for the Web method.

See Also

http://msdn.microsoft.com/Webservices/

19.2. Consuming a Web Service using a WSDL Generated Proxy

You want to use WSDL.EXE to create a proxy class to use to consume a Web service in your application.

Technique

In order to consume the Web service, you must first create a proxy class. The proxy class will provide you with early binding and will pass messages to the Web service so that you don't have to worry about this detail. You create the proxy class by using a little tool called WSDL.EXE, which is included in the .NET Framework installation. In order to create a proxy class, WSDL.EXE needs to know the interfaces provided by the Web service. By adding ?WSDL to the end of the Web service URL, you can get the Web service's WSDL interface, which WSDL.EXE then uses to create the proxy class.

```
Syntax: WSDL.EXE <parameters> <URL or Path>
```

This example assumes path is configured to access WSDL.EXE assembly from anywhere. Now open the command prompt. Go to your file location and type this code:

```
wsdl /l:vb /o:recipe1902vb.vb http://localhost/cookbook/recipe1901vb.asmx?wsdl
➥/n:recipe1902vb
```

You have to type your URL location in place of `http://localhost/cookbook/recipe1901vb.asmx?wsdl`. The /n: recipe1902vb part of the command helps by giving a namespace to the generated proxy class. This example uses recipe1902vb as the namespace. Also, the /l:vb portion of the code tells WSDL to create the proxy in VB.NET. After running the previous command, you should see this result:

```
Microsoft (R) Web Services Description Language Utility
[Microsoft (R) .NET Framework, Version 1.0.3705.0]
Copyright (C) Microsoft Corporation 1998-2001. All rights reserved.

Writing file 'recipe1902vb.vb'.
```

The recipe1902vb.vb file is generated in the specified directory. You now have to compile this code into a .NET assembly/DLL, so that you can use it in your applications. The following command compiles the code into an assembly:

```
vbc /out:recipe1902vb.dll /t:library /r:system.web.dll,system.dll,
system.xml.dll,system.web.services.dll recipe1902vb.vb
```

After running this command, you should see the following result:

```
Microsoft (R) Visual Basic .NET Compiler version 7.00.9466
for Microsoft (R) .NET Framework version 1.00.3705
Copyright (C) Microsoft Corporation 1987-2001. All rights reserved.
```

Now you have your DLL. To use it, you copy it into the /bin directory under your application directory. If the /bin directory is not there, create that directory and copy recipe1902vb.dll into it. To consume the Web service using this proxy, you can use the following simple ASP.NET page, which calls the Web service in the button's click event:

```vb
<%@ Page Language="vb" debug="True" %>
<%@ Import namespace="recipe1902vb" %>
<script language="vb" runat="server">

Public Sub CallWS(sender as System.Object, e as System.EventArgs)
   Dim CookWS as new recipe1902vb.recipe1901vb()
   CookWS.Timeout = 5000
   lblResult.Text = CookWS.GreetCustomer(TextWho.Text)

End Sub

</Script>

<html>
  <body>
   <form id="Form1" method="post" runat="server">
   <center><b>Welcome to Cook Center</b><br>
   Please enter your name
   <asp:TextBox id="TextWho" runat="server"></asp:TextBox><br>
   <asp:Button id="ForWSCall" runat="server" Text="Invoke"
      OnClick="CallWS"></asp:Button><br>
   <asp:Label id="lblResult" runat="server" Width="100%"></asp:Label>
   </form>
   </body>
</html>
```

See Also

WSDL at MSDN—http://msdn.microsoft.com/library/en-us/dnwebsrv/html/wsdlexplained.asp

19.3. Consuming a Web Service Using a VS.NET Web Reference

You want to add a Web reference using Visual Studio .NET and then use this Web reference to consume a Web service.

Technique

In Visual Studio.NET (VS.NET), a *Web reference* describes when you have a reference to an XML Web service. In the previous section you learned how to use WSDL.EXE to create a proxy class, and then to use that proxy class in your ASP.NET project. VS.NET's Add Web Reference tool essentially does this for you. It automatically creates the proxy class for you to consume in your ASP.NET project.

The first step, after you have created or opened your ASP.NET project in VS.NET, is to right-click the specific project and choose Add Web Reference. You are prompted with a form that allows you to specify the URL of any Web service.

Alternatively, you can dive into the UDDI directories to find your service. The Web service used in this example is at `http://rob.santra.com/webservices/public/solace/index.asmx`. Copy and paste the URL into the address bar in the Add Web Reference dialog box, and then press Enter to load the service.

You will notice that VS.NET displays the page on the left, and gives you the following options:

- View Contract
- View Documentation

You can explore both of these options on your own.

Press the Add Reference button to add this Web service to your ASP.NET project. The new node named Web References is then added to your project under the Solution Explorer.

Right-click the `com.santra.rob` node in the tree, and choose Properties. Change the Folder Name property to `AI`. This will force the namespace of the proxy class to be `AI`.

Let's examine how you'll consume this Web service in the ASP.NET project. First, you add a TextBox (`InputTextBox`), a button (`SubmitButton`), and a label (`ResponseLabel`) to the form. And the SubmitButton's `Click` event:

```
Dim solace As New Recipe1903cs.AI.Solace()
ResponseLabel.Text = solace.speak(InputTextBox.Text)
```

19.4. Returning an Image from a Web Service

You want to return an image from a Web service.

Technique

You must, of course, first retrieve your image from some location. Refer to Chapter 22, "Generating and Manipulating Images," to learn how to dynamically create images on the fly. For this example, you can simply pull an image from the file system, and then stream the image back out via the Web service.

```
<WebService
➡(Namespace:="http://www.aspalliance.com/webservices/public/images/")>
Public Class Images
Inherits System.Web.Services.WebService
```

```
<WebMethod(Description:="Get an Image using Base64 Encoding")>
➥Public Function GetImage() As Byte()
    Return getBinaryFile(Server.MapPath("aspalliance_logo.gif"))
End Function 'GetImage

Public Function getBinaryFile(ByVal filename As String) As Byte()
    If File.Exists(filename) Then
    Try
        Dim s As FileStream = File.OpenRead(filename)
        Return ConvertStreamToByteBuffer(s)
    Catch e As Exception
        Return New Byte(0) {}
    End Try
    Else
    Return New Byte(0) {}
    End If
End Function 'getBinaryFile

Public Function ConvertStreamToByteBuffer _
(ByVal theStream As System.IO.Stream) As Byte()
    Dim bytes(theStream.Length) As Byte
    theStream.Read(bytes, CInt(0), CInt(theStream.Length))
    Return bytes
End Function 'CStreamToByte

End Class
```

Now, in order to use this Web service, you must use the WSDL.EXE tool to generate a proxy, and then use the proxy to retrieve and spit out the image:

```
    Dim i As New Images()
    Page.Response.BinaryWrite(i.GetImage())
```

Comments

Notice that the return type of the GetImage() method is a byte[]. When the .NET Framework recognizes this, it will automatically apply Base64 encoding to the data being sent over the wire. Base64 encoding is a pretty common encoding format for encoding data within XML documents.

See Also

Base64 Content-Transfer-Encoding—http://www.freesoft.org/CIE/RFC/1521/7.htm

20

LDAP/ADSI Directory Services

20.0. Introduction

Directory stores are becoming an increasingly common piece of the enterprise application. Active Directory is just one such directory store, and the Lightweight Directory Access Protocol (LDAP) provides access to many others. The .NET Framework's support for directory store access is mainly contained within the System.DirectoryServices namespace. This chapter's recipes demonstrate the most common operations you need to perform using the classes contained in this namespace.

> **See Also**
>
> Using System.DirectoryServices to Search the Active Directory—http://msdn.microsoft.com/library/en-us/dndotnet/html/dotnetadsearch.asp

20.1. Connecting to a Directory Store

You want to connect to and/or disconnect from a directory store using LDAP/ADSI.

Technique

The DirectoryServices namespace provides the developer with many avenues. There are four service providers you can use with DirectoryServices:

Directory Store	Access Format
Windows NT version 5.0, Windows 2000 and later	`"WinNT://path"`
Lightweight Directory Access Protocol (LDAP)	`"LDAP://path"`
Novell Netware Directory Service	`"NDS://path"`
Novell Netware 3.x	`"NWCOMPAT://path"`

This chapter focuses on WinNT and LDAP.

With WinNT, you can access domains, computers, print queues, and sessions. With LDAP, you can access organizations, locality, and root DS entry (`rootDSE`) objects.

Creating a connection is as simple as writing one line of code, although you must keep certain things in mind. For instance, if you only intend to read data from the directory, you don't have to set a login and password. Note that by not setting a login and password, the connection will use the default logged in account in the current session. In the case of an ASPX page, it will use the account set for the site, which will default to the standard `asp.net account`.

In order to edit the contents of the directory store, you log in using an `admin` account or an account that has administrative permissions.

You must add the reference `System.DirectoryServices.dll`, and make sure you have ADSI 2.5 installed. This is installed by default in Windows 2000 and later. If you want to make things easier and not have to type the whole address each time, you can place the line `Imports System.DirectoryServices` at the top of the VB code block. The following code demonstrates how to connect to a directory store:

```
Dim Entry As System.DirectoryServices.DirectoryEntry

Try
    Entry = New System.DirectoryServices.DirectoryEntry("WinNT://DomainName"
)
    'Notice that we are using the WinNT provider
    'Note that if you wish to get access to the local computers
    'accounts you would do DomainName/ComputerName

    'Note that no Login or password was set, this line would end up
    'using the default account as stated above.
    'Dim Entry As New System.DirectoryServices.DirectoryEntry(
➡"WinNT://DomainName",Login,Password)
    'This will log in using the account specified
    'Note you can also set the authentication type as the 4th parameter.
    Dim child As DirectoryServices.DirectoryEntry
    For Each child In Entry.Children
        Response.Write(child.Name.ToString() & "<br>")
    Next
Catch
    'Error message
```

```
Finally
   Entry.Close()
   'This will close the connection
End Try
```

Comments

As you can see, it is a simple matter to gain a connection, and an even simpler matter to close it. Active Directory is a tree structure. That means that each node or object contains a set of other nodes. You can traverse, search, and even modify the tree.

See Also

Section 20.2, "Authenticating a User Using Directory Services"

20.2. Authenticating a User Using Directory Services

You want to use Directory Services to authenticate a user.

Technique

As noted in the previous section, you must have certain permissions to do certain things. When using the WinNT provider, you can search though the collections to a point until permissions are required. This is all depending on how your network is set up. If you reach an object that needs certain permissions, the system will then use your login and password. As long as objects within the path are open for everyone to access, you don't need to be authenticated.

This example shows the use of LDAP to search though the directory. The new objects you will learn about include `DirectorySearcher` and `SearchResult`.

```
Function ValidateUser(ByVal Login As String, _
ByVal Password As String) As Boolean
    Dim Entry As DirectoryEntry
    Try
      Entry = New DirectoryEntry("LDAP://DomainName", Login, Password)
         'DirectorySearcher can only be used when using the LDAP provider.
         'If we were searching for something specific we
         'could put it in the path above.
         'Of course you don't need to do it there; you could also
         'use the filter property of the DirectorySearcher object.

         Dim Search As DirectorySearcher = New DirectorySearcher(Entry)
```

```
    'Notice that now we want to retrieve the results,
    'we then must use the SearchResult object.
    'When retrieving results there are two objects "SearchResult"
    'and "SearchResults" depending on how you retrieve the results
    'depends will tell what to use.

    Dim results As SearchResult = Search.FindOne

    'Since we are only looking to authenticate we don't want to take
    'too long so we are only searching for one, which in this case
    'decides which search object to use.

    Return True
    'If it authenticates and the user and password is valid then you
    'return true, else it will throw an Exception and return false
Catch
    Return False
Finally
    'Finally we close the entry which will close all resources using entry
    Entry.Close()
End Try
End Function
```

Comments

As you can see, this process is a fairly simple matter. You might wonder why you can't just compare using the user information. Mainly because you must have admin rights to search though user information.

See Also
Section 20.3, "Reading a Value from a Directory Store"

20.3. Reading a Value from a Directory Store

You want to read values from a directory store using Directory Services.

Technique

To read from a directory store, you must first know the name of the property you want to read. You can then read the value of that property. This example uses the LDAP provider; using this provider, you can specify which user you want to edit. Keep in mind that if the current login doesn't have read permissions, you cannot obtain the desired values. The following example shows how to read a particular user's home phone number property.

```
Sub Page_Load(ByVal sender As System.Object, _
ByVal e As System.EventArgs)
    'Put user code to initialize the page here

    'Note that this is getting a pre filtered result for the desired User
    Dim User As System.DirectoryServices.DirectoryEntry
    Try
      User = New System.DirectoryServices.DirectoryEntry( _
"LDAP://CN=Username, CN=users, DC=DomainName")
        Dim Value As String
        Value = User.Properties(&quot;HomeNumber&quot;).Item(0)
        'Now that value contains the value of that property you
        'can use it however you see fit.
        'Note also that each property might contain more then one
        'value depending on the property
        'That is why we used a zero above in item to get the first value.
    Catch
        'Show error message
    Finally
        User.Close()
    End Try
End Sub
```

Comments

As you can see, reading values is simple. However, the real issue is how to get the property names. There is a `PropertyNames` property on `User` that is a collection holding all of the property names for this object. Using a `For Each` loop, you can easily iterate through all of the supported properties. Note, however, that numeric indexers (for example, `User.Properties(2).Item(0)`) will not work.

See Also
Section 20.4, "Writing a Value to a Directory Store"

20.4. Writing a Value to a Directory Store

You want to write a value to a directory store using Directory Services.

Technique

Writing to an entry in the directory store involves nearly the same code as reading a value, other than the actions to actually set and save the value.

```
Sub Page_Load(ByVal sender As System.Object, _
ByVal e As System.EventArgs)
    'Put user code to initialize the page here

    'Note that this is getting a pre filtered result for the desired User
    Dim User As System.DirectoryServices.DirectoryEntry
    Try
        User = New System.DirectoryServices.DirectoryEntry( _
"LDAP://CN=Username, CN= users, DC=DomainName")
        User.Properties("HomeNumber").Item(0) = "8501234567"
        'Now that value contains the value of that property you can
        'use it however you see fit.
        'Note also that each property might contain more then one value
        'depending on the property
        'That is why we used a zero above in item to get the first value.
        User.CommitChanges()
        'This saves the changes
    Catch
        'Show error message
    Finally
        User.Close()
    End Try
End Sub
```

Comments

If you consider the connection example in example 20.1, you can see that it isn't set to any path other than the domain name. You can then go to the children and use the Add method to add a new entry. In the present example, you narrowed the nodes to one user. Instead of editing it, you can remove this entry. Use the `DeleteTree` method of the object `User.DeleteTree` to delete that entry and all its sub-entries. If you have many entries, you can delete a child entry by using `children.remove(EntryObject)`.

See Also

Section 20.1, "Connecting to a Directory Store"

Section 20.3, "Reading a Value from a Directory Store"

Internet Tasks and Techniques

21.0. Introduction

Many Web applications require specific network resources to perform their functions. Uploading files, sending or retrieving email, and making HTTP requests are some of the most common Internet tasks that Web applications must perform. In this chapter, you will find a variety of examples describing how you can utilize standard Internet protocols in your applications with the help of the .NET Framework's class library.

21.1. Screen Scraping the Contents of a Web Page

You want to "screen scrape" the contents of a Web page.

Technique

This example screen scrapes, or retrieves the content of, another page and displays the results.

The ASPX page is as follows:

```
<form runat="server">
  <asp:Button Runat="server" ID="SubmitButton"
Text="Get CNN.com Home Page" OnClick="SubmitButton_Click"/><br>
  <asp:TextBox Runat="server"  id="WebResponseText" Width="780" Height="300"
TextMode="MultiLine"/>
  <asp:Label Runat="server" ID="WebResponseLabel"/>
</form>
```

This example creates a Web request that scrapes the contents of the specified Web page and displays the results.

In `<script runat="server" />` block or codebehind:

```
Sub SubmitButton_Click(ByVal sender As System.Object, _
ByVal e As System.EventArgs)
  Dim RequestUrl As String = "http://www.cnn.com"

  Dim WebRequestObject As HttpWebRequest
  Dim sr As StreamReader
  Dim WebResponseObject As HttpWebResponse

  Try
    WebRequestObject = CType(WebRequest.Create(RequestUrl), HttpWebRequest)
    WebRequestObject.Method = "GET"

    WebResponseObject = CType(WebRequestObject.GetResponse(), HttpWebResponse)
    sr = New StreamReader(WebResponseObject.GetResponseStream)

    Dim Results as string = sr.ReadToEnd
    WebResponseLabel.Text = Results
    WebResponseText.Text = Results
  Finally
    Try
      sr.Close()
    Catch
    End Try

    Try
      WebResponseObject.Close()
      WebRequestObject.Abort()
    Catch
    End Try
  End Try
End Sub
```

Comments

Screen scraping grabs the contents of an external Web page. An HTTP Web request is created and the target Web page is requested and returned through an HTTP Web response object. A `StreamReader` object is extracted from the HTTP Web response object containing the string contents of the requested page. The response from the target Web page can then be parsed and displayed to the client. This can all occur within a single postback, thus allowing you to incorporate content from other pages.

A reference to the `System.Net` namespace is required for the `HttpWebRequest` and `HttpWebResponse` objects. Similarly, a reference to the `System.IO` namespace is required for the `StreamReader` object.

See Also

Section 1.4, "Submitting Data to Another Page Using ASP.NET"

Section 21.2, "Screen Scraping the Contents of a Web Page that Requires Post Information"

21.2. Screen Scraping the Contents of a Web Page that Requires Post Information

You want to "screen scrape" the contents of a Web page that requires a postback.

Technique

Here, you create a page that will accept the post information and display the results. This example screen scrapes Amazon.com's search results page.

The ASPX page is as follows:

```
<form runat="server">
  Search Amazon for: <asp:TextBox Runat="server" ID="SearchText" />
  <asp:Button Runat="server" ID="SubmitButton"
Text="Get Amazon.com Search Results" OnClick="SubmitButton_Click"/><br>
  <asp:TextBox Runat="server"  id="WebResponseText" Width="780" Height="300"
TextMode="MultiLine"/>
  <asp:Label Runat="server" ID="WebResponseLabel"/>
</form>
```

You create a Web request to post to the target Web page from within the current page's postback and then display the screen-scraped information to the client.

In `<script runat="server" />` block or codebehind:

```
Protected Sub SubmitButton_Click(ByVal sender As System.Object, _
ByVal e As System.EventArgs)
  Dim RequestUrl As String = _
   "http://www.amazon.com/exec/obidos/search-handle-form"
  Dim Post As String = "field-keywords=" & SearchText.Text
  Dim Writer As StreamWriter = Nothing

  Dim WebRequestObject As HttpWebRequest
  Dim sr As StreamReader
  Dim WebResponseObject As HttpWebResponse

  Try
    WebRequestObject = CType(WebRequest.Create(RequestUrl), HttpWebRequest)
    WebRequestObject.Method = "POST"
    WebRequestObject.ContentType = "application/x-www-form-urlencoded"
```

```
    WebRequestObject.ContentLength = Post.Length
    Writer = New StreamWriter(WebRequestObject.GetRequestStream())
    Writer.Write(Post)
    Writer.Close()

    WebResponseObject = CType(WebRequestObject.GetResponse(), _
HttpWebResponse)
    sr = New StreamReader(WebResponseObject.GetResponseStream)

    Dim Results as string = sr.ReadToEnd
    WebResponseLabel.Text = Results
    WebResponseText.Text = Results
  Finally
    Try
      sr.Close()
    Catch
    End Try

    Try
      WebResponseObject.Close()
      WebRequestObject.Abort()
    Catch
    End Try
  End Try
End Sub
```

Comments

Screen Scraping can be used to grab the contents of an external Web page. Some Web pages, such as search pages, require user input before returning results (these pages require information to be posted to them before the page results are returned).

In this example, an HTTP Web request is created and the post data (the search string you are interested in) is written to the request. This request is then sent to the target Web page and the results are returned through an HTTP Web response object. A `StreamReader` object is extracted from the HTTP Web response object containing the string contents of the requested page. The response from the post results can then be parsed and displayed to the client.

A reference to the `System.Net` namespace is required for the `HttpWebRequest` and `HttpWebResponse` objects. Similarly, a reference to the `System.IO` namespace is required for the `StreamReader` object.

See Also

Section 1.4, "Submitting Data to Another Page Using ASP.NET"

Section 21.1, "Screen Scraping the Contents of a Web Page"

Section 21.3, "Screen Scraping the Contents of a Web Page that Requires Cookies"

21.3. Screen Scraping the Contents of a Web Page that Requires Cookies

You want to screen scrape the contents of a Web page that requires certain cookies.

Technique

This example screen scrapes a page that requires cookies and displays the results. The ASPX page is as follows:

```
<form runat="server">
  <asp:Button Runat="server" ID="SubmitButton"
Text="Get Page Requiring Cookies" OnClick="SubmitButton_Click"/><br>
  <asp:TextBox Runat="server" id="WebResponseText" Width="780"
Height="300" TextMode="MultiLine"/><br>
  <asp:Label Runat="server" ID="WebResponseLabel"/>
</form>
```

The example creates a Web request, adds the required cookie, and then scrapes the contents of the specified Web page.

In `<script runat="server" />` block or codebehind:

```
Protected Sub SubmitButton_Click(ByVal sender As System.Object, _

ByVal e As System.EventArgs)
  Dim RequestUrl As String = _
Request.Url.GetLeftPart(System.UriPartial.Authority) & _
Request.ApplicationPath & "/Recipe2103Cookie.aspx"

  Dim WebRequestObject As HttpWebRequest
  Dim sr As StreamReader
  Dim WebResponseObject As HttpWebResponse

  Try
    WebRequestObject = CType(WebRequest.Create(RequestUrl), HttpWebRequest)
    WebRequestObject.Method = "GET"

    Dim CookieContainerObject as New System.Net.CookieContainer()
    Dim Cookie as New System.Net.Cookie()

    Cookie.Name = "userid"
    Cookie.Value = "1234567890"
    Cookie.Domain = Request.ServerVariables("HTTP_HOST")  'www.somedomain.com
    Cookie.Secure = True
    CookieContainerObject.Add(Cookie)
```

```
      WebRequestObject.CookieContainer = CookieContainerObject

      WebResponseObject = CType(WebRequestObject.GetResponse(), HttpWebResponse)

      sr = New StreamReader(WebResponseObject.GetResponseStream)

      Dim Results as string = sr.ReadToEnd
      WebResponseLabel.Text = Results
      WebResponseText.Text = Results
    Finally
      Try
        sr.Close()
      Catch
      End Try

      Try
        WebResponseObject.Close()
        WebRequestObject.Abort()
      Catch
      End Try
    End Try
End Sub
```

Comments

Screen scraping grabs the contents of an external Web page. Some Web pages require user data, in the form of a cookie, to be present before returning the page.

In this example, an HTTP Web request is created and the required cookie is included in the request. This request is then sent to the target Web page and the results are returned through an HTTP Web response object. A `StreamReader` object is extracted from the HTTP Web response object containing the string contents of the requested page. The response from the post results can then be parsed and displayed to the client.

The cookie's domain should be set to the domain name of the target page that is requiring cookies. In this example, it just happens to be the same as the sample page, so server variables are used for simplicity.

Remember you do not have access to the client's cookies for another domain. For example, the site `www.acme.com` requires a `userid` cookie. You are trying to scrape a page from `www.acme.com/somepage.aspx`. You are attempting to scrape acme's page from your page located at `www.mysite.com/scraper.aspx`. When a user visits `www.mysite.com/scraper.aspx`, the scraper page will only have access to the user's cookies in the domain `www.mysite.com`; there is no way for your page to view the cookies of `www.acme.com`. Therefore, you cannot pass the user's `userid` cookie for `www.acme.com` through your page at `www.mysite.com`; you would have to explicitly create the cookie with the correct name and value in the page `www.mysite.com/scraper.aspx`.

A reference to the `System.Net` namespace is required for the `HttpWebRequest` and `HttpWebResponse` objects. A reference to the `System.IO` namespace is required for the `StreamReader` object.

> ### See Also
>
> Section 1.4, "Submitting Data to Another Page Using ASP.NET"
>
> Section 21.2, "Screen Scraping the Contents of a Web Page that Requires Post Information"
>
> Section 21.4, "Screen Scraping the Contents of a Web Page that Requires Windows Authentication"

21.4. Screen Scraping the Contents of a Web Page that Requires Windows Authentication

> You want to "screen scrape" the contents of a Web page that requires Windows authentication.

Technique

This example screen scrapes a page that requires Windows authentication and displays the results.

The ASPX page is as follows:

```
<form runat="server">
  <asp:Button Runat="server" ID="SubmitButton"
Text="Get Page Requiring Windows Authentication"
OnClick="SubmitButton_Click"/><br>
  <asp:TextBox Runat="server"  id="WebResponseText" Width="780"
Height="300" TextMode="MultiLine"/><br>
  <asp:Label Runat="server" ID="WebResponseLabel"/>
</form>
```

The code creates a Web request, adds the required cookie, and then scrapes the contents of the specified Web page.

In `<script runat="server" />` block or codebehind:

```
Protected Sub SubmitButton_Click(ByVal sender As System.Object, _
ByVal e As System.EventArgs)
  Dim RequestUrl As String = _
Request.Url.GetLeftPart(System.UriPartial.Authority) & _
Request.ApplicationPath & "/Recipe2104Auth.aspx"

  Dim WebRequestObject As HttpWebRequest
  Dim sr As StreamReader
  Dim WebResponseObject As HttpWebResponse
```

```
  Try
     WebRequestObject = CType(WebRequest.Create(RequestUrl), HttpWebRequest)
     WebRequestObject.Method = "GET"

     Dim CredCache As New CredentialCache()
     CredCache.Add(New System.Uri(_
Request.Url.GetLeftPart(System.UriPartial.Authority)), "NTLM", _
New NetworkCredential("username", "password", "DOMAIN"))
     WebRequestObject.Credentials = CredCache

     WebResponseObject = CType(WebRequestObject.GetResponse(), HttpWebResponse)

     sr = New StreamReader(WebResponseObject.GetResponseStream)

     Dim Results as string = sr.ReadToEnd
     WebResponseLabel.Text = Results
     WebResponseText.Text = Results
  Finally
    Try
      sr.Close()
    Catch
    End Try

    Try
      WebResponseObject.Close()
      WebRequestObject.Abort()
    Catch
    End Try
  End Try
End Sub
```

Comments

Screen scraping grabs the contents of an external Web page. Some Web pages restrict user access using the built-in IIS security mechanisms—Basic or Windows Authentication. In either case, the target page being screen scraped requires proper credentials before the contents will be returned.

In this example, an HTTP Web request is created and the required authentication credentials are included in the request. This request is then sent to the target Web page and the results are returned through an HTTP Web response object. A `StreamReader` object is extracted from the HTTP Web response object containing the string contents of the requested page. The response from the post results can then be parsed and displayed to the client.

A reference to the `System.Net` namespace is required for the `HttpWebRequest` and `HttpWebResponse` objects. A reference to the `System.IO` namespace is required for the `StreamReader` object.

See Also

Section 1.4, "Submitting Data to Another Page Using ASP.NET"

Section 21.3, "Screen Scraping the Contents of a Web Page that Requires Cookies"

Section 21.5, "Screen Scraping the Contents of a Web Page that Requires a Proxy"

21.5. Screen Scraping the Contents of a Web Page that Requires a Proxy

You want to "screen scrape" the contents of a Web page that requires a proxy.

Technique

This example screen scrapes a page that requires a proxy and displays the results. The ASPX page is as follows:

```
<form runat="server">
  <asp:Button Runat="server" ID="SubmitButton"
Text="Get Page Requiring Proxy" OnClick="SubmitButton_Click"/><br>
  <asp:TextBox Runat="server"  id="WebResponseText" Width="780"
Height="300" TextMode="MultiLine"/><br>
  <asp:Label Runat="server" ID="WebResponseLabel"/>
</form>
```

Here, you create a Web request, add the required cookie, and then scrape the contents of the specified Web page.

In `<script runat="server" />` block or codebehind:

```
Protected Sub SubmitButton_Click(ByVal sender As System.Object, _
ByVal e As System.EventArgs)
  Dim RequestUrl As String = "http://www.cnn.com"

  Dim WebRequestObject As HttpWebRequest
  Dim sr As StreamReader
  Dim WebResponseObject As HttpWebResponse

  Try
    WebRequestObject = CType(WebRequest.Create(RequestUrl), HttpWebRequest)
    WebRequestObject.Method = "GET"

    WebRequestObject.Proxy = New WebProxy("http://myproxy:80/")

    WebResponseObject = CType(WebRequestObject.GetResponse(), HttpWebResponse)

    sr = New StreamReader(WebResponseObject.GetResponseStream)
```

```
      Dim Results as string = sr.ReadToEnd
      WebResponseLabel.Text = Results
      WebResponseText.Text = Results
   Finally
     Try
       sr.Close()
     Catch
     End Try

     Try
       WebResponseObject.Close()
       WebRequestObject.Abort()
     Catch
     End Try
   End Try
End Sub
```

Comments

Screen scraping can be used to grab the contents of an external Web page. Some companies require all Internet traffic to route through a proxy. In this case, it is necessary to specify the proxy to use to request the Web page.

In this example, an HTTP Web request is created and the correct proxy information is included in the request. The request is then sent to the target Web page and the results are returned through an HTTP Web response object. A `StreamReader` object is extracted from the HTTP Web response object containing the string contents of the requested page. The response from the post results can then be parsed and displayed to the client.

A reference to the `System.Net` namespace is required for the `HttpWebRequest` and `HttpWebResponse` objects. A reference to the `System.IO` namespace is required for the `StreamReader` object.

See Also

Section 1.4, "Submitting Data to Another Page Using ASP.NET"

Section 21.4, "Screen Scraping the Contents of a Web Page that Requires Windows Authentication"

Section 21.6, "Screen Scraping the Contents of a Web Page that Requires a Specific Browser"

21.6. Screen Scraping the Contents of a Web Page that Requires a Specific Browser

You want to "screen scrape" the contents of a Web page that requires a specific browser.

Technique

This example screen scrapes a page that requires a specific browser and displays the results.

The ASPX page is as follows:

```
<form runat="server">
   <asp:Button Runat="server" ID="SubmitButton"
Text="Get Page Requiring Specific Browser Settings"
OnClick="SubmitButton_Click"/><br>
   <asp:TextBox Runat="server" id="WebResponseText" Width="780"
Height="300" TextMode="MultiLine"/><br>
   <asp:Label Runat="server" ID="WebResponseLabel"/>
</form>
```

You create a Web request, add the required user agent field, and then scrape the contents of the specified Web page.

In `<script runat="server" />` block or codebehind:

```
Protected Sub SubmitButton_Click(ByVal sender As System.Object, _
ByVal e As System.EventArgs)
  Dim RequestUrl As String = _
Request.Url.GetLeftPart(System.UriPartial.Authority) & _
Request.ApplicationPath & "/Recipe2106Browser.aspx"

  Dim WebRequestObject As HttpWebRequest
  Dim sr As StreamReader
  Dim WebResponseObject As HttpWebResponse

  Try
    WebRequestObject = CType(WebRequest.Create(RequestUrl), HttpWebRequest)
    WebRequestObject.Method = "GET"

    WebRequestObject.UserAgent = _
"Mozilla/4.0 (compatible; MSIE 6.0; Windows NT 5.1; .NET CLR 1.0.3705)"

    WebResponseObject = CType(WebRequestObject.GetResponse(), HttpWebResponse)
```

```
    sr = New StreamReader(WebResponseObject.GetResponseStream)

    Dim Results as string = sr.ReadToEnd
    WebResponseLabel.Text = Results
    WebResponseText.Text = Results
  Finally
    Try
      sr.Close()
    Catch
    End Try

    Try
      WebResponseObject.Close()
      WebRequestObject.Abort()
    Catch
    End Try
  End Try
End Sub
```

Comments

Screen scraping can be used to grab the contents of a Web page. Some Web sites require a certain level browser before allowing the user to browse. In this case, it is necessary to specify the user agent as part of the request for the page.

In this example, an HTTP Web request is created and a valid up-level user agent is included in the request. The request is then sent to the target Web page and the results are returned through an HTTP Web response object. A `StreamReader` object is extracted from the HTTP Web response object containing the string contents of the requested page. The response from the post results can then be parsed and displayed to the client.

A reference to the `System.Net` namespace is required for the `HttpWebRequest` and `HttpWebResponse` objects. A reference to the `System.IO` namespace is required for the `StreamReader` object.

See Also

Section 1.4, "Submitting Data to Another Page Using ASP.NET"

Section 21.5, "Screen Scraping the Contents of a Web Page that Requires a Proxy"

Section 21.7, "Avoiding Redirects While Screen Scraping a Web Page"

21.7. Avoiding Redirects While Screen Scraping a Web Page

> You want to stop getting redirected when trying to screen scrape the contents of a Web page.

Technique

Display the redirect information instead of actually getting redirected when screen scraping.

The ASPX page is as follows:

```
<form runat="server">
  <asp:Button Runat="server" ID="SubmitButton"
Text="Get Redirecting Page" OnClick="SubmitButton_Click"/><br>
  <asp:TextBox Runat="server" id="WebResponseText" Width="780"
Height="300" TextMode="MultiLine"/><br>
  <asp:Label Runat="server" ID="WebResponseLabel"/>
</form>
```

You must create a Web request, add the required cookie, and then scrape the contents of the specified Web page.

In `<script runat="server" />` block or codebehind:

```
Protected Sub SubmitButton_Click(ByVal sender As System.Object, _
ByVal e As System.EventArgs)
  Dim RequestUrl As String = _
Request.Url.GetLeftPart(System.UriPartial.Authority) & _
Request.ApplicationPath & "/Recipe1207Redirect.aspx"

  Dim WebRequestObject As HttpWebRequest
  Dim sr As StreamReader
  Dim WebResponseObject As HttpWebResponse

  Try
    WebRequestObject = CType(WebRequest.Create(RequestUrl), HttpWebRequest)
    WebRequestObject.Method = "GET"

    WebRequestObject.AllowAutoRedirect = False

    WebResponseObject = CType(WebRequestObject.GetResponse(), HttpWebResponse)

    sr = New StreamReader(WebResponseObject.GetResponseStream)

    Dim Results as string = sr.ReadToEnd
    WebResponseLabel.Text = Results
    WebResponseText.Text = Results
```

```
   Finally
     Try
       sr.Close()
     Catch
     End Try

     Try
       WebResponseObject.Close()
       WebRequestObject.Abort()
     Catch
     End Try
   End Try
End Sub
```

Comments

Screen scraping can be used to grab the contents of a Web page, even when the page redirects to another page. The automatic redirections can be stopped, as illustrated in this example.

In this example, an HTTP Web request is created and the allow automatic redirects property is set to `false`, therefore not allowing the request to be redirected. The request is then sent to the target Web page and the results are returned through an http Web response object. A `StreamReader` object is extracted from the HTTP Web response object containing the string contents of the requested page. The response from the post results can then be parsed and displayed to the client.

A reference to the `System.Net` namespace is required for the `HttpWebRequest` and `HttpWebResponse` objects. A reference to the `System.IO` namespace is required for the `StreamReader` object.

See Also

Section 1.4, "Submitting Data to Another Page Using ASP.NET"

Section 21.6, "Screen Scraping the Contents of a Web Page that Requires a Specific Browser"

Section 21.8, "Viewing the Headers and Cookies of a Screen-Scraping Page"

21.8. Viewing the Headers and Cookies of a Screen-Scraping Page

You want to view the headers and cookies of a page you are screen scraping.

Technique

This example shows you how to view the headers and cookies when screen scraping a page.

The ASPX page is as follows:

```
<form runat="server">
  <asp:Button Runat="server" ID="SubmitButton"
Text="Get Headers and Cookies" OnClick="SubmitButton_Click"/><br>
  <asp:TextBox Runat="server"  id="HeadersText" Width="780" Height="300"
TextMode="MultiLine"/><br>
  <asp:TextBox Runat="server"  id="WebResponseText" Width="780"
Height="300" TextMode="MultiLine"/><br>
  <asp:Label Runat="server" ID="WebResponseLabel"/>
</form>
```

You must create a Web request, scrape the contents of a page, and then view the headers and cookies collections.

In `<script runat="server" />` block or codebehind:

```
Protected Sub SubmitButton_Click(ByVal sender As System.Object, _
ByVal e As System.EventArgs)
  Dim RequestUrl As String = "http://www.ebay.com"

  Dim WebRequestObject As HttpWebRequest
  Dim sr As StreamReader
  Dim WebResponseObject As HttpWebResponse

  Try
    WebRequestObject = CType(WebRequest.Create(RequestUrl), HttpWebRequest)
    WebRequestObject.Method = "GET"

    WebResponseObject = CType(WebRequestObject.GetResponse(), HttpWebResponse)

    Dim i As Integer
    HeadersText.Text = ""
    For i = 0 to WebResponseObject.Headers.Count-1
      HeadersText.Text &= ControlChars.Cr & "Header Name: " & _
WebResponseObject.Headers.Keys(i) & "   Value :" & _
WebResponseObject.Headers(i)
    Next

    Dim myCookieCollection As CookieCollection = WebResponseObject.Cookies
    For i = 0 To myCookieCollection.Count - 1
      HeadersText.Text &= ControlChars.Cr & "Cookie Name: " & _
myCookieCollection(i).Name & "   Value= " & myCookieCollection(i).Value
    Next i

    sr = New StreamReader(WebResponseObject.GetResponseStream)

    Dim Results as string = sr.ReadToEnd
    WebResponseLabel.Text = Results
    WebResponseText.Text = Results
```

```
    Finally
      Try
        sr.Close()
      Catch
      End Try

      Try
        WebResponseObject.Close()
        WebRequestObject.Abort()
      Catch
      End Try
    End Try
End Sub
```

Comments

Screen scraping can be used to grab the contents of a Web page. Occasionally, it is useful to view the contents of the headers or cookies being returned in the response.

In this example, an HTTP Web request is created and sent to the target Web page. The results are returned through an HTTP Web response object. The Cookie and Headers collections of the returned response object are then displayed.

A reference to the `System.Net` namespace is required for the `HttpWebRequest` and `HttpWebResponse` objects. A reference to the `System.IO` namespace is required for the `StreamReader` object.

> **See Also**
>
> Section 1.4, "Submitting Data to Another Page Using ASP.NET"
>
> Section 21.7, "Avoiding Redirects While Screen Scraping a Web Page""

21.9. Performing a DNS Lookup

> You want to perform a DNS lookup for a particular Fully Qualified Domain Name (FQDN).

Technique

You use the `IPHostEntry` and `Dns` classes from the `System.Net` namespace to perform a DNS lookup for a particular FQDN. The code to perform the lookup is as follows:

```
Try
  LblHostName.Text = ""
  Dim  GetIPHost As IPHostEntry
  GetIPHost = Dns.GetHostByName(TxtInput.Text)
  Dim ip as IPAddress
```

```
Dim HostIpaddress As long
LblValue.Text = "DNS LookUp as : " & "<Br>"
For Each ip In GetIPHost.AddressList
  HostIpaddress = ip.Address
  LblValue.Text &= HostIpaddress.ToString() & " -- "
  LblValue.Text &= ip.ToString() & "<br>"
Next ip

LblHostName.Text = "Host Name is: " & GetIPHost.HostName

Catch ex as Exception
  LblValue.Text = "<font color=red>Error:" & ex.Message
End Try
```

Comments

The IPHostEntry class provides a container class for Internet host address information. The host information from the DNS query is returned with the help of GetHostByName, in an instance of the IPHostEntry class. If the specified host has more than one entry in the DNS database, IPHostEntry builds an array having multiple IP addresses and aliases.

See Also

IPHostEntry Class Information—http://msdn.microsoft.com/library/en-us/cpref/html/frlrfSystemNetIPHostEntryClassTopic.asp

Dns Class Information—http://msdn.microsoft.com/library/en-us/cpref/html/frlrfsystemnetdnsclasstopic.asp

21.10. Performing a Reverse-DNS Lookup

You want to get the domain name of a particular IP address using a reverse DNS lookup.

Technique

Use the IPAddress and Dns classes from the System.Net namespace to perform a DNS query to get the host information. The relevant code is listed here:

```
Try
  Dim myIP As IPAddress = IPAddress.Parse(TxtInput.Text)
  Dim GetIPHost As IPHostEntry = Dns.GetHostByAddress(myIP)
  LblHostName.Text = "Host Name is: " & GetIPHost.HostName

Catch ex As Exception
  LblHostName.Text = ex.Message
End Try
```

Comments

The IPAddress class provides an Internet Protocol (IP) address. Dns.GetHostByAddress gets DNS host information into an instance of the IPHostEntry class.

See Also

IPAddress Class Information—http://msdn.microsoft.com/library/en-us/cpref/html/frlrfsystemnetipaddressclasstopic.asp

Dns Class Information—http://msdn.microsoft.com/library/en-us/cpref/html/frlrfsystemnetdnsclasstopic.asp

21.11. Uploading a File Using HTTP

You want to allow your users to upload a file through HTTP and save the file to the server.

Technique

First add the enctype property to the form tag and set it to multipart/form-data:

```
<form id="Form1" method="post" runat="server" enctype="multipart/form-data">
```

Then use the html input tag and set the type to file; also set runat="server" and add an ID value for the tag:

```
input type="file" runat="server" id="fileinput">
```

Add a quick ASP.NET button control to save the file:

```
  <asp:Button id="UploadButton" runat="server" Text="Upload"
onclick="UploadButton_Click"></asp:Button></P>
```

You save the file in your code by using the PostedFile property of the file input tag and the SaveAs method:

```
Private Sub UploadButton_Click(ByVal sender As System.Object, _
ByVal e As System.EventArgs) Handles UploadButton.Click
 If Not (FileInput.PostedFile Is Nothing) Then
  Try
   FileInput.PostedFile.SaveAs("c:\test.txt")
    Catch exc As Exception
    Response.Write(exc.Message)
  End Try
 End If
End Sub
```

Before calling the SaveAs method, it is a good idea to make sure that the PostedFile property is not null. Be careful to contain the saving in a try..catch in case there is a file or access exception. Because the file is being posted to the server through HTTP, the size of the file is limited to the maximum allowable HTTP request size. By default, this is set to 4MB, but you can modify this setting very easily by delving into the machine.config on your server:

```
<httpRuntime executionTimeout="90" maxRequestLength="4096"
useFullyQualifiedRedirectUrl="false" minFreeThreads="8"
minLocalRequestFreeThreads="4" appRequestQueueLimit="100"/>
```

Find this setting and simply modify the `maxRequestLength` value to the number of bytes that you need.

Comments

ASP.NET makes it very easy to include uploading functionality in your application, but be careful when allowing users to upload files. It's best not to allow users to specify the names of their files or to save the files using the posted filenames, because doing so can pose a major security risk. You will also want to be sure to give the ASP.NET user account `write` access to the directory you want to use before attempting to save files.

See Also

Chapter 17 "Working with Files and Folders"

File Uploading with .NET—`http://aspalliance.com/damianm/article/2/`, by Damian Manifold

21.12. Sending an Email Message

You want to send an email message using ASP.NET.

Technique

The first thing you need to do is import the `System.Web.Mail` namespace:

```
Imports System.Web.Mail
```

Next, you create an instance of the `MailMessage` class and fill the applicable properties:

```
Dim EMail As New MailMessage()
EMail.To = "dev@null.com"
EMail.From = "reader@aspnetcookbook.com"

EMail.Cc = "someoneelse@somebody.com"
EMail.Subject = "Test AspNetCookbook Email"
EMail.Body = "Here is the body of our email"
```

With your email ready to go, you specify what server to use in order to send it. This example uses `localhost`, but you can also use an IP address of any Windows 2000 server. Before the email will send successfully, you need to configure relaying on your SMTP server.

```
SmtpMail.SmtpServer = "localhost"
```

And finally, you send the email:

```
Try
  SmtpMail.Send(EMail)
Catch exc As Exception
  Response.Write("Send failure: " + exc.ToString())
End Try
```

Comments

Sending emails with ASP.NET is much easier than with ASP, but the downside is that it is simply a wrapper for CDONTS. If you are sending a small number of emails, this method works great, but if you want to send large numbers of emails or use more advanced email functions, a third-party .NET component might be the way to go.

See Also

AspNetMail, an excellent third-party .NET mail component—`http://www.aspnetmail.com`

Reading POP3 Email with ASP.NET—`http://www.aspalliance.com/chrisg/default.asp?article=93`

21.13. Sending Email with Attachments

You want to send an email with one or more file attachments.

Technique

The `System.Web.Mail` consists of three classes—`MailAttachment`, `MailMessage`, and `SmtpMail`. Example 21.12 shows `MailMessage` and the `SmtpMail` class. In example 21.12, you learned how to send emails through ASP.NET; this example extends that topic and demonstrates how to add attachments to your emails.

The ASPX page is as follows:

```
<html>
<head>
    <title>Recipe2211</title>
</head>
<body>
    <form runat="server">
      <asp:Literal id="MessageLiteral" runat="server"></asp:Literal>
```

```
        </form>
      </body>
    </html>
```

In `<script runat="server" />` block or codebehind:

```
Sub Page_Load(Sender As Object, E As EventArgs)

  MessageLiteral.Text = ""

  Dim _Message As New MailMessage()

  With _Message
        .To = "Recipients Email"
        .From = "Your Email"
        .Subject = "How to send emails through ASP.NET"
        .Body = "Your Message goes here..."
  End With
  'Create a MailAttachment, specifying path to file to attach
  Dim _Attachment As New MailAttachment("c:\myfile.txt")

  'Attach the MailAttachment to the Message
  _Message.Attachments.Add(_Attachment)

  'Specify the name of the SMTP gateway server
  SmtpMail.SmtpServer="mail.myserver.com"

  Try
    SmtpMail.Send(_Message)
  Catch Err As Exception
    Response.Write(Err.Message())
  End Try

End Sub
```

21.14. Retrieving Messages from a POP3 Mailbox

You want to retrieve email messages from a POP3 mailbox using TCP/IP.

Technique

This example uses the `System.Net.Sockets.TcpClient` class to connect to a POP3 email server and retrieve messages.

Import the following namespaces into your page:

```
<%@ Import Namespace="System.Text" %>
<%@ Import Namespace="System.Net.Sockets" %>
<%@ Import Namespace="System.Threading" %>
```

In `<script runat="server" />` block or codebehind:

```
Sub Page_Load(Sender As Object, E As EventArgs)
  Dim tcpClient As TcpClient = New TcpClient()
  Dim hostname As String = "Host"
  Dim username As String = "User"
  Dim userpassword As String = "Password"
  Dim messagenumber As String = "1"
  Dim Returnmessage As String
  Try
    tcpClient.Connect(hostname, 110)
    Dim networkStream As NetworkStream = tcpClient.GetStream()
    Dim bytes(tcpClient.ReceiveBufferSize) As Byte
    Dim sendBytes As Byte()

    networkStream.Read(bytes, 0, CInt(tcpClient.ReceiveBufferSize))

    sendBytes = Encoding.ASCII.GetBytes("USER " + username + vbCrLf)
    networkStream.Write(sendBytes, 0, sendBytes.Length)

    networkStream.Read(bytes, 0, CInt(tcpClient.ReceiveBufferSize))

    sendBytes = Encoding.ASCII.GetBytes("PASS " + userpassword + vbCrLf)
    networkStream.Write(sendBytes, 0, sendBytes.Length)

    networkStream.Read(bytes, 0, CInt(tcpClient.ReceiveBufferSize))

    sendBytes = Encoding.ASCII.GetBytes("STAT" + vbCrLf)
    networkStream.Write(sendBytes, 0, sendBytes.Length)

    networkStream.Read(bytes, 0, CInt(tcpClient.ReceiveBufferSize))

    sendBytes = Encoding.ASCII.GetBytes("RETR " + messagenumber + vbCrLf)
    networkStream.Write(sendBytes, 0, sendBytes.Length)

    Thread.Sleep(500)

    networkStream.Read(bytes, 0, CInt(tcpClient.ReceiveBufferSize))
    Returnmessage = Regex.Replace(Encoding.ASCII.GetString(bytes), _
vbCrLf, "&lt;br/&gt;")
    EmailContent.Text = Returnmessage

    sendBytes = Encoding.ASCII.GetBytes("QUIT" + vbCrLf)
    networkStream.Write(sendBytes, 0, sendBytes.Length)
```

```
    tcpClient.Close()

  Catch
    EmailContent.Text = "Could not retrieve email or your inbox is empty."
  End Try

End Sub
```

The ASPX page is as follows:

```
<html>
  <body>
      <asp:Literal id="EmailContent" runat="server />
  </body>
</html>
```

Comments

You can use the `System.Threading.Thread.Sleep` method to allow the buffer time, in milliseconds, to receive the entire email message.

See Also

TcpClient Class—`http://msdn.microsoft.com/library/en-us/cpref/html/ frlrfSystemNetSocketsTcpClientClassTopic.asp`

Pausing and Resuming Threads—`http://msdn.microsoft.com/library/en-us/cpguide/ html/cpconworkingwiththreads.asp`

Encoding.GetBytes Method—`http://msdn.microsoft.com/library/en-us/cpref/html/ frlrfSystemTextEncodingClassGetBytesTopic2.asp`

Section 21.12, "Sending an Email Message"

Sending Emails in ASP.NET—`http://aspalliance.com/hrmalik/2002/200206/ 20020601.aspx`, by Haroon Rasheed Malik

VI

Advanced .NET Framework Tasks

Generating and Manipulating Images

22.0. Introduction

The .NET Framework class library includes an API for working with images, called GDI+. The classes that comprise GDI+ are mainly found in the System.Drawing namespace. This graphics library can be very useful within Web applications, allowing dynamic manipulation or generation of charts, buttons, drawings, and images. In this chapter, you will find recipes covering many of these techniques.

22.1. Creating an Image Programmatically

You want to dynamically create an image from a Web URL.

Technique

This example uses members of the System.Drawing namespace to draw shapes on a bitmap and then delivers the bitmap to the user's browser.

At the top of your .ASPX page, insert the following so that the required namespaces are referenced:

```
<%@ Page language="vb" %>
<%@ Import Namespace="System.Drawing" %>
<%@ Import Namespace="System.Drawing.Imaging" %>
<%@ Import Namespace="System.Drawing.Drawing2D" %>
<%@ Import Namespace="System.Drawing.Text" %>
```

In <script runat="server" /> block or codebehind:

```
Public Sub Page_Load(sender as object, e as System.EventArgs )
```

```
'create a new bitmap image
Dim OutputBitmap = new Bitmap(320,200)
Dim DrawGraphic = Graphics.FromImage(OutputBitmap)

'blank the bitmap
DrawGraphic.Clear(Color.Beige)

'create pens and brushes
Dim RedBrush = new SolidBrush(Color.Red)

'draw output
DrawGraphic.FillEllipse(RedBrush, 50,50,50,50)

' set the mime type
Response.Clear()
Response.ContentType="image/jpeg"

' send the image to the viewer
OutputBitmap.Save(Response.OutputStream, ImageFormat.Jpeg)

' clean up
OutputBitmap.Dispose()
DrawGraphic.Dispose()

End Sub
```

Comments

The goals of this example are to create and deliver an image in server memory and format and deliver the binary data to the user's browser with the correct MIME type.

See Also
GDI+ Articles—http://aspalliance.com/chrisg/

22.2. Creating Images from Strings

You want to create an image based on the contents of a string, or add some text to an existing image.

Technique

This example uses members of the System.Drawing namespace to create a bitmap and then uses the DrawString method of the System.Drawing.Graphics class to draw the string on to the image.

At the top of your .ASPX page, insert the following so that the required namespaces are referenced:

```
<%@ Page language="vb" %>
<%@ Import Namespace="System.Drawing" %>
<%@ Import Namespace="System.Drawing.Imaging" %>
<%@ Import Namespace="System.Drawing.Drawing2D" %>
<%@ Import Namespace="System.Drawing.Text" %>
```

In `<script runat="server" />` block or codebehind:

```
Public Sub Page_Load(sender as object, e as System.EventArgs )

'create a new bitmap image
Dim OutputBitmap = new Bitmap(320,200)
Dim DrawGraphic = Graphics.FromImage(OutputBitmap)

'blank the bitmap
DrawGraphic.Clear(Color.Beige)

'set smoothing
DrawGraphic.SmoothingMode = SmoothingMode.AntiAlias
DrawGraphic.TextRenderingHint = TextRenderingHint.AntiAlias

'create message string
Dim MessageString as String = System.DateTime.Now.ToString()

'draw string on graphic
DrawGraphic.DrawString(MessageString, _
   new Font("arial",18,FontStyle.Bold), _
   Brushes.DarkBlue, new PointF(20,20))


' set the mime type
Response.Clear()
Response.ContentType="image/jpeg"

' send the image to the viewer
OutputBitmap.Save(Response.OutputStream, ImageFormat.Jpeg)

' clean up
OutputBitmap.Dispose()
DrawGraphic.Dispose()

End Sub
```

Comments

The goal of this example is to create and deliver to the user an image consisting of a dynamically created text message.

See Also

GDI+ Articles—http://aspalliance.com/chrisg/

22.3. Loading an Existing Image

You want to load an existing image so that you can manipulate it.

Technique

This example creates an image based on an existing file using the System.Drawing namespace. It discovers the file system's filename using Server.MapPath along with the relative path within the Web site.

At the top of your .ASPX page, insert the following so that the required namespaces are referenced:

```
<%@ Page language="vb" %>
<%@ Import Namespace="System.Drawing" %>
<%@ Import Namespace="System.Drawing.Imaging" %>
<%@ Import Namespace="System.Drawing.Drawing2D" %>
<%@ Import Namespace="System.Drawing.Text" %>
```

In <script runat="server" /> block or codebehind:

```
Public Sub Page_Load(sender as object, e as System.EventArgs )
    'create a new bitmap image
    Dim OutputBitmap = new

Bitmap(Server.MapPath("recipe2203.jpg"))
    Dim DrawGraphic = Graphics.FromImage(OutputBitmap)

    'set smoothing
    DrawGraphic.SmoothingMode = SmoothingMode.AntiAlias
    DrawGraphic.TextRenderingHint = TextRenderingHint.AntiAlias

    'create message string
    Dim MessageString as String = System.DateTime.Now.ToString()

    'draw string on graphic
    DrawGraphic.DrawString(MessageString, _
        new Font("arial",8,FontStyle.Bold), _
```

```
        Brushes.DarkBlue, new PointF(10,22))

    ` set the mime type
    Response.Clear()
    Response.ContentType="image/jpeg"

    ` send the image to the viewer
    OutputBitmap.Save(Response.OutputStream, ImageFormat.Jpeg)

    ` clean up
    OutputBitmap.Dispose()
    DrawGraphic.Dispose()
End Sub
```

Comments

The goal of this example is to create and deliver an image based on an existing file found in the local Web directory.

See Also

GDI+ Articles—http://aspalliance.com/chrisg/

22.4. Resizing Images Dynamically

You want to change the width or height of an image programmatically.

Technique

This example uses members of the System.Drawing namespace to draw a new image at the required size based on your original image.

At the top of your .ASPX page, insert the following so that the required namespaces are referenced:

```
<%@ Page language="vb" %>
<%@ Import Namespace="System.Drawing" %>
<%@ Import Namespace="System.Drawing.Imaging" %>
<%@ Import Namespace="System.Drawing.Drawing2D" %>
<%@ Import Namespace="System.Drawing.Text" %>
```

In <script runat="server" /> block or codebehind:

```
    Public Sub Page_Load(sender as object, e as System.EventArgs )
        `create a new bitmap image
        Dim InputBitmap as Bitmap = New _
Bitmap(Server.MapPath("aspalliance_logo.gif"))
```

```
        ` create a new image from original
        Dim newWidth as integer = 100
        Dim newHeight as integer = 100
        Dim OutputBitmap as Bitmap = New _
Bitmap(InputBitmap, newWidth, newHeight)

        ` set the mime type
        Response.Clear()
        Response.ContentType="image/Gif"

        ` send the image to the viewer
        OutputBitmap.Save(Response.OutputStream, ImageFormat.Gif)

        ` clean up
        OutputBitmap.Dispose()
        InputBitmap.Dispose()
    End Sub
```

Comments

The goals of this example are to create and deliver an image at a set size based on an existing image and to deliver the binary data to the user's browser with the correct MIME type.

See Also

GDI+ Articles—`http://aspalliance.com/chrisg/`

22.5. Creating Thumbnail Images Without Distortion

You want to limit images to a certain size of thumbnail without distorting the original image (that is, maintaining the original aspect ratio).

Technique

This example uses members of the System.Drawing namespace to draw a new image at the required size based on your original image while maintaining the aspect ratio.

At the top of your .ASPX page, insert the following so that the required namespaces are referenced:

```
<%@ Page language="vb" %>
<%@ Import Namespace="System.Drawing" %>
<%@ Import Namespace="System.Drawing.Imaging" %>
<%@ Import Namespace="System.Drawing.Drawing2D" %>
```

In `<script runat="server" />` block or codebehind:

```
Public Sub Page_Load(sender as object, e as System.EventArgs )
   ' Initialize variables.
   Dim boxWidth As Integer = 100
   Dim boxHeight As Integer = 100
   Dim scale As Double = 0

   ' Set the filename.
   Dim fileName As String
   fileName = Server.MapPath("aspalliance_logo.gif")


   ' create a new bitmap image
   Dim InputBitmap As Bitmap = New Bitmap(fileName)


   ' work out new sizes
   If(InputBitmap.Height < InputBitmap.Width) Then
      scale = (boxHeight)/InputBitmap.Width
   Else
      scale = (boxWidth)/InputBitmap.Height
   End If

   ' Set new width and height.
   Dim newWidth As Integer = CInt(scale*InputBitmap.Width)
   Dim newHeight As Integer = CInt(scale*InputBitmap.Height)

   ' create a new image from original
   Dim OutputBitmap As Bitmap = New Bitmap(InputBitmap, newWidth, newHeight)

   ' set the mime type
   Response.Clear()
   Response.ContentType="image/Gif"

   ' send the image to the viewer
   OutputBitmap.Save(Response.OutputStream, ImageFormat.Gif)

   ' clean up
   OutputBitmap.Dispose()
   InputBitmap.Dispose()
End Sub
```

See Also

GDI+ Articles—http://aspalliance.com/chrisg/

22.6. Cropping, Flipping, and Rotating Images

You want to crop an image, and then flip it horizontally or vertically, or rotate it.

Technique

GDI+ provides several tools for altering graphics. In the following example, you learn how to crop, flip, and rotate an image. First, open an existing image from the hard drive and store it in the `originalImage` object. Then create a new bitmap to store the new image and call it `newImage`. Now create a `Graphics` object called `graph` from the `newImage`. Use `graph.Clear` to set the background color.

Cropping

Create a new rectangle called `rect` and set the `x`, `y`, `width`, and `height` properties to the section of the original image you want to crop. Now use `graph.DrawImage` to place this cropped section of the original image into the new image. Pass in the `originalImage` object, a new rectangle specifying where to place the selection in the new image, and the rectangle you cropped from the `originalImage`. Specify `Pixel` for the `GraphicsUnit`. This example crops the bottom-right 90×50 pixels from the original image.

Flipping

To flip or rotate the image predefined degrees, use the `RotateFlip` method of `originalImage`. Just specify the `RotateFlipType`. This example uses `RotateNoneFlipY` to flip the image vertically. Now use `DrawImage` to add the flipped image to the `newImage`.

Rotating

You can rotate the image using the `RotateTransform` method of the `graph` object. Specify positive or negative degrees for rotation. Then, use `graph.DrawImage` to output the new image to `newImage`.

In `<script runat="server" />` block or codebehind for the list page:

```
Sub Page_Load(sender As Object, e As EventArgs)
    Dim originalImage As System.Drawing.Image
    Dim newImage As System.Drawing.Bitmap
    Dim graph As System.Drawing.Graphics
    Dim rect As System.Drawing.Rectangle


    originalImage=System.Drawing.Image.FromFile(
➥Server.MapPath("aspalliance_logo.gif"))
    newImage=new System.Drawing.Bitmap(250,350)
```

```
graph=System.Drawing.Graphics.FromImage(newImage)
graph.Clear(System.Drawing.Color.White)


'Crop
rect=new System.Drawing.Rectangle(
➥originalImage.Width-90,originalImage.Height-50,90,50)
    graph.DrawImage(originalImage,new
System.Drawing.Rectangle(0,0,90,50),rect,System.Drawing.GraphicsUnit.Pixel)

'Flip
originalImage.RotateFlip(System.Drawing.RotateFlipType.RotateNoneFlipY)
graph.DrawImage(originalImage, new System.Drawing.Point(0,51))

'Rotate
graph.RotateTransform(45)
graph.DrawImage(originalImage, new System.Drawing.Point(130,50))

Response.ContentType="image/gif"
newImage.Save(Response.OutputStream,System.Drawing.Imaging.ImageFormat.Gif)
End Sub
```

Comments

When using `RotateTransform`, you also rotate the x and y axes. Placing the image at (130,50), for example, is 130 pixels at a 45 degree down-right angle, and 50 pixels at a down-left angle.

See Also

Section 22.3, "Loading an Existing Image"

Section 22.4, "Resizing Images Dynamically"

GDI+ Tutorial—`http://www.aspalliance.com/chrisg`

22.7. Applying Textures to Images

You want to apply a texture to an image.

Technique

This example shows you how you can easily apply a texture to an image. This is accomplished with the `TextureBrush` class.

```
Private Sub Page_Load(sender As Object, e As System.EventArgs)
   Dim outputBitmap As New Bitmap(400, 400)
   Dim drawGraphics As Graphics = Graphics.FromImage(outputBitmap)

   Dim image As System.Drawing.Image = _
System.Drawing.Image.FromFile(Server.MapPath("recipe2207.gif"))
   Dim textureBrush As New TextureBrush(image)
   drawGraphics.FillRectangle(textureBrush, 0, 0, 400, 400)

   Response.ContentType = "image/jpeg"
   outputBitmap.Save(Response.OutputStream, ImageFormat.Jpeg)
   image.Dispose()
   drawGraphics.Dispose()
   outputBitmap.Dispose()
End Sub
```

Comments

Remember to add `Import` directives for `System.Drawing`, `System.Drawing.Drawing2D`, and `System.Drawing.Imaging`.

See Also

Section 22.1, "Creating an Image Programmatically"

Section 22.3, "Loading an Existing Image"

22.8. Blurring and Sharpening Images

You want to blur or sharpen an image.

Technique

This example looks at some algorithms for blurring and sharpening images. Let's start by taking a look at the blur algorithm:

```
Private Sub BlurImage()
   Dim outputBitmap As New Bitmap(Server.MapPath("recipe2208.jpg"))
   Dim repetitions As Integer = 5
   Dim red As Integer = 0
   Dim green As Integer = 0
   Dim blue As Integer = 0

   Dim i As Integer
   For i = 0 To repetitions - 1
      Dim x As Integer
```

```
        For x = 1 To (outputBitmap.Width - 1) - 1
           Dim y As Integer
           For y = 1 To (outputBitmap.Height - 1) - 1
               red += outputBitmap.GetPixel(x, y - 1).R
               red += outputBitmap.GetPixel(x, y + 1).R
               red += outputBitmap.GetPixel(x, y).R
               red += outputBitmap.GetPixel(x + 1, y).R
               red += outputBitmap.GetPixel(x - 1, y).R
               red = red / 5

               green += outputBitmap.GetPixel(x, y - 1).G
               green += outputBitmap.GetPixel(x, y + 1).G
               green += outputBitmap.GetPixel(x, y).G
               green += outputBitmap.GetPixel(x + 1, y).G
               green += outputBitmap.GetPixel(x - 1, y).G
               green = green / 5

               blue += outputBitmap.GetPixel(x, y - 1).B
               blue += outputBitmap.GetPixel(x, y + 1).B
               blue += outputBitmap.GetPixel(x, y).B
               blue += outputBitmap.GetPixel(x + 1, y).B
               blue += outputBitmap.GetPixel(x - 1, y).B
               blue = blue / 5

               outputBitmap.SetPixel(x, y, Color.FromArgb(red, green, blue))

               red = 0
               green = 0
               blue = 0
           Next y
        Next x
     Next i

     Response.ContentType = "image/jpeg"
     outputBitmap.Save(Response.OutputStream, ImageFormat.Jpeg)
     outputBitmap.Dispose()
End Sub
```

Basically, this algorithm makes each pixel's red, green, and blue components an average of that pixel and the pixels above, below, left, and right of it. In this particular instance, the process is repeated five times so you can clearly see the blur effect.

Next, let's check out the sharpening algorithm:

```
Private Sub SharpenImage()
   Dim outputBitmap As New Bitmap(Server.MapPath("sample.jpg"))
   Dim repetitions As Integer = 1
   Dim red As Integer = 0
```

```
Dim green As Integer = 0
Dim blue As Integer = 0

Dim i As Integer
For i = 0 To repetitions - 1
   Dim x As Integer
   For x = 3 To (outputBitmap.Width - 3) - 1
      Dim y As Integer
      For y = 3 To (outputBitmap.Height - 3) - 1
         ' red
         red += -1 * outputBitmap.GetPixel(x + 1, y + 1).R
         red += -2 * outputBitmap.GetPixel(x, y - 1).R
         red += -1 * outputBitmap.GetPixel(x + 1, y - 1).R
         red += -2 * outputBitmap.GetPixel(x - 1, y).R
         red += 16 * outputBitmap.GetPixel(x, y).R
         red += -2 * outputBitmap.GetPixel(x + 1, y).R
         red += -1 * outputBitmap.GetPixel(x - 1, y + 1).R
         red += -2 * outputBitmap.GetPixel(x, y + 1).R
         red += -1 * outputBitmap.GetPixel(x + 1, y + 1).R
         red = red / 4
         If red > 255 Then
            red = 255
         End If
         If red < 0 Then
            red = 0
         End If

         ' green
         green += -1 * outputBitmap.GetPixel(x + 1, y + 1).G
         green += -2 * outputBitmap.GetPixel(x, y - 1).G
         green += -1 * outputBitmap.GetPixel(x + 1, y - 1).G
         green += -2 * outputBitmap.GetPixel(x - 1, y).G
         green += 16 * outputBitmap.GetPixel(x, y).G
         green += -2 * outputBitmap.GetPixel(x + 1, y).G
         green += -1 * outputBitmap.GetPixel(x - 1, y + 1).G
         green += -2 * outputBitmap.GetPixel(x, y + 1).G
         green += -1 * outputBitmap.GetPixel(x + 1, y + 1).G
         green = green / 4
         If green > 255 Then
            green = 255
         End If
         If green < 0 Then
            green = 0
         End If

         ' blue
```

```
          blue += -1 * outputBitmap.GetPixel(x + 1, y + 1).B
          blue += -2 * outputBitmap.GetPixel(x, y - 1).B
          blue += -1 * outputBitmap.GetPixel(x + 1, y - 1).B
          blue += -2 * outputBitmap.GetPixel(x - 1, y).B
          blue += 16 * outputBitmap.GetPixel(x, y).B
          blue += -2 * outputBitmap.GetPixel(x + 1, y).B
          blue += -1 * outputBitmap.GetPixel(x - 1, y + 1).B
          blue += -2 * outputBitmap.GetPixel(x, y + 1).B
          blue += -1 * outputBitmap.GetPixel(x + 1, y + 1).B
          blue = blue / 4
          If blue > 255 Then
             blue = 255
          End If
          If blue < 0 Then
             blue = 0
          End If
          outputBitmap.SetPixel(x, y, Color.FromArgb(red, green, blue))

          red = 0
          green = 0
          blue = 0
       Next y
    Next x
  Next i

  Response.ContentType = "image/jpeg"
  outputBitmap.Save(Response.OutputStream, ImageFormat.Jpeg)
  outputBitmap.Dispose()
End Sub
```

This algorithm is a bit more advanced then the blur algorithm. This algorithm takes away a portion of each pixel by adding the values of each pixel's surrounding pixels and applying a matrix that, depending on the X and Y coordinate relationship to the pixel, adds either a positive or negative value.

Comments

Remember to add Import directives for System.Drawing, System.Drawing.Drawing2D, and System.Drawing.Imaging.

See Also

Section 22.1, "Creating an Image Programmatically"

Section 22.3, "Loading an Existing Image"

22.9. Gray-scaling an Image

You want to convert a color image into a grayscale image.

Technique

This example explains a simple algorithm that converts a color image into a grayscale one.

```
Private Sub Page_Load(ByVal sender As Object, _
ByVal e As System.EventArgs) Handles MyBase.Load
    Dim outputBitmap As New Bitmap(Server.MapPath("recipe2209.jpg"))
    Dim gray As Integer = 0

    Dim x As Integer
    For x = 0 To outputBitmap.Width - 1
        Dim y As Integer
        For y = 0 To outputBitmap.Height - 1
            gray = outputBitmap.GetPixel(x, y).R
            gray += outputBitmap.GetPixel(x, y).G
            gray += outputBitmap.GetPixel(x, y).B
            gray = gray / 3

            outputBitmap.SetPixel(x, y, Color.FromArgb(gray, gray, gray))
        Next y
    Next x

    Response.ContentType = "image/jpeg"
    outputBitmap.Save(Response.OutputStream, ImageFormat.Jpeg)
    outputBitmap.Dispose()
End Sub
```

This algorithm is really simple, but very effective—all it does is make the current pixel an average of the pixel's red, green, and blue values.

Comments

Remember to add Import directives for System.Drawing, System.Drawing.Drawing2D, and System.Drawing.Imaging.

See Also

Section 22.1, "Creating an Image Programmatically"

Section 22.3, "Loading an Existing Image"

22.10. Creating a Photo Negative of an Image

You want to create a photographic negative of an image.

Technique

This example creates a simple algorithm that converts an image into a photographic negative.

```
Private Sub Page_Load(ByVal sender As Object, _
ByVal e As System.EventArgs) Handles MyBase.Load
   Dim outputBitmap As New Bitmap(Server.MapPath("sample.jpg"))
   Dim invertedRed As Integer = 0
   Dim invertedGreen As Integer = 0
   Dim invertedBlue As Integer = 0

   Dim x As Integer
   For x = 0 To outputBitmap.Width - 1
      Dim y As Integer
      For y = 0 To outputBitmap.Height - 1
         invertedRed = 255 - outputBitmap.GetPixel(x, y).R
         invertedGreen = 255 - outputBitmap.GetPixel(x, y).G
         invertedBlue = 255 - outputBitmap.GetPixel(x, y).B

         outputBitmap.SetPixel(x, y, Color.FromArgb(invertedRed, _
invertedGreen, invertedBlue))
      Next y
   Next x

   Response.ContentType = "image/jpeg"
   outputBitmap.Save(Response.OutputStream, ImageFormat.Jpeg)
   outputBitmap.Dispose()
End Sub
```

This algorithm simply subtracts a pixel's value for red, green, and blue from 255. This results in red, green, and blue values that are opposite of the original values. The result of this conversion is a photographic negative.

Comments

Remember to add Import directives for System.Drawing, System.Drawing.Drawing2D, and System.Drawing.Imaging.

See Also

Section 22.1, "Creating an Image Programmatically"

Section 22.3, "Loading an Existing Image"

22.11. Loading an Animated GIF

You want to load an animated GIF image.

Technique

First, you need to create a page that lists each frame. To do this, create a string called `fileName` that contains the filename you want to display. Create a new `Image` object and load the specified filename. Create a new `FrameDimension` object to store the frames of the animated GIF. You can use the `GetFrameCount` method of the `Image` object to retrieve the number of frames. Finally, loop through each frame and write an `<img>` tag pointing to the viewer and passing the frame index.

In `<script runat="server" />` block or codebehind for the list page:

```
Sub Page_Load(sender As Object, e As EventArgs)
    Dim i, frameCount As Int32
    Dim fileName As String
    Dim img As System.Drawing.Image
    Dim frameDim As System.Drawing.Imaging.FrameDimension

    fileName="recipe2212.gif"
    img = System.Drawing.Image.FromFile(Server.MapPath(fileName))
    frameDim = New _
System.Drawing.Imaging.FrameDimension(img.FrameDimensionsList(0))
    frameCount=img.GetFrameCount(frameDim)
    Response.Write("<img src=""" & fileName & """><BR>")
    Response.Write("Frame Count: " & frameCount.ToString() & "<BR>")
    For i=0 To frameCount-1
        Response.Write("<img src=""recipe2612bvb.aspx?fileName=" & _
fileName & "&frame=" & i.ToString() & """><BR>")
    Next
End Sub
```

To create the viewer, first request the filename and frame number and store them in the variables, `fileName` and `frame`, respectively. Create an image and a `FrameDimension` object as in the list page. Next, use the `SelectActiveFrame` method of the `Image` object to set the frame to the requested one. Set the output type as `image/jpeg`. Then call the `Save` method and pass in the output stream to output the image.

In `<script runat="server" />` block or codebehind for the image viewer:

```
Sub Page_Load(sender As Object, e As EventArgs)
    Dim frame As Int32
    Dim fileName As String
    Dim img As System.Drawing.Image
    Dim frameDim As System.Drawing.Imaging.FrameDimension
```

```
    fileName = Convert.ToString(Request("fileName"))
    frame=Convert.ToInt32(Request("frame"))

    img = System.Drawing.Image.FromFile(Server.MapPath(fileName))
    frameDim = New +
System.Drawing.Imaging.FrameDimension(img.FrameDimensionsList(0))
    img.SelectActiveFrame(frameDim,frame)
    Response.ContentType="image/jpeg"
    img.Save(Response.OutputStream,System.Drawing.Imaging.ImageFormat.Jpeg)
    img.Dispose()
End Sub
```

See Also

Section 22.3, "Loading an Existing Image"

GDI+ Tutorial—http://www.aspalliance.com/chrisg

22.12. Saving an Image with Web Safe Colors

You want to save an image so that it only uses Web safe colors.

Technique

This example converts an image into a format that uses only Web safe colors.
First, you need to add a little function that gets a palette:

```
Private Function GetColorPalette() As ColorPalette
    Dim bitmap As New Bitmap(1, 1, PixelFormat.Format8bppIndexed)
    Dim palette As ColorPalette = bitmap.Palette
    bitmap.Dispose()

    Return palette
End Function
```

As you can see, all you do is to create a new bitmap instance that is 1×1 pixels big and
has 256 colors in its indexed palette. Otherwise, the only way to get a `ColorPalette`
object is from an instance of the `Image` class or one of the classes that derives from it.

```
Private Function ReColorGif(image As System.Drawing.Image) As Bitmap
    Dim colors As Integer = 255
    Dim width As Integer = image.Width
    Dim height As Integer = image.Height

    Dim bitmap As New Bitmap(width, height, PixelFormat.Format8bppIndexed)
    Dim palette As ColorPalette = GetColorPalette()
```

```vbnet
    Dim oleColors As New SortedList()
    Dim safeColors() As Integer = {0, 51, 102, 153, 204, 255}

    Dim count As Integer = 0
    Dim r As Integer
    For r = 0 To safeColors.Length - 1
        Dim g As Integer
        For g = 0 To safeColors.Length - 1
            Dim b As Integer
            For b = 0 To safeColors.Length - 1
                palette.Entries(count) = Color.FromArgb(255, safeColors(r), _
safeColors(g), safeColors(b))
                oleColors(ColorTranslator.ToOle(palette.Entries(count))) = count
                count += 1
            Next b
        Next g
    Next r
    palette.Entries((colors - 1)) = Color.FromArgb(0, 255, 255, 255)

    bitmap.Palette = palette
    Dim bmpCopy As New Bitmap(width, height, PixelFormat.Format32bppArgb)
    If (True) Then
        Dim g As Graphics = Graphics.FromImage(bmpCopy)
        g.PageUnit = GraphicsUnit.Pixel
        g.DrawImage(image, 0, 0, width, height)
        g.Dispose()
    End If

    Dim bitmapData As BitmapData
    Dim rect As New Rectangle(0, 0, width, height)
    bitmapData = bitmap.LockBits(rect, ImageLockMode.WriteOnly, _
PixelFormat.Format8bppIndexed)

    Dim pixels As IntPtr = bitmapData.Scan0
    Dim bits As Byte()
    Dim pBits As Int32

    If (bitmapData.Stride > 0) Then
        pBits = pixels.ToInt32()
    Else
        pBits = pixels.ToInt32() + bitmapData.Stride * (Height - 1)
    End If

    Dim stride As Integer = Math.Abs(bitmapData.Stride)
    ReDim bits(Height * stride)

    Dim row As Integer
```

```vb
Dim col As Integer

For row = 0 To Height - 1
    For col = 0 To Width - 1

        Dim pixel As Color
        Dim i8BppPixel As Integer = row * stride + col

        pixel = BmpCopy.GetPixel(col, row)

        Dim index As Double

        Dim entry As Integer = 0
        If ColorTranslator.ToHtml(pixel) = "#ffffff" Then
            index = (colors - 1)
        ElseIf oleColors.ContainsKey(ColorTranslator.ToOle(pixel)) Then
            index = oleColors(ColorTranslator.ToOle(pixel))
        Else
            Dim red As Integer
            Do While safeColors(entry) < pixel.R
                entry += 1
            Loop
            red = safeColors(entry)
            entry = 0

            Dim green As Integer
            Do While safeColors(entry) < pixel.G
                entry += 1
            Loop
            green = safeColors(entry)
            entry = 0

            Dim blue As Integer
            Do While safeColors(entry) < pixel.B
                entry += 1
            Loop
            blue = safeColors(entry)
            entry = 0

            index = oleColors(ColorTranslator.ToOle(Color.FromArgb(red, _
green, blue)))

        End If

        bits(i8BppPixel) = CByte(index)

    Next col
```

```
   Next row

CopyArrayTo(pBits, bits, bits.Length)
bitmap.UnlockBits(bitmapData)

Return bitmap

bitmap.Dispose()
bmpCopy.Dispose()
End Function
```

This function is the core of this example, because this is where all the color reduction happens. This example created the palette using a simple color algorithm. This is simple because all Web safe colors are made up of six fixed values for red, green, and blue: 0, 51, 102, 153, 204 and 255.

Near the end of the `ReColorGif` function, there's a call to a method called `CopyArrayTo`. This method is in fact a call to a kernel method—you use this to change the palette in the image.

Take a look at the method:

```
<DllImport("KERNEL32.DLL", EntryPoint:="RtlMoveMemory", _
    SetLastError:=True, CharSet:=CharSet.Auto, _
    ExactSpelling:=True, _
    CallingConvention:=CallingConvention.StdCall)> _
Public Shared Sub CopyArrayTo(<[In]()(), MarshalAs(UnmanagedType.I4)> _
    ByVal hpvDest As Int32, <[In]()(), Out()> ByVal hpvSource() As Byte, _
    ByVal cbCopy As Integer)
End Sub
```

All that is left now is to load the image and pass it through the `ReColorGif` method.

```
Private Sub Page_Load(sender As Object, e As System.EventArgs)
    Dim outputBitmap As New Bitmap(Server.MapPath("sample.jpg"))

    outputBitmap = ReColorGif(outputBitmap)

    Response.ContentType = "image/gif"
    outputBitmap.Save(Response.OutputStream, ImageFormat.Gif)

    outputBitmap.Dispose()
End Sub
```

Comments

Remember to add `Import` directives for `System.Runtime.InteropServices`, `System.Drawing`, `System.Drawing.Drawing2D`, and `System.Drawing.Imaging`.

See Also

Section 22.1, "Creating an Image Programmatically"

Section 22.3, "Loading an Existing Image"

22.13. Overlaying One Image Over Another

You want to overlay one image on top of another image.

Technique

This example uses members of the System.Drawing namespace to draw an image on top of a bitmap and then deliver the bitmap to the user's browser.

At the top of your .ASPX page, insert the following so that the required namespaces are referenced:

```
<%@ Page language="vb" %>
<%@ Import Namespace="System.Drawing" %>
<%@ Import Namespace="System.Drawing.Imaging" %>
<%@ Import Namespace="System.Drawing.Drawing2D" %>
```

In <script runat="server" /> block or codebehind:

```
Public Sub Page_Load(sender as object, e as System.EventArgs )
    'create bitmaps
    Dim InputBitmap as Bitmap = New Bitmap(Server.MapPath("deviq.gif"))
    Dim BaseBitmap as Bitmap = New _
Bitmap(Server.MapPath("aspalliance_logo.gif"))

    ' create a new image from original
    Dim OutputBitmap as Bitmap = new Bitmap(BaseBitmap, 320, 200)

    ' draw the overlay image
    Dim DrawGraphic as Graphics = Graphics.FromImage(OutputBitmap)
    InputBitmap.MakeTransparent(Color.White)
    DrawGraphic.DrawImage(InputBitmap,5,5)

    ' set the mime type
    Response.Clear()
    Response.ContentType="image/Gif"

    ' send the image to the viewer
    OutputBitmap.Save(Response.OutputStream, ImageFormat.Gif)

    ' clean up
    OutputBitmap.Dispose()
```

```
            InputBitmap.Dispose()
            BaseBitmap.Dispose()
            DrawGraphic.Dispose()
        End Sub
```

See Also

GDI+ Articles—`http://aspalliance.com/chrisg/`

22.14. Using Custom Fonts in the Text of an Image

You want to use custom fonts in the text of an image.

Technique

You can easily load a custom font in your Web application without requiring any work from the system administrator. The font just needs to be uploaded to the server, not installed. Once you have uploaded your font, you begin by creating a new bitmap named `pic` and specifying the dimensions. Next, you create a new `Graphics` object named `graph` from the `pic`. You also need to create a new brush. Next, create a new `PrivateFontCollection` to store your custom font.

Use the `AddFontFile` method to load the font family from the file and add it to your `PrivateFontCollection`. Then get the font family from the `PrivateFontCollection` by returning the first item in the `Families` collection. Create a new font using that font family and specifying the size, the `FontStyle`, and the `GraphicsUnit`. Be sure to clear the image with the color white before writing your text so you're not writing black on black. Now use the `DrawString` method and specify your string, font, brush, and X and Y coordinates to draw your text. Finish by setting the content type and writing out the image.

In `<script runat="server" />` block or codebehind for the list page:

```
Sub Page_Load(sender As Object, e As EventArgs)
    Dim pic As System.Drawing.Bitmap
    Dim graph As System.Drawing.Graphics
    Dim brush As System.Drawing.Brush
    Dim privateFontCollection As System.Drawing.Text.PrivateFontCollection
    Dim family As System.Drawing.FontFamily
    Dim myFont As System.Drawing.Font

    pic = new System.Drawing.Bitmap(200, 50)
    graph = System.Drawing.Graphics.FromImage(pic)
    brush = new System.Drawing.SolidBrush(System.Drawing.Color.Black)
```

```
   privateFontCollection= new System.Drawing.Text.PrivateFontCollection()
   privateFontCollection.AddFontFile(Server.MapPath("recipe2615.ttf"))
   family = privateFontCollection.Families(0)
   myFont = new System.Drawing.Font(family, 32, _
System.Drawing.FontStyle.Regular, System.Drawing.GraphicsUnit.Pixel)
   graph.Clear(System.Drawing.Color.White)
   graph.DrawString("Hello World", myFont, brush, 5,5)

   Response.ContentType = "image/gif"
   pic.Save(Response.OutputStream, System.Drawing.Imaging.ImageFormat.Gif)
End Sub
```

See Also

Section 22.1, "Creating an Image Programmatically"

Section 22.2, "Creating Images from Strings"

GDI+ Tutorial—`http://www.aspalliance.com/chrisg`

22.15. Loading an Image from a Remote Server

You want to load an image from a remote server.

Technique

This example uses the drawing and networking capabilities of .NET to load an image from a remote server and deliver it to the browser.

At the top of your .ASPX page, insert the following so that the required namespaces are referenced:

```
<%@ Page language="vb" %>
<%@ Import Namespace="System.Drawing" %>
<%@ Import Namespace="System.Drawing.Imaging" %>
<%@ Import Namespace="System.Drawing.Drawing2D" %>
<%@ Import Namespace="System.Net" %>
```

In `<script runat="server" />` block or codebehind:

```
   Public Sub Page_Load(sender as object, e as System.EventArgs )
      ' Initialize the web object
      Dim webC as WebClient = new WebClient()

      ' Set the URL of the file.
      Dim strFilename as String = _
"http://aspalliance.com/images/aspalliance_logo.gif"
```

```
        ' create a new image from original
        Dim OutputBitmap as Bitmap = New Bitmap(webC.OpenRead(strFilename))

        ' set the mime type
        Response.Clear()
        Response.ContentType="image/Jpeg"

        ' send the image to the viewer
        OutputBitmap.Save(Response.OutputStream, ImageFormat.Gif)

        ' clean up
        OutputBitmap.Dispose()
        webC.Dispose()
    End Sub
```

See Also
GDI+ Articles—http://aspalliance.com/chrisg/

22.16. Creating Transparent GIF Images

You want to create a transparent GIF using GDI+.

Technique

This example explains how you can create transparent GIFs using GDI+.

First, you add a little function that you'll use to get a palette. See Example 22.12 for more on this function:

```
Private Function GetColorPalette() As ColorPalette
    Dim bitmap As New Bitmap(1, 1, PixelFormat.Format8bppIndexed)
    Dim palette As ColorPalette = bitmap.Palette
    bitmap.Dispose()

    Return palette
End Function

Private Function ReColorGif(image As System.Drawing.Image) As Bitmap
    Dim colors As Integer = 255
    Dim width As Integer = image.Width
    Dim height As Integer = image.Height

    Dim bitmap As New Bitmap(width, height, PixelFormat.Format8bppIndexed)
    Dim palette As ColorPalette = GetColorPalette()
```

```vbnet
    Dim oleColors As New SortedList()
    Dim safeColors() As Integer = {0, 51, 102, 153, 204, 255}

    Dim count As Integer = 0
    Dim r As Integer
    For r = 0 To safeColors.Length - 1
        Dim g As Integer
        For g = 0 To safeColors.Length - 1
            Dim b As Integer
            For b = 0 To safeColors.Length - 1
                palette.Entries(count) = Color.FromArgb(255, safeColors(r), _
safeColors(g), safeColors(b))
                oleColors(ColorTranslator.ToOle(palette.Entries(count))) = count
                count += 1
            Next b
        Next g
    Next r
    palette.Entries((colors - 1)) = Color.FromArgb(0, 255, 255, 255)

    bitmap.Palette = palette
    Dim bmpCopy As New Bitmap(width, height, PixelFormat.Format32bppArgb)
    If (True) Then
        Dim g As Graphics = Graphics.FromImage(bmpCopy)
        g.PageUnit = GraphicsUnit.Pixel
        g.DrawImage(image, 0, 0, width, height)
        g.Dispose()
    End If

    Dim bitmapData As BitmapData
    Dim rect As New Rectangle(0, 0, width, height)
    bitmapData = bitmap.LockBits(rect, ImageLockMode.WriteOnly, _
PixelFormat.Format8bppIndexed)

    Dim pixels As IntPtr = bitmapData.Scan0
    Dim bits As Byte()
    Dim pBits As Int32

    If (bitmapData.Stride > 0) Then
        pBits = pixels.ToInt32()
    Else
        pBits = pixels.ToInt32() + bitmapData.Stride * (Height - 1)
    End If

    Dim stride As Integer = Math.Abs(bitmapData.Stride)
    ReDim bits(Height * stride)

    Dim row As Integer
```

```
    Dim col As Integer

For row = 0 To Height - 1
    For col = 0 To Width - 1

        Dim pixel As Color
        Dim i8BppPixel As Integer = row * stride + col

        pixel = BmpCopy.GetPixel(col, row)

        Dim index As Double

        Dim entry As Integer = 0
        If pixel.A = 0 Then
            index = (colors - 1)
        ElseIf oleColors.ContainsKey(ColorTranslator.ToOle(pixel)) Then
            index = oleColors(ColorTranslator.ToOle(pixel))
        Else
            Dim red As Integer
            Do While safeColors(entry) < pixel.R
                entry += 1
            Loop
            red = safeColors(entry)
            entry = 0

            Dim green As Integer
            Do While safeColors(entry) < pixel.G
                entry += 1
            Loop
            green = safeColors(entry)
            entry = 0

            Dim blue As Integer
            Do While safeColors(entry) < pixel.B
                entry += 1
            Loop
            blue = safeColors(entry)
            entry = 0

            index = oleColors(ColorTranslator.ToOle(Color.FromArgb(red, _
green, blue)))

        End If

        bits(i8BppPixel) = CByte(index)

    Next col
```

```
    Next row

    CopyArrayTo(pBits, bits, bits.Length)
    bitmap.UnlockBits(bitmapData)

    Return bitmap

    bitmap.Dispose()
    bmpCopy.Dispose()
End Function
```

This function is the core of this example, because this is where all the transparency and color reduction happens. This example created the palette using the color algorithm for Web safe colors.

Near the end of the `ReColorGif` function, there's a call to a method called `CopyArrayTo`. This method is in fact a call to a kernel method—you use this to change the palette in the image.

Take a look at the method:

```
<DllImport("KERNEL32.DLL", EntryPoint:="RtlMoveMemory", _
    SetLastError:=True, CharSet:=CharSet.Auto, _
    ExactSpelling:=True, _
    CallingConvention:=CallingConvention.StdCall)> _
Public Shared Sub CopyArrayTo(<[In](), MarshalAs(UnmanagedType.I4)> ByVal _
hpvDest As Int32, <[In](), Out()> ByVal hpvSource() As Byte, _
ByVal cbCopy As Integer)
End Sub
```

All that is left now is to draw some graphics onto the image and pass the image through the `ReColorGif` method.

```
Private Sub Page_Load(sender As Object, e As System.EventArgs)
    Dim outputBitmap As New Bitmap(200, 200, PixelFormat.Format24Rgb)

    Dim blackPen As New Pen(Color.Black, 2)
    Dim bluePen As New Pen(Color.Blue, 5)
    Dim greenPen As New Pen(Color.Green, 10)
    Dim redBrush As New SolidBrush(Color.Red)
    Dim g As Graphics = Graphics.FromImage(outputBitmap)

    g.Clear(Color.FromArgb(0, 255, 255, 255))
    g.SmoothingMode = SmoothingMode.AntiAlias
    g.DrawString("Aqua", New Font("Arial", 24, FontStyle.Bold), redBrush, _
New PointF(50, 60))
    g.DrawEllipse(greenPen, 40, 40, 110, 80)
    g.DrawEllipse(bluePen, 30, 30, 130, 100)
    g.DrawEllipse(blackPen, 23, 23, 144, 113)
```

```
    outputBitmap = ReColorGif(outputBitmap)

    Response.ContentType = "image/gif"
    outputBitmap.Save(Response.OutputStream, ImageFormat.Gif)

    outputBitmap.Dispose()
End Sub
```

Comments

Remember to add `Import` directives for `System.Runtime.InteropServices`, `System.Drawing`, `System.Drawing.Drawing2D`, and `System.Drawing.Imaging`.

See Also

Section 22.1, "Creating an Image Programmatically"

Section 22.3, "Loading an Existing Image"

Section 22.12, "Saving an Image with Web Safe Colors"

23

Threading, Remoting, Reflection, and CodeDOM

23.0. Introduction

To wrap up, a few of the more advanced topics are discussed in this final chapter. As you've no doubt realized, the .NET Framework provides a huge amount of built-in functionality. This chapter includes examples that demonstrate the framework's support for threading, reflection, and CodeDOM (Code Document Object Model). Although you most likely won't use these recipes every day, they're definitely good to have on hand when the need arises.

23. 1. Starting a Process in a Separate Thread

You want to start a process in its own thread.

Technique

Starting a process in a separate thread can be extremely useful when you have a long-running process such as connecting to an XML Web service, or running a DB query. A separate thread allows your program to continue executing other work while waiting for the long-running process to finish.

You create a `ThreadStart` object called `myThreadStart` and point it to the address of the `DoSomething` method. This object indicates which method to run when the thread is started. Next, you create a new thread and pass it `myThreadStart`. Call `myThread.Start` to start the thread you created and execute the `DoSomething` method. Normally the application would wait for the `DoSomething` method to complete before running the next line in `Page_Load`, but because it was called in a separate thread, the current thread can continue running.

In this example, `Page_Load` counts from 1 to 10 and `DoSomething()` count from 11 to 20. Notice that when you run the example, the results are intermixed. This is because both threads are running simultaneously.

The ASPX page is as follows:

```
<HTML>
   <body>
      <form id="form1" method="post" runat="server">
         <asp:Label ID="myLabel" Runat="server"></asp:Label>
      </form>
   </body>
</HTML>
```

In `<script runat="server" />` block or codebehind:

```
Sub Page_Load(sender As Object, e As EventArgs)
   Dim i as Integer
   Dim myThread As System.Threading.Thread
   Dim myThreadStart As System.Threading.ThreadStart

   myThreadStart=new System.Threading.ThreadStart(AddressOf DoSomething)
   myThread=new System.Threading.Thread(myThreadStart)
   myThread.Start()
   For i=1 To 10
      System.Threading.Thread.Sleep(100)
      myLabel.Text+=i & "<BR>"
   Next
End Sub

Sub DoSomething()
   Dim i As Integer
   For i=11 To 20
      System.Threading.Thread.Sleep(100)
      myLabel.Text+=i & "<BR>"
   Next i
End Sub
```

Comments

The `System.Threading.Thread.Sleep(100)` statement pauses execution for 100 milliseconds on each loop. This is necessary in this example because creating the new thread requires a small amount of overhead, and without the pause, the page would finish rendering before the `DoSomething` event was complete.

See Also

Section 16.14, "Pausing Your Program"

Section 23.2, "Terminating a Thread"

Using Threads—`http://msdn.microsoft.com/library/en-us/dv_vstechart/html/vbtchUsingThreads.asp`

23.2. Terminating a Thread

You want to terminate a thread in order to kill all processes running on that thread.

Technique

Occasionally, you might need to kill a thread. The `Abort` method of the thread object provides an easy way to do this. First, load the code from example 23.2. Modify the loop in `Page_Load` to run only from one to five. Then call `myThread.Abort()`. You'll notice when you run the code, the output from `DoSomething()` is stopped after the loop in `Page_Load` finishes.

The ASPX page is as follows:

```
<HTML>
   <body>
      <form method="post" runat="server">
         <asp:Label ID="myLabel" Runat="server"></asp:Label>
      </form>
   </body>
</HTML>
```

In `<script runat="server" />` block or codebehind:

```
Sub Page_Load(sender As Object, e As EventArgs)
   Dim i as Integer
   Dim myThread As System.Threading.Thread
   Dim myThreadStart As System.Threading.ThreadStart

   myThreadStart=new System.Threading.ThreadStart(AddressOf DoSomething)
   myThread=new System.Threading.Thread(myThreadStart)
   myThread.Start()
   For i=1 To 5
      System.Threading.Thread.Sleep(100)
      myLabel.Text+=i & "<BR>"
   Next
   myThread.Abort()
End Sub
```

```
Sub DoSomething()
   Dim i As Integer
   For i=11 To 20
      System.Threading.Thread.Sleep(100)
      myLabel.Text+=i & "<BR>"
   Next i
End Sub
```

See Also

Section 16.14, "Pausing Your Program"

Section 23.1, "Starting a Process in a Separate Thread"

Using Threads—`http://msdn.microsoft.com/library/en-us/dv_vstechart/html/vbtchUsingThreads.asp`

23.3. Retrieving Metadata Information from an Assembly

You want to retrieve metadata information from an assembly using reflection.

Technique

Use reflection to find detailed information about an assembly, such as the code base, the location, the full name, resource names, and information about the modules in the assembly.

The ASPX page is as follows:

```
<asp:button id="RetrieveInfo" onclick="RetrieveInfo_Click"
runat="server"
   Text=" Retrieve Assembly Info "></asp:button>
   <br><br>
   <asp:label id="OutputClass" runat="server"></asp:label>
```

In `<script runat="server" />` block or codebehind:

```
Private Function GetAssemblyInfo() As String
   Dim sb As StringBuilder = New StringBuilder()
   Try
      'Use c:\Windows\... on Windows XP
      Dim assemblyFile As String = _
"C:\WINNT\Microsoft.NET\Framework\v1.0.3705\mscorlib.dll"
      Dim assemblyInfo As System.Reflection.Assembly = _
System.Reflection.Assembly.LoadFrom(assemblyFile)
```

```
        sb.Append("CodeBase: ")
        sb.Append(assemblyInfo.CodeBase)
        sb.Append("<br>Location: ")
        sb.Append(assemblyInfo.Location)
        sb.Append("<br>FullName: ")
        sb.Append(assemblyInfo.FullName)
        sb.Append("<br>Manifest Resource Names: ")

        Dim resourceNames() As String = _
assemblyInfo.GetManifestResourceNames()
        Dim i As Integer
        For  i = 0 To resourceNames.Length-1
          Dim name As String = resourceNames(i)
          If  i > 0 Then sb.Append(",")
          sb.Append(name)
        Next

        Dim types() As Type =  assemblyInfo.GetTypes()
        Dim typeInfo As Type
        For Each typeInfo In types
          sb.Append("<h2>" + typeInfo.FullName + "</h2>")
          sb.Append("Number of Constructors: ")
          sb.Append(typeInfo.GetConstructors().Length.ToString())
          sb.Append("<br>Number of Properties: ")
          sb.Append(typeInfo.GetProperties().Length.ToString())
          sb.Append("<br>Number of Fields: ")
          sb.Append(typeInfo.GetFields().Length.ToString())
          sb.Append("<br>Number of Events: ")
          sb.Append(typeInfo.GetEvents().Length.ToString())
          sb.Append("<br>Number of Methods: ")
          sb.Append(typeInfo.GetMethods().Length.ToString())
          sb.Append("<br>Is Class: ")
          sb.Append(typeInfo.IsClass)
          sb.Append("<br>Is Interface: ")
          sb.Append(typeInfo.IsInterface)
          sb.Append("<br>Is Enum: ")
          sb.Append(typeInfo.IsEnum)
          sb.Append("<br>Attributes: ")
          sb.Append(typeInfo.Attributes)
          sb.Append("<br>GUID: ")
          sb.Append(typeInfo.GUID.ToString())
        Next
      Catch ex As Exception
        sb.Append("Error: " + ex.ToString())
      End Try
```

```
        Return sb.ToString()
    End Function


    Protected  Sub RetrieveInfo_Click(ByVal sender As Object, _
ByVal e As System.EventArgs)
        OutputClass.Text = GetAssemblyInfo()
    End Sub
```

Comments

There are many ways to load an assembly. This example uses the `Assembly.LoadFrom` method, which takes a path to the assembly. Another alternative is to use the `Assembly.Load` method, making it possible to just use the assembly name, such as `mscorlib` if the application running this code knows about the assembly. After the assembly is loaded, the program reads assembly metadata using methods and properties from the `Assembly` object, such as `CodeBase`, `Location`, `FullName`, and `GetManifestResourceNames()`. Getting the types of the `Assembly` object using the `GetTypes` method allows the program to retrieve information about the assembly's modules.

See Also

An Introduction to Reflection in C#—`http://www.codeguru.com/cs_misc/Reflection.html`

`System.Reflection` Namespace—`http://msdn.microsoft.com/library/en-us/ cpref/html/frlrfSystemReflection.asp` in .NET Framework Class Library

Assembly Class—`http://msdn.microsoft.com/library/en-us/cpref/html/ frlrfSystemReflectionAssemblyClassTopic.asp` in .NET Framework Class Library

23.4. Retrieving Information About a Class and its Members

You want to gather information about a class and its members using reflection.

Technique

Use reflection to find the constructors, fields, properties, and methods of the selected class.

Create a `Type` object from a class using the `GetType` method. Using the `Type` object, retrieve the constructors (`GetConstructors`), the fields (`GetFields`), the properties (`GetProperties`), and the methods (`GetMethods`). Display the results in a DataGrid.

In `<script runat="server" />` block or codebehind:

```
      Private Sub ShowConstructors(ByVal type As Type)
        Dim constructorsTable As DataTable = New DataTable()
        constructorsTable.Columns.Add("Constructor",
➥type.GetType("System.String"))
        constructorsTable.Columns.Add("Parameters",
➥type.GetType("System.String"))
        Dim constructors() As MemberInfo = type.GetConstructors()
        Dim constructor As ConstructorInfo
        For Each constructor In constructors
          Dim dr As DataRow = constructorsTable.NewRow()
          dr("Constructor") = constructor.DeclaringType.Name
          Dim sb As StringBuilder = New StringBuilder()
          Dim pi() As ParameterInfo = constructor.GetParameters()
          sb.Append("( ")
          Dim i As Integer
          For i = 0 To pi.Length - 1 Step i + 1
            If i > 0 Then
              sb.Append(", ")
            End If
            Dim p As ParameterInfo = pi(i)
            sb.Append(p.ParameterType.Name)
            sb.Append(" ")
            sb.Append(p.Name)
          Next
          sb.Append(" )")
          dr("Parameters") = sb.ToString()
          constructorsTable.Rows.Add(dr)
        Next
        Dim constructorsView As DataView = constructorsTable.DefaultView
        constructorsView.Sort = "Constructor"
        ConstructorsGrid.DataSource = constructorsView
        ConstructorsGrid.DataBind()
      End Sub

      Private Sub ShowFields(ByVal type As Type)
        Dim fieldsTable As DataTable = New DataTable()
        fieldsTable.Columns.Add("Type", type.GetType("System.String"))
        fieldsTable.Columns.Add("FieldName", type.GetType("System.String"))
        Dim fields() As MemberInfo = type.GetFields()
        Dim field As FieldInfo
        For Each field In fields
          Dim dr As DataRow = fieldsTable.NewRow()
          dr("Type") = field.FieldType.Name
          dr("FieldName") = field.Name
          fieldsTable.Rows.Add(dr)
        Next
        Dim fieldsView As DataView = fieldsTable.DefaultView
```

```
      fieldsView.Sort = "FieldName"
      FieldsGrid.DataSource = fieldsView
      FieldsGrid.DataBind()
   End Sub


   Private Sub ShowProperties(ByVal type As Type)
      Dim propertiesTable As DataTable = New DataTable()
      propertiesTable.Columns.Add("Type", type.GetType("System.String"))
      propertiesTable.Columns.Add("PropertyName",
➥type.GetType("System.String"))
      Dim properties() As MemberInfo = type.GetProperties()
      Dim property1 As PropertyInfo
      For Each property1 In properties
         Dim dr As DataRow = propertiesTable.NewRow()
         dr("Type") = property1.PropertyType.Name
         dr("PropertyName") = property1.Name
         propertiesTable.Rows.Add(dr)
      Next
      Dim propertiesView As DataView = propertiesTable.DefaultView
      propertiesView.Sort = "PropertyName"
      PropertiesGrid.DataSource = propertiesView
      PropertiesGrid.DataBind()
   End Sub


   Private Sub ShowMethods(ByVal type As Type)
      Dim methodsTable As DataTable = New DataTable()
      methodsTable.Columns.Add("ReturnType", type.GetType("System.String"))
      methodsTable.Columns.Add("MethodName", type.GetType("System.String"))
      methodsTable.Columns.Add("Parameters", type.GetType("System.String"))
      Dim methods() As MethodInfo = type.GetMethods()
      Dim method As MethodInfo
      For Each method In methods
         Dim dr As DataRow = methodsTable.NewRow()
         dr("ReturnType") = method.ReturnType.Name
         dr("MethodName") = method.Name
         Dim sb As StringBuilder = New StringBuilder()
         Dim pi() As ParameterInfo = method.GetParameters()
         sb.Append("( ")
         Dim i As Integer
         For i = 0 To pi.Length - 1 Step i + 1
            If i > 0 Then
               sb.Append(", ")
            End If
            Dim p As ParameterInfo = pi(i)
            sb.Append(p.ParameterType.Name)
            sb.Append(" ")
            sb.Append(p.Name)
         Next
```

```
        sb.Append(" )")
        dr("Parameters") = sb.ToString()
        methodsTable.Rows.Add(dr)
    Next
    Dim methodsView As DataView = methodsTable.DefaultView
    methodsView.Sort = "MethodName, Parameters"
    MethodsGrid.DataSource = methodsView
    MethodsGrid.DataBind()
End Sub


    Private Sub RetrieveInfo_Click(ByVal sender As Object, ByVal e As
➡ System.EventArgs)
        Dim selectedClass As String = ListOfClass.SelectedItem.Value
        OutputClass.Text = selectedClass
        Dim type As Type = type.GetType(selectedClass)
        ShowConstructors(type)
        ShowFields(type)
        ShowProperties(type)
        ShowMethods(type)
    End Sub
```

The ASPX page would include:

```
<asp:Button id="btnGenerate" runat="server" Text="Create Code"
OnClick="btnGenerate_Click"></asp:Button><br>
<br>
<asp:Label id="Result" runat="server"></asp:Label>
<asp:HyperLink ID="link" Runat="server"/>
```

See Also

Type Class—`http://www.aspalliance.com/aspxtreme/sys/TypeClass.aspx`

`System.Reflection` Namespace—`http://msdn.microsoft.com/library/en-us/ cpref/html/frlrfSystemReflection.asp` in `.NET Framework Class Library`

23.5. Generating a Class Using the CodeDOM

You want to generate a class dynamically using the Code Document Object Model (CodeDOM).

Technique

Using CodeDOM, you can have code that generates code. In this example, a class is created that calculates the area of a circle, the area of a sphere, and the volume of a sphere.

This code starts out using an `ICodeGenerator` for a specific language (in this case, VB). The `GenerateCodeFromCompileUnit` method of the `ICodeGenerator` generates code using the Code Document Object Model that is built up. To start building the Code Document Object Model, you use `CodeNamespace`. To that, you attach the main class called `Round Measures`. To `Round Measures`, you attach the subclass `Round` and a method. You attach several methods, a field, and a property to the class `Round`. The Code Document Object Model is like a container that has containers, each of which can have containers and so on.

The ASPX page is as follows:

```
    <asp:Button id="btnGenerate" runat="server" Text="Create Code"
OnClick="btnGenerate_Click"></asp:Button><br>
    <br>
    <asp:Label id="Result" runat="server"></asp:Label>
```

In `<script runat="server" />` block or codebehind:

```
    Public Function CreateVbCode(ByVal filepath As String) _
As String
        Dim sw As StreamWriter = Nothing
        Try
          sw = File.CreateText(filepath)

          Dim codeProvider As VBCodeProvider = New VBCodeProvider()
          Dim codeGenerator As ICodeGenerator = _
codeProvider.CreateGenerator(sw)
          Dim options As CodeGeneratorOptions = New CodeGeneratorOptions()

          'Create namespace and references
          Dim usingSnippet1 As CodeSnippetCompileUnit = _
New CodeSnippetCompileUnit("Imports System")
          codeGenerator.GenerateCodeFromCompileUnit(usingSnippet1, sw, options)
          sw.WriteLine()
          Dim recipesNamespace As CodeNamespace = New CodeNamespace("Recipes")

          'Create RoundMeasures Class Declaration
          Dim roundMeasures As CodeTypeDeclaration = New CodeTypeDeclaration()
          roundMeasures.IsClass = True
          roundMeasures.Name = "RoundMeasures"
          roundMeasures.TypeAttributes = TypeAttributes.Public

          'Create Round Class Declaration
          Dim round As CodeTypeDeclaration = New CodeTypeDeclaration()
          Dim roundComment As CodeComment = New CodeComment()
          roundComment.Text = "Round calculates the Area of a Circle,
▶the Area of a Sphere, and the Volume of a Sphere"
```

```
            Dim roundCommentStatement As CodeCommentStatement = _
New CodeCommentStatement(roundComment)
            round.Comments.Add(roundCommentStatement)
            round.IsClass = True
            round.Name = "Round"
            round.TypeAttributes = TypeAttributes.Public

            'Create Class Member Field m_radius
            Dim radiusMember As CodeMemberField = New _
CodeMemberField(type.GetType("System.Double"),"m_radius")
            radiusMember.Attributes = MemberAttributes.Private
            radiusMember.Comments.Add(New CodeCommentStatement( _
"The radius used to calculate areas and volume."))
            round.Members.Add(radiusMember)

            'Create Round Class Constructor
            Dim roundConstructor As CodeConstructor = New CodeConstructor()
            roundConstructor.Attributes = MemberAttributes.Public
            Dim roundConParameter As CodeParameterDeclarationExpression = _
                New CodeParameterDeclarationExpression(type.GetType(_
"System.Double"),"pRadius")
            roundConstructor.Parameters.Add(roundConParameter)
            roundConstructor.Statements.Add(New CodeSnippetStatement(_
"Me.m_radius = pRadius"))
            round.Members.Add(roundConstructor)

            'Create Radius Property
            Dim radiusProperty As CodeMemberProperty = New CodeMemberProperty()
            radiusProperty.Attributes = MemberAttributes.Public
            radiusProperty.Type = _
New CodeTypeReference(type.GetType("System.Double"))
            radiusProperty.Name = "Radius"
            radiusProperty.HasGet = True
            radiusProperty.GetStatements.Add(New _
CodeSnippetExpression("Return m_radius"))
            radiusProperty.HasSet = True
            radiusProperty.SetStatements.Add(New _
CodeSnippetExpression("m_radius = value"))
            round.Members.Add(radiusProperty)

            'Create CircleArea Method
            Dim circleAreaMethod As CodeMemberMethod = New CodeMemberMethod()
            circleAreaMethod.Comments.Add(New _
CodeCommentStatement("Calculates the area of a circle."))
            circleAreaMethod.Name = "CircleArea"
            circleAreaMethod.ReturnType = New _
```

```
CodeTypeReference(type.GetType("System.Double"))
        circleAreaMethod.Attributes = MemberAttributes.Public
        circleAreaMethod.Statements.Add(New _
CodeSnippetStatement("Return Math.PI * m_radius * m_radius"))
        round.Members.Add(circleAreaMethod)

        'Create SphereArea Method
        Dim sphereAreaMethod As CodeMemberMethod = New CodeMemberMethod()
        sphereAreaMethod.Comments.Add(New _
CodeCommentStatement("Calculates the area of a sphere."))
        sphereAreaMethod.Name = "SphereArea"
        sphereAreaMethod.ReturnType = _
New CodeTypeReference(type.GetType("System.Double"))
        sphereAreaMethod.Attributes = MemberAttributes.Public
        sphereAreaMethod.Statements.Add(New _
CodeSnippetStatement("Return 4 * CircleArea()"))
        round.Members.Add(sphereAreaMethod)

        'Create SphereVolume Method
        Dim sphereVolumeMethod As CodeMemberMethod = New CodeMemberMethod()
        sphereVolumeMethod.Comments.Add(New _
CodeCommentStatement("Calculates the volume of a sphere."))
        sphereVolumeMethod.Name = "SphereVolume"
        sphereVolumeMethod.ReturnType = New _
CodeTypeReference(type.GetType("System.Double"))
        sphereVolumeMethod.Attributes = MemberAttributes.Public
        sphereVolumeMethod.Statements.Add(New _
CodeSnippetStatement("Return SphereArea() * m_radius / 3"))
        round.Members.Add(sphereVolumeMethod)

        'Add Round class to RoundMeasures class
        roundMeasures.Members.Add(round)

        'Create Main Method
        Dim mainMethod As CodeMemberMethod = New CodeMemberMethod()
        mainMethod.Name = "Main"
        mainMethod.Attributes = MemberAttributes.Public
        mainMethod.Attributes = MemberAttributes.Static
        mainMethod.Statements.Add(New _
CodeSnippetStatement("Dim r As Double = 5.0"))
        mainMethod.Statements.Add(New _
CodeSnippetStatement("Dim rnd As Round = New Round(r)"))
        mainMethod.Statements.Add(New _
CodeSnippetStatement("Console.WriteLine(""Radius of Circle: {0:f1}"", _
rnd.Radius)"))
        mainMethod.Statements.Add(New _
```

```
CodeSnippetStatement("Console.WriteLine(""Area of Circle: {0:f1}"", _
rnd.CircleArea())"))
        mainMethod.Statements.Add(New _
CodeSnippetStatement("Console.WriteLine(""Area of Sphere: {0:f1}"", _
rnd.SphereArea())"))
        mainMethod.Statements.Add(New _
CodeSnippetStatement("Console.WriteLine(""Volume of Sphere: {0:f1}"", _
rnd.SphereVolume())"))
        roundMeasures.Members.Add(mainMethod)

        'Add RoundMeasures class to Recipe namespace
        recipesNamespace.Types.Add(roundMeasures)

        'Generate Source Code File
        codeGenerator.GenerateCodeFromNamespace(recipesNamespace, _
sw, options)

        Return filepath & " was successfully created."
      Catch ex As Exception
        Return "Error: " & ex.Message
      Finally
        'Close StreamWriter
        If Not sw Is Nothing Then
          sw.Close()
        End If
      End Try
    End Function



    Protected Sub btnGenerate_Click(ByVal sender As Object, _
ByVal e As System.EventArgs)


Result.Text = CreateVbCode( Server.MapPath("Round.vb"))
    End Sub
```

Comments

CodeDOM enables you to generate code on the fly. Building a Code Document Object
Model will seem familiar to most programmers because it is similar to building an XML
document or adding controls that have controls, which can also have controls. After the
CodeDOM is built, most of the work is done. The ICodeGenerator uses the
CodeDOM and generates the code.

See Also

Microsoft .NET CodeDom Technology—Part 1—`http://www.15seconds.com/issue/020917.htm`

System.CodeDom Namespace—`http://msdn.microsoft.com/library/en-us/cpref/html/frlrfSystemCodeDom.asp` in .Net Framework Class Library

System.CodeDom.Compiler Namespace—`http://msdn.microsoft.com/library/en-us/cpref/html/frlrfSystemCodeDomCompiler.asp` in .Net Framework Class Library

23.6. Compiling a Class using the CodeDOM

You want to compile a class using the CodeDOM.

Technique

Using CodeDOM, you can have code that generates and compiles code. In this example, a class is generated that calculates the area of a circle, the area of a sphere, and the volume of a sphere. The generated code is contained in a `CodeCompileUnit`. The code then compiles the CodeDOM tree contained in the `CodeCompileUnit` using an `ICodeCompiler`.

The ASPX page is as follows:

```
    <asp:Button id="btnGenerate" runat="server"
Text="Create Code" OnClick="btnGenerate_Click"></asp:Button><br>
    <br>
    <asp:Label id="Result" runat="server"></asp:Label>
```

In `<script runat="server" />` block or codebehind:

```
    Public Function CreateVbCode() As String
      Try
          'Language specific code provider
          Dim codeProvider As VBCodeProvider = New VBCodeProvider()

          'Create Code Compile Unit
          Dim compileUnit As New CodeCompileUnit()

          'Create namespace
          Dim recipesNamespace As New CodeNamespace("Recipes")

          'Create namespace references
          recipesNamespace.Imports.Add(New CodeNamespaceImport("System"))

          'Create Round Class Declaration
          Dim round As CodeTypeDeclaration = New CodeTypeDeclaration()
```

```vbnet
            Dim roundComment As CodeComment = New CodeComment()
            roundComment.Text = "Round calculates the Area of a Circle,
➥the Area of a Sphere, and the Volume of a Sphere"
            Dim roundCommentStatement As CodeCommentStatement = _
New CodeCommentStatement(roundComment)
            round.Comments.Add(roundCommentStatement)
            round.IsClass = True
            round.Name = "Round"
            round.TypeAttributes = TypeAttributes.Public

            'Create Class Member Field m_radius
            Dim radiusMember As CodeMemberField = New _
CodeMemberField(type.GetType("System.Double"),"m_radius")
            radiusMember.Attributes = MemberAttributes.Private
            radiusMember.Comments.Add(New CodeCommentStatement(
➥"The radius used to calculate areas and volume."))
            round.Members.Add(radiusMember)

            'Create Round Class Constructor
            Dim roundConstructor As CodeConstructor = New CodeConstructor()
            roundConstructor.Attributes = MemberAttributes.Public
            Dim roundConParameter As CodeParameterDeclarationExpression = _
                New CodeParameterDeclarationExpression(_
type.GetType("System.Double"),"pRadius")
            roundConstructor.Parameters.Add(roundConParameter)
            roundConstructor.Statements.Add(New CodeSnippetStatement(_
"Me.m_radius = pRadius"))
            round.Members.Add(roundConstructor)

            'Create Radius Property
            Dim radiusProperty As CodeMemberProperty = New CodeMemberProperty()
            radiusProperty.Attributes = MemberAttributes.Public
            radiusProperty.Type = New _
CodeTypeReference(type.GetType("System.Double"))
            radiusProperty.Name = "Radius"
            radiusProperty.HasGet = True
            radiusProperty.GetStatements.Add(New _
CodeSnippetExpression("Return m_radius"))
            radiusProperty.HasSet = True
            radiusProperty.SetStatements.Add(New _
CodeSnippetExpression("m_radius = value"))
            round.Members.Add(radiusProperty)

            'Create CircleArea Method
            Dim circleAreaMethod As CodeMemberMethod = New CodeMemberMethod()
            circleAreaMethod.Comments.Add(New _
CodeCommentStatement("Calculates the area of a circle."))
```

```
            circleAreaMethod.Name = "CircleArea"
            circleAreaMethod.ReturnType = _
New CodeTypeReference(type.GetType("System.Double"))
            circleAreaMethod.Attributes = MemberAttributes.Public
            circleAreaMethod.Statements.Add(New _
CodeSnippetStatement("Return Math.PI * m_radius * m_radius"))
            round.Members.Add(circleAreaMethod)

            'Create SphereArea Method
            Dim sphereAreaMethod As CodeMemberMethod = New CodeMemberMethod()
            sphereAreaMethod.Comments.Add(New _
CodeCommentStatement("Calculates the area of a sphere."))
            sphereAreaMethod.Name = "SphereArea"
            sphereAreaMethod.ReturnType = New _
CodeTypeReference(type.GetType("System.Double"))
            sphereAreaMethod.Attributes = MemberAttributes.Public
            sphereAreaMethod.Statements.Add(New _
CodeSnippetStatement("Return 4 * CircleArea()"))
            round.Members.Add(sphereAreaMethod)

            'Create SphereVolume Method
            Dim sphereVolumeMethod As CodeMemberMethod = New CodeMemberMethod()
            sphereVolumeMethod.Comments.Add(New _
CodeCommentStatement("Calculates the volume of a sphere."))
            sphereVolumeMethod.Name = "SphereVolume"
            sphereVolumeMethod.ReturnType = New _
CodeTypeReference(type.GetType("System.Double"))
            sphereVolumeMethod.Attributes = MemberAttributes.Public
            sphereVolumeMethod.Statements.Add(New _
CodeSnippetStatement("Return SphereArea() * m_radius / 3"))
            round.Members.Add(sphereVolumeMethod)

            'Add Round class to Recipe namespace
            recipesNamespace.Types.Add(round)

            'Add Namespace to Code Compile Unit
            compileUnit.Namespaces.Add(recipesNamespace)

            'Create ICodeCompiler
            Dim compiler As ICodeCompiler = codeProvider.CreateCompiler()

            'input parameters for the compiler
            Dim compilerParams As New CompilerParameters()
            Dim filepath As String = _
Path.GetDirectoryName(Request.PhysicalPath)
            compilerParams.OutputAssembly = filepath + "\Round.dll"
            compilerParams.ReferencedAssemblies.Add("System.dll")
            compilerParams.GenerateExecutable = False 'dll not exe
```

```
         'Compile the assembly using the Compile Unit
         Dim results As CompilerResults = _
compiler.CompileAssemblyFromDom(compilerParams, compileUnit)

         Dim sb As New StringBuilder()
         Dim compError As CompilerError
         For Each compError In  results.Errors
             sb.Append(compError.ErrorText)
             sb.Append("<br>")
         Next compError

         Dim output As String
         For Each output In  results.Output
             sb.Append(output)
             sb.Append("<br>")
         Next output

         Return "Round Class compiled. " + sb.ToString()
      Catch ex As Exception
         Return "Error: " + ex.Message
      End Try
   End Function


   Protected Sub btnGenerate_Click(sender As Object, _
e As System.EventArgs)
      Result.Text = CreateVbCode()
   End Sub
```

Comments

CodeDOMenables you to generate and compile code on the fly. After the
CodeCompileUnit is built, the code can be compiled using the ICodeCompiler
CompileAssemblyFromDom method. A new assembly file is generated based on the
CodeCompileUnit. If you have a file that you want to compile instead of a
CodeCompileUnit, you can use the CompileAssemblyFromFile method.

See Also

Building .NET Assemblies Dynamically—
http://www.csharpfriends.com/Articles/getArticle.aspx?articleID=118

JIT Coding—http://www.c-sharpcorner.com/Code/2002/Mar/JITCodingFB.asp

System.CodeDom Namespace—http://msdn.microsoft.com/library/en-us/cpref/
html/frlrfSystemCodeDom.asp in .Net Framework Class Library

System.CodeDom.Compiler Namespace—http://msdn.microsoft.com/library/en-us/
cpref/ html/frlrfSystemCodeDomCompiler.asp in .Net Framework Class Library

Index

C

How can we make this index more useful? Email us at indexes@samspublishing.com

How can we make this index more useful? Email us at indexes@samspublishing.com

X-Y-Z

XML files

    converting between datasets, 157-158

    creating classes from, 158-161

    finding nodes, 153-154

    navigating, 166-168

    opening, 151-152

    reading, 162-163

    storing on file system, 154-155

    transforming with XSLT, 155-157

    writing, 164-166

XML Web services

    consuming

        using VS.NET, 324-325

        using WSDL.EXE, 323-324

    creating, 321-322

    returning images from, 325-326

XmlTextReader class, 162-163

XmlTextWriter class, 164-166

XPathNavigator class, 166-168

XSD.EXE, 158-161

XSLT, transforming XML documents, 155-157

Your Guide to Computer Technology

www.informit.com

Sams has partnered with **InformIT.com** to bring technical information to your desktop. Drawing on Sams authors and reviewers to provide additional information on topics you're interested in, **InformIT.com** has free, in-depth information you won't find anywhere else.

ARTICLES

Keep your edge with thousands of free articles, in-depth features, interviews, and information technology reference recommendations—all written by experts you know and trust.

POWERED BY

Safari

ONLINE BOOKS

Answers in an instant from **InformIT Online Books'** 600+ fully searchable online books. Sign up now and get your first 14 days **free**.

CATALOG

Review online sample chapters and author biographies to choose exactly the right book from a selection of more than 5,000 titles.

 www.samspublishing.com

SAMS DEVELOPER'S LIBRARY

Cookbook   Handbook   Dictiona

PHP
DEVELOPER'S COOKBOOK

Sterling Hughes and
Andrei Zmievski

ISBN: 0-672-32325-7
$39.99 US/$59.95 CAN

Python
DEVELOPER'S HANDBOOK

André Lessa

ISBN: 0-672-31994-2
$44.99 US/$67.95 CAN

Perl
DEVELOPER'S DICTION

Clinton Pierce

ISBN: 0-672-32067-3
$39.99 US/$59.95 CAN

OTHER DEVELOPER'S LIBRARY TITLES

ColdFusion MX
DEVELOPER'S COOKBOOK

Brad Leupen,
Peter Freitag,
Christopher Reeves

ISBN: 0-672-32462-8
$39.99 US/$59.95 CAN

mod_perl
DEVELOPER'S HANDBOOK

Barrie Slaymaker
and James Smith

ISBN: 0-672-32132-7
$39.99 US/$59.95 CAN
(Available Spring 2002)

JavaScript
DEVELOPER'S DICTIONARY

Alexander Vincent

ISBN: 0-672-32201-3
$39.99 US/$59.95 CAN
(Available Spring 2002)

PostgreSQL
DEVELOPER'S HANDB

Ewald Geschwinde
Hans–Jürgen Schön

ISBN: 0-672-32260-9
$44.99 US/$67.95 CA

ALL PRICES ARE SUBJECT TO CH

SAMS
www.samspublishing.com